THE MAN
from the
RIO GRANDE

Harry Love, "the Black Knight of the Zayante."
Sailor, soldier, dispatch rider, explorer,
and leader of the California Rangers who tracked down
Joaquín Murrieta. *Bancroft Library.*

THE MAN
from the
RIO GRANDE

A biography of
HARRY LOVE
*Leader of the California Rangers
who tracked down Joaquín Murrieta*

by William B. Secrest

UNIVERSITY OF OKLAHOMA PRESS
NORMAN

For Shirley . . .

Library of Congress Cataloging-in-Publication Data
Secrest, William B., 1930-
The man from the Rio Grande : a biography of Harry Love, leader of the California rangers who tracked down Joaquín Murrieta / by William B. Secrest.
   p. cm. — (Western frontiersmen series ; 32)
Includes bibliographical references and index.
ISBN 978-0-8061-9299-4 (paper)
1. Love, Harry, 1810-1868. 2. Pioneers—Southwest, New—Biography. 3. Soldiers—Southwest, New—Biography. 4. Soldiers—California—Biography. 5. Murieta, Joaquín, d. 1853—Adversaries. 6. Frontier and pioneer life—Southwest, New. 7. Explorers—Rio Grande Valley—Biography. 8. Pioneers—California—Santa Cruz Region—Biography. 9. Frontier and pioneer life—California—Santa Cruz Region. 10. Santa Cruz Region (Calif.)—Biography. I. Title. II. Series.
F786.L85S43 2005
979.4'7104'092--dc22

2004022035

Library of Congress Cataloging-in-Publication Data as is Copyright © 2005 by William B. Secrest.

Originally published in hardcover in the Western Frontiersmen Series by the Arthur H. Clark Company, Spokane, Washington. Paperback published 2023 by the University of Oklahoma Press, Norman, Publishing Division of the University. Manufactured in the U.S.A.

The paper in this book meets the guidelines for permanence and durability of the Committee on Production Guidelines for Book Longevity of the Council on Library Resources, Inc.

All rights reserved. No part of this publication may be reproduced, stored in a retrieval system, or transmitted, in any form or by any means, electronic, mechanical, photocopying, recording, or otherwise-except as permitted under Section 107 or 108 of the United States Copyright Act-without the prior written permission of the University of Oklahoma Press.

Contents

Acknowledgements	9
Introduction	13
1 The Wolf	19
2 The Road to Camargo	25
3 Sonora	49
4 On the Rio Grande	63
5 California Calls	73
6 Ruddle	87
7 Los Angeles	97
8 Death on the Trail	105
9 Ranger Days	121
10 The Long Trail to Cantua Creek	135
11 Heads You Win	149
12 Mary	173
13 A Place Called Zayante	183
14 Byrnes	199
15 The Violent Land	209
16 Santa Cruz	221
17 Flash Floods and Fierce Fires	231
18 The End	245
Epilogue	263
Bibliography	277
Index	287

Maps and Illustrations

Harry Love, "the Black Knight of the Zayante" . . . . *frontispiece*
The United States Army camp at Corpus Christi, Texas 24
Street scene in Mobile, Alabama 26
Map showing the area around Fort Brown, Texas, and Matamoros, Mexico 29
Matamoros, Mexico 29
Map of Harry Love's West 32
Maj. William W. Chapman 37
Harry Love's bounty land application 40
Mrs. Helen Chapman 44
A keelboat such as the one Love operated on the Rio Grande . . 47
Sonora, California, in the early 1850s 51
Map segment thought to have been based on maps made by Harry Love 62
Map of Harry Love's California 72
San Francisco in the early 1850s 86
Home of Joaquín Murrieta and his wife 89
Knife purported to have been owned by Joaquín Murrieta . . . 90
The Niles Canyon home of Joaquín Murrieta 93
Woodcut of Harry Love 96
Joseph S. Mallard 99
San Gabriel, California 100
The hanging of Rafael Escobar in 1855 106
Joaquín Murrieta fleeing from a pursuing posse 109
Frank Salazar 116
The mining town of Mariposa, California 120
William J. Howard and Isabelle Holton 125
William W. Byrnes 126
Judge Walter Harvey 127
Patrick E. Connor 138
Cantua Creek, California 141

William Henderson	142
The death of Joaquín Murrieta	145
A dramatic rendering of Joaquín Murrieta's death	146
Harry Love	147
Samuel A. Bishop	152
Dr. William F. Edgar	154
A portion of the log book of Mariposa Sheriff John Boling	157
Broadside advertising the first exhibition of Joaquín Murrieta's head	161
The head of Joaquín Murrieta	162
Sacramento newspaper advertisement	167
Mary Bennett Love	174
Downtown Santa Cruz, California, in 1866	177
Scene in the San Lorenzo Valley, California	186
Map of area around Santa Cruz, California	208
Charles F. Bludworth	211
Stage road in the rugged Santa Cruz Mountains	232
Mary Love's home in Santa Clara, California	253
The Santa Clara shootout between Harry Love and Chris Eiverson	254
Winston Bennett	259
Harry Love's grave	260
Displays at Dr. Jordan's Museum	262
A fraudulent wax "head" of Joaquín Murrieta	264
Mariana Andrada	271

Acknowledgements

Following the tracks of Harry Love has been an experience that matches his life. It has been a trail of ups and downs, satisfying discoveries, and many disappointments. For years, as I gathered bits and pieces of the Joaquín Murrieta story, the shadowy figure of his destroyer, Harry Love, lurked in the background. Who was he? He seemed to have appeared in California like some mysterious Paladin, at a time when he was particularly needed. Then, his job done, he again faded into obscurity. Where did he come from? What was his life before, and after, the Murrieta affair? My interest in this mysterious man gradually superseded my other pursuits, and I began rooting out his story. It was a frustrating but enjoyable task of many years.

I could do little of my historical work without the help of my wonderful wife. Besides accompanying me on research trips, Shirley assumes most of the chores around the house and provides the solid base of our home and family. Men as lucky as I am should be grateful indeed.

In California, my good friend John Boessenecker was never too busy with his own projects to keep an eye out for Love material. Over the years he has provided counsel and useful information, as well as reading and offering constructive criticism of the manuscript. He kept me on the trail when I wandered afield. Everyone should have as good a friend as John Boessenecker.

Richard Dillon also read and edited the manuscript. An always-helpful friend of many years, his encouragement, expertise, and interest is much appreciated.

I am most grateful, also, to Carlo M. DeFerrari, the eminent Tuolumne County historian, who has shared his own research with me for many years. Fellow researchers Mrs. Fay Ellis and Troy Tuggle have generously helped and provided encouragement, which is very much appreciated. My thanks also to Mrs. Lorrayne Kennedy, former Archivist of the Calaveras County Museum and Archives; Jerry and Joyce Wilson; the late Bertha Schroeder; Dianne Klyn; Phil and Josh Reader; Charles Callison; James F. Varley; Robert Chandler; Dr. James Secrest; Gladys Hansen and Frank Quinn of the San Francisco Archives; Mr. L. Taylor Graham; James R. Smith; Brenda Davis, Santa Clara County Recorder's Office, San Jose; Richard C. Neal, Recorder, Santa Cruz County Recorder's Office; Santa Cruz County Clerk's Office, Santa Cruz, California; Special Collections, University of California at Santa Cruz, Santa Cruz; and Ms. Daryl Morrison, Special Collections, University of the Pacific Library, Stockton.

Allan R. Ottley, Sybille Zemitis, and many others of the California State Library staff have been most helpful over the years. A copy of my first Love document, the California Rangers muster roll, was obtained in the late 1950s from Colonel N. O. Thomas of the Office of the Adjutant General of California. Much more material was located over the years at the California State Archives thanks to W. N. Davis, Jr., Joseph P. Samora, and other always-helpful staff members. Grace E. Baker provided material from the library of the Society of California Pioneers in San Francisco.

A special debt of gratitude is owed to Caleb Coker, whose great-great-grandfather hired Harry Love as an army dispatch rider on the Texas frontier. Along with much encouragement, Caleb provided copies from rare original documents in his possession to help with details of Love's services in Texas.

Charles A. Shaughnessy, Navy and Old Army Branch, Military Archives Division of the National Archives and Records Service in Washington, located the Quartermaster records that led to many additional documents pertaining to Love's Texas service. Others who helped were Kent Carter, Chief, Archives Branch, Federal Archives and Records Center, Fort Worth, Texas; Michael E. Pilgrim, Archives/Reference Branch, Textual Reference Division, National Archives, Washington, D.C.; and Rose Mary Kennedy, Archives Technician of the National Archives-Pacific Sierra Region in San Bruno, California.

In Texas I was helped in great and small ways by J. Milton Nance of Texas A&M University at College Station; Mrs. Eddie Williams and

Donaly E. Brice of the Texas State Library at Austin; William H. Richter, Assistant Archivist at the University of Texas Library at Austin; Jane Baker, Museum Director, Daughters of the Republic of Texas, Austin; Mrs. Elaine Schoenfeld, Records Research Division, General Land Office, Austin; Llerena Friend of Wichita Falls, Texas; and Susan M. Golden and Brenda S. McClurkin, Special Collections, University of Texas Library, Arlington. I am most grateful to Madison Love Jamison, Jr., of Hearne, Texas, who provided the clue that led to the discovery of the Texas records of Love's Rio Grande days.

Information on the Alabama Volunteers and the Mexican War was provided by George H. Schroeter of the Mobile Public Library; the State of Alabama Department of Archives and History, Montgomery; Steven R. Butler, President, the Descendants of Mexican War Veterans; Wilburn Keith Miller, University of South Alabama Archives; and the New Orleans Public Library.

Others who have helped in various capacities are Lee Goodwin, Archivist, New Mexico State Records Center and Archives, Santa Fe; Maudean Neill, C.G.; Marion Pokriots; Paul F. Johnston, Ph.D., Curator of Maritime History, Peabody Museum, Salem, Massachusetts; Carol A. Juneau, Whaling Museum, New Bedford, Massachusetts; Lori A. Garcia; Conrado Family Archives; Eric Carlson; Vian Viola Kill, Genealogist; Deborah W. Boles, Missouri Historical Society; and Mrs. J. F. Parsons, Vermont Historical Society, Montpelier, Vermont.

Bob Clark and Ariane Smith were a pleasure to work with and always encouraging. A big thanks to my son, Bill Secrest, Jr., for indexing and much critical editorial work. A better scholar and historian than I will ever be, he is always there when I need him.

To you all, and anyone I may have overlooked, my grateful appreciation.

WILLIAM B. SECREST
Fresno, California

Introduction

In the 140 years since his death, Joaquín Murrieta has become one of the most renowned outlaws in American history. His story, a mixture of fact, legend, and conjecture for so long, has been clarified to some extent in recent years by a cadre of dedicated historians and grassroots researchers. It has not always been so, however.

For many years, historians researching the Murrieta story were discouraged by the theories of Joseph Henry Jackson whose book, *Bad Company,* appeared in 1949. Jackson, a writer and a literary editor for the *San Francisco Chronicle,* convinced himself and many others that Murrieta was the quasi-fictional creation of one John Rollin Ridge, a Cherokee newspaperman of the 1850s and 60s. Ridge had written and published a rousing biography of Murrieta that had appeared the year after the bandit's death. Utilizing Ridge's booklet, some contemporary accounts, and a great deal of supposition, Jackson managed to shape his sources into a scenario whereby the Murrieta legend was "created" by Ridge at a time when California needed such a bandit-hero myth in its past.

It was 1949, the one hundredth anniversary of the great California gold rush. Jackson's provocative theory was just right for the time, as was Ridge's story so many years before. More importantly, Jackson's skillful prose suggested a validity and depth of research that, under close scrutiny, was just not there. An accomplished writer, his style made his theories seem wonderfully plausible and convincing. Many historians of the time were impressed and startled at Jackson's conclusions, and few questioned his findings. Because so little research had been done on the subject, critics and historians such as Ramon Adams were persuaded that Jackson had indeed discovered the long-hidden reality that California's most famous outlaw was a largely fictional character. Actually, except for conversations and other fictional devices of the time, the Ridge tale was largely true.

Today, thanks to the work of such dedicated researchers as John Boessenecker, the late Frank Latta, Ray Wood, James Varley, and others, we are learning more and more of the real Murrieta story. But even as information emerges about California's famous bandit, the Ranger leader who tracked him down, Harry Love, remains an enigmatic and shadowy figure. Ridge knew little of Love, as did all subsequent writers, including Latta. Love was a mysterious figure who appeared when needed, then faded into obscurity. It turns out that even the meager biographical information provided in newspaper obituaries was largely false.

Even with the dearth of information on Love, he has always been fair game for those who sought to sensationalize his career. He had "mean eyes," was a "prevaricator," a "killer," and an "illiterate coward." When he commanded the California Rangers in 1853, various newspapers, antagonistic towards California governor John Bigler, accused Love of getting up the Joaquín campaign as a money-making scheme, of killing the wrong man and even murdering prisoners. Later, Love was accused of participating in the killing of a passenger while on a trip east in 1854. Incredibly, a recent, ill-informed writer even claimed that Love murdered his wife. Assuming such incidents to be factual without further research, a prominent California historian referred to Love as "a cruel and vindictive hardcase," a description he hardly merits.

A more current writer, offering nothing more than a fertile imagination for evidence, slyly suggests that Love murdered the two prisoners taken at the time of the Cantua Creek fight—this to cover up the fact that they had killed the wrong man. He further "suspects" that a Mariposa document concerning the prisoner José Ochoa is "bogus." This is nonsense, all gotten up for sensational effect to establish a preconceived agenda of conspiracies that never existed. But, perhaps it helps sell books.

The reasons for the constant maligning of Love seems to be that so little was known of his life and character that his career could be exaggerated and sensationalized and no one would know the difference. He did indeed live an adventurous life, but Love was no "killer" or "hardcase." Actually, the last thirteen years of his life were spent operating a sawmill and farm, trying desperately to live a normal existence.

Contemporary writers, even those unacquainted with Love, could be even more outrageous. Writing in his own sleazy publication, the Sacramento *Phoenix*, in 1858, Edward McGowan related a story of Love's participation in the Texas battle of San Jacinto in 1836. According to McGowan, when General Sam Houston's small army charged Santa Ana's troops that day, shouting, "Remember the Alamo," every man but one rushed into the fight, in which the Mexicans were thoroughly defeated. The lone deserter, according to McGowan, was Harry Love. After the battle, Houston called Love in front of the troops and dismissed him from the service, saying there was no room for cowards in the Army of Texas. As a parting bit of advice, Houston told Love if he ever married, to marry into a fighting family "and probably the anticipated young Loves might inherit the blood of the mother and not be all poltroons."

McGowan, a politician chased out of town by the 1856 San Francisco vigilantes, neglected to give the source of his anecdote. The sole purpose of his little scandal sheet the *Phoenix* was to vilify the vigilantes who had "persecuted" him in the bay city. Obtaining the scandalous material in his publication from those opposed to the vigilantes, McGowan received all sorts of stories of varying degrees of authenticity. The former judge accused Love of being one of the San Francisco vigilantes—all the reason he needed to make the old Ranger a target in his vulgar publication.

This same incident, however, is reported in the July 24, 1846, issue of the *American Flag*, a newspaper published at Matamoros, Mexico, during the war. Under the heading "Gen. Houston's Advice to a Coward," it is related that Houston had told his troops to charge the Mexican lines, but when they saw the match applied to the cannon, they were to fall to the ground so the shot would pass harmlessly overhead. They would then jump to their feet and attack the breastworks before the enemy could reload. One man, however, did not understand the plan. When he saw all his comrades fall and heard the cannon he assumed they were killed and retreated as fast as he could. After the battle Houston sent for the man. "My friend, are you a married man?" "No sir," replied the soldier. "Well then, take my advice—go off immediately and marry into a brave family, for you are a large man and may make good children." The article concluded by reporting the man was no coward, but actually assumed his comrades had all been killed and that it was folly to attack the breastworks alone. *The name of the man is not reported.*

As apochryphal as this tale sounds, there appears to be some element of truth to it. Captain William Heard, one of Houston's company commanders at San Jacinto, later reported that his men would fall to the ground when they thought the cannon was to be fired, then raised up and "sprint like bucks" directly after the artillery had boomed. Heard's story, however, mentions no coward refusing to fight.

This is obviously the basis for McGowan's tale. He had no doubt obtained it from someone who remembered the Texas story, and McGowan then made Harry the villain as a matter of revenge. The irresponsibility of McGowan's tale was further emphasized by a revealing article appearing in the *Flag* a few days later:

> In our previous edition we published an anecdote, in the way of filling up, relative to a conversation between Gen. Houston and a soldier after the battle of San Jacinto. In the recital, and particularly the caption, we place the gentleman in an unenviable light. We have learned since then, that he is here in the army, serving the country, and since the time alluded to has been in a number of campaigns against both Indians and Mexicans, and his comrades speak of his actions as indicative of a brave and daring man. A friend of his called at our office yesterday morning, and informed us that he was the person alluded to and gave us to understand that for the sake of a little mirth we had wounded the feelings of a sensitive man who had proved his courage in twenty battles. We expressed much regret at our sinning and assured the friend of our ignorance as to the particulars of the affair. . . .

So there we have it! McGowan, who was not even a veteran of the Mexican War, gleefully published an unverified tale, apparently doctoring it up to make Love the villain. It was just the sort of tale McGowan relished. When the truth is known, the coward of the yarn turns out to be a hero who might very well have been Harry Love, who was in the area of Matamoros in July 1846. Love is not known to have been in the Texas army in 1836, however, and since he never applied for bounty land, the chances of his being this man are rather slim. On such flimsy material from unreliable characters as McGowan is the stuff of history made if we are not cautious.

Actually, Love's Texas years were a high point in his life. His adventures as an army courier and explorer of the Rio Grande were widely published and discussed. An indication of his popularity at the time is reported in the contemporary letter of a Brownsville army officer's wife, who described him in the following rather lyrical tones:

> I wish I could picture him to your vision, as he came dashing down the street, well mounted as he always is, sitting his horse as if he were a part of the noble animal he rides, his long black curls flowing in the wind, his

chest thrown out, his expression cool, frank and resolute, his saber and spurs clashing, his clothes torn by the chaparral and covered with dust....

Although not a distinguished man in any sense of the word, Harry Love was a builder of the West and a small reflection of his times. As a sailor he visited California as early as 1839, and when volunteers were first called for the Rio Grande, Harry needed no prodding to enlist. He gained nationwide fame with his exploring feats and dangerous rides carrying dispatches for the army after the war. In California he gained even wider fame as the destroyer of the bloodiest bandit of gold rush days. But he had pushed back the frontier of a society in which he found it difficult to exist. His later years were spent more or less in seclusion, as a pioneer sawmill operator and farmer in the Zayante Valley, near Santa Cruz, California.

In telling the story of Harry Love, I have given much space to the story of Joaquín Murrieta for several reasons. It goes without saying that without Murrieta there would not have been a Harry Love as we know him. It was both the high point and the turning point of his life. I felt it was time to give a more complete story of California's most famous outlaw, based on my own and others' research. More important, it was time to show that the real Murrieta had indeed been killed by Harry Love's Rangers that hot July day in 1853.

Indications are that Love yearned for a stable home and environment after his years of wandering. However, an antagonistic and manipulative wife, disappointing business ventures, and various calamities combined to reduce him to a shell of his former self. Rather than walk away from his troubles, he chose to confront them head on, as he always had. Plus, there are suggestions that he sought refuge in the bottle as his world crumbled around him.

"Love is a gallant fellow," wrote an army officer after Harry's long and dangerous 1849 ride from the Rio Grande. Those unfamiliar with Love's complete story find it difficult to reconcile this "gallant fellow" with the destitute, drunken old man who ran amuck in Santa Clara one afternoon in 1868. And, in fact, they were not the same person.

Harry Love's story is of a man who knew the heights and depths of life. He was not perfect, but if he is to be remembered, his successes deserve equal billing with his failures. In revealing for the first time a more complete biography of the man, perhaps at last we can give him a modicum of the credit that has so long escaped him.

I

The Wolf

JOAQUIN CAPTURED, BEHEADED, AND HIS BODY IN THE HANDS OF HIS CAPTORS—It has just been reported here that the company of Rangers, commanded by Captain Harry Love, met with the notorious murderer and robber, Joaquin and six of his equally infamous band, at Panocha Pass, [*sic*] and after a desperate running fight, Joaquin and one of his gang were killed and two taken prisoners: three managed to make their escape, but one of their horses were killed and several captured. Captain Love is now on his way down with his prisoners and the head of Joaquin preserved in spirits. . . . In Haste yours, T.C.A.   Quartzburg, July 27, 1853
New York Daily Times, August 24, 1853

The head of Joaquín! As the news was carried around the country in late 1853, it must have startled a great many people. In more primitive countries, such treatment of bandits and pirates was understood. It was done for a very specific reason. Indeed, it was considered necessary to show the public, children and adults alike, the inevitable conclusion to a life of crime.

But the young United States was coming into the industrial age and as such it decried such colonial methods used in the Far East, South America, Africa, and other less developed societies. Now, suddenly, it was brought home that America was not so sophisticated after all. Our frontiers were still quite primitive. When events demanded it, Americans did what was necessary, whether it was lynching a man who seemed obviously guilty or cutting off a bandit's head, even though he had not been convicted of a crime.

What kind of man could have led such an expedition? Captain Harry Love was a familiar name in Texas, but to most he was merely a frontier ranger who had committed an atrocity—albeit to a bandit. Many Mexican War veterans recalled the fearless army dispatch rider who had carried news between the Texas border posts during and after the war. Others recalled his daring exploration of the Rio Grande River. Was this the same Harry Love?

To most Americans, Love was just a name. He had cut off a man's head to be placed in a bottle and exhibited. Circumstances did not matter. It was a terrible thing to do. Some press accounts mentioned Love's Mexican War service and work as an army courier during and after the war. But few said more than that. Actually, no one knew much more than that—except Harry Love. And when it came to himself, Harry was a man of few words.

• • •

Born in Vermont in 1810, Henry Love came from pioneering stock.[1] The name Love is thought to be a derivation of the French *le loup*, meaning "the wolf." From Loup, the name evolved into Lou, Louf, Luff, Luef, Luv, Lov, and Love.[2] The first Loves to arrive in America were of British and Irish descent, including a John Love who settled at Boston, Massachusetts, in 1635. Other Loves were soon sprinkled up and down the Eastern seaboard.

Henry Love's paternal grandfather reportedly fought at Bennington during the Revolutionary War, while his mother was said to have been related to the noted Ethan Allen.[3] A big, ungainly youth, young Henry grew up hiking the pine-choked hills of Vermont and learning to love the solitude of the creeks and valleys of his home state. Schools were scattered and crude, but he managed to obtain a rudimentary education, although his handwriting and spelling were always quite poor.

Children worked nearly as hard as adults in those faraway times. There were always chores to do whether one lived in a village or a rural area;

---

[1] Harry Love's year and place of birth are established by the United States Census Population Schedules, Santa Cruz County, California, 1860, as well as the Santa Clara census and his voter registration for the same year.

[2] George W. Allen, *Love History and Genealogy* (La Porte, Ind.: Allen Press, 1937), 5–13.

[3] Harry Love's minimal family history is taken from the *Santa Cruz Sentinel* of July 4, 1868, quoting from a "brief history of his life as written by J. D. Hyde in 1865." This "history" has not been located, either as a booklet or an article in the *Sentinel*. Hyde was a Santa Cruz attorney who owned the *Sentinel* for a time. See also Margaret Koch, *Santa Cruz County, Parade of the Past* (Fresno, Calif.: Valley Publishers, 1973), 190.

any playtime took place during such moments as school recess. It was a time when most everyone made their own soap and candles, built their own furniture, and raised their own food. Children were doing adult chores by the time they were five or six years old.

Eli Canfield recalled his Vermont boyhood in the 1820s:

> I never had any playthings, not even a hand sled, until I was large enough to make one myself. I never owned a pair of skates. I had a ball, but I picked up old woolen stockings and would use the ravelings to make it, and covered it myself when I was nine or ten years old. I remember throwing it for Herman Dyer to knock . . . and we went behind the barn for this performance as we knew that both my parents would regard it as a foolish waste of precious time.[4]

There was never enough time and always too much to do. Money was scarce, and people did what they could to make ends meet. Barter was a way of life, and everyone traded whenever possible for what was needed. Shoemakers traveled from village to village, staying with families while making their shoes. Those who had cows traded milk for what they needed, and pay was often in goods of one kind or another. The principal items stocked in stores were tea, tobacco, rum, buttons, indigo, utensils of all kinds, spices, and such luxuries as sugar (ordinarily, sweetening was done with maple syrup or molasses). Blacksmiths made anything constructed of metal. Economy and self-restraint was a way of life for all but the most wealthy in frontier Vermont.[5]

Like other youths of his time, young Henry Love probably "picked wool" by candlelight in the evenings. This entailed pulling the fleece apart with his fingers so it would be light and fluffy for carding. Well-to-do families had their own looms to make their clothing, while most others would furnish the wool and trade for the service. Henry Love's boyhood world, as described by Eli Canfield, was simple and quite primitive:

> Wind on the water and the domestic animal on land were the principal motors for travel or transportation. Little machinery was used, most of that except such as was employed to saw or grind grain was propelled by human strength. Wood was the only fuel known in the country. Tallow candles or whale oil were the only sources of artificial light. A spark from the percussion of flint and steel was the only known way of originating

---

[4] Eli Canfield, "In the Twilight of His Years, Eli Canfield Recalls his Boyhood in Arlington, 1817–1831," *Vermont History*, Spring 1972.

[5] For life in pioneer Vermont, see Barrows Mussey, *A Book of Country Things* (Battleboro, Vt.: Stephen Greene Press, 1965), 1–157.

fire. A man could go no faster than a horse could run, and news could go no faster than a man could carry it. Steamboats were used here and there, but railroads had not been thought of. There was hardly any money in circulation and first class farm hands were glad to work for 50¢ a day, and take their pay in shoes or at the store.[6]

Henry lost his mother at an early age. When his father remarried, there was apparently a natural hostility toward his stepmother, and it was not long before the boy refused to conform to her "petty tyranny."[7] Perhaps, too, he felt a stirring to travel suggested by another Vermont native some years later. Stephen Douglas, in a debate with Abraham Lincoln in 1858, stated, "My friends, Vermont is the most glorious spot on the face of this globe for a man to be born in, provided he *emigrates* when he is very young."[8] In any case, young Henry left home.

The boy reportedly made his way to the East Coast, probably seeking work in one of the larger ports—Portsmouth, Maine, or perhaps Boston. An early account states he sought out an uncle in the maritime service and obtained a berth on his ship. Years later, he would regale a Texas acquaintance with a more romantic version of his leaving home:

> At a seaboard town, he sought and obtained a situation as a cabin-boy on a vessel bound for the West Indies. When fairly out at sea, he discovered that he formed part of a buccaneer crew, whose exploits on the Spanish Main he would only allude to vaguely in after years. Over all attempts to trace his career through the vicissitudes incident upon this piratical life he studiously threw the veil of taciturnity.[9]

There is little doubt the boy grew up at sea, although there are vague rumors that he participated in the Blackhawk and Florida Indian troubles. Big and brawny at an early age, he reportedly captained a ship at the age of fifteen and later worked as a keelboatman on the Mississippi between the various river towns and New Orleans.[10] Whatever his travels, he spent much time on the water and first saw what later became the

---

[6]Canfield, "In the Twilight of his Years . . . ," *Vermont History*.
[7]Teresa Griffin Vielé, *Following the Drum* (New York: Rudd and Carlton, 1858), 227. Mrs. Vielé obtained these stories from her husband, Lieutenant Egbert Vielé, who had served with Love in Texas as related in the text.
[8]Duane Smith, "Vermont Remembered: 'Silver King' Tabor Recalls his Boyhood," *Vermont History*, Spring 1972.
[9]Vielé, *Following the Drum*, 227.
[10]Koch, *Santa Cruz County, Parade of the Past*, 114.

state of California in October 1839.[11] Strong and over six feet tall, he was twenty-nine years of age at this time, and with his long hair and black beard was undoubtedly a dashing figure. Whether on a whaling vessel or a trading expedition, young Henry must have been thrilled to be visiting the opposite side of the continent.[12]

• • •

In time Love, now known as Harry, decided to quit the sea. It must have been shortly after his California visit, and his next line of work was quite probably on a ranch in Louisiana or Texas. Weary of the heaving deck of a ship, he now found he was much more at home on the back of a horse, and soon was roping cattle as though he had been born to the saddle. For the next few years he learned his trade and was as skilled a ranch hand as any of the more seasoned vaqueros.

It must have been in early 1846 while on a trip to Mobile, Alabama, perhaps for supplies, that he was smitten by a local beauty.[13] Wishing to have some time for courting, Harry obtained work as a stevadore on the local waterfront and was so engaged when festering troubles between the United States and Mexico took a serious turn.

---

[11]Love's visit to California in 1839 was the basis of his admittance to the Society of California Pioneers in 1866. See the *Constitution and Bylaws of The Society of California Pioneers and List of Members since its Organization* (San Francisco: published by Order of Board of Directors, 1912), 132. Only five American ships were recorded as visiting in California during 1839, according to William Heath Davis, *Seventy-Five Years in California* (San Francisco: John Howell Books, 1967), 149.

[12]The trade in sea otter skins between China and California had been quite profitable in the past, but at this time it was tapering off. Hides, tallow, and some lumber were the principal trading items of the Mexican province, and at certain times of the year there was a brisk business. D. Mackenzie Brown, ed., *China Trade Days in California, Selected Letters from the Thompson Papers, 1832–1863* (Berkeley and Los Angeles: University of California Press, 1947), 1–52.

Great, multi-masted schooners, barques, and frigates anchored off San Diego, San Pedro, Santa Barbara, and Monterey as bundles of dried and stiffened hides were rafted out to fill their holds. Often these trading ships would be stocked with pots, pans, clothes, and furniture from the States that would be bartered to the Californians for "Yankee bank notes"—the 500-pound bags of tallow and bundles of hides. The visiting ships frequently avoided the high duties of the custom houses by conducting their business in secluded coves without government sanction. For the society and economy of early California, see such first-hand accounts as Walter Colton, *Three Years in California* (Stanford, Calif.: Stanford University Press, 1949); William Robert Garner, *Letters from California, 1846–1847* (Los Angeles: University of California Press, 1970); and Robert Glass Cleland, *The Cattle on a Thousand Hills* (San Marino, Calif.: The Huntington Library, 1951).

[13]The author is speculating on just how Harry Love turned up in Mobile, Alabama, in 1846. It is known that he had experience with keelboats on the rivers, but he must have worked on cattle ranches also to be able to use a rope as he later did. See Vielé, *Following the Drum*, 228.

The United States Army camp at Corpus Christi, Texas, where General Zachary Taylor waited for the inevitable war. Love and the Alabama Volunteers landed at Point Isabel, some miles to the south. *National Archives.*

2

The Road to Camargo

When the United States Congress formally annexed Texas in December 1844, it was to forestall British influence and allay the constant border dissension along the Rio Grande. Mexico still insisted that the future of Texas was tied to the mother country, while Texans were growing increasingly weary of their insecure situation. Feeling they must take a stand on the matter, the Mexican government was adamant that the border of the two countries was the Nueces River, which bisected the southern tip of Texas. Both the United States and Texas insisted the border was the Rio Grande, further to the south. President Polk and most politicians thought Mexico too politically factionalized to even consider going to war over such a matter. All failed, however, to consider the nationalism and pride of the Mexican people.[1]

When Texas agreed to annexation in June 1845, General Zachary Taylor had been ordered to lead a 3,500-man army to the new territory in order to guarantee safety to the inhabitants. Establishing his camp and headquarters at Corpus Christi, Taylor awaited orders. Primarily a pressure tactic, the troops were also there to keep an eye on any Mexican troops in the area. At this time, the United States Army was armed with inferior flintlocks and a variety of other weapons. Supplies were scanty and of poor quality. Although Taylor did have some good heavy and light artillery commanded by West Point graduates, his army had never operated as a unit, and neither the commander nor his subordinates had experience in the mass movement of troops. When a large Mexican force was reported heading north, a jittery U.S. government began giving real consideration to the possibility of war.

---

[1] For a good layman's understanding of the troubles leading up to the Mexican War, see Bernard DeVoto, *The Year of Decision, 1846* (Boston: Little, Brown and Company, 1943), 5–484.

Street scene in Mobile, Alabama, as it appeared in Harry Love's time. The city hall, with cupola, is flanked by markets and other shops. *Ballou's Pictorial, 1857.*

After five months of waiting, on February 3, 1846, Taylor was ordered to move his army some 150 miles south into the disputed territory. He set up a supply depot at Point Isabel, near the mouth of the Rio Grande, then moved his main force upstream across the river from the Mexican town of Matamoros. As the Mexican military troops at Matamoros kept a wary eye on the invaders across the river, Taylor's men were set to work drilling and building an earthworks fort.

On August 23, 1845, General Taylor had been authorized by the War Department to call on the governors of Louisiana and Texas for troops in case of an emergency. It was not until the move opposite Matamoros and a discouraging skirmish with Mexican troops took place that the seriousness of the situation was realized by both Taylor and the nation.

A squadron of the Army's Second Dragoons under Captain Seth B. Thornton was sent out to scout the route between the coast and Taylor's men. Surprised by a large Mexican force, Thornton's whole command was captured after sixteen dragoons were killed. The country was horrified and humiliated. There was no doubt now that a state of war existed between the two nations. The *New Orleans Picayune* parroted the dismay of newspapers and the public all across the country:

> It is a mortifying reflection that an American army should be beleaguered, on our own soil, by a Mexican force. The bare announcement of such a fact ought to arouse a spirit that nothing could appease but a thorough and withering chastisement of the invaders.... It is useless to waste time in speculating upon the causes of the perilous attitude of the American troops upon the frontier; it is enough to know that unless succor is speedily forwarded, the consequences may be disastrous to our army and humiliating to the national pride.[2]

A field artillery piece was hauled into New Orleans' Lafayette Square, where it was fired, and a Captain Forno began soliciting recruits. Enlistments were also being taken at the Carrollton Railroad Depot, the Franklin House, and other locations. Surrounding states also began mustering volunteer units.[3]

The same degree of excitement prevailed in Mobile, Alabama. The mayor called a public meeting at a local theater on the evening of May 3, and a committee was appointed to adopt measures for the relief of General Taylor. Five places of enlistment were set up.[4]

A regiment of Alabama volunteers had been previously organized under Colonel John I. Seibels, but a disagreement among its officers resulted in the unit being abandoned. Remnants of the group formed a battalion of three-month volunteers under Lt. Colonel Phillip H. Raiford. A second group made up of three independent companies of six-month volunteers was also formed. The three company commanders were Robert Desha, William H. Platt, and Rush Elmore.[5]

Harry Love promptly signed up for a six-month tour of duty in Captain Desha's company. Although his service record lists his muster date as May 6, he was obviously enlisted earlier, as noted in the *Mobile Register* of May 5:

> The Troops for the Rio Grande ... One company of fresh volunteers was organized yesterday, to the number of over one hundred, elected their offi-

---

[2] *New Orleans Picayune*, May 3, 1846.
[3] Ibid. The gathering of volunteer units from other states is also mentioned in this and succeeding issues of the same paper.
[4] *Picayune*, May 6, 1846.
[5] Steven R. Butler, "Alabama Volunteers in the Mexican War, part two," *Alabama Genealogical Society Magazine*, vol. 23, 1991.

cers, Gen. Robt. Desha, Captain, mustered into the service of the U. States, and started for New Orleans.[6]

On May 5, the *New Orleans Picayune* noted: "Yesterday a company of seventy-six fine, noble-looking fellows from Mobile arrived in this city under command of Gen. R. Desha, and in the afternoon marched down to the U.S. Barracks, all in excellent spirits."[7]

The three companies arrived on the Texas coast on May 13 and set up a hasty camp at Point Isabel, the army supply depot near the mouth of the Rio Grande. They were welcomed by General Taylor himself, fresh from the battles of Palo Alto and Reseca de la Palma on May 8 and 9. The actions had been resounding American victories, and the volunteers eagerly looked forward to their first engagement. A *Picayune* correspondent recorded the volunteers' arrival:

> Fort Polk, Point Isabel, May 13, 1846
> ... This morning part of the 1st artillery, 1st Infantry and some volunteers from your city and Mobile arrived, others being hourly expected. A company of mounted Texan rangers also arrived, a large number being daily expected to join the army opposite Matamoros. A large quantity of subsistence, arms, ordinance and ammunition is being taken to the army above, and soon the General will be able to open upon Matamoros.[8]

Despite a variety of rumors, the Alabama boys were told they would be leaving for Fort Brown, the new post across the Rio Grande from Matamoros, Mexico. The next day they were attached to a unit of regulars and Louisiana volunteers to begin the march, accompanied by a long train of artillery and supply wagons. The post was located some twenty-five miles upriver.

As the balance of the caravan proceeded on the American side of the river, General Taylor dispatched Lt. Colonel Wilson with four companies of regulars and Louisiana volunteers, along with Captain Desha's Alabama company, to cross the river and investigate reports of enemy troop movements at the pueblo of Burita. The U.S. steamer *Neva*, with a small detach-

---

[6] State of Alabama, Department of Archives and History, Montgomery, Alabama; letter dated August 22, 1985. Enlistment record shows Love to have been mustered into Captain Desha's Company on May 6, 1846, at Mobile, Alabama; appointed 4th sergeant July 2, 1846; and mustered out at New Orleans, August 3, 1846. A later bounty land application, based on this service, gives his enlistment date as May 3, which is probably more accurate. [7] *Picayune,* May 20, 1846.
[8] Ibid., May 23, 1846, and Butler, "Alabama Volunteers in the Mexican War, part two," *Alabama Genealogical Society Magazine,* Vol. 23, 1991.

The Road to Camargo 29

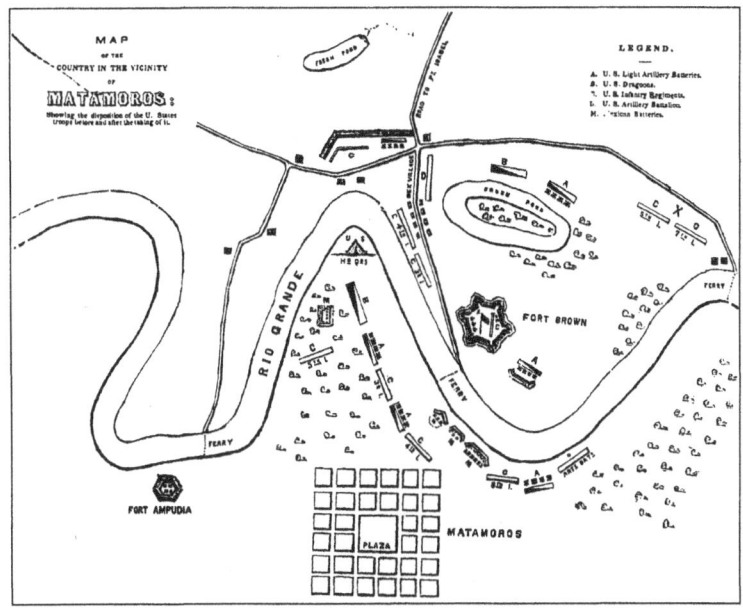

Map showing the area around Fort Brown and Matamoros, Tamaulipas, Mexico, indicating the American positions both before and after occupation by U.S. forces. *New Orleans Picayune, June 28, 1846.*

A woodcut rendition of Matamoros, as it looked from Fort Brown across the Rio Grande. *Chronicles of the Gringos.*

ment of troops and a field piece, accompanied Wilson's expedition. No enemy troops were sighted, and the town was secured without firing a shot. Four days later, General Taylor was back at Fort Brown and crossed the river to take Matamoros, but found the enemy there had also fled.

Although he had two heady battlefield victories, General Taylor had a burgeoning set of problems to contend with. The swamps skirting Point Isabel were a source of fevers that had prostrated many of the troops and volunteers bivouacked there. "It was here," wrote a correspondent, "that the mosquitos commenced their attack on us in full force—none of your common Louisiana mosquitos, but the genuine Mexican gallinippers. They came in clouds, fairly encrusting our horses and filling our eyes, noses and mouths, and biting."[9]

In late June and early July the rains came in torrents for two weeks. All along the Rio Grande, from Fort Brown and Matamoros and on to Camargo, Mexico, soldiers and volunteers did what they could to stay dry in a sea of mud and rain. "The volunteer camp on the opposite side of the river," wrote a correspondent from Matamoros on July 9, "... was disagreeable enough before the heavy rains commenced, but now it is a perfect mud puddle.... The tents of the volunteers are made of cotton, which allows a sufficiency of water to pass through to saturate everything inside."[10]

An unforseen problem was the hordes of volunteers that kept arriving. Taylor had neither the supplies nor the transportation to handle all these troops, and with no campaigns underway yet, the resulting inactivity was encouraging desertions, drinking, and other problems. Supplies promised by the government were far behind schedule.[11]

Symptomatic of the problems engendered by the restless troops was the capture in Mobile of two deserters from Desha's company. In late June there had been a dispute between the officers and men of the company over assigned duties. Two volunteers named Chandler and Kern were arrested and confined to quarters, but managed to escape and make their way back to Mobile, where they were promptly captured.[12] A portion of the company were in sympathy with the two deserters, but a letter from Captain Desha to the Mobile *Register and Journal* of July 10 made it clear the men were in serious trouble:

---

[9]*Picayune*, July 7, 1846.
[10]Ibid., July 12, 1846. Matamoras was generally spelled with the last 'o' as 'a' by the Americans, but on Mexican maps it was spelled "Matamoros."
[11]George Winston Smith and Charles Judah, *Chronicles of the Gringos: The U.S. Army in the Mexican War, 1846–1848* (Albuquerque: University of New Mexico Press, 1968).   [12]*Picayune*, July 12, 1846.

> Camp opposite Matamoros, June 28, 1846
>
> Dear Sir: Sergeant James Chandler, of my Company, who joined said Company in Mobile, after behaving very unsoldierlike and after being under arrest for grave offenses, and after a court martial had been organized for his trial, deserted last night and it is believed he took with him a horse that did not belong to him inasmuch as mine was missing this morning. It is thought he left here with Sergeant Kern who also deserted on yesterday from my company, and no doubt exists but they left together from a previous arrangement. This man Kern, it appears, was a deserter at the time he joined my company, from the 6th Regiment of U.S. Infantry, which fact the day previous to his desertion was ascertained and made known to him by myself. . . .
>
> Very respectfully,
> Robert Desha
> Captain Company Mobile Volunteers
>
> P.S. Since writing the above a friendly Mexican has come in and says this fellow Chandler borrowed his saddle about 8 o'clock last night under the pretense of coming to camp and had my horse.[13]

On July 14, Taylor's forces took the Mexican town of Camargo, situated some three miles south of the Rio Grande on the San Juan River. A correspondent of the *Picayune* sent the following dispatch:

> Camargo, July 15, 1846
>
> Gentlemen: I am happy to inform you that Camargo is now a port of entry, we having entered and taken possession of it yesterday morning about ten o'clock. The land forces—3 company's 7th Infantry, one section of artillery, and McColloch's company—came in this morning. . . .
>
> This town is a perfect ruin, the recent flood having destroyed nearly all the buildings.[14]

It was Taylor's plan to consolidate all his forces at Camargo, one hundred miles upriver. Here some 15,000 troops set up camp outside the old stone village, drilling when possible, digging latrines, pulling sentry duty, or going out on patrol. Dysentery and other diseases in the baking heat cut a terrible swath through the troops, and every day the burial parties went out to the cemetery and dropped the blanketed corpses into their desert graves. The sad drum rolls and firing of military salutes soon became a part of daily routine. By the time General Taylor began his move to the

---

[13]*Mobile Register and Journal*, July 10, 1846. More news of the deserters appeared in the *Register and Journal* on July 11 and 27, 1846.
[14]*Picayune*, July 26, 1846.

Author's art.

interior, only 370 of 795 Georgians were present for duty, and only 324 of 754 Alabamans. An estimated 1,500 men had died there.[15]

Love and his Alabama comrades baked in the heat and choking dust and shivered in the drenching rain, as climate and disease did much more damage than the Mexican muskets had done in battle. Apparently the Alabamans kept busy with patrol and occupation duty between Camargo and the coast.

In late July Captain Desha and his men were ordered back to Fort

---

[15]The great many deaths among the American troops at Camargo is noted in John S. D. Eisenhower, *So Far from God, The U.S. War with Mexico, 1846–1848* (New York: Random House, Inc., 1989), 110, and in the letters of Lt. John J. Peck as published in *The Sign of the Eagle*, Foreword and Commentary by Richard F. Pourade (San Diego: A Copley Book, 1970), 34.

Brown and boarded the brig *Empresario* for the trip down the Rio Grande.[16] Still hoping to see some action, Love and the other volunteers had no sooner disembarked than they received news that all three- and six-month enlistments had been invalidated by Congress. All who had enlisted under those terms were to be discharged, but with the option to re-enlist for a one-year term if they wished to do so.[17]

Around the campfire that night, Harry and his comrades discussed their situation. Rumors and newspaper reports confirmed what had happened. When Taylor had issued his first call for volunteers, he had only been authorized to solicit Louisiana and Texas for troops, which he had done. However, General Edmund Gaines, the overzealous commander of the Army's Western Division, requested the states of Alabama, Kentucky, Missouri, and Mississippi to also send volunteers.[18] Taylor's army was quickly glutted by a horde of volunteers he could neither supply nor move.[19]

The volunteers instinctively felt they were not appreciated—that they had only been used as a stopgap in an emergency. They had boldly rushed to Taylor's aid when he was threatened, but now were being discarded as no longer needed. Many of them were disgusted and ready to return home. To date, the war had been nothing but dust, blistering heat, mud, torrential rain, sickness, and disease. Death was from dysentery, measles, and other maladies—not in glorious battle.

They were at least partially placated by a general order issued by Taylor on July 21: "The general cannot forget that with an enthusiasm seldom exhibited in any country, they were the first to flock to his standard when he was menaced with a superior force. That with a generous disregard of self they sacrificed the highest personal interests to aid in sustaining the reputation of American arms."

Harry had been appointed sergeant on July 2, but he would have to re-enlist as a private. In the end, he opted to return home with most of his pals. Besides, there was the matter of his lady waiting for him at Mobile.

---

[16] *Picayune*, August 2, 1846.
[17] The General Order announcing the re-enlistment or discharge of the three- and six-month volunteers was published in the *Mobile Register and Journal* of August 10, 1846.
[18] A full discussion of the situation created by General Gaines appeared in the *Mobile Register and Journal*, August 24, 1846.
[19] A letter from General Taylor to the adjutant general of the Army on May 20, 1846, complains of Gaines' actions, stressing that he had only called for volunteers from the two authorized states. Gaines was later given a mild court martial for his impulsive actions. See *29th Congress, 2nd Session. House Executive Document 119: Message from the President of the United States, etc.* (Washington, D.C.: Ritchie and Heiss, Printers, 1847), 27–31.

Sergeant Love was discharged and officially mustered out at New Orleans on August 3, 1846. On the 10th the Mobile *Register* had a brief item on the returning volunteers:

> A portion of Captain Desha's Company came over from New Orleans on Saturday, where they had been paid off and mustered out of service. They look none the worse for wear, and are generally in fine health. The gallant old captain (Desha), now the hurry is over, is loitering behind at the watering places on the Gulf.

Captain Desha returned to Mobile on August 12.[20] A veteran of the War of 1812, this had been his last campaign, and he must have enjoyed meeting members of his company in the saloons of Mobile where the Texas expedition seemed much more important than it turned out to be.

Back in town, Harry was doubly disappointed to discover his lady love had strayed after his departure. A Texas acquaintance later wrote,

> Alas for human constancy, he found the fair object of his love had proved false during his absence, and bestowed herself on a less patriotic admirer. Harry, in a fit of misanthropic disgust, returned to the army, and throughout the war performed the most reckless feats of bravery. He never became entirely cured of his disappointment, which seemed to have taken a hold on his heart that neither time nor the instigation of common sense could entirely eradicate.[21]

Love may well have sadly ruminated over his lost love, but he did not join the army, except perhaps as a civilian employee. He may have also returned to ranch work, or even enlisted as a Texas Ranger. In light of his later career as an army dispatch rider and guide, he must have engaged in one of these occupations to come to know the country as well as he obviously did.

Sam Chamberlain, a trooper in the First Regiment of United States Dragoons during the Mexican War, later penned his memoirs of those exciting days. In recalling the exploits of the Texas Rangers he remembered the names of Captain Baylor, M. B. "Mustang" Gray, Ben McCulloch, and Captain Harry Love as being among those who inspired the most fear in the Mexican populace. The records of that colorful service are scattered and incomplete, and Chamberlain's memoir is the only known evidence that Love was indeed a prominent Ranger.[22]

Although the Ranger scenario is interesting, it is far more likely that

---

[20]*Mobile Register and Journal*, August 14, 1846.   [21]Vielé, *Following the Drum*, 228–229.
[22]Samuel E. Chamberlain, *My Confession* (New York: Harper & Brothers, Publishers, 1956), 177.

Love signed on as an army employee after his brief volunteer stint. A general order issued at Matamoros on July 10, 1846, noted that all volunteers were eligible to remain with the army as employees of the Quartermaster's Department, or elsewhere.[23] There were always civilians attached to army units—packers, guides, mechanics, couriers, teamsters, and blacksmiths employed by the army quartermasters. Harry was hired as a dispatch carrier and express rider between commands in the field and various military posts. By the time Mexico had capitulated and the Treaty of Guadalupe Hidalgo was signed on February 2, 1848, Love had established himself as one of the most daring and reliable couriers along the border. The *Matamoros Flag* of October 9, 1848 refers to "Mr. Henry Love, well known as having proved himself a good and faithful soldier, and one of the most trustworthy and fearless express-riders on this line." The implication is that he had been on the job for some time. It was a lonely and dangerous job, and occasional stints as guide for military patrols furthered his knowledge of the country. Harry undoubtedly preferred the solitude of his job to army life, entailing as it did a minimum of order-taking, military discipline, and routine.

Love was employed by Captain William Chapman, United States Army quartermaster stationed at Matamoros. A veteran of the Florida Indian War and Taylor's Mexican campaign, Chapman served as quartermaster for General John E. Wool's army for eighteen months. After the war, Chapman was very much involved in the occupation of Matamoros, supervising the schools, collecting local taxes, improving the roads, and establishing a local police force. The captain's wife, Helen, had joined him in January 1848, and the two lived comfortably in several rooms of the large home of a prominent Matamoros Mexican señora.[24]

Love's duties took him through Mexico, New Mexico, and Texas. He generally took two horses and carried military dispatches, mail, and often newspapers from Fort Brown and Matamoros to other outposts. Upon arrival he would report to the commanding officer and pick up new dis-

---

[23] *Picayune*, August 2, 1846.

[24] There is no record of just when Captain Chapman hired Harry Love, but the Matamoros newspaper article seems to indicate that Love had been in service for some time. For information on Captain Chapman, see Caleb Coker, ed., *The News from Brownsville, Helen Chapman's Letters from the Texas Military Frontier, 1848–1852* (Austin, Texas: State Historical Association, 1992), xi–xxvi. This book, the ably-edited letters of Chapman's wife to her parents in Massachusetts, presents a wonderfully detailed chronicle of Harry Love's Texas by one who knew him well. Caleb Coker, the great-great-grandson of Helen and William Chapman, was most helpful in supplying documents and information for this work.

patches for the return trip. Often he would travel to several posts before returning to the Rio Grande.

During the summer of 1848 Captain Chapman was transferred to Fort Brown, across the river from Matamoros. The post was primarily concerned with the transfer of government property from Mexico; due to all of the activity, the village of Brownsville quickly came into being also. At one point, Love, or one of the other dispatch riders, had to ride into the dangerous deserts of Mexico to give a returning American unit the distasteful news that, instead of returning home, they were being transferred to California.[25]

In September, Love was given dispatches to carry to Chihuahua across a dangerous stretch of desert called the *Trevesía*. It was a particularly inhospitable land of jagged mountains, interrupted only by rough salt hardpan described even today by a modern traveler as "the most desolate country backroads in the western hemisphere."[26] After delivering his dispatches, Love rested briefly before the return trip to Fort Brown with some mail.

Leaving Chihuahua at a steady gallop, Love had just passed the village of Parras when he stopped to rest at a Mexican rancho. Here he was informed that a large Comanche war party had stolen some animals and wounded several of the local inhabitants. After resting for twenty-four hours, Harry felt the Indians had moved on and again took the trail accompanied by an American traveler named William Sherman. It was deemed safer to travel by night, and at about eight o'clock in the evening the two riders saw a group of horsemen approaching across the desert skyline. It was dark but, assuming the approaching group to be a party of Mexicans, Love hailed them—only to be greeted by a volley of arrows.

Startled, Harry and his companion veered their horses off the road and into some mountains, hoping to lose their attackers. They hid out that night, then, believing they were safe the following day, returned to the road, only to have the Indians quickly pick up their trail. Whipping their horses again off the road, the two men dodged down into an arroyo and quickly prepared for a defense. Recent rains had swelled the few creeks

---

[25]The incident of the returning army unit being transferred to California instead of going home undoubtedly refers to six units of dragoons and a battery of light artillery, all under the command of Lt. Colonel John Washington. See Henry F. Dobyns, ed., *Hepah, California!, The Journal of Cave Johnson Coutts* (Tucson: Arizona Pioneers Historical Society, 1961), 29–45.

[26]The "modern traveler" across the *Trevesía* was Caleb Coker, who made the trip in the course of editing *The News from Brownsville*. Caleb Coker to the author, March 30, 1994.

Major William W. Chapman, the army quartermaster who hired Love as a dispatch rider and spearheaded the expedition up the Rio Grande River. A daguerrotype made in about 1849. *Caleb Coker Collection.*

and arroyos in the area and a rushing stream gushed behind Love and Sherman as they sighted their rifles over the rim of the gorge.

Firing as the Indians came into range, Love saw what he took to be a chief go down as his followers reined up and milled around.[27] Quickly mounting again, the two Americans urged their horses into the flooded stream, but the rushing water was too much for Sherman's animal, which had been wounded the day before and was weak from loss of blood. As the horse was swept away, it was dashed over a waterfall just as Love threw his lariat over the floundering Sherman. The two men made it across the stream, Sherman mounting Love's second horse as they quickly outdistanced the discouraged Indians. "Mr. Love," noted a newspaper account of the affair, "who has made several excursions on this route, as also others, states that he has uniformly met with kind and hospitable treatment from the higher classes of the inhabitants."

Some equipment had been lost in crossing the stream, and at the village of Mapimí the two riders stopped and looked up the local magis-

---

[27]*American Flag,* October 9, 1848. The Indians that Love encountered were probably roving Comanche, who regularly invaded Mexico that time of year. Ruxton says the month of September on the Comanche calendar is known as the "Mexico Moon."

trate. The town was merely a collection of adobe houses inhabited by several thousand miners and farmers, all living in dread of the Indians.[28] Knowing he could be charged for any missing government property, Love had Sherman dictate the circumstances of the loss to the official, who wrote up the affidavit in Spanish:

> I certify with all the formality of the law, that in this my court, personally appeared the foreigner William Shearman [sic], who made oath according to the form used by those of the religion he professes that coming in company with Harry Love in the direction of the port of Matamoros where they are sent by the government, in the desert at a place called San Antonio, they were attacked by a party of barbarians of from thirty to thirty-five, that having fought with them, his horse was wounded and continuing their flight and on arriving at the Tinaja de los Dragones, they threw themselves into the creek, wherein it being swollen, the horse fell, he being wounded and weak, and could not get out nor was it possible to get him out and with the horse which was grey were lost the saddle, a percussion carbine, a rifle the same and a pair of pistols; all these arms being such as are used by the army and at request of the party interested and for the uses for which he may need it, I give the present on common paper, as he stated that it would be useful to him.   Mapime, September 13, 1848
> (Signed) Carmine Gonzales[29]

Back at Fort Brown, Love reported to Captain Chapman, giving him the Chihuahua mail and the affidavit. One of the lost weapons belonged to another officer at the post, and he was appraised of what happened to get Harry off the hook.[30]

In late January 1849, Love was assigned to carry dispatches to Santa Fe in New Mexico Territory. Passports were obtained from the Mexican authorities and the American consul, and he was issued a Colt revolver, a powder flask, two horses and saddle blankets, a saddle, bridle, two surcingles, and a valise. His pay at the time was seventy-five dollars per month plus all expenses, a considerable amount at that time. Major Chapman advanced him two months' pay and authorized the quartermaster at Santa Fe to pay him any expense money should he need it. It was an important trip. Besides carrying dispatches from Major General William Worth to

---

[28]George Frederick Ruxton, *Adventures in Mexico* (New York: Outing Publishing Company, 1915), 87. Ruxton writes of his travels throughout Mexico in 1846.

[29]The carbine lost by Love on this trip belonged to Captain Reuben P. Campbell; W. W. Chapman to R. P. Campbell, October 10, 1848. Copies furnished by Caleb Coker.

[30]Ibid.

Colonel John M. Washington at Santa Fe, Love was to return via San Antonio, where he was to report directly to General Worth. Chapman's specific orders to Love were as follows:

> Mr. Harry Love,
> January 30, 1849.
> Sir.
>   You will proceed tomorrow morning to Santa Fe, as bearer of dispatches from Major General Worth, Commanding 8th & 9th Military Departments, to Colonel Washington, Commanding Officer at Santa Fe.
>   Your dispatches convey military orders having reference mainly to such disposition of troops as will fulfill our treaty stipulations in restricting the Indians residing within our borders from committing depredations in the Mexican States.
>   On your return from Santa Fe, you will take the most practical route to San Antonio, Texas, and report in person to Maj. General Worth at the latter place. You will make every possible inquiry which may be useful to the Commanding General in regard to the roads, the water and grass and the resources and character of the country.[31]

Harry had recently received word that he was eligible for Mexican War bounty land, and on January 31 he called on Justice of the Peace G. M. Armstrong at his office in Brownsville. Love had acquired little of this world's goods up to this point, but he must have realized the danger of his occupation. If anything happened to him, he wanted something to leave behind for his family—even if it was a mere dusty plot of Texas land.[32] Dictating a note in which he directed that the approved bounty land grant should be "issued to the care" of his friend, W. P. Wallace, a Brownsville merchant, Harry then finished preparations for his trip.

It was not until early on the morning of February 8 when Love cantered his horse out of Fort Brown and headed northwest along the Rio Grande. He may have stopped at Ringgold Barracks some ten or twelve miles above Fort Brown, then crossed the muddy Rio Grande on a rope ferry into Mexico, galloping easily along the road to Camargo. The road leading towards the old town undoubtedly brought back bitter memories of that disastrous summer of 1846. Passing an occasional cart or a

---
[31]Two letters of Major Chapman, one to Harry Love and the other to Colonel Washington, give instructions and the purpose of the Santa Fe trip. Both letters are from the Chapman letter book, copies furnished by Caleb Coker.
[32]Texas State Archives, Austin, Texas; letter from Mrs. Eddie Williams, Texas State Archives, June 10, 1981, including copy of document.

Declaration to obtain Bounty Land.

State of TEXAS, County of *Cameron*
ON THIS *thirty-first* day of *January* in the year one thousand eight hundred and *forty-nine* personally appeared before me, the undersigned, a Justice of the Peace for the county and State above mentioned, *Henry Love* who, being duly sworn according to law, declares that he is the identical *Henry Love* who was a *Sergeant* in the company commanded by Captain *Robert Desha* in the ~~Regiment~~ *Alabama Vol. (attached to 1st W.S. Inf.)* commanded by *Lt. Col. H. Wilson (at that time)* That he enlisted on the *fourth* day of *May* 1846 for the term of *six months* and was discharged at *New Orleans La.* on the *sixth* day of *August* 1846 by reason of *the company being disbanded*

Henry Love

Harry Love's bounty land application, based on his Mexican War service. If approved, he could obtain 160 acres of land. Harry had the Justice of the Peace fill out the form, then he validated it with his easily-identified signature.
Texas State Library, Austin.

reboso-clad senorita on a mule, the expressman kept up a steady pace along the shrub and brush-lined road, and soon the village's cathedral tower was in view.

Camargo was an ancient village of mostly one-story stone houses with flat roofs. The town surrounded the usual Spanish plaza, with the barred windows of the buildings giving the impression of a prison. "This precaution," noted a visitor referring to the bars, "is taken that the whole house may be thrown open and yet protected."[33]

Soon he had ridden through and was on his way again, moving at a steady gallop toward Monterrey. From there he followed the military road to Chihuahua, where he stopped for six days. The whole country had been devastated by the Indians, with ranchos burned and most of the stock

---
[33] A. Wislizenus, M.D., *Memoir of a Tour to Northern Mexico* (Glorieta, New Mexico: The Rio Grande Press, Inc., 1969), 147.

driven off.[34] He was strongly advised not to leave town without an escort, but he insisted on heading for El Paso alone. He was twice chased by Indians, but arrived at Santa Fe on March 24, being twenty-eight days from Camargo to his destination. He reported to Colonel Washington at his headquarters in town, the officer quite pleased to receive a packet of late newspapers Major Chapman had sent along.

Love had brought along other news also, as reported in a letter from Colonel Washington to Major Chapman: "It had been rumored here from Chihuahua that Genl. T[aylor] was elected, but the fact was not positively known until announced by your expressman."[35]

Love was in town nearly a week and must have enjoyed the *cantinas* of old Santa Fe after his long ride. Fort Marcy, the military post, was a defensive position overlooking the town, but the troops were all quartered in the village. The plaza was lined with adobe structures, including the old Palace of the Governors, which had been built in 1606 and was the oldest building in the United States. Surrounded by beautiful, rolling hills, Colonel Washington described the dirty little village as "by no means a desirable residence.... It can boast but little of honest men or bonny ladies. Society is at a low ebb. The American portion of it consists mainly of gamblers and merchants scratching tight for a living with frequent occurrences of unexpected failures and sudden elopements, leaving those behind them minus a book account, a horse, gun, coat or some other article of value."[36]

Everywhere along his route Harry had heard talk of the California gold discoveries; Santa Fe was no different. If he, too, was bitten by the gold bug, he had to put aside such inclinations for the moment. He reported to Quartermaster Captain Thomas L. Brent, who replaced his two travel-worn mounts with fresh animals. Brent also assigned a Cherokee Indian scout named Rodgers to accompany Love on the return trip to get through what he termed "really a most hazardous & perilous journey." Brent would comment in a letter to Chapman that "Love is a gallant fellow and I hope will reach you safely."[37]

Leaving Santa Fe on the morning of April 3, 1849, Love and the Cherokee Rodgers traveled south, making the 370-mile trip to El Paso in thir-

---
[34]*Corpus Christi Star*, June 2, 1849.
[35]Letter from Colonel Washington to Major Chapman dated Santa Fe, March 29, 1849.
[36]Ibid. Love carried this letter back to Fort Brown.
[37]Chapman letter book, copies furnished by Caleb Coker.

teen days. Here they joined forces with Lieutenant William H. C. Whiting, who had led an army engineering expedition to survey the best route to El Paso from San Antonio.[38] A party of California gold rushers had accompanied Whiting who was now preparing to return to San Antonio.[39]

A twenty-five-year-old shavetail who had arrived in Texas late the previous year, Whiting and Lieutenant William F. Smith had left San Antonio on February 12, 1849, with a party of some sixteen civilian guides and packers. They had encountered particularly sparsely watered country during their expedition and now planned to alter their return route accordingly. Besides ease of travel, the projected road had to have available water and grass for both military and civilian wagon trains.

With Harry and his Cherokee accompanying them, Whiting's party left El Paso on April 19. They headed south, along the Rio Grande, passing through the villages of Isleta, Socorro, and San Elizario. The weather was becoming very warm, and they would soon be traveling at night to spare their animals.

After striking their old trail on April 23, the party made their way through some grassy plains and camped near a landmark called Eagle Mountain. While meals were being prepared, one of the men was carrying some embers to another campsite when the grass caught fire and winds quickly spread the flames. Everyone turned out with blankets and water to fight the spreading fire; after some singed hair and beards, it was finally brought under control. "These accidents," wrote Whiting in his journal, "are very dangerous, both from the alarm they always give to the Indians and the risk to packs, arms and animals."[40]

After making a dry camp the expedition was on the move in search of water early the next day. By 3:30 they had reached the Rio Grande after having traveled about twenty-five miles. They were in rocky hills and mountains now, and any future road in this country would entail considerable work to make it practical.

By April 29 they were in mountainous oak and pine forests. The country was rugged, and in a canyon of high, dark bluffs and spires, they found a human skeleton. That morning a mule had been lost by Allen, one of the packers. Harry and the Cherokee Rodgers helped track the animal and they rejoined the party that evening at their creekside camp.

---

[38] *Corpus Christi Star,* June 2 and August 11, 1849.   [39] *Houston Telegraph,* February 15, 1849.
[40] Ralph Bieber and Averam B. Bandel, eds., *Exploring Southwestern Trails, 1846–1854* (Glendale, Calif.: The Arthur H. Clark Company, 1938), 314–350.

By May 1 they were following a wide Indian trail and soon reached the abandoned site of a large camp. While riding along nearby Limpia Creek, great black clouds swept overhead as lightning lit up the area. The group was suddenly struck by a fierce hail- and rainstorm, forcing them to seek shelter among the willow and cottonwood thickets along the creek. Wrapping themselves in their wet blankets, the men tried to sleep through a night that Whiting later characterized as "one of the most uncomfortable" he had ever spent. A few days later, they were caught in another violent hailstorm while camping on an open plain. The men had to hold their saddles over their heads for protection and now longed for the tents they had long ago cut up to make pack pads for their animals.

On the 6th they encountered a truculent band of Lipan Indians, but tough talk and threats convinced them to be more sociable. On May 15, Whiting sent several of his men ahead to San Antonio to announce their safe arrival in the area. Love was impatient at the slow traveling, but agreed to remain with the larger main group. By the time they struck the Woll military road on May 20, however, Harry decided to go on ahead, leaving early the following morning. It was a mere ninety miles to San Antonio now, and he arrived at the district army headquarters on May 23, 1849. Whiting's party had slowed Love down considerably and he later told Major Chapman that, traveling alone, he could have made the trip from El Paso to San Antonio in sixteen or eighteen days.

Love was informed that General Worth had died of cholera on May 7, and after reporting to the acting commander of the department, he set out on the last leg of his return trip to Fort Brown.[41] On the way down he was interviewed for an article in the *Corpus Christi Star* of June 2, 1849:

> FROM SANTA FE—Harry Love, the celebrated express rider, arrived here on Wednesday last from San Antonio, to which place he accompanied the U.S. Topographical Engineers from El Paso. Mr. Love is thus the first man who came by the direct route from El Paso to the Gulf Coast, which trip he says can easily be made in twenty days to this point.
>
> He represents the country around Santa Fe as being entirely overrun with hostile Indians. So bold had they become that a party of Apaches had entered the corral of the U.S. troops stationed at Don Llano, sixty miles above El Paso, and stole thirteen American horses under the very noses of the sentries....
>
> The day before Mr. Love left San Antonio news had been received there

---

[41] *Houston Telegraph*, May 24, 1849.

Mrs. Helen Chapman, shown with her son William, was Harry Love's biggest fan in frontier Texas and mentioned him in many of her letters home. A daguerrotype made about 1846. *Caleb Coker Collection.*

of several murders having been committed in the vicinity of the town by Indians and Gen. Harney had sent out a party of dragoons in pursuit, with orders to take no prisoners. . . . Mr. L. left on Thursday for Fort Brown.[42]

Helen Chapman reported Harry's return to the post in a letter to her mother dated June 8, 1849:

> Harry Love came dashing up to the office last week, his horse covered with foam, bearing dispatches from Colonel Washington. He is a perfect specimen of the Border Dandy, browned by exposure to wind and weather, of magnificent physical proportions, and altogether bearing himself with a dashing easy kind of grace that would astonish you. We had heard he had been murdered and the joy of his safe return was unbounded. He brings us accounts of the Indians ravaging the whole line above.

The American Flag of May 16 had indeed reported Harry's murder in Monclova, Mexico, but on June 2 the paper reported the "well-known and daring express rider" was not dead as rumor had suggested. Report-

---

[42]Major Chapman to his superior, Major General Thomas S. Jesup, June 8, 1849. Records Group 92, Consolidated Correspondence File of the Office of the Quartermaster General; letter from Charles A. Shaughnessy, August 20, 1981, Navy and Old Army Branch, Military Archives Division, National Archives, Washington, D.C.

ing to Major Chapman at the fort, Love soon discovered he was a national celebrity. The story of his ride was repeated in the New Orleans and New York newspapers, and when he told Chapman he would like an increase from seventy-five to one hundred dollars a month plus expenses for his services, the major readily agreed.[43] He had other plans for his now-famous express rider.

In early August, Major Chapman sent Love north with dispatches to Austin and San Antonio. One night, on the way to Corpus Christi, the express rider was suddenly confronted with seven men who appeared ahead of him on the road. Reining up, the expressman waved his hand and shouted, "Clear the road gentlemen, or I must do it for myself." Love heard his name passed among the intruders, who suddenly vanished into the chaparral. It was thought the supposed highwaymen were from around Brownsville and were afraid of being recognized.[44]

Communication was so difficult and time consuming along the frontier that it was customary for teamsters, stagecoach lines, and express companies to carry the latest newspapers from town to town, and Harry was no exception. "To Captain Harry Love," reported the *Corpus Christi Star* on August 11, "who has arrived from the Rio Grande, we are indebted for late Brownsville papers."

As if frequent Indian raids nearby were not enough of a concern, Brownsville was a rough and wild town with a floating population of soldiers, gamblers, teamsters, and merchants. "The population of Brownsville," noted the *New Orleans Daily Delta*, "of all colors, at the present time is 5,000. It is a right bustling, business place . . . several two and three story brick houses are going up."[45]

When new Fort Brown was constructed across the river from Matamoros, Major Chapman and his wife moved into quarters at the post and watched as the nearby village of Brownsville grew into a flourishing trading center. Like most frontier towns, drinking and gambling were the popular pastimes, and Helen Chapman sorely missed her cultured New England home. A native of Massachusetts, where she obtained a good education, Mrs. Chapman was trained as a teacher and was a skilled and articulate observer of her times.[46] "At last," she wrote her mother in Feb-

---

[43]*New Orleans Bee*, June 19, 1849, and the *New York Herald*, June 28, 1849.
[44]Letter dated August 24, 1849, Coker, ed., *The News from Brownsville*, 146.
[45]*New Orleans Daily Delta*, March 22, 1850.
[46]Helen Chapman's letters at this time describing life in Matamoros and Fort Brown are fascinating glimpses of life along the early Rio Grande.

ruary 1849, "to my great joy they have got a school started in Brownsville to be kept by a very excellent, and I should think, well educated young man, a member of the Methodist Church. He has organized a Sunday School and I trust this is the dawn of better things."

By August 19 Love was back in town, as noted by Mrs. Chapman:

> Last Sunday while on my way to a prayer meeting in Brownsville, I discovered dashing down the street, to my great delight, our dashing and favorite express rider, Harry Love. He had been sent by the Major to headquarters in Texas and also to Austin. It was a perilous journey and we had again been troubled by fears for his safety. But here he was again, safe and sound.
>
> I wish I could picture him to your vision, as he came dashing down the street, well mounted as he always is, sitting his horse as if he were a part of the noble animal he rides, his long black curls flowing in the wind, his chest thrown out, his expression cool, frank and resolute, his saber and spurs clashing, his clothes torn by the chaparral and covered with dust, one of Colt's revolvers, a six shooter, fastened to his side and an additional brace of pistols in his holsters. These are his usual accouterments....
>
> "How do you do, Harry? What's the news? Just arrived?" and so on were the exclamations from all sides as he entered the town....
>
> As we met in the street, I smiled and he took his cap from his head and bowed very low; but I was too glad for such a salutation merely and I held out my hand with "How do you do, Mr. Love? We are delighted to see you back again."[47]

After talking briefly with Mrs. Chapman, Love rode over to the fort and reported to her husband. He had brought the major's leave papers from San Antonio and quickly briefed him on other matters before retiring to his quarters. Mrs. Chapman saw him later, surrounded by friends and others inquiring about the news and his latest trip. "He has unbounded popularity both with gentlemen and the rabble," she wrote.

There is little doubt but that Love was in his element. He was as important to the average Texan as any town mayor or general overseeing a garrison. He brought the news—the lifeblood of any of the isolated frontier posts and towns scattered across the Texas border. In addition, he was envied as one who worked alone on his own terms and was respected by the army officers, who often looked down their noses at common folk.

---

[47]Letter dated August 24, 1849, Coker, ed., *The News from Brownsville*, 145–146. She also writes of the discussions with her husband concerning transfers to the West Coast. Neither relished the idea.

A keelboat such as the one Love operated on the Rio Grande. The pole handlers faced in the opposite direction from which the boat was traveling. *Harpers New Monthly Magazine, December 1855.*

That Love had also cherished the formative years of his Vermont youth was made clear when he learned of the new Sunday School in town. Mrs. Chapman wrote:

> I must tell you while I think of it of quite a touching little incident concerning our famous Harry. You know before he came down the river, he was reported and mourned as dead. But he came as usual and during that visit to Brownsville he heard of the Sunday School. He expressed himself as much interested in its success, and Lo! The next Sunday, he made his appearance divested of all his border trappings and dressed in a handsome suit of black. They say he displayed the delight of a child and said he had not had an opportunity for many years of seeing such a sight.[48]

Love watched with interest as a constant stream of gold rushers passed through the town headed for El Paso and the southern Gila Trail to California. Major Chapman had discussed California with his courier, Harry no doubt describing his visit there in 1839. Chapman dreaded being sent

---
[48]Ibid., 147.

to that far corner of the country so much that he applied for further service at Fort Brown. As crude as their current post was, California or Oregon seemed much worse to both he and his wife, and it made more sense to stay with a known quantity.

But Chapman could see the far-away look in Love's eyes, and he knew gold fever was becoming a magnet his expressman could not resist much longer. Well aware of Harry's maritime experience and hoping to keep him as long as he could, Major Chapman put him in charge of a keelboat on the upper Rio Grande.[49] The craft was christened the *Harry Love* and plied the river between various army posts delivering supplies. It was, however, strictly a device for keeping the frontiersman handy.

Steamboats and other small craft had regularly traversed the Rio Grande from the gulf to Fort Brown, but much beyond that point, little was known of the practicality of the river's navigation. Chapman had obtained authorization to build two keelboats for the purpose of exploring the upper reaches of the river. If successful, these boats would be a much more practical way of supplying upriver towns and military posts.

When he told Love of the venture, he saw the frontiersman's eyes sparkle with interest. The two men must have huddled together for hours discussing plans, and it was agreed that Love would construct a model to the agreed-upon specifications.[50]

Meanwhile, the Chapmans planned to leave in late September 1849 for a trip home and a reunion with their young son, Willie.

---

[49]Major Chapman to his superior, Major General Thomas S. Jesup, June 8, 1849. Records Group 92, Consolidated Correspondence File of the Office of the Quartermaster General; letter from Charles A. Shaughnessy, August 20, 1981, Navy and Old Army Branch, Military Archives Division, National Archives, Washington, D.C.

For a discussion of Chapman's and others' efforts at navigation of the Rio Grande, see Pat Kelley, *River of Lost Dreams* (Lincoln and London: University of Nebraska Press, 1986), 42–93.

[50]Major Chapman to Captain E. B. Babbitt, January 24, 1849; letter in Chapman letter book, courtesy Caleb Coker.

3

Sonora

Although the Mexican province of Sonora lay to the west of Love's noted ride to Santa Fe, conditions all along the border were pretty much the same. Indian raids were constant and brutal, and burned ranches and *haciendas* dotted the landscape. Both the Mexican government and the state officials of Sonora were so factionalized, poor, and unable to offer any significant aid, and the frontier was largely unprotected. When news of the California gold discoveries began to spread in early 1848, the inhabitants of Sonora began looking around at their situation. Although there were some rich mines in the state, working many of them was an isolated and dangerous way of life. The Apaches and Yaquis constantly picked off straggling ranchers, miners, and supply trains. Life in the harsh desert country was a constant struggle.

California offered hope. Many Sonorans saw little choice between remaining in their current hopeless condition and making the move north with the hope of acquiring wealth. When large parties of Sonorans began making the trek to Alta California, the Mexican authorities became alarmed. The weak and impoverished state would become even more vulnerable to Indian raids with so many men leaving, but there was little they could do.[1]

Dragoon First Lieutenant Cave J. Couts accompanied an army column being transferred from Mexico to California in the summer of 1848. After crossing the Colorado River into California, he noted the droves of emigrants in his journal:

---

[1] An excellent overview of the situation in Mexico's Sonora province during the California gold rush is Sister M. Colette Standart, O.P., "The Sonora Migration to California, 1848–1856: A Study in Prejudice," *Southern California Quarterly* 58, no. 3 (Fall 1976).

Persons, Mexicans from Sonora, are passing us daily on their way to the abundancia, the gold mines. This is all we can hear, The Mines!

... The whole state of Sonora is on the move, are passing us in gangs daily, and say they have not yet started. Naked and shirtailed Indians and Mexicans or Californians, go and return in 15 or 20 days with over a pound of pure gold each, per day, and say "they had bad luck and left...."[2]

• • •

There is every indication that Joaquín Murrieta was born and raised in the Mexican state of Sonora. His mother, Eduviges Hipólito, was married to Juan Carrillo and the couple had two sons—Joaquín Manuel and Jesús Carrillo. The father died when the boys were still quite young. The Indians were extremely troublesome around Ures where the widow Carrillo lived, and a brother, Don Jesús Hipólito, moved both his own and his sister's family to the Pueblo de Murrieta, near the Sinaloa border, where it was more safe. Here Rosa remarried a man named Joaquín Murrieta and began raising an extended family. A son, Joaquín, later to be so famous in California, was born here about 1830, along with José, Jesús, and several sisters. According to family tradition, these Murrietas were fair-skinned, with some of them having brown hair and blue eyes. Don Jesús Hipólito moved with his own family to upper California in 1848, after the Mexican War.[3]

Joaquín Murrieta reportedly came to California in 1849 as a young man of about seventeen years. A good-looking boy, he wore his hair long and confined in a bandana under his wide-brimmed hat. He had heavy eyebrows and a broad jaw tapering to a firm chin. His light and scraggly beard indicated that he had never shaved.

Travelling with the caravan was a collection of Murrieta and Carrillo family friends and relatives, some eighteen people in all. Reportedly,

---

[2]Dobyns, ed., *Hepah, California!* 86–88.
[3]Although a birth certificate or other evidence of Murrieta's Sonora nativity has yet to be discovered, there seems little reason to doubt the research and interviews of Frank Latta among Murrieta descendants in the area. His extensive travels, many documentary photographs, and other data acquired over many years of research all add up to the best evidence yet on the noted bandit's origins. See Frank F. Latta, *Joaquín Murrieta and His Horse Gangs* (Santa Cruz, Calif.: Bear State Books, 1980), 145–254. Despite the fact that a good portion of the book should have been relegated to footnotes, Latta's work is the starting place for any serious Murrieta research. See also the *San Francisco Call-Bulletin,* April 28, 1934, for the story of Robert J. Richards, whose mother was a cousin of Joaquín Murrieta. An interesting account of a scholar on the trail of Murrieta is Raymund F. Wood, "New Light on Joaquin Murrieta," *Pacific Historian,* Winter 1970.

Sonora, California, in the early 1850s was a booming gold rush town, scattered between the Tuolumne County hills in the lower Sierra Nevadas. Murrieta and many of the early Mexican miners came into this area and many residents recognized Joaquín's head when it was exhibited there. *California State Library.*

Joaquín's young wife, Rosa Féliz, along with her brothers Reyes, Claudio, and Jesús, were members of the group. They came north over the old Anza trail, in a caravan large enough to insure protection against Indians. There were many such groups on the trail that spring, some riding and some walking, while a few *carretas* and wagons were utilized. Most provisions and property were packed by mule back, however.[4]

The trip was through a raw and hostile desert country, over a trail labeled *El Camino del Diablo*—The Road of the Devil. Sonorans raised in this country, however, thought nothing of the trip, so long as one took the proper precautions and carried plenty of water. Teodora Arredondo, who made the journey several times during this period, remembered the bones of an unprepared party that had preceded them. Still, her fondest memories were

---

[4]The Murrieta caravan to California is based on Latta's researches as detailed in his book, pp. 145–254. The Féliz family lived near the Murrieta home in Sonora. Although Latta never learned the true identity of Claudio, various newspaper references leave little doubt that he and Reyes Féliz were brothers, and the confession of Teodore Basquez (noted later) provides final confirmation. See the *San Joaquin Republican*, August 11, 1853, and the *Placerville Herald*, August 13, 1853.

of a pleasant nature—night camps on the desert, with guitars and violins wailing and spirited dancing on carpets thrown on the ground.[5]

It took the group about three months to make the trip; by the time they were well into California, Rosa Féliz was ill with scurvy. Joaquín visited his uncles and aunts in Monterey, then worked in the San Jose area while Rosa recuperated. As soon as possible, the couple headed east into the foothills of the Sierra Nevada Mountains.

Most of the Mexicans who came north with the gold rush were skilled miners and ranchers, and the Murrietas were no exception. A large Mexican population was centered in Tuolumne County, along the Stanislaus River, and at the "Sonoranian Camp," soon to be named Sonora. The Murrieta group probably stopped there to look over the country. Both Carrillos and Murrietas are listed in the 1850 Tuolumne County census, as well as José Ochoa, who later claimed to have come to California with the Murrieta group.[6]

Joaquín's movements and experiences during this early period of his California sojourn are difficult to establish. The unsettled climate of the time helps validate the traditional tales of violence that turned him into an outlaw. Mexicans were among the first into the mines, since they had the shortest distance to travel. Also, the native Californians were, for all practical purposes, Mexicans and had quickly occupied some of the choice mining locations in the gold country.

California had just been acquired from Mexico with the Treaty of Guadalupe Hidalgo and many of the gold-rushing Americans felt Mexicans had no rights in their new territory. Most American soldiers discharged in California after the war also flocked to the mines. Stevenson's Regiment was sprinkled liberally with New York criminals and thugs, and these, together with others who had little regard for the rights of Mexicans and other foreigners, felt they had every right to drive Mexicans

---

[5]The Arredondo interview was in F. F. Latta, "Murrieta Rides Again," *The Pony Express*, September 1962.

[6]U.S. Census Population Schedules, 1850 Census, Tuolumne County. For life in the mining camp of Sonora and the strong Mexican tinge to the population, see William Perkins, *William Perkins' Journal or Life at Sonora, 1849–1852* (Berkeley and Los Angeles: University of California Press, 1964), 20–26; and Thomas Robertson Stoddart, *Annals of Tuolumne County*, ably edited and annotated by Carlo M. De Ferrari (Sonora, Calif.: Tuolumne County Historical Society, 1963), 54–55. Both of the above works have much discussion of the Foreign Miner's Tax, as does Raymund F. Wood's *California's Agua Fria: The Early History of Mariposa County* (Fresno, Calif.: Academy Library Guild, 1954), 61–65.

from their claims. They were bolstered in this feeling in April 1850 when the state legislature passed the Foreign Miners' License Act, which levied a fee of twenty dollars per month on foreign miners. Unjust and poorly executed, this act set the stage for much of the racial violence that occurred in the mines. The fee was reduced to four dollars per month in 1853, but was still subject to much abuse, as indicated by an article in the San Francisco *Alta* of August 15 of that year:

> FOREIGN MINERS' TAX—The Chinamen and other foreigners are subjected to the grossest imposition and extortion in some parts of the mines by villains who pretend to be collectors of the Foreign Miners' Tax. Aside from the profits of the business, the imposition and outrage is looked upon as capital sport. If the poor Chinamen make opposition to the demands of the voluntary tax collectors, the "tax" is doubled, and they get flogged into the bargain.

The tax and individual acts of intolerance caused many a Mexican to turn to crime in retaliation. But just as there were criminals among the Americans, there were those Mexicans who sought an easier way to make a living than by the drudgery of mining. Taken all together, this combination of factors made for an explosive decade in California, and a climate in which a Joaquín Murrieta was almost inevitable.

Whatever the implications of legend and popular history, apparently Joaquín's first documented brush with the law took place in late 1850. On November 28 he was arrested in Stockton and charged with the theft of a pair of boots from the shop of merchant Hyman Mitchell. When questioned in the City Recorder's Court, the defendant gave the following responses:

Q. "What is your name and age?"
A. "Joaquin Murieta, age 18."
Q. "Where were you born?" (or been)?
A. "In Placers Seco and mile of American Camp."
Q. "Where do you reside & how long have you resided there?"
A. "In Stockton, in the street, been there about five months."
Q. "What is your business or profession?"
A. "A miner."
(By recorder:) Give any explanation you may think proper of the circumstances appearing in the testimony against you and state any facts which you think will tend to your exculpation.

A. "Another man gave me the boots. I didn't take them myself."

his X
Joaquin Murieta
mark[7]

Although some of the queries are difficult to read, the answers clearly indicate the question. The prisoner was illiterate and would not have known that the recorder had spelled his surname with one 'r' instead of two. More importantly, the document notes that he had been living in the area of the "American camp," as Columbia was known at the time. "Placers Seco," or "dry diggings," was another name for the area. It was recalled by many in later years that Joaquín had lived in this vicinity.

Tried in the San Joaquin County Court of Sessions before Judge Benjamin Williams, Joaquín was given a jury trial and convicted as charged. In mid-December 1850, he was sentenced to three months in the county jail. At that time, the city of Stockton utilized city prisoners in chain gangs to work on various municipal projects. Joaquín and others probably went to work on the local levee, which needed constant upkeep.[8]

The future bandit chief may or may not have served out his term. There was a jail break on February 24, 1851, and eleven prisoners escaped.[9] Two of the fugitives were recaptured. The nine others disappeared into the countryside, but it is not known if young Murrieta was among them. Either then, or when his term was up, Joaquín sought out his in-laws, Claudio and Reyes Féliz, and learned of their murderous forays of the previous December.

• • •

Ben Marshall was born in Kentucky and came to California after a stint as a cavalryman in the Mexican War. He was elected constable at Murphys in Calaveras County on May 18, 1850. Marshall claimed to have

---

[7] In the late 1950s, Carlo M. De Ferrari was researching boundary litigation between Alpine and Tuolumne County in Stockton. While going through an old court of sessions index, he noticed an entry "Peo. vs. Joaquin Muliati." As an historian, he was interested in the similarity to the name of the famous bandit. Later, he checked the court records and found the name "Muliati" had been crossed out and "Murieta" inserted instead. Mr. De Ferrari had a photographic copy of the documents made, although it turned out to be unsatisfactory. Later, he discovered these old court records had been destroyed. He had made a startling discovery, however, and published his findings many years later in *CHISPA*, The Quarterly of the Tuolumne Historical Society, Jan./Mar. 2003. Mr. De Ferrari, the premier historian of Tuolumne County and an old friend of the author, kindly permitted me to use material from his article at a meeting we had in April 2003.

[8] *Stockton Journal*, January 4, 1851, and *Stockton Times*, January 4, 1851.

[9] *Stockton Journal*, January 4 and March 22, 1851.

known Murrieta, who was mining in the area during the day and running a monte game at night. When a gang of toughs began harassing Murrieta and threatened to tear down his gambling tent, Constable Marshall interfered. He told the thugs if they bothered the young Mexican again, he would throw them all in jail. Grateful to the lawman for his help, young Joaquín gave Marshall a daguerreotype of himself which had been made during a trip to Sonora. The picture remained in the Marshall family for many years, but disappeared in the 1930s.[10]

Marshall was also authority for the story of Joaquín's other clash with a group of miners. A half-brother, Jesús Carrillo Murrieta, had bought a mule from a man named Lang, who later claimed the mule had been stolen. When a crowd of angry miners confronted the brothers on the creek where they mined, Jesús was seized and hanged, while Joaquín was tied to the same tree and flogged, then told to leave the area. This was not the first time young Murrieta had been run off a mining claim, and he was quite bitter about the incident. Ben Marshall reportedly wrote in his diary:

Murphys, New Diggins—
There was bad blood between Sam Green and Bill Lang over the lynching of Jesus Murrieta, Joaquin's brother, in Murphys New Diggins when Lang accused Jesus Murrieta of stealing a mule that he, Lang had sold to Jesus Murrieta for cash. Sam Green some time after this meets Bill Lang and as Green was in his cups, denounced him. "You cowardly cur, you had nothing on them Murrieta boys, Jesus paid you for that mule. You are a born scoundrel. You never was no good, I ought to kill you and I guess I will." Out came his six-shooter and he killed Bill Lang.[11]

The San Francisco *Daily Alta California* reported the shooting at Murphys on June 20, 1852. Newspaper accounts report that Lang had been

---

[10] For material on Benjamin F. Marshall and Murrieta, see the *Stockton Record*, September 3, 1932, and the *Calaveras Prospect*, August 12, 1982. See also an interview between Judy Cunningham, director/curator, Calaveras County Museum and Archives, and Manuel and Thomas Marshall, grandsons of Ben Marshall, in the Calaveras County Archives, San Andreas, California.

The alleged likeness of Murrieta handed down in the Marshall family and now in the Murphys Museum is not the same daguerreotype sketched by Walter Noble Burns in the 1920s while researching his book, *The Robin Hood of El Dorado* (New York: Coward McCann, Inc., 1932). According to John Boessenecker, the Burns notebooks (now housed in the University of Arizona Library Special Collections, Tucson) include a pencil sketch of the Marshall Murrieta image, showing a young man in 1850s attire. The bogus Murrieta likeness appears to have been taken in the 1860s or later. It has been published in several works, including this author's *Joaquin, Bloody Bandit of the Mother Lode* (Fresno, Calif.: Saga-West Publishing Company, 1967). It has been suggested that the photo is actually one of Marshall's sons.

[11] The Marshall diary entry is quoted from Latta, pp. 286–289. There are reasons for believing this particular entry is fictionalized, and it has been questioned by several reputable historians.

shot in the back, however, in a dispute over a bad debt. There could have been other problems, such as the Murrieta lynching, but this is undocumented. Ben Marshall was sheriff of the county at this time and had a scaffold erected at the base of French Hill, outside town. After a trial, Green was hanged on July 31 by Sheriff Marshall.[12]

Despite numerous confrontations between Mexicans and Americans, the Marshall anecdote seems unlikely to have happened. Still, it might have happened, and if so, it perhaps took place during the summer of 1850.

Joaquín's brother-in-law, Claudio Féliz, made his initial foray into crime at Sonora about this same time. Still a teenager, he has been described as light-complexioned, about five feet, four inches in height, and quick and agile in his movements. In the spring of 1849 he was working at a mining camp when a cook was suspected of stealing some gold dust and sentenced to be flogged. Later, when Claudio disappeared, it was realized that he was the thief. He turned up in Stockton a short time later, where he was caught stealing some gold and jailed. When he escaped, he fled to the foothills, where he gathered a band of desperados anxious for plunder. It is not clear whether Murrieta was with him at this time, but he was probably in the Stockton jail, as noted previously. What is clear is that this band of disgruntled Sonorans and criminals were ready for murder if anyone stood in the way of their pillaging.[13]

At about noon on December 5, 1850, Claudio and two companions rode up to the adobe ranch house of John Marsh, located west of Stockton. A Massachusetts native who settled in California in 1836, Marsh parlayed his Harvard diploma into a California career as a physician, although he had no medical degree. He took his fees in cattle, and maintained a large farm and cattle ranch on the San Joaquín River, where he built rodeo grounds, a slaughter house, and other outbuildings. Steamboats stopped at Marsh's Landing, and travelers and friends often visited in the area. To Claudio and his bandits, it was a place ripe for plunder.

Portraying themselves as vaqueros looking for stray stock, the outlaws spent the afternoon talking to the ranch hands as they kept an eye out

---

[12] *Republican*, August 4, 1852.

[13] Claudio Féliz's early foray into crime at Sonora is recounted in Stoddart's previously-cited *Annals of Tuolumne County*, 85–87. Originally published as a series of articles in the *Tuolumne Courier* beginning in February 1861, Stoddart began residing in Tuolumne County during 1857 and gathered historical material from early newspapers and other sources, as well as pioneer settlers. The book version, published in 1963, was made much more valuable by the editing and annotations of Tuolumne County historian Carlo M. De Ferrari.

for property they could steal. Claudio claimed to be an Argentinean who had traveled in Europe and resided for some time in Mexico. He spoke French and English imperfectly and was no doubt trying to confuse his identity. Marsh, who traveled frequently, may or may not have been home. At about three o'clock that afternoon, the bandits left and rejoined their comrades in the surrounding hills.

All the gang, with the exception of Claudio, had blackened their faces when they returned to the Marsh ranch that night. An account of the affair was reported in the *Alta* of December 22, 1850:

> They returned about 8 o'clock, some 14 or 20 in number, surrounded the house, and detached a party to surround the tent of Mr. Harrington, which was occupied by Mr. Mortimer Wilson and Mr. Seaburn Abernathy. The noise of the approaching party attracted the attention of the inmates of the tent. Three guns were then immediately fired into it. Mr. Harrington stepped to the door, and the other two gentlemen escaped from the back part of the tent in the hope of reaching the house. They discovered, however, that it was surrounded by horsemen. At this moment Mr. Harrington was seen by his companions to emerge from the tent, pursued by two horsemen. He was shot in the shoulder by them, pierced with eight lance wounds, and is supposed to have died instantly. He was found dead next morning, lying upon his face. At the same instant that the firing upon the tent commenced, the doors of Dr. Marsh's house were broken in, the inmates knocked down and bound, and the house rifled of money, watches and guns.[14]

Claudio was described in the report as "a young man of short stature, very fair complexion, and black eyes and hair. His manners are pleasing and his appearance rather prepossessing." Heading south, the bandits quickly disappeared into the night, while the people at Marsh's sent a hasty dispatch to Gov. Peter Burnett, advising him of the murderous assault.

On Sunday, December 15, the bandits struck again. A man named Hamilton, who ranched near San Jose, heard an explosion at about seven o'clock in the evening. Outside, the sky was lit up in the vicinity of a house owned by a man named Bester. Rushing to the scene, Hamilton found the place enveloped in flames, and he was unable to see if anyone was inside. The next morning, a horrible scene was discovered in the smoldering embers of the fire. Digby Smith, an owner of the ranch, was found with his arms and legs nearly burnt off and his skull crushed. The cook,

---

[14] *Alta*, December 18 and 20, 1850.

a man named Wood, was found in a similar condition with his head missing. Beneath him lay the blackened body of E. G. Barber, whose skull had been split open by an ax. A coroner's inquest the next day determined there was no clue as to who had committed the brutal murders.

Claudio would later confess to a cell mate that he and seven others had committed the crime, making off with some $1,500.[15] By now, the countryside was becoming alarmed, and a posse started out from San Jose. A Californian had been murdered near the Kell ranch the following Wednesday—probably by the Claudio gang as well. When the posse caught a suspicious Mexican, under threats of a "cravat made of a *riata*," he gave up the names of several whom he claimed were involved in the crime—including his own father.[16] The *Alta* saw a dangerous pattern in the raids:

> It cannot fail to be noticed that there are many most desperate characters in the country, who, failing to realize their expectations in the mines by honest labor, are determined to grasp the earnings of other men at all hazards.... It cannot be doubted that there is in this country more than one systematic gang of villains whose bloody actions thus far can only be traced by the bloody stains they have left after them.[17]

Murrieta had not been involved in the Marsh and San Jose incidents, but he must have decided to lay low for a while. He probably returned to mining at Sonora. He was again assaulted and driven from his claim. Later, he was quoted that these troubles had turned him into an outlaw. The *San Francisco Herald* reported that he had stopped at a ranch on the Salinas plains one night in April 1853. When asked if he had any news of the robber Joaquín who was then being hunted, the well-armed man replied that he was Joaquín and would not be taken alive:

> Without any further ceremony, and perfectly unexcited, the robber went on to relate the reasons of his conduct in his late career—he had been oppressed, robbed and persecuted by the Americans in the placers—had lost $40,000—been driven from a piece of land which he was working with an American companion—had been insulted and grossly mistreated without justice—had been flogged—and he was determined to be revenged for his wrongs fourfold.[18]

---

[15] *Benicia Gazette*, February 21, 1852. This remarkable document was discovered by James F. Varley while researching his book, *The Legend of Joaquin Murrieta* (Twin Falls, Idaho: Big Lost River Press, 1995), 174–179. [16] San Francisco *Daily Alta California*, December 22, 1850.
[17] Ibid., December 18, 1850.
[18] *San Francisco Herald*, April 18, 1853.

Assuming this interview to be valid, and allowing for the usual exaggeration and justification of criminals for their conduct, this follows the traditional accounts of Joaquín's beginnings in crime, and certainly rings true for that racially-troubled time. Corroboration of sorts for the above was furnished by William T. Henderson, one of the California Rangers who would later pursue Joaquín and his gang. Subsequently, Henderson gave this parallel account of Murrieta's beginning in crime:

> Joaquin used to live in Sonora [California] in early days, with Col. Acklin. Joaquin found a very rich claim in the town of Sonora, but he was driven out by the Americans. He gave it up with a struggle. Subsequently he found another claim near by and was working it one day when a couple of Irishmen came to it and ordered him off. Joaquin refused to go, when one of the men, who had a bottle of whiskey in his hand, struck him a fearful blow in the face, opening a frightful wound, and stunning him. They then took possession of the claim. Joaquin was taken by Col. Acklin to his home, and his wound dressed and attended to by that gentleman. From that day Joaquin seemed a changed man.[19]

This incident parallels a documented occurrence when a gang of Mexicans murdered a miner named Snow at a mining camp near Sonora on June 10, 1851. The particularly brutal murder and robbery outraged the local miners, and agitated posses of Americans, led by the victim's brother, were quickly in the field. When several suspects were captured in Sonora and confessed to their cruel crime, they were lynched at once by the infuriated mob.

During the excitement, feelings between the races were running high in town. When City Marshal Jim McFarland tried to arrest a drunken Chilean miner in the street, a gunfight took place in which the Chileño was shot down by deputy John Sheldon. "A scene the most intensely exciting and dreadful," commented a newspaper account, "immediately commenced. Firearms were discharged from all directions; knives were drawn and a fearful contest was kept up for a considerable time, in which two Mexicans were killed and three others seriously wounded."[20]

On June 13, another riot took place at the nearby village of Melones. When an American gambler and a Mexican had an argument, it erupted into a general racial brawl, as noted in a local miner's journal:

---
[19] *Fresno Expositor*, November 12, 1879.
[20] *Alta*, June 18 and 20, 1851.

It appears that the Mexicans had prepared themselves for a contest and as soon as it commenced they shouted "kill all the Americans." Capt. Wm. M. Acklin, of Alabama, tried to make peace between them and he was attacked; at the moment of assault a number of Mexicans cried out not to kill the Captain, but a Mexican ran him through the body with a long knife. The fight now became general, the Americans fighting in self-defense. . . .

The keeper of a monte table lost his bank, about $1200, during the principal row. . . .

Captain Acklin was the only American injured in the melee, and he, it is thought, cannot survive. One Mexican has died of his wounds and two others . . . will also die. This morning, early, a number of Americans started out in pursuit of the Mexicans who were engaged in the attack.[21]

The mention of "Captain Acklin" in both this contemporary account and by Henderson some years later is significant. Between these two accounts and the *Herald* article, all the traditional elements of the events causing Murrieta's slide into banditry are present. We must now consider that Joaquín was ejected from his claim in Sonora, involved in these riots, and probably abused in the general fighting. It might very well have been both the Murphys and the Sonora incidents that caused his ultimate turn to crime. The real question seems to be whether Murrieta turned outlaw before or after he was allegedly abused in the mines.

Whatever his misadventures in the gold country, no one could blame Joaquín for wanting to give up mining and start fresh somewhere. His first move apparently was to get his wife out of the way. At some point he took up some land in a secluded Alameda County canyon called Cañada Molino Vallejo.[22] The property was probably acquired from owner José de Jesús Vallejo, and included a good-sized adobe by Alameda Creek. He planned to go into the wild horse business, neccessitating a headquarters. Rosa lived there while her brother, Jesús Féliz, worked the place when not carrying messages for Joaquín. Reportedly his half-brother, Joaquín Carrillo, also helped out.[23]

---

[21] Ibid.

[22] To date no documentation for Murrieta's residence in Alameda County has surfaced. The primary evidence consists of Frank Latta's interviews with early pioneers of the area, who recalled Joaquín and his wife living there. Latta's witnesses seem credible, and Murrieta has traditionally been associated with the area. See Latta, *Joaquín Murrieta and His Horse Gangs*, 619–640. See also "Spanish Pioneer Houses of California," *Magazine of American History*, vol. 23, January and June 1890, and "History of Rural Alameda," *WPA Typescript*, Alameda County Library, 1937, 377–399.

[23] Verification of José de Jesús Vallejo's property holdings in the area can be found in Mildred Brooke Hoover, Hero Eugene Rensch, and Ethel Grace Rensch, *Historic Spots in California*, *(continued)*

The plains of the San Joaquín Valley were swarming with herds of wild horses at this time, as noted by traveler James H. Carson in 1852:

> The Tulare Valley, perhaps, contains a larger portion of wild horses than any other part of the world of the same extent. On the western side of the San Joaquin, they are to be seen in bands of from two hundred to two thousand. . . . The traveler, in going from the mouth of the lake slough to the head of (Tulare) lake—four days travel—can see the plains covered with these fine animals as far at the eye can reach, in every direction. . . . The wild horse of the Tulares ranks amongst the finest of his species. . . . The Spaniards frequently travel on one of them from seventy-five to one hundred miles per day.[24]

The *San Francisco Alta* reported in July 1852:

> MUSTANGS—Judge Marvin informs us that on his way down from the Frezno [*sic*] he saw several gangs of Spaniards on the plains, between the Merced and the San Joaquin, engaged in catching wild horses which they drive into corrals. One or two thousand mustangs are sometimes seen in bands on these plains. The Spaniards were apparently very successful, having caught a large number. They sold them, after breaking, for from fifteen to thirty dollars per head.[25]

There were probably several reasons Joaquín changed the emphasis of his mustang project. One reason was undoubtedly the burning resentment occasioned by his treatment in the mines. He would not want to deal with Americans for obvious reasons, and that left only the Californio rancheros, who had horse herds of their own. That meant driving the horses down into Mexico—a long, difficult, and dangerous drive.

The answer was simple enough. Why not make that long drive into Mexico more worthwhile by stealing some good, blooded stock from the Americans? He went ahead with plans for his mustang venture, but never passed up an opportunity to do a little rustling on the side. If young Joaquín had indeed accompanied Claudio and Reyes on any of the recent bloody raids, he knew he had crossed a line from which he could never turn back.

3rd edition, rev. by William N. Abeloe (Stanford, Calif.: Stanford University Press, 1966), 18–19. See also *History of Washington Township, Alameda County*, compiled and published by the Country Club and Women's Club of Washington Township, 1965.

[24]The Carson quote is taken from his original 1852 newspaper series in the Stockton *Republican*, March 20, 1852. The complete series is published in Peter Brown, ed., *Bright Gem of the Western Seas* (Lafayette, Calif.: Great West Books, 1991), 85.

[25]*Alta*, July 13, 1852.

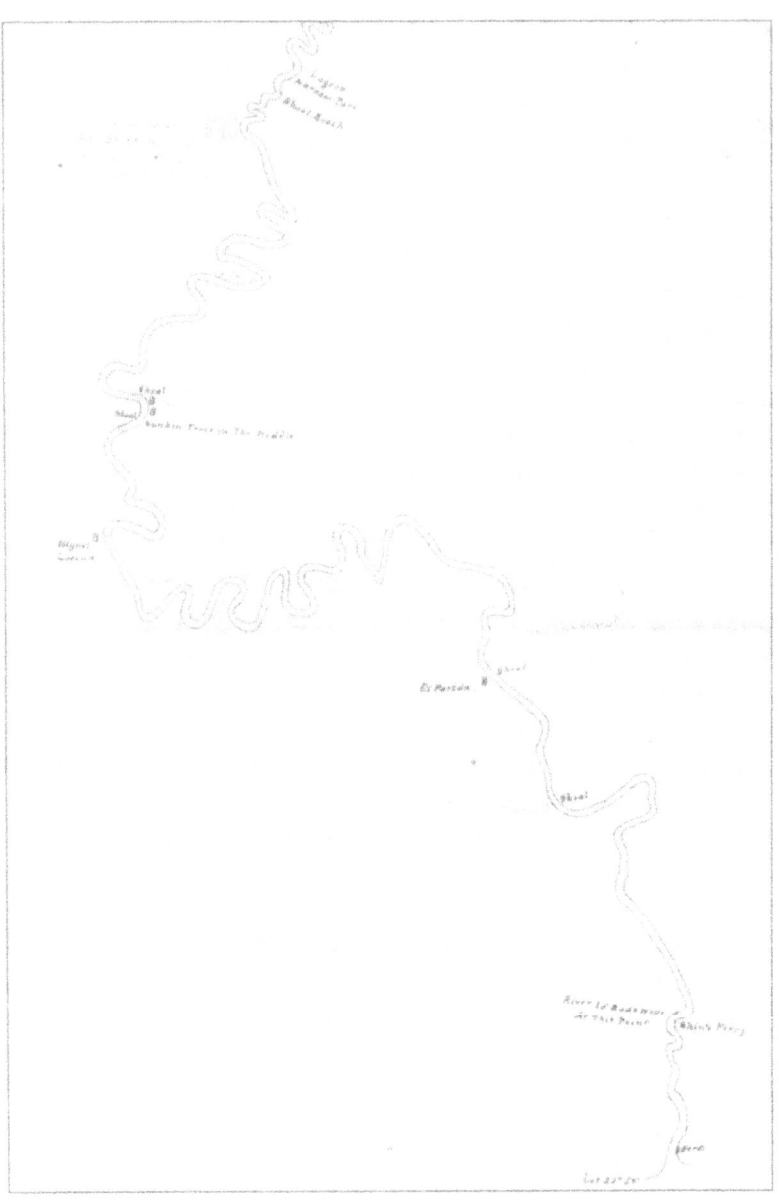

Map segment thought to have been based on crude maps made by Harry Love while on his Rio Grande exploring expedition, or perhaps drawn under his supervision. This shows a stretch of the river between Matamoros and the gulf. Love had visited with Lieutenant Plummer after his Rio Grande exploring expedition and discussed the trip. The maps are part of the Joseph Bennett Plummer Letter Book, Special Collections, The University of Texas at Arlington Libraries. *Used by permission.*

4
On the Rio Grande

When Major Chapman returned from his leave, he was upset to learn that his boat project had languished in his absence. On January 24, 1850, he reported on the progress of his venture to Major E. B. Babbitt:

> The two new keel boats were not completed as I had expected, but this was occasioned by the difficulty of obtaining promptly the right kind of oak lumber from New Orleans. However, they are now rapidly progressing, and the smaller one will be finished in 15 days and other soon after.
>
> As soon as the smaller one is ready, I shall direct Harry Love to take her and ascend the Rio Grande to the highest possible point. From his previous hasty examinations of the River he is of the opinion that he can go with her to within 150 miles of El Paso—If this proves true, it will save the government an immense amount in land transportation. On his return I shall make a detailed report of his expedition and make such suggestions as the facts he will procure may warrant.[1]

Chapman had tactfully christened Love's new craft *The Major Babbitt*, after his immediate superior at San Antonio. He anxiously awaited news from Brazos Santiago of the completion of the two keel boats; by early March, Love's boat was ready for the water. Chapman had the craft towed to Fort Brown by the steamer *Mentoria;* from there, it would be towed to Ringgold Barracks.

The *Major Babbitt* was fifty feet long by thirteen feet wide and could carry up to one hundred barrels of flour. It would draw but thirteen inches of water when loaded, and only four inches when light. Although smaller

---
[1] Chapman to Major E. B. Babbitt, chief quartermaster, 8th Dept., San Antonio, Texas, January 24, 1850. Records Group 92, Records of the Office of the Quartermaster General, Consolidated Correspondence File, 1794–1890, National Archives.

craft were rapidly being replaced on the major rivers by the big steamboats and packets, the uncharted and shallower waterways were only safe with keelboats, flatboats, and other light-draft small craft.[2]

Keelboats had a mast and sail and differed from flatboats in that they had a keel and both the prow and stern were pointed, allowing movement either up or down river. When going upstream, they stayed close to the banks and out of the swifter current of the river. Men, holding steel-tipped poles to their shoulders, moved the craft by treading a cleated walk along the sides of the boat toward the stern. When the river bottom was too unstable or deep for poling, the boat was propelled by cordelling—pulled by men on the bank by means of a long rope tied to the mast. When practical, the craft could be moved upstream by sail, poling, and cordelling—all at once.

Fifteen miles a day might be covered by cordelling, but speed hinged on a variety of elements. When both sail and poling failed, warping might be utilized. This consisted of rowing a skiff several hundred feet upstream, where the cordelle was anchored to a snag or tree. Then the crewmen would reel in the line, pulling the boat forward. The hard routine nature of the work made keelboatmen a tough and rowdy group.[3]

On March 4, 1850, Major Chapman gave Captain Love written instructions for the trip. He was to draw enough provisions at Ringgold Barracks to take him to Eagle Pass, draw three months' worth of provisions, and proceed upriver without delay with his ten crewmen to the highest point he could reach. He was issued twenty-two muskets and rifles, along with forty rounds of ammunition per man, and was cautioned to keep his weapons ready and not waste any bullets. He was given a new American flag for his masthead and told to lower it at sunset and hoist it every dawn. "It is necessary to direct you," penned the major, "to cause this flag to be at all times respected by both Mexicans and Indians."[4]

Each night there would be three watches, and no freight or passengers would be allowed, so as to keep the boat as light as possible. Captain Love was to keep a daily journal of the trip, stating the course of the river, its depth, falls, rapids, and the types of rocks found in the bed and along the

---

[2]Chapman to Captain E. B. Babbitt, January 24, 1849; letter in Chapman's letter book as reported in Coker, ed., *The News from Brownsville*, 381 note 3.
[3]Data on keelboats in general is taken from Frank Donovan, *Riverboats of America* (New York: Thomas Y. Crowell Co., 1966), 25–29, and Paul O'Neal, *The Rivermen* (New York: Time-Life Books, 1975), 20, 64–67.
[4]Chapman to Love, letter dated March 4, 1850. Records Group 92, Records of the Office of the Quartermaster General, Consolidated Correspondence File, 1794–1890, National Archives.

banks. He was to make notes of fords and streams and any farms or settlements along the way, what livestock and crops were in the area, and in general make note of anything of value to the military, ranchers, and other settlers.

At the highest point of keelboat navigation he was to examine the site as a possible location for a military depot or post. Chapman closed his instructions by telling Harry, "The successful accomplishment of this pioneer enterprise will bring into exercise all your energy, perseverance and judgement. Much is expected of you and I feel confident that the department will not be disappointed."[5]

The day after Love's departure from Brazos Santiago, Major Chapman received an alarming message from headquarters at San Antonio. The army engineers were to assume command of Love's expedition. Chapman was horrified; this was his project—his and Harry Love's! They had worked long and hard on it and now, near the time of fruition, it had been wrested from their control. A frustrated Major Chapman penned a frantic letter to Major Babbitt at San Antonio on March 5:

> Yesterday I started Harry Love with the Major Babbitt from Brazos Santiago with full instructions, a copy of which I herewith enclose. Today I received your letter of Feb. 18th by Mr. Clements containing instructions to turn Harry and his beautiful craft over to the Engineers. I was sadly disappointed that this enterprise commenced by our Department should change hands just at this time and also because we lose the services of Harry Love.
>
> Harry has only been kept from going to California by a promise that he should have charge of the expedition and if successful should command our fleet on the Rio Grande hereafter. He has entered into it with more zeal and enthusiasm than either you and myself and now he says "that his hopes of frontier fame are blasted and he shall seek his fortunes on the Pacific shores." One of the Engineer boats goes up with the Major Babbitt tomorrow morning. All the others will leave here for Ringgold Barracks in about 20 days from this time. Harry is now in complete readiness to proceed to El Paso, his crew which is a picked one, on board under pay and engaged to go with him. If he leaves, they will probably all leave.[6]

Major Chapman decided to take a calculated risk. Love positively refused to participate in the revamped expedition, and Chapman knew from experience the engineers would not only take much longer to com-

---

[5] Ibid.
[6] Chapman to Major Babbitt at San Antonio, dated March 5, 1850. Records Group 92, Records of the Office of the Quartermaster General, Consolidated Correspondence File, 1794—1890, National Archives.

plete the project, but would be less competent than an experienced keelboatman such as Love. Despite his new orders, he decided to start Love anyway with the proviso that he could resign at Eagle Pass, if need be. He advised Major Babbitt that he was proceeding with the original plan. "An express from San Antonio," concluded Chapman, "would reach Eagle Pass about the time his boat will, so that no time will be lost if the general permits him to proceed as I confidently hope he will."[7]

As Love moved upriver he stationed himself on top of the keelboat's cabin, at the stern where he guided the craft's rudder. Poling upstream, the crewmen moved the craft nearly a full length as they walked along the sides of the boat. It was slow, grueling work, rewarded at the end of the day by a plate of beans, venison or salt pork, hardtack, and coffee. At night, the men might have sat around a campfire telling stories, danced to some fiddle music, or passed around a jug of *aguardiente* to forget the pain of their aching muscles.

Harry paused frequently to rest the men and prowl the riverbanks, checking for minerals, looking for Indian signs, and talking to any nearby settlers. He made notes on the vegetation and commented on farming prospects. When necessary, the explorers stopped to hunt game for their larder. At Eagle Pass he undoubtedly waited a day or so to see if a courier from San Antonio showed up, then again headed upriver.[8]

• • •

Second Lieutenant Egbert Vielé probably did not relish his role in a scouting expedition for some Indian horse thieves in April 1850. He was eagerly looking forward to a leave and trip east, where he was to be married. He had put in for recruiting duty and hoped to honeymoon in a civilized New England environment.[9] Most young officers would jump at the

---

[7]Ibid.

[8]Mrs. William L. Cazneau, *Eagle Pass or Life on the Border*, ed. Robert Crawford Cotner (Austin: Pemberton Press, 1966). Mrs. Cazneau (Jane McManus) originally published her book in 1852 under the pen name of Cora Montgomery. This is an excellent book describing the country traversed by Love.

[9]Lieutenant Egbert L. Vielé graduated from West Point on July 1, 1847. He served briefly in Mexico and took up his duties at Camp Crawford (later, Fort McIntosh) in March 1849. Lieutenant Vielé married Teresa Griffin at Buffalo, New York, on June 3, 1850, and the couple honeymooned in the East while the new bridegroom pursued his recruiting duties. In January 1851 the couple moved back to Texas, when the young officer was assigned to Ringgold Barracks on the Rio Grande. Mrs. Vielé's book, *Following the Drum: A Glimpse of Frontier Life* (New York: Rudd & Carleton, 1858) is a fascinating view of early army life by an observant and articulate woman. Information on Lieutenant Vielé is from James M. Day's introduction to the 1968 edition of Mrs. Vielé's book, published by the Steck-Vaughn Company, Austin, Texas.

chance for an Indian chase in the rugged country around Fort McIntosh—such patrols were the only relief from the endless monotony of drill and military routine, not counting passes to the dirty little village of Laredo to the south. Suddenly, life seemed very precious, and the risks of this raw frontier country took on a new meaning to Lieutenant Vielé.

Fort McIntosh was close to the Rio Grande, another of the posts designed to help control the Indian troubles on both sides of the border. Garrisoned by two companies of the First Infantry, the post was commanded by Captain John H. King. The troops were housed in tents, while scattered about the parade ground were occasional brush shelters to provide some relief from the unrelenting sun.[10] When several local ranchers reported an Indian raid and the loss of some stock, Captain King quickly assembled two patrols from G Company.

The troopers, a mounted infantry unit, were gathering their gear when they noticed Captain King and Lieutenant Vielé talking to Harry Love in front of the officer's quarters. The famous express rider was pointed out to some of the new recruits, and all wondered about the latest news. The troopers, busily rolling blankets and stuffing saddlebags, probably were not aware of Love's exploring expedition at this time.

Love and his keelboat crew must have put in at Fort McIntosh for a few days' rest and perhaps to restock their larder. At this point they had come two hundred miles in some twenty days—nearly ten miles per day. This was extraordinarily good time and could only be accounted for by the low stage of the river, utilization of the sail, and the freshness of the crew. Since there was nearly always a strong southeast wind blowing, the sails must have been used frequently, if not constantly.[11]

Love had previously carried dispatches to the post and had apparently scouted for Lieutenant Vielé in the past. The young officer later described Love to his wife as "a real 'Green Mountain Boy,' six feet three, and stalwart and robust in proportion, as bold and intrepid as a lion, with a voice of thunder, and a mild blue eye, which softened the otherwise fierce aspect of his rough, sun-burnt face, which was half concealed by a flowing beard and heavy mustache."[12]

---

[10] Herbert M. Hart, *Pioneer Forts of the West* (Seattle: Superior Publishing Company, 1967), 46–48.
[11] The fast time made by Love's keelboat was unusual, but could be done under suitable circumstances. A dispatch from Matamoros in the *New Orleans Picayune*, August 5, 1846, notes that "The winds here are very drying and are always blowing. They prevail constantly from the S. and E." This means the keelboat could have utilized its sail, besides poling. The low state of the river at that time would also add to the speed of the craft. Data on keelboat mileage were obtained from Donovan, *Riverboats of America*. [12] Vielé, *Following the Drum*, 227.

Making his way from the landing to the post, Harry called on his soldier acquaintances and was told of the Indian-hunting expedition being formed. He was familiar with the country and the officers urged him to go along, since no scouts were available at the time. After being assured they would be out only a few days, Love agreed. Even if nothing exciting happened, the patrol would be a welcome break from the river.[13]

The rustled ranches were some eighteen miles below the fort, and on April 3 Love and the troopers rode out and quickly picked up the trail. Lieutenant Walter Hudson was apparently in command, with Lieutenants Samuel B. Holabird and Vielé along in case the unit had to split up in the search. The raiders seemed to be making for the Nueces River to the north, and on the second day they were spotted camped on the other side of the river. Fleeing at the approach of the soldiers, the hostiles left all but two of the stolen animals.

Sending a party across the Nueces to swim back the stock, the officers held a conference on their next move. Apparently Love found two Indian trails leading from the area and it was decided Lieutenant Hudson would take one trail with a detachment of men, while Vielé, Holabird, and Love would follow the other tracks and see where they led. Not knowing how large a band they were following, Love's group would swing back and meet up with Hudson's men if the two trails became too far apart.

After the two groups had separated, Hudson's patrol found itself following a trail leading in the direction of Fort McIntosh. What happened next is dramatically recounted in Captain King's official report:

> On the fourth day out from the Post (7th of the month) [Lt. Hudson] met another party of fifteen Indians who commenced running at the first sight of the troops. This officer gave the command to gallop and took the lead at full speed—The Indians retreated to a chaparal [sic] thicket and as Lieut. H. and three or four of his men rode up, they fired at them with rifles and arrows. Private M. Leahy was killed, but not till after he had fired at his Indian. Lieut. H. received a wound in the leg and Sergeant Ling a very severe one in the chest. O'Donnell & Turley were slightly wounded. Lieut H. then dashed up to an Indian who was on foot and fired at him three times, and two balls he thinks took effect—he now dismounted from his horse as he found him difficult to manage to make an attack upon another Indian, but he had hardly got to the ground before this one, with three others, rushed upon him and shot him with three arrows. Lieut. H. cut

---
[13]Ibid., pp. 226–234. Mrs. Vielé gives a good account of the Indian scout, which must have been related by her husband to her later, as she was not married or even in Texas at that time.

the string of one bow and caught a second man by the throat and gave him two cuts over the face with his sabre, he was, however, too weak to do him much injury.[14]

The balance of the soldiers had by now galloped up and the Indians fled. The troopers took after them, but with both Hudson and the only non-commissioned officer down, they quickly returned to look after their wounded comrades. Hudson had several nasty wounds, the most dangerous being an arrowhead buried deep in his chest. Although the officer had lost both his horse and six-shooter in the fight, several guns and horses of the hostiles had been captured. Three of the company mounts had run off and could not be found. Looking about, the troopers found the saddle and saddlebags belonging to the Corpus Christi mail rider who had recently disappeared. Several letters were recovered.

Retracing their trail to the last waterhole, the wounded were made as comfortable as possible and a rider was sent to the post for aid. They were found there the following morning by Love and Vielé's command. Later the same morning, the assistant surgeon arrived from Fort McIntosh with an ambulance and wagon and the trek back to the post was begun.

With the recovered stock returned to the owners, Lieutenant Vielé must have been grateful that he had come through the expedition unscathed. Harry was anxious to return to the river. His men, restless and no doubt hung-over from the deadfalls of Laredo, were soon poling again up the Rio Grande. Later, Love learned that Lieutenant Hudson had died on the 19th.

After spending the summer working their way upriver, Love and his crew found rocky rapids beyond which their craft could not go. Leaving some crew with the boat, Love took four others and carried their skiff up to where they could again enter the water. They rowed on from this point, but reached another stopping place preventing further travel. It was late summer by the time they made their way downhill and back to the keelboat for the journey home.

It was August 11, 1850, when Love and his crew cruised downriver and stopped briefly at the Ringgold Barracks landing. After another brief halt at Brownsville, they travelled down to the Gulf of Mexico, where Harry reported to Major Chapman at Brazos Santiago on the 25th.

---

[14]Captain John H. King to Brevet Major George Deas, asst. adjutant general, report dated Fort McIntosh, Texas, April 10, 1850. It is the only document located relative to this patrol and action. There is no mention of Love in the report. Letters Received, Western Department and Department Records of U.S. Army Continental Commands, Records Group 393.

Always extremely busy, Chapman must have dropped everything to hear the explorer's first report of the trip. Handing over his book of notes, Love announced that he had taken the *Major Babbitt* as far upstream as he could go before being forced to halt by what he termed "impassable falls," actually rapids. The explorers had managed to proceed overland to quieter water and rowed some 47 miles in their skiff before being stopped by more falls. By Harry's reckoning they had gone some 1,014 miles above Ringgold Barracks, or to within 150 miles of El Paso.

The major was elated. He had proved that many of the towns and military posts along the Rio Grande could be supplied by water, thus opening up much of the area for more settlers. Pouring the explorer a drink, Chapman excitedly thumbed through his notes as Love described his journey. He had found evidence of extensive bituminous coal deposits above Fort Duncan, talked to many settlers, and otherwise gathered much valuable information. With some work on the more difficult channels, steamboats would be able to traverse much of the river. The country was alive with game, Love reporting herds of black-tailed deer numbering two or three thousand each.

Not mentioning his unscheduled foray out of Fort McIntosh, Harry announced he had seen no Indians, but many signs of them. He had passed what he termed a "Grand Indian Crossing" where the Comanche and others crossed over into Mexico for their frequent raids. A post at this point could be instrumental in controlling such movements. The Brownsville *Sentinel* reported an interview with the doughty captain on August 21:

> One act of this daring man we cannot refrain from noticing here. After having, at great labor and mental trouble, carried his frail bark far up into the mountains, through which our noble river holds its way, and having come to obstructions which it was beyond the power of man to overcome, at which his ascent by water must stop, he planted, fast in the solid rock, a staff, bearing proudly to the winds the stars and stripes of his country's banner—fit memento of the gallant daring of himself and his brave little band.[15]

---

[15] W. W. Chapman, brevet major and assistant quartermaster to Major General T. S. Jesup, quartermaster general, Washington, D.C., Brazos Santiago, Texas, September 5, 1850. Published in the Brownsville *Rio Grande Sentinel*, November 27, 1850. This report was also published in Washington, New Orleans, and Mexico City.

On September 5, 1850, Major Chapman wrote a glowing report of the expedition to Major General T. S. Jesup, quartermaster general at Washington, D.C. Under the title EXPLORATION OF THE RIO GRANDE, the report was widely published and appeared in the Washington; Brownsville;New Orleans; Sandusky, Ohio; and Mexico City presses. Harry Love had achieved the "frontier fame" he had sought after all. But he had his cake and ate it, too, when he left for California that fall of 1850. There was no future for him on the Rio Grande now. The army would be taking over his project, and he had put off his California trip for too long. Getting together his meager belongings, Harry said goodbye to his friends and bid farewell to the Rio Grande.[16]

---

[16] Several letters report on Love's exploring expedition up the Rio Grande: Major E. B. Babbitt to Major General T. S. Jesup, quartermaster general, Washington, D.C., San Antonio, August 9, 1850; and Major W. W. Chapman to Major E. B. Babbitt, chief quartermaster, 8th Military Department, San Antonio, Texas, Brazos Santiago, September 14, 1850. Records Group 92, Records of the Office of the Quartermaster General, Consolidated Correspondence File, 1794–1890. See also W. W. Chapman, brevet major and assistant quartermaster to Major General T. S. Jesup, quartermaster general, Washington, D.C., Brazos Santiago, Texas, September 5, 1850, published in the Brownsville *Rio Grande Sentinel*, November 27, 1850. The *Sandusky* (Ohio) *Clarion* of September 23, 1850, also published an account of the expedition, picked up from the *Rio Grande Sentinel* of August 21, 1850.

Author's art.

5
California Calls

Traveling across Mexico, Captain Love boarded a coastal steamer at Mazatlan for the trip north. He is listed among the passengers of the *New Orleans*, which arrived in San Francisco on December 11, 1850.[1] The frontiersman must have been astounded at the city that had grown up on the site of the sleepy Mexican village of Yerba Buena. Every nationality in the world was here, either establishing a business or preparing to go to the mines. Horsemen, groups of prospectors, packtrains, and a few wagons struggled through the muddy roads that bisected the rows of tents, shacks, and new brick buildings that made up the burgeoning town. An arrival of the time described the place in discouraging tones:

> Everything bore evidence of newness, and the greater part of the city presented a makeshift and temporary appearance, being composed of the most motley collection of edifices in the way of houses which can well be conceived.... There were ... occasionally some substantial brick buildings, but the great majority were nondescript, shapeless, patchwork concerns in the fabrication of which sheet-iron, wood, zinc, and canvass seemed to have been employed indiscriminately.[2]

Of course, such a place was a tinderbox; the fledgling town had been destroyed several times by fire. The very year Harry arrived there were several serious conflagrations with much property loss.[3] Despite the fires and rag-tag appearance of portions of the town, the local *Evening Picayune* looked forward to a bright future:

---
[1] Louis J. Rasmussen, *San Francisco Passenger Lists*, vol. 2 (Colma, Calif.: San Francisco Historic Records, 1966), 78.
[2] J. D. Borthwick, *Three Years in California* (Edinburgh, Scotland: William Blackford and Sons, 1857), 36.
[3] Frank Soulé, John H. Gihon, and James Nisbet, *The Annals of San Francisco* (New York: D. Appleton and Company, 1854), 274–275.

We have laid before us a beautiful Lithographic view of Portsmouth Square, taken from the southern side of it. . . . It will be likely to give to those abroad who may be so fortunate as to receive copies of it, some surprise at the evidence it affords, not only of the advancement of our city . . . but also of the degree of perfection to which we have arrived in the cultivation and practice of the Arts.[4]

Like most of the gold rushers, Love found the village too expensive for an extended stay. He must have had several thousand dollars saved from his Texas days and was soon prowling through the mining country, looking for investment or mining opportunities. We know little of his movements, but the following year he was reported supervising the construction of a dam in Placer County.[5] In early 1852, while seeking opportunities in Tuolumne County, he was approached to join a prospecting party going into the Gila River region. When this project fell through, he moved further south, this time searching for business or mining prospects in Mariposa County.[6]

A lone man could get by very reasonably in those days. Occasionally buying some flour, bacon, and beans, Harry could shoot game and camp out in a sheltered tent even in the winter. He was used to being alone. Camping near a mining settlement, he could spend the daylight hours looking around and the evenings in a warm saloon. His horse would get a good feed once a week and the rest of the time subsist on the countryside.

He found the mining camps overcrowded, rough—and dangerous. Although most of the miners were honest and hard working, thieves, claim jumpers, con men, and outlaws found the primitive conditions to be ideal for looting. Officers were few and scattered, and laws were difficult to enforce. Suspects were often seized by mobs and either lynched, flogged, had their heads shaved, or were banished, depending on the crime. Convicts from Australia, thugs and criminals from New York's slums, and footloose ex-soldiers and sailors all contributed to the lawlessness that shocked and dismayed the diggers for gold.

---

[4] *San Francisco Evening Picayune,* December 10, 1850.

[5] Little is known of Love's movements between his arrival in California and the spring of 1852. Much of this time he was undoubtedly doing what nearly every arrival did: prospecting for gold. He is noted as supervising the construction of a mining dam in Placer County in 1849, but the year is wrong; see Myron Angel and M. D. Fairchild, *History of Placer County* (Oakland: Thompson and West, 1882), 67–72.

[6] The exploring party of Captain H. H. Clark and other "gentlemen of Tuolumne County" is reported in the *Sacramento Daily Union,* February 28, 1852.

While it is true that many Mexicans and native Californians sought to justify a life of crime after being mistreated in the mines, there were also many of the criminal class that came to California with no intention of working for their gold. Young Joaquín Murrieta supposedly evolved into a bandit after his bitter experiences in the mines. Although he obviously gathered about him what friends and relatives could be inveigled into a life of crime, many who rode with him were already outlaws looking for the safety of a gang affiliation.

The ease with which Claudio and Joaquín incorporated various relatives into their gangs suggests some kind of criminal bent to the whole family. This may or may not be the case, however. These men were all Sonorans, used to looking out for themselves. Back home they could not depend on the Mexican government for anything and they learned to take care of their own problems, be it Indians, politics, or crime. They quickly discovered that in California they were no better off than they had been at home. Unable to look to the Americans for help, they reacted as they would in Mexico and took the law into their own hands. In a violent age and a raw new land, the Mexican avengers were quickly infused with horse thieves, murderers, and desperadoes; Joaquín, perhaps, found himself at a point of no return.

It is important to remember, too, that most of Murrieta's men were part-time criminals who would join in sporadic raids and then hide out, working as gamblers, miners, or vaqueros, until another opportunity for plunder was offered. That these outlaws came and went and exchanged information and stolen property at a hidden mountain rendezvous is indicated by a notice in the May 22, 1852, *San Joaquin Republican*:

> GANG OF HORSE THIEVES ON THE SAN JOAQUIN.
> Mr. Gibbes, who returned yesterday from the Coast Range, informs us that upwards of 100 horses were stolen from the ranches on the San Joaquin on Monday night last. A party of Mexicans were engaged in catching wild horses on the plains, and their animals were also driven off. One portion of them gave information of the affair to the rancheros and another portion tracked the robbers to their hiding place in the mountains on this side of Pacheco's Pass. They counted 25 robbers—Mexicans, Americans and Indians, who were headed by the notorious "Spencer," brother to Spencer who was hung for mutiny on board the brig Somers. The Mexicans were not strong enough to attack that body so they hastened back to the river, where, in a very short time 20 men were mustered and well armed, left

immediately to attack the lair of these desperadoes. If they are caught, no mercy will be shown.

Although the account refers to the "hiding place" as being between Stockton and Pacheco Pass, this might very well be a confused reference to Joaquín's hideout at Las Tres Piedras, which is farther south. This may or may not be a reference to Murrieta's gang, but it indicates the existence of the criminal bands that roamed the state at this time.

An even stronger indication of the prevalence of such marauders was a law enacted in early 1851 which made grand larceny—even horse theft—a capital offense. A section of the new law read:

> Robbery is the felonious and violent taking of money, goods, or other valuable things from the person of another by force or intimidation. Every person guilty of robbing shall be punished by imprisonment in the State Prison for a term not less than one year, not more than ten years, or by death in the discretion of the jury.[7]

There was no doubt that the new law meant business. When horse thieves "Mountain Jim" Wilson and Frederick Salkmar were captured in Stockton in early June 1851, they were given a trial and then unceremoniously hanged the following November. Three others captured at the same time were given prison sentences. The stakes for Joaquín and his men were now high indeed.[8]

In November 1851, Murrieta, the Féliz brothers, and several others were active in Yuba County. Fresh from the Sonora troubles of the preceding June, they were determined to resume their careers as highwaymen. "Scarcely had we announced in our last," announced the *Sacramento Union*, "the murder of two men, when we heard of the murder of three more, about four miles from Natchez, on Honcut Creek. There is reason to believe that there is a band of Mexicans engaged in robbing in the coun-

---

[7] The most obvious indication that crime was out of control by 1851 is Gov. Peter Burnett's annual message to the California State Legislature, recommending an amendment to the criminal code to make grand larceny and robbery punishable by death at the discretion of the jury. See the *Stockton Times*, February 5, 1851. The problem was exacerbated by a lack of local jails or even a state prison and the rise of vigilance committees. See the Sacramento *Daily Union*, September 27, 1851, and June 21, 1852; the *Marysville Herald*, January 21, 1851; the *Stockton Times*, April 1, 1851; and the San Francisco *Daily Alta California*, January 23, 1852.

[8] An account of the capture and trial of James "Mountain Jim" Wilson, Frederick Salkmar, and three other horse thieves appeared in the Stockton *San Joaquin Republican*, June 4, 1851. The *Republican* reports the hanging of Wilson and Salkmar on November 29, 1851.

try above us, and that they are the same men who murdered Gallagher and the black man on Feather River."⁹

A teamster named George Mather had been stopped and was being assaulted on the road by a gang of Mexican bandits when two unarmed American travelers came up and tried to interfere. All three men were then brutally murdered and robbed. The *Union* account continued:

> Mather had his throat cut horribly, was stabbed in the right arm, and his forehead was terribly bruised. All three of the murdered men had marks of a lariat upon their neck, having been dragged out of the road by that means.
>
> P.S. Since writing the above we learn that six other men have been found murdered near the same place . . . the men appear to have been killed by the same means and instruments as Mather, Jenkinson and Gardiner.¹⁰

Yuba County Sheriff Robert B. "Buck" Buchanan, Deputy Isaac Bowen, and several others immediately left for a nearby Mexican settlement known as the "Sonorian Camp," where the suspected parties had been seen. It was a moonlit evening and, as the sheriff was easing himself through the bars of a rail fence, he was fired upon from the rear. Buchanan was hit in the spine, the bullet coming out near the hip. Allowing the ambushers to escape, Bowen lugged the desperately wounded sheriff to the road, where a passing carriage was hailed.

Posses were immediately formed in Marysville, a local shop even opening their doors and offering weapons to any unarmed men. It was quickly learned the wanted parties had fled the scene, but they were traced to a large patch of chaparral on the east side of the Yuba River. As the brush was being searched, several shots were fired and it was thought best to leave a guard while reinforcements were sought. When more men arrived the next morning, it was discovered the guard had left and the fugitives were gone. "A number of the Vigilance Committee, however," noted the *Marysville Herald*, "arrested a man at a house on this side of the river, above the Sonorian Camp, who is supposed to have intelligence of the murderers. . . . Another Mexican and an American were arrested yesterday. . . . They also are in the hands of the Vigilance Committee for examination."¹¹

---

⁹Sacramento *Daily Union*, September 27, 1851, and June 21, 1852. ¹⁰Ibid.
¹¹The Yuba County murders are detailed in the Sacramento *Daily Union*, November 14 and 18, 1851. See also the *San Francisco Herald*, November 13–15, 18, and 20, and the San Francisco *Alta*, November 16, 1851.

It was thought Buchanan's wound was fatal, but by November 18 it was reported by his physician that "You may bet on Buck now!" The press reported that he "still lives to lend his efficient aid in ridding this community of the bands of murderers, cut-throats, robbers and thieves which at present infest it." The Vigilance Committee was reported still in session, deciding the fate of four or five suspects. In mid-December the *Sacramento Union* reported other suspects had been picked up in that city:

> THE MEXICAN PRISONERS—Considerable excitement prevailed at Marysville on the arrival of the three Mexicans who had been arrested in this city for being concerned in the murderous assault on Sheriff Buchanan. The Herald states that a large crowd gathered at the U.S. Hotel when the stage arrived there, all anxious to get a peep at the supposed murderers. Sheriff Buchanan recognized them as the men he saw at the Sonorian Camp, one of whom shot him.[12]

There is little doubt that Joaquín was indeed involved in these killings. Early the following year Claudio Féliz was picked up on a murder charge in San Jose and placed in a cell with one Teodore Vasquez. Tried as a horse thief in December 1851, Vasquez was convicted by a jury that deliberated only twenty minutes. The jury probably knew he had received thirty-five lashes just two weeks previously for the same offense under another name. The "deeply affected" prisoner was promptly sentenced to death under the newly amended grand larceny law.

As he awaited his execution, Vasquez had obtained some interesting revelations from Claudio. One day an officer came to the jail and asked to look over the prisoners. Afterwards, Claudio told Vasquez that the lawman had been looking for his brother, Reyes Féliz, who had a noticeable scar on his face. Vasquez later related what Claudio had told him—a damning admission of the recent murderous events near Marysville:

> At the river Yuba we murdered six Americans; the first American was a poor, unhappy fellow, whom we murdered and robbed of 2 ounces; the second American was travelling with his wagon, whom we killed and robbed of $500; and after we left the cart, we fell in with two Americans who inquired of us for the one with the wagon; after sending them away we went back to them and asked for fire and murdered and took from them two ounces of gold and a watch, which was all they had; after finishing the murder of these men, we saw a company of ten Americans coming;

---

[12]Sacramento *Union*, December 17, 1851. Another account is in William Henry Chamberlain and Harry L. Wells, *History of Yuba County, California* (Oakland: Thompson and West, 1879), 125–126.

we then ran away to the mountains ... and in the night we went to Marysville and were nearly taken prisoner, but by killing an American [Sheriff Buchanan?] we made our escape by swimming the river Yuba with our horses.[13]

Claudio's bloody recital to Vasquez tallies almost exactly with events surrounding the Buchanan shooting. He further states that some of the men connected with the gang at that time were his brother Reyes, Trinidad, Gabriel, Soliz, and several others. Joaquín *Gurietta* is also mentioned as a member, seemingly a misspelling or typo for Murrieta. Claudio also described to Vasquez the Marsh raid and the San Jose slaughter in December 1850.

After fleeing the area, the gang committed other crimes while moving south. There is some indication that Murrieta himself took a horse herd to Mexico that winter. For skilled Mexican vaqueros, taking a herd of horses south could be a hard but fast journey. Eighty to one hundred miles a day could be covered when the riders changed horses as their mount tired. Still, it was a good two-month round trip, and on his return he reportedly brought his mother and father, a sister and nephew, and some dozen others with him. His parents were apparently left in Los Angeles with a married daughter, while his sister Vicenta and her son were taken to the Alameda County ranch to live with Rosa. It had been a long ride—some twelve hundred miles—and, after a few days' rest, Joaquín again headed east into the gold country, where he soon located his gang.[14]

Whether it was the murderous Yuba County bandits again, or if it was a different group altogether, by early April the *Sacramento Union* was reporting a flurry of stock thefts in Calaveras County. A letter from Mokelumne Hill reported a desperate encounter with these rustlers on April 5:

> On Sunday night several horses were stolen, and on Monday morning a man by the name of Clark and one by the name of Cochran, went in pursuit of the thieves. They succeeded in tracing the horses through the Valley to the Willow Springs by the peculiar shape of one of the shoes. At the Willow Springs they found the horses and four Mexicans who had stolen them, dining there. Clark and Cochran determined to arrest them at all hazards. They accordingly stationed a man at the back door with an

---
[13]*Benicia Gazette*, February 21, 1852. Details of his trial are taken from the *San Jose Visitor* of December 31, 1851.
[14]Murrieta's trip to Mexico and return are conjectural, but Latta cites such a trip after interviewing an aged Sonoran who remembered selling the outlaw some goods along the route (pp. 176–178).

axe, that he might prevent their escape from that quarter, and they entered at the front.

As soon as the Mexicans found that they were to be arrested, they commenced firing upon their pursuers; Clark was shot through and instantly killed. A colored man connected with the house shot one of the Mexicans and killed him on the spot, and the others made a rush from the house and mounted their horses. Cochran pursued and nearly succeeded in lassoing one of the desperadoes, when he was fired upon and wounded in the thigh, and the scoundrels succeeded in making good their escape. Nearly every man in the Valley is in pursuit of the murderers and are determined to capture them.[15]

Apparently these bandits split up to hinder their pursuers, but the *Sacramento Union* reported the capture of at least one of the suspects on April 21. "Joaquín, one of the Mexicans who shot Mr. Clark at the Willow Springs on the Jackson road a short time since, was arrested, we are informed, on Monday at Jackson. He was taken to the Willow Springs where it was thought summary punishment would be dealt out to him."[16] It is not known if this was Murrieta but, in any case, he apparently escaped later from the posse.

"He lived on horseback," commented an early California pioneer speaking of the Mexican and Californian vaqueros," and you might almost say he was born on horseback and better horsemen the world never saw."[17] Murrieta and his men stole the best horseflesh in the state for themselves and, as they dashed across the foothills and plains, stealing fresh animals as needed, it was nearly impossible for posses to catch them. By the spring of 1852, the miners scattered along the creeks and rivers of the gold rush country were becoming increasingly concerned with the problem.

The extent of Murrieta's leadership among this Mexican banditti is not at all clear. At first glance it does not make sense that a large organization would be effectively commanded by a twenty-year-old, no matter how motivated he might be. Still, the legend persists, and the young Joaquín may have been a born leader who worked in conjunction with one or several horse gangs running stolen stock and mustangs down into Mexico. His own immediate gang of highwaymen and robbers were men he could depend on and trust. Any other gangs of confederates were led

---

[15]Sacramento *Union*, April 13.
[16]Ibid., April 21, 1851. See also the *San Francisco Herald,* April 10, 1851.
[17]Stockton *Republican*, 1852 series of letters written by James H. Carson. The complete series was published in Peter Brown, ed., *Bright Gem of the Western Seas* (Lafayette, Calif.: Great West Books, 1991), 53–111.

by trusted friends and relatives who were independent, and pretty much did as they pleased.

Ascertaining the names of the outlaws associated with Murrieta, despite the pioneering work of Frank Latta, is difficult in the extreme. Some of them can indeed be identified, however, and their lives clearly indicate the off-and-on aspects of their criminal activities. Joaquín Juan and Martin Murrieta were cousins of the bandit chieftain and operated a pack station near Mariposa when they were not riding with their relative. Reyes Féliz was still a teenager when he rode with his brother Claudio and Joaquín in the early 1850s. José Ochoa had come up from Sonora with Joaquín and was a miner before he traded his pick and shovel for a bandit's life. Joaquín Valenzuela and several brothers were also reportedly related to Murrieta. Other gang members were Bernardino Garcia, called Three-fingered Jack by the Americans, and Pedro Gonzales, said to have been a noted horse thief. Antonio López had a wife and several children living at Las Juntas, on the San Joaquín River. He was with the horse gangs and may have ridden on bandit raids also. Others among the outlaws at one time or another were Juan Salazar, Ramon Soto, Antonio Valencia, Miguel Escobosa, José Borella, and Pedro Sánchez. There were many others, including Americans.[18]

After his escape from the San Jose jail, Claudio fled to the Sierra foothills. When not with Murrieta, he led his own band of cutthroats and robbers in the area around Sonora, Saw Mill Flat, and Columbia. He was on a horse-stealing expedition in late March 1852 when he and his men camped in a secluded canyon of the North Fork of the Stanislaus River. Caleb Dorsey, a lawyer bitten by the prospecting bug, was camped in the same canyon and was asked by the Mexicans to share their evening meal. Later the group sat around the campfire and sang ballads, led by a one-eyed musician.

The next morning several of the vaqueros told Dorsey to forget he had seen them or he would be sought out and killed. Shaken, the attorney made his way back to Sonora and forgot the incident.

Later the one-eyed bandit turned up in the Sonora jail on a horse-stealing charge and demanded counsel to represent him. When Caleb Dorsey appeared as his lawyer, both men were surprised. Promising his best efforts in the outlaw's defense, Dorsey was told that despite his efforts

---

[18]Names of the Murrieta gang members were all taken from contemporary newspapers. Latta lists some sixty members in his book—names he acquired during nearly fifty years of interviewing old timers and bandit descendants, pp. 77–143.

to capture local outlaws, if he got him off he would never be molested by the bandits. When no indictment was returned, both the thief and the lawyer were pleased.[19]

In early April 1852 Reyes Féliz was accused of stealing two pistols and was arrested by Constable John Leary. A notice of the incident was reported in the *Stockton Journal:*

> An officers' posse from Columbia had arrested a Mexican for theft at a camp called Humbug on Wood's Creek, three miles above Sonora, and were conveying him to the former place to be tried when they were suddenly surprised by a party of Mexicans who attempted a rescue. Several shots were fired by the Mexicans, but without effect. The Americans returned the fire, and two Mexicans fell, one of them mortally and the other severely wounded. The Mexicans fled, leaving these two in the hands of the Americans. The prisoner escaped.[20]

Reyes' brother Claudio, Joaquín Murrieta, and several others had attempted the rescue. After a brief exchange of gunfire, Reyes and his rescuers made their escape. Claudio, however, was cut off and kept up a running fight to the top of a hill. Here, with his two empty pistols in his hands, he collapsed with several serious wounds. As Leary and others rushed up to the fallen outlaw, the constable put his pistol to Claudio's head, but Caleb Dorsey pushed it aside and saved his life.

When Claudio was well enough to talk, he thanked Dorsey for saving his life and asked that he represent him at his arraignment. He also assured the lawyer that if he obtained his release, he would take his outlaw band to Mexico and never return. Dorsey asked why he should believe him. "Sir," answered Claudio proudly, "you have the word of honor of a highwayman!"[21]

Constable Leary hauled his prisoner before Justice of the Peace Joseph Carly for a preliminary hearing. Carly's recommendation to the Grand Jury was as follows:

THE PEOPLE VS. CLARIA FARLIA

The above named defendant was brought before me this 6th day of April, 1852, by John Leary, Constable, charged with stealing two pistols. The said

---

[19]Herbert Lang, *History of Tuolumne County* (San Francisco: B. F. Alley Company, 1882), 207–216.
[20]The arrest of Reyes Féliz by Constable John Leary and the resulting gunfight and capture of Claudio Féliz is detailed in the *Stockton Journal* (no date given) and reprinted in the *San Francisco Herald,* April 11, 1852. See also Margaret Hanna Lang, *Early Justice in Sonora* (Sonora, Calif.: The Mother Lode Press, 1963), 78–84.   [21]Lang, *History of Tuolumne County,* 207–216.

pistols was stolen about one year since. And also an attempt to rescue a prisoner from a public officer, and shooting at said office. The said defendant is in my charge. I would further request that the Court of Sessions to order said prisoner before the Grand Jury as soon as convenient. The defendant is badly wounded.[22]

During the course of Claudio's trial, the court clerk seldom got his name right. Besides Farlia, he was referred to as Claude Felice, Claude Felix, Claude Féliz, and Claude Fellis. When Dorsey did indeed manage to secure an acquittal for the outlaw, he was roundly criticized in the local *Sonora Herald*.[23]

Claudio's word was worth just what might be expected, as noted in the *San Joaquin Republican* of September 4, 1852:

> There is no doubt as to the existence of a formidable band of guerillas in the mountains around Sonora. We have received several communications from which we learn that the party is guided by one "Cloudy," a noted Mexican guerilla chief. Two daring robberies have been committed and they number some 40 strong. The first robbery was committed at the Chinese Camp on the 26th, ultimo. The victims were a party of Mexicans, one of whom was killed by the villains.
>
> The second robbery was committed on the 30th of August at Sullivan's Creek from which they stole a large amount of money. A party has gone out from Sonora in pursuit.

One can only wonder if Mr. Dorscy was one of those in pursuit. Claudio found the area too hot for him now. In early September 1852 he and some six or eight of his men drove a herd of stolen cattle to the coast. Another notice of "Cloudy," or Claudio, appeared in the *San Francisco Alta* that same month:

> We have seen a letter addressed to a gentleman of this city which states that at Yorktown Gulch, near Camp Seco, a lawless band of fifty Mexicans have started for the lower country on a plundering expedition. They have stolen about eighty animals in that part of the country, committed several robberies and two or three murders and are now on their way to Los Angeles to join a party who are waiting for them at that place. They are headed by a Mexican named Cloudy who was in jail in Sonora last winter and who is represented as one of the most desperate villains in the

---

[22]"The People vs. Claria Farlia" is quoted from a document reproduced in Lang, *Early Justice in Sonora*, 77–79.

[23]Carlo M. DeFerrari generously shared his notes from the Claudio trial records with the author; letter, June 23, 1995.

country. He has a brother named Reyas [*sic*] now in jail in Monterey and it is said that Cloudy and his party have it in view to release him by force

This is the same party who a few days since stole Col. James Douglas' animals and four belonging to Mr. A.B. Beaurais. It is rumored that four men have been murdered and robbed.[24]

Claudio might have had a particularly good reason to leave the area at this time. Alf Doten, who operated a store at Big Bar on the Calaveras River, wrote in his journal September 1, 1852, of two Mexicans who took a six-year-old girl into the chaparral. One of them attempted to rape her. The two were discovered by a party of Americans who seized one of the culprits, while the rapist made a successful getaway. "Men are scouring the country," Doten wrote, "for the other one, named Clondy." This was quite possibly Claudio of the many names.[25]

Claudio and his men were probably going to join Joaquín and Reyes, who were now in the Los Angeles area, but Claudio's race had been run. After being repelled during an attack on the home of J. W. Kottinger in the Livermore Valley, the gang made other raids, including the robbery of a Mexican traveler named Agapito on the Salinas road.[26] The incident was quickly reported to Monterey justice of the peace Henry Cocks, who put together a posse. Cocks was a tough English sailor who had lived at Monterey since 1848. He took no nonsense from outlaws, in-laws, governors, or anyone else.

Gathering a posse of eight native Californians, including the later-notorious Anastacio Garcia, Cocks and his men rode up to the house of Manuel Espinosa in the Salinas Valley. It was early in the evening on September 12, 1852. As the posse galloped up, dogs began barking and lights in the house were quickly extinguished. A volley of pistol shots greeted the lawmen, and during the resulting shootout, two of the bandits escaped.

With his pistol emptied, Claudio himself had rushed from the house into the arms of Cocks, who held on to him. "I surrender, sir," said the bandit chief. "I have no arms." But Cocks had caught his movement as he pulled a concealed dagger. There was a roar of gunfire and a moment later, Claudio lay dead on the ground. He had been shot just under the left eye and in the femoral artery of his left leg. Pablo Valdez, who had a wife and child living at the Espinosa home, was also killed. Various local stolen horses were found in possession of the outlaws.

---

[24]*Alta*, September 4, 1852.
[25]Walter Van Tilburg Clark, ed., *The Journals of Alfred Doten, 1849–1903* (Reno: University of Nevada Press, 1973), 123. [26]*Pleasanton Times*, January 17, 1891.

Esteban Silva, who had escaped after the initial burst of gunfire, was wounded and returned to the house the following morning. Seeking to retrieve some property left behind, he resisted capture by Espinosa and several others and was killed when he again tried to escape. The colorful serape he wore was splattered with the blood of a half-dozen stab wounds. A native of Los Angeles, he was about twenty-two years old.

A report from Monterey dated September 15, 1852, proved to be the obituary of one who, if he had lived, would have undoubtedly been as noted as his brother-in-law, Joaquín Murrieta:

> The verdict of the jury was—That Claudio, Valdez and Silva came to their deaths by wounds inflicted with balls and knives while resisting arrest as further set forth in the testimony.
>
> This Claudio is said to be the same man who has been robbing and murdering within the last three years around San Jose and the placers of the Stanislaus and Tuolumne. He is a light complected, small made man, said to be a native of Hermosillo in Sonora, 5 ft. 4 in., about 19 years old, was very quick and agile, and made a desperate resistance with a revolver and bowie knife, has an old wound under the right ribs and two others about his stomach. Some of the witnesses knew him at the Sonorean Camp [Sonora] three years ago. . . .
>
> The bodies of Claudio and Silva were buried near Espinosa's house, under the direction and inspection of the Coroner and that of Valdez was delivered to his wife at her request.[27]

Mateo Andrade, the other escaped bandit, was captured on the 17th, nearly dead from starvation and loss of blood from a leg wound. He was booked into the Monterey jail on September 18, 1852. Only twenty-one years old at the time, Andrade was sentenced to eleven years at San Quentin. After escaping two years later, he was reportedly lynched at San Luis Obispo.[28]

After Claudio's capture and trial the previous April, Joaquín promptly left the area and headed south with several gang members. It was, apparently, the last time he saw his lieutenant and brother-in-law alive.

---

[27] *San Francisco Herald*, September 18, 1852. See also the Stockton *Republican*, September 29, 1852, and the *Sacramento Daily Union*, June 2, 1874.

[28] *Marysville Herald*, September 24, 1852. A copy of the old Monterey jail register owned by John Boessenecker contains the name of Andrade, as does the *List of Convicts on Register of State Prison at San Quentin* (Sacramento: State Printing Office, 1889), which notes his escape in 1854.

San Francisco in the early 1850s was the gold rush boom town of the Far West. *Society of California Pioneers.*

6

Ruddle

Love was probably working along Burns Creek in late April 1852 when word arrived of a brutal murder on the Stockton road. Too well aware of the burgeoning crime problem, the Texas veteran quickly decided on a course of action.

John and Allen Ruddle came to California in 1849 and began mining near Hornitos, in Mariposa County. Natives of Massachusetts, the brothers were great-nephews of the poet William Cullen Bryant. Allen had a college education, was a poet himself, and kept a journal while crossing the plains. When their claim petered out, the brothers established a farm on the Merced River. They still had only the crudest of quarters when their parents, brothers, and sisters joined them in early 1852.[1]

Strangely enough, a brother of Julia Ward Howe and a former friend and companion of Longfellow named Sam Ward was working at Belt's Ferry and store at this time. Located on the Merced River in Mariposa County, Belt's trading post operation supplied the surrounding mining camps and farms, as well as nearby Indian rancherias. On the afternoon of April 27, 1852, Ward was riding along the Stockton road when he noticed wagon wheel tracks turning off towards the river. "It struck me," Ward would later recall, "as a capital spot for an ambuscade, and I intuitively loosened the revolver in my belt, and kept 'my eyes skinned' until I again reached level ground."[2]

Ward was having a meal at a roadhouse a short time later when a rider

---
[1] Frank Latta interview with Ann Elisabeth Ruddle, *Fresno Bee,* June 2, 1935. A sister-in-law of the slain Allan, Mrs. Ruddle had valuable first-hand information on the murder obtained from her husband.

[2] Carvel Collins, *Sam Ward in the Gold Rush* (Stanford, Calif.: Stanford University Press, 1949), 169–170. This book is based on Ward's reminiscences, as published serially in the New York *Porter's Spirit of the Times* in 1861. An excellent account of Joaquín Murrieta's career is in John Boessenecker's recent *Gold Dust & Gunsmoke* (New York: John Wiley & Sons, Inc., 1999), 73–99.

galloped up with the news that a teamster had been murdered down the road. Some six hundred dollars had been stolen, and the rider was on his way to the next ferry to see if any suspicious persons had passed recently. Ward shuddered, for the murder was undoubtedly committed a short time before he had seen those tell-tale tracks.

Again mounting his horse, Ward headed north towards Dickenson's ferry on the Tuolumne River. As he reached the outpost, two heavily-armed riders galloped up, announcing they were in pursuit of the killers. While crossing the river, they told Ward the victim was Allen Ruddle, who had been on his way to Stockton to buy furniture. He had left the farm the day before, but when his oxen returned home that evening, the family went in search of him. After searching all night, a servant had found the body in the wagon, which had been driven off the road.

"Allan [sic] had only gone about two miles toward Stockton when he was killed," recalled his sister-in-law. "He had resisted to the last, the butt of his whip being battered and the ground giving evidence of a struggle. He had been both shot and beaten. He had not been knifed." He had refused when his family urged him to take a weapon, although Ward had pontificated that "No one walked a rod in that region without a revolver in his belt."[3]

The *Stockton Journal* published an account of the murder, as reported in a letter from Belt's Ferry:

> On the Plains, April 29
> ... A young man named Allen B. Ruddle, who was driving a wagon to Stockton for supplies, was found dead on the road on Monday last, having been shot through the head and breast. He had about four hundred dollars in his possession when he left home, of which he was robbed. The deceased leaves an aged father, mother, brothers and sisters to mourn his untimely end.... There is good reason for supposing that the murder was perpetrated by Spaniards.[4]

Although unidentified by Ward, the two-man posse that crossed the river with him was undoubtedly Harry Love and a partner.[5] The Rud-

---

[3] For a typical, exaggerated account of the murder, see the San Francisco *Daily Evening Bulletin*, July 23, 1905, complete with conversations between the killers and their victim.
[4] The *Stockton Journal* account of the murder was republished in the San Francisco *Alta*, May 3, 1852. See also the Sacramento *Daily Union*, May 6, the *San Joaquin Republican*, May 15, and the *San Francisco Herald*, May 7, 1852.
[5] It is not known what Love was doing in the area at the time of the Ruddle murder. He may have been prospecting or merely visiting an acquaintance, since there were many Mexican War veterans in California at that time.

Thought to have been the home of Murrieta and his wife, this old adobe was in Niles Canyon, near the present town of Fremont in Alameda County. Located on the land grant of José de Jesús Vallejo, the structure had disappeared by 1919. *Author's collection.*

dle family and friends had quickly offered a reward for the killers. Love knew time was of the essence in such a pursuit, and while other posses were being organized, he and his friend left while the sign was still fresh. Following the trail towards the watering hole at the San Luis Gonzaga ranch, the men were soon at the foot of the Coast Range, near Pacheco Pass.

Since Allen had been alone on his trip, no one but the bandits witnessed the tragedy, although Joaquín Murrieta has always been blamed for the killing. Several Mexicans had been seen in the vicinity, however, and they were the immediate suspects. A letter written from Fort Miller, on the San Joaquín River, was published in the Stockton *San Joaquin Republican* and indicated the killers had indeed been identified:

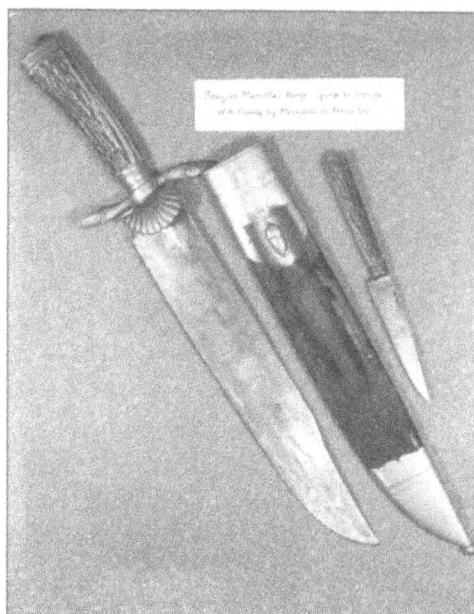

This knife, purported to have been owned by Murrieta, was given to Mariposa County Sheriff R. A. Prouty by Mexican residents of Hornitos. *Photograph in author's collection.*

The Indians are quiet, but the white horse thieves and Mexicans are occasionally practising to keep their "hands in." There is a body of Mexicans down the river about thirty miles, in a very secret camp, almost invisible, who have a large number of tame animals—report says nearly a hundred. They number between twenty and thirty, and no doubt their scouts are out continually. And that is the grand depot of stolen animals in all this section of country. It is also supposed that the two Mexicans who shot young Ruddle, a week ago, have taken refuge in this camp; there are about thirty men, in different parties, in pursuit of the murderers, and they will not escape apprehension, as they are known.[6]

They were indeed known and identified by description. A few weeks earlier, on April 4, another young teamster had been murdered on the same road. He had been traveling with an older man who stopped at a roadhouse while his companion went on. Later he found the body of his young friend, murdered, in the middle of the road. Three Mexican riders had been following them earlier in the day. The teamster was con-

---

[6]*Republican*, May 15, 1852.

vinced they were the killers and was able to give good descriptions of the suspects.[7]

William Perkins, a Sonora merchant, was returning home from Stockton the next day on this same stretch of road. At Dent's Ferry he heard of the murder and listened to the descriptions of the suspects. Not wanting to wait for his stage in the morning, he rented a horse from Dent and proceeded on his way. It was still light when about three miles down the road he saw the described trio of vaqueros riding towards him.

"I'm not ashamed to admit," Perkins later wrote,

> that my heart jumped to my throat.... I drew the pommel of my revolver to the front, grasped it ... and cocked it in its pouch.... The minuteness of the description given by the old man left no doubt as to the identity of these men with those who followed ... and who had assuredly murdered the young man.... I walked my horse past them [and] expected every moment to hear the report of a pistol and the whiz of a ball. As soon as I had got to a respectable distance, I dug the spurs into my fat horse's side and got him into a gallop.[8]

The three Mexican riders were not mere travelers, as they had been seen on both sides of the river for several days. A guess as to the identity of the trio would be Murrieta, Reyes Féliz, and Pedro Gonzales. Perkins ascribed his narrow escape to the fact that he was going towards the mines, and not leaving, and the vaqueros assumed he would not be worth robbing. Love and his partner had these "minute" descriptions to aid them in their search.

Although he may have received reinforcements by the time he approached the creek at San Luis Gonzaga, Love probably still only had his one companion. They were trailing the same two riders, who had now been joined by a third horseman. Being well armed, Harry and his partner still felt able to handle any situation. Indications are, however, they were about to ride straight into the campground of Murrieta's bandit gang.[9]

It was dark when the two-man posse rode up to the single adobe that served as the ranch headquarters of Juan Perez Pacheco. The building was alongside Cottonwood Creek, a tree-lined waterway that served as a watering hole for miles around. Besides the trail over Pacheco Pass that

---

[7]Perkins, *William Perkins' Journal or Life at Sonora, 1849–1852*, 326.   [8]Ibid., 327–328.
[9]John Rollin Ridge (Yellow Bird), *The Life and Adventures of Joaquin Murrieta* (Norman: University of Oklahoma Press, 1955), 34–41. Originally published in 1854, the year after Murrieta's death, Ridge's book was thought to be highly fictionalized until recently, when many of the incidents portrayed were validated by modern research.

led to the coast and San Jose, the roads from Mariposa and Stockton also converged here. Travelers often camped in the area, and it seemed a likely spot to check for the fugitives.[10]

Remaining on his horse, Love banged on the door of the adobe, but was undoubtedly told by the inhabitants that they knew nothing. Ygnacio Villegas, who lived on another nearby Pacheco ranch, admitted years later that "every large rancho in the country would assist Murrieta or any of his gang. They had to or be wiped out!"[11] The isolated ranchos were easy targets of retribution for the outlaws, and Villegas reported that most of the larger ranches had spies who quickly reported anyone who collaborated with the lawmen.

Spotting horses grazing along the creek, Love galloped over to check them out. He quickly noticed some tents in the brush and, seeing several figures scampering away in the darkness, assumed they had flushed their quarry. Firing their pistols, the two men rode among the horses, scattering them, but quickly lost the fleeing figures in the darkness and brush.

Many years later, an aged Avelino Martinez, one of the outlaws, told historian Frank Latta about the incident. Martinez remembered Joaquín Murrieta being present, as well as Ramon Soto, Joaquín Valenzuela, Juan Salazar, "Three-fingered Jack," Juan Mendez, Tony Villegas, and several women from the village of Las Juntas. Murrieta's brother-in-law, Reyes Féliz, was there, along with Pedro Gonzales. Not knowing how many were in the posse, the outlaws scattered, some heading south for their hideout at Las Tres Piedras, while others hid in the brush up the creek. Valenzuela and several others had given the first alarm and galloped out of the area quickly. Others lost their horses and saddles. Riding double, without saddles, Murrieta and several others rode north, telling the women to hide in the brush, where they would be retrieved later.[12]

It had been a narrow escape. There was little Love and his partner could do in the darkness, and they knew better than to split up and be ambushed. They would wait until morning and see if they could pick up a trail.

---

[10]Mildred Brooke Hoover, Hero Eugene Rensch, and Ethel Grace Rensch, *Historic Spots in California*, 3rd edition, rev. by William N. Abeloe (Stanford, Calif.: Stanford University Press, 1966), 202–203; and the *Los Banos Enterprise*, January 27, 1933.

[11]Ygnacio Villegas, edited by Dr. Albert Shumate, *Boyhood Days* (San Francisco: California Historical Society, 1983), 43.

[12]Latta, *Joaquín Murrieta and His Horse Gangs*, 363–373. Latta, however, makes no mention of the Ruddle killing causing Love's pursuit and places the incident a year later, in 1853.

The Niles Canyon home of Murrieta as it appeared in 1872. Reportedly, Rosita lived here while her husband ravaged California's mining country. *Dianne C. Klyn.*

Not knowing what had happened to the others, Joaquín's party headed north. It was imperative that they secure more horses and riding gear. They headed for the foothills along Orestimba Creek, where they knew rancher Yrenero Corona had some of the best stock in the area.

The outlaws apparently watched for Corona to leave before they brazenly rode into his corral and ran six of his best horses into the barn. Here they were saddled and bridled, while several lookouts kept watch to avoid any surprise interruptions. They were in no time ready to ride. Bolting out of the barn, the bandits headed down the creek towards the San Joaquín plains.

Helping a neighbor work cattle at the time, Corona was eating lunch with some vaqueros when the outlaws came out of the hills and headed south. He recognized his stock from a distance and was about to go after them when he realized he had to first ride home and check on his wife. The rancher lost some valuable time, but found his wife unhurt and quickly prepared to take the rustlers' trail.

Joaquín and his men now retraced their steps to Cottonwood Creek, where they picked up the women. Afraid that the posse might be scouring the foothills around their hideout at Las Tres Piedras, Joaquín headed for Los Angeles.

As they rode south down the valley, Joaquín and his compatriots stopped at a small Mexican settlement located where the town of Visalia was established the following year. They had seen no sign of a posse and felt safe partying at a *fandango* house that night. The next day they again headed south for Tejon Pass, already looking forward to the cantinas of San Gabriel and Los Angeles.

As the *bandidos* approached the lower foothills of the Tehachapi Mountain range, they spotted a camp of Indian vaqueros herding stock. They were familiar with this campground at Los Alamos, which was sprinkled with big shade trees and a good waterhole. Joaquín and one of his men rode up first, but as they were talking to the Indians, Three-fingered Jack galloped up, beating the Indians with his lariat and making them run away. Laughing, he then sat down and began wolfing down the meal they had just prepared. The other outlaws watched the Indian vaqueros either run or ride off, then sat down and helped themselves also. It was a serious miscalculation.

The Indians made their way back to the vaquero main camp at Chief Zapatero's house on Tunis Creek. The chief quickly gathered a posse, including two of his sons, and sent them back to Los Alamos with all of the rifles they had. The Indians watched the Murrieta encampment until nightfall, then crept slowly down to where the bandits slept. At a signal, rifles were jammed into the sleeping bandit's ribs and stern voices informed them they were prisoners. Stripping them of every stitch of clothing, down to their socks, the Indians then hog-tied the prisoners and wrapped their loot in the bandits' blankets. Leaving Murrieta and his group where they lay, all their supplies were taken, as well as the bandits' horses and riding rigs. One of the women had screamed and fought like a wildcat and ran off, stark naked, into the brush and trees.

Back at Zapatero's camp, the Indians spent most of the night dividing their loot. The chief suspected the stock was stolen and wanted to talk to the prisoners, but when they returned to Los Alamos the captives were nowhere to be seen; the woman who had escaped had returned and freed her friends. Now they were all gone.

The rancher Corona arrived at the Indian camp a short time later and was glad to retrieve his stolen stock and gear from the Indians.[13] It was early June before word of the incident filtered over the Tehachapis and a brief item appeared in the *Los Angeles Star*: "Jose Zapatero, another chief, has since taken a number of horses from some Sonoreans which were pursued to the Tejon, and delivered them over to the authorities."[14]

---

[13] Latta obtained the Yrenero Corona story from a man named José Aguila, who had heard the story from Corona himself and several Murrieta men. He also interviewed descendants of the Indians involved in the Murrieta capture. Again, he gives no date (Latta, *Joaquín Murrieta and His Horse Gangs*), 373–394. With minor discrepancies, the whole scenario of the routing of the outlaws at the San Luis Gonzaga ranch, the theft of Corona's horses, his pursuit, and the Indian capture of the outlaws was first reported in Ridge's biography of Murrieta, 34–41.

[14] *Los Angeles Star*, June 12, 1852.

A woodcut of Harry Love in Ridge's *The Life and Adventures of Joaquín Murrieta* shows him in his trail clothes as he must have appeared while tracking the Ruddle killers. The likeness is good enough to assume it was made from a daguerrotype. *Author's collection.*

7
Los Angeles

Dusty and weary, Harry Love and his partner were still on the trail. After the gang had split up, there was little choice but to pick a trail and follow it. The skills learned in Texas were put to good use now as they tracked several of the gang south through the San Joaquín Valley, past Tulare Lake and over the Tehachapis to Los Angeles. They were following the hoofprints of a particular animal. The two men followed several false leads, then made their weary way down the coast towards San Buenaventura (now Ventura).

On June 18, 1852, Love and his partner appeared before Justice of the Peace Joseph S. Mallard at Los Angeles. In a prepared affidavit they stated they were in the area "for the purpose of apprehending a couple of Sonorans who were charged with having committed murders and robberies in Mariposa County and for whom a large reward had been offered." They had tracked two of the gang to a San Buenaventura roadhouse and, after a brief exchange of gunshots, had captured one of the suspects—thought to be Pedro Gonzales, a Murrieta gang member. The two possemen began the trek back to Los Angeles, herding their captive on foot while they rode. The *Los Angeles Star* reported what happened next as given in the affidavit:

> The prisoner, being on foot, complained of fatigue and made several ineffectual attempts to escape. When about 8 miles this side of the river he complained of thirst and pointing to a ravine near at hand, told his conductor that there was plenty of water a little way up. Accordingly, Mr. Lull [Love] dismounted and proceeded with the man til they came to a small clump of bushes, when the prisoner darted forward into them and would have made his escape—Mr. L's botas and spurs preventing him from giving chase—but the latter, in endeavoring to knock him down with his pis-

tol, accidently [*sic*] discharged it and shot him through the head, killing him instantly.[1]

They had undoubtedly brought the dead prisoner into town and, after calling on the local officers, they prepared for the long trip back to Mariposa. Love was gone when the *Star* corrected the misspelling of his name a few days later. "Mr. Love," commented the paper, "was one of the most fearless of Gen. Taylor's express riders at the time of the Mexican War, in which capacity he rendered great and arduous services."[2] It was a comment Harry was to read frequently in future years.

Murrieta and his group, meanwhile, had made their way to a rendezvous where a fellow bandido was able to get them all into clothes again. It had been a harrowing experience. Reyes Féliz had a disagreement with a bear while in the mountains and was badly chewed up, but he later joined his friends at San Gabriel, a small village some nine miles from Los Angeles.

It is not known what Murrieta and his men did for the next few months, but some of them may have made a hurried trip to Mexico. The *Los Angeles Star* of December 4, 1852, noted that "Los Angeles County has been infested with a gang of robbers and murderers for a long time past," indicating others remained at San Gabriel. When they wanted a place to stay, they simply appeared at a friend's adobe with a hunk of rustled beef on their shoulder. More often than not, they probably slept in the open where they could keep an eye out for posses. In this manner they lolled about the San Gabriel cantinas, drinking away the hours until they again ran low on coin.

The village had grown up around the San Gabriel Mission, which at this time housed, of all things, a saloon in its southwest corner. Called The Headquarters, the saloon was operated by a former San Diego mayor, one Joshua Bean. San Gabriel was described as a rowdy place when visited by Horace Bell during this period:

> At the time there were three great grog-shops at the Mission; all kept by Americans; all doing a smashing business, especially on Sundays, when from early dawn till late at night these devil's workshops would be surrounded by a mass of drunken, howling Indians. About sundown the smashing business would begin in good earnest; that is to say, these gentle aboriginal Christians would commence to smash in each other's skulls. Now

---

[1]Under the heading "Prisoner Shot," the *Los Angeles Star,* June 19, 1852, reported Love and his partner made a statement to Justice of the Peace Joseph S. Mallard regarding the killing of Pedro Gonzales.   [2]Love's name was corrected in the *Star,* June 26, 1852.

Joseph S. Mallard was the justice of the peace at Los Angeles to whom Love reported the death of his prisoner. *Author's collection.*

you see the kind of a smashing business carried on by our three honorable countrymen in addition to getting the Indian's coin.³

Others were not quite so sarcastic in their commentary. Edward G. Buffum saw the village as "one of the prettiest spots in California," the banks of the San Gabriel River being "girdled with grape vines" for miles.⁴

General Bean was a Kentuckian who had served in the Mexican War and later came west with the gold rush. Always prominent in civic affairs, Bean was a major general of the California Militia and commander of a local contingent of Rangers.⁵ The Rangers had been prominent in quelling a recent Indian uprising and had done much to hold down the depredations of Indian horse thieves. That the Rangers were not ones to fool with horse thieves, Indian or otherwise, was indicated by a May 1851 item in the *Star*:

---

³Horace Bell, *Reminiscences of a Ranger* (Santa Barbara, Calif.: Wallace Hebberd, 1927), 84.
⁴Edward Gould Buffum, *Six Months in the Gold Mines* (Los Angeles: The Ward Ritchie Press, 1959), 122.
⁵C. L. Sonnichsen, *Roy Bean, Law West of the Pecos* (New York: The Macmillan Company, 1943), 27–33. See also the *Corpus Christi Star*, November 14, 1848, and the *Los Angeles Star*, November 13, 1852.

In late 1852, San Gabriel, California, was a collection of adobe homes and shops surrounding the old mission building, a portion of which was then being utilized as Joshua Bean's saloon. The village was also a hotbed of outlaws. *California State Library.*

Gen. Bean has moved his camp from the Cajon Pass to a point some fifteen miles to the south.... A scouting party sent to the San Francisco ranch, returned to the Cajon yesterday. They made one prisoner, and subsequently shot him. The Indians were not to be met with in any numbers.[6]

According to the *Star*, Bean had disbanded his Rangers in July 1851, but may have been preparing to re-activate them, given the increase in crime, in late 1852. Bean's brother Roy was in San Gabriel now and could be counted on to run the saloon if Josh were to again take his Rangers out. After engaging in a horseback duel in San Diego in February 1852, Roy had done some time in the local bastille, then escaped one night and fled to San Gabriel. Here he could bask in the reflected glory of his popular brother and help out in the saloon when occasion demanded.[7]

---

[6] *Star,* May 24, 1851.
[7] William L. Roper, "The Duel on Horseback: Roy Bean in Old Town," *San Diego Magazine,* October 1972. See also the *Star* of February 28, 1855, and the *San Francisco Daily Alta California,* March 24, 1855.

Any infestation of criminals was not reflected in the local press that summer of 1852, the only significant crime being the murder of several travelers from San Diego. The two murderers were quickly caught and hanged. When Murrieta and his men limped into San Gabriel, they apparently laid low until the fall when they again became active, as noted by the *Star* in November:

> HORSE STEALING. Numerous cases of horse stealing are reported in this neighborhood. A gentleman who had occasion to make some inquiries yesterday ascertained that no less than fourteen horses and mules were stolen on the previous night.[8]

A much more serious incident happened on the evening of November 7. There had been a *maromas*, or rope dance, part of a traveling Mexican circus in San Gabriel. Consequently, the village was even rowdier than usual. Joaquín and a young woman named Ana Benítez had attended the circus and afterwards returned to the home of one Juan Rico, a mutual friend. Besides Rico's family, there were others in the adobe that night, and all were asleep when several shots were heard outside, as recalled later by Ana:

> At a later part of the night, I heard some shots, and during the three shots heard voices; could not, however, distinguish whether they were Americans or Mexicans. A short moment afterwards I heard some more shots, the voice of Gen. Bean, who arrived crying "Rico! Rico! Rico!" I then sat up and saw Bean, who came dragging a cloak, Senora Jesus opened the door and Juanita Rico was already holding him in his arms and said, "Mother, it is General Bean." ... First, three were fired; then a single shot, which was fired when the General came crying out towards the house.
>
> I told Joaquin Murieta [*sic*] to go in search of a doctor, but in the first place an alcalde, in order that they might see what had taken place.[9]

Bean died that night. When such a prominent citizen could be shot down in the streets, people were outraged! Posses were quickly in the field, but it was several weeks before any suspects could be isolated. "His death," noted the *Star*, "has created a deep sensation in this community, and his remains were followed to their last resting place by a procession of citizens much more numerous than ever before witnessed in this city."[10]

Ana Benítez was picked up, as was Joaquín's brother-in-law, Reyes Féliz.

---

[8] *Star*, November 13, 1852.   [9] Ibid., December 4, 1852.
[10] Ibid., November 13, 1852. See also *Star*, December 4, 1852, and the *San Joaquin Republican*, December 4, 1852.

Benito López, said to be a member of the Salomón Pico gang, was also arrested, along with one Cypriano Sandoval, who was accused by Ana Benitez of being the actual killer of Bean. Felipe Read, the half-breed son of a prominent local rancher, was picked up also, but was quickly released. Juan Rico, José Alviso, and someone named Eleuterio were also caught up in the dragnet. Joaquín Murrieta avoided capture, if indeed he was being sought, and his disappearance certainly lent credence to his involvement in the affair. In his flight to avoid capture, he callously abandoned his brother-in-law, Reyes Féliz, although there was little he could have done to save him.

A Los Angeles letter dated November 11, 1852, gave yet another possible reason for Bean's death:

> It appears that soon after the evacuation of the city of Mexico, Gen. Bean and Judge Stakes, at a place called Roma, arrested ten cut-throat villains, and these wretches have frequently since that time threatened their lives. It has been well known that they resided lately in the lower country and probably had renewed their intentions of revenging themselves.

Because of inadequate facilities, the authorities agreed to let the local vigilance committee hold the prisoners and punish them. One by one the suspects were taken to a small, two-room adobe in Los Angeles and questioned, then either released or locked up for further investigation. The seven-man vigilance examining committee questioned some dozen witnesses for a week before narrowing down their list to six men. Féliz, young as he was, was hard as nails and admitted to having murdered a man at the Tuolumne County mining camp of Sonora. His confession corroborates the Corona raid, the run-in with the Indians at the Tejon, and even Love's killing of Pedro Gonzales:

> My name is Reyes Feliz, am 15 or 16 years old, was born at the Real de Bayareca, State of Sonora; did not know General Bean; don't know who killed him. Here in Los Angeles, I heard some gentlemen, whose names I do not know, say that Murieta's [sic] woman had said that Joaquin Murieta [sic] had killed him. I live at San Gabriel. . . . I belonged to the company of Joaquin Murieta [sic] and the late Pedro, who was killed by Americans in the "Cuesta del conejo." I was not then with Pedro; I was then ill in the Tulares of the effects from bites of a bear. We robbed, Joaquin Murieta, [sic] the late Pedro and myself. In Avisimba, "orilla de la Sierra," [foot of the mountains] in front of the Pueblo of San Jose, we robbed 20

horses, which we brought to the "Tejon." There the Indians took some of them from us; others, the owner took, who went in pursuit of us. I don't know his name, he was a Mexican. I have not robbed any more, I did not kill anybody else. I know nothing more about the death of Gen. Bean.[11]

The vigilantes could not directly tie him to the Bean killing, but his confession of the Sonora murder resulted in his being condemned to death. In his examination before the vigilance committee, young Reyes had made other damaging disclosures, according to a correspondent of the *San Francisco Herald*:

> There can be no doubt as to the guilt of the first named prisoner [Reyes] ... as he acknowledged that he ought to die as a punishment for his varied crimes. He confessed to be a murderer and a robber, but denied that he had killed General Bean. He was connected with the murder of the Riddle [*sic*] family, and is no doubt a finished villain. A large reward has been offered for him in Mariposa County.[12]

The following day he was taken to Prospect Hill, where he bravely accepted his fate. Addressing the crowd, he admitted his punishment was justly merited and cautioned his listeners about putting faith in women. Still insisting he knew nothing of Bean's death, young Féliz was hanged by the crowd.

Benito López found himself in much the same situation. He admitted to several murders, and when he took several vigilantes to the bones of his victims, his fate was also sealed. But he made some serious allegations about the elusive Joaquín:

> I know that Ana belonged to the gang of robbers because she herself told me that she was the woman of Joaquin. She told me that Joaquin had gone to the Tulares to sell about 30 horses he has stolen, and that he would be back in about 20 days.[13]

Ana was quite probably one of the women who accompanied Joaquín and his men from San Luis Gonzaga to the Tejon and San Gabriel. She had effectively thrown suspicion from Joaquín onto Cypriano Sandoval, who was hanged along with López and a murderer named Barumas. Years later, Felipe Read was discovered to have been the real killer. According to Horace Bell, General Bean had been killed for seducing Read's mistress.[14]

[11]*Star*, December 4, 1852.
[12]*San Francisco Herald,* December 6, 1852.
[13]*Star*, December 4, 1852.
[14]Bell, *Reminiscences of a Ranger*, 9–10.

A notice in the *Star* undoubtedly refers to Joaquín's southern California exit:

> On the night of Tuesday, the 25th ult., the entire stock of horses belonging to Messrs. White & Courtney, consisting of about one hundred head, together with some few owned by emigrants who have recently arrived in the country, were stolen from San Gabriel. At first the robbery was supposed to have been committed by Indians, but from present indications it seems more probable that the same band of outlaws who have so long infested this county, and a part of whom, there is every reason to believe, are now in the hands of the people, are the guilty ones. . . . Four or five men have started on their track.[15]

---

[15] *Star*, December 4, 1852.

8

Death on the Trail

By early 1853 crime had become a burgeoning problem throughout the mines. Highwaymen, robbers, and horse thieves, many of them members of Joaquín's gangs, were particularly active in Calaveras County. The past June two Frenchmen had been assaulted in their tent and robbed at Jackson; one of them died. The local vigilance committee offered a $300 reward for the suspects, who were brought in and delivered to the officers the following day. Both were Mexicans, one known as Cheverino Cruz and the other as Mariano.[1]

That night the two suspects were taken from the jail by a mob of Frenchmen and others who prepared to lynch them. When two witnesses argued that Mariano had been asleep at their house during the time of the murder, some Americans stepped in and persuaded the crowd to release him and he was returned to the officers. The lynching of Cruz was a particularly ugly affair, as reported by an eyewitness:

> It was a most brutal scene. The prisoner was first raised from the ground with his hands not tied behind. He clutched the rope with both hands, and thus preserved his life for perhaps ten minutes, when he was let down, his hands tied behind him, and again swung up, which terminated the tragedy. He confessed that he was one of the murderers. We expect that tomorrow night two other Mexicans will be brought up from your city (Sacramento) who participated in the murder and will probably meet the same fate.[2]

Even horse thieves were given short shrift by the embattled ranchers and miners. When some stock was stolen in Ione Valley in September

---
[1] The murder of the two Frenchmen and resulting events were reported in the *Calaveras Chronicle* and reprinted in the Sacramento *Daily Union*, May 24, 1852.
[2] The Jackson correspondence was published in the *Union*, June 12, 14, and 16, 1852.

In 1853, one of Murrieta's men was lynched from this same tree in Jackson. This lithograph seems to have been made from a daguerrotype and depicts the hanging of Rafael Escobar in 1855.
Courtesy the Huntington Library.

1852, the ranchers reported a description of the animals to officers in Jackson. Before long, a Mexican had offered one of the stolen animals for sale and was seized. A posse went out and managed to capture his accomplice, along with other stolen animals.[3] When a deputy sheriff then sent for the owners of the stock and deputized them to deliver the prisoners to Mokelumne Hill, the exasperated ranchers had other ideas, as reported in the *Calaveras Chronicle*:

> They bound the captives to their horses, and instead of taking the road to the Hill, went full gallop towards Ione Valley. At the latter place, the citizens assembled in large numbers on Wednesday, and decreed that the prisoners should expiate their offence by hanging. This sentence was carried

---
[3]Stockton *San Joaquin Republican*, September 22, 1852.

into execution on Wednesday evening. The names of the unfortunate Mexicans were Jesus Brisano and Antonio Duartes.[4]

Despite these summary executions, however, the outlaws did not appear to have gotten the message by the time Murrieta and his men arrived in mid-January 1853.

The death of General Bean and resulting events in southern California had been widely reported in the press. Joaquín Murrieta knew by now that his brother-in-law, young Reyes Féliz, was dead, and that Claudio had also been killed the previous September. Pedro Gonzales had been killed by Harry Love after the long chase from San Luis Gonzaga, and other members of his band had been lynched or captured in the past few months. Only twenty-two years old at this time, the young outlaw must have had a gut feeling that he was on a collision course with disaster himself.

Sending out small parties of robbers, Joaquín began his bloody vendetta. The *San Joaquin Republican* called attention to the results in January 1853:

ROBBERY—For some time back a band of robbers have been committing depredations in the southern section of our county, the Chinamen being the principal sufferers. During the week a party of three Mexicans entered a Chinese tent at Yackee [Yaqui] camp, near San Andreas, and ransacked everything, despite the opposition of the inmates, carrying off two bags of gold dust, one containing $110 and the other $50.

... Three armed Mexicans—supposed to be the same who committed the above outrage—entered another Chinese tent in the same vicinity, assaulted its inhabitants, holding loaded pistols at their heads to keep them quiet, and robbed them of two bags of gold dust, $90 and $60. One of the Chinamen, named Akop, refused to give up his money and attempted to defend himself, when one of the ruffians drew his knife and run the unfortunate celestial through the body, causing almost instant death. The party then escaped with their booty.[5]

For some time Joaquín and his men had apparently camped on the outskirts of Yaqui Camp, but their presence was now known.[6] Another *Repub-*

---

[4] *Calaveras Chronicle*, May 24, 1852.   [5] *Republican*, January 29, 1853.
[6] Murrieta's secluded camp was above San Andreas, according to a writer in the San Francisco *Argonaut*, June 29, 1878. A physician who signed his article "B.R." was once summoned to attend an injured man in the mountains back of town. Accompanying a "rough-looking Spaniard" to a local landmark called Bear Mountain, the doctor was then blindfolded and taken to Joaquín's camp, where he attended a wounded outlaw. He described Joaquín as having a "delicate beauty of profile, its almost feminine freshness of appearance was marred by a terrific scar on the forehead which had slightly disfigured the upper part of the nose.... He was below the medium height, delicately, but firmly knit, and his eyes were perfectly luminous."

lican article noted that the place was a rendezvous for some "notorious Mexican desperadoes" and a San Andreas constable had recently been attacked there. "The place . . . ," continued the article, "should be inevitably visited by the authorities and this band of villains broken up ere they effectively organize for their summer depredations." But it was now too late.

After cataloguing a fearful series of murders, robberies, and rustling operations, the *Republican* reported suspicions that were becoming more credible every day:

> The band is led by a robber named Joaquin, a very desperate man, who was concerned in the murder of 4 Americans sometime ago, at Turnerville (the killings connected to the Buchanan shooting). He levied his "Blackmail" generally upon the Chinese population, a very peaceable and industrious class. With his band, he would frequently enter their tents and compel them to cook for him and his accomplices whatever food they required. This has been done in many instances.
>
> On Friday night another man was murdered at Yackee [*sic*] Camp and about the same time, a Chinaman was found dead at Bay State Ranche and an American at Foreman's Ranche.[7]

Miners and isolated camps and villages were terribly vulnerable, and posses began to organize. Five men rode out from Yaqui Camp on Saturday morning, January 22, hot on the trail of the marauders. Near San Andreas, they discovered a dozen of the outlaws with a large drove of stolen animals in their possession. The posse felt they were outgunned and quickly rode into San Andreas for reinforcements.

Flushed with the success of their recent raids, Joaquín sent his men and animals south to their hideout in the Coast Range, then rode to the nearby Phoenix Quartz Mills with his remaining gang members. Firing their pistols as they galloped up, the bandits were quickly engaged in a gunfight with Peter Woodbeck and another mill operator who had been sleeping in the canvas-roofed house. One of the bandits dismounted and, climbing up some boxes and barrels, lifted up the canvas and shot and killed one of the defenders. The sniper was spotted and took a shotgun blast in the shoulder, but managed to kill the other man before dropping to the ground and crawling off into the surrounding brush. Surprised by the resistance, Joaquín and his men ransacked the place, then galloped off, abandoning their wounded comrade.

---

[7] *Republican*, January 29, 1853.

This scene, depicting Joaquín Murrieta fleeing from a pursuing posse, took place many times during the winter of 1852–53. The *California Police Gazette* of October 8, 1859, featured this illustration on its front page. *Author's collection.*

The following morning, Constable Charles Ellis received word of the Phoenix Mill attack and organized a posse hastily. At the scene, the two bodies were cared for and a trail of blood was followed to a small mining camp at Las Muertos. The wounded bandit was discovered hiding in a tent and was soon in custody. Four shotgun pellets were found in his body, but he was taken to San Andreas, where he was questioned closely by Ellis and others. A shouting and frustrated mob then lynched him.[8] The Mokelumne Hill *Calaveras Chronicle* reported:

> The Mexican that was hanged at San Andreas on Sunday last made a confession which discovered a plan of a well organized banditti throughout the state. He was of Joaquin's party, but not a conspicuous or leading member. His obligations confined him to a certain district, out of which he dare not travel.... He was bound to shelter and protect any of the brethren who were in danger, to procure horses and assist them in their escape at all hazards.... Such a combination as this cannot easily be broken up, and

---
[8] *Republican*, January 26, 1853. See also the *San Francisco Herald*, February 8, 1853, and John R. Andrews, *Ghost Towns of Amador* (New York: The Carlton Press, Inc., 1967), 120.

it shows a skillful generalship in the leaders greater than they have been given credit for. From this statement we can easily understand how Joaquin obtains his splendid animals. These agents know where the best horses are kept, make themselves familiar with the locality, and on the arrival of the band are required to procure them forthwith. Thus they have always fresh horses and generally the best in the country. The leaders of the band were Joaquin, Claudio, and Reiz [sic]. These were the party who killed the Sheriff of Yuba, Claudio having fired the first shot. He was at Monterey when last heard from, wither he had gone to drive cattle. Reiz [sic] is still with Joaquin.[9]

Neither Claudio nor his brother Reyes were with the party, of course, since they were both dead. The *Sacramento Union* noted that the bandit "made a full confession and gave an accurate description of Joaquín and thirteen of the party."[10]

Other crimes were committed this same night and the following Sunday morning, January 30, some three hundred miners assembled, sending armed groups to the Stanislaus and Calaveras rivers to guard the ferries. Posses were systematically combing the brush- and tree-choked hills and gullies for the outlaws now. Frustrated and angry, they burned many Mexican houses and disarmed every Hispanic they met, ordering them to leave the area. The entire Mexican population was driven from San Andreas and the forks of the Calaveras River.

This same Sunday morning a Mexican tied his horse at the Bay State Ranch and went into the house to inquire about breakfast. John Hall, the owner, told him to sit down while he stepped out the door to talk to a man named Rains, who operated the ferry. Hall told the ferryman he thought the Mexican's horse was stolen, and the two decided to hold him. Meanwhile, the Mexican saw them talking from the window, quickly slipped out the back door, and began walking down the road. As the two men ran after the fugitive, three magnificently mounted vaqueros swept out of the roadside chaparral and took their companion up double behind one of them. As they galloped off down the road, Hall and Rains promptly armed themselves and sent for help. They then proceeded after the suspected outlaws.

When Constable Ellis, Jeff Gatewood, and Ike Betts joined the pursuit, the reinforced posse soon spotted the outlaws on a nearby mountain top. Closing in, Ellis and his men charged up the hill, but the Mexicans

---
[9] *Calaveras Chronicle* as re-printed in the *Republican*, March 2, 1853.
[10] Sacramento *Union*, February 24, 1853.

fled down the side after one of the party was wounded. Seeing the bandits preparing to charge back up the hill, the posse dismounted and sought what shelter they could find as the outlaws swept by firing their pistols. "There was lots of shooting," reported the *Republican*, "and three of the Mexicans were wounded, but the Americans had to leave when they ran out of ammunition."[11]

But Joaquín was taking more casualties. The *Republican* reported, "We are glad to hear that one of the gang has been caught at Yackee [*sic*] Camp and another at Cherokee Ranch. Both were inevitably strung up."[12]

Always on the move, Joaquín and his men galloped swiftly through the bitter cold nights and camped near the mining town of Jackson. On the Cosumnes River they robbed and killed a number of Chinese, then stole three fine horses, leaving several broken down animals in their place. On February 13 a number of Chinese miners came into Jackson, complaining of being robbed by a gang of Mexican bandits. Shortly after this, another group of Chinese came in saying they, too, had been robbed and one of their party killed. A hastily-organized posse had no sooner galloped out of town when a third group of Chinese victims arrived, bringing the bodies of two of their murdered companions. A February 13 dispatch to the *Sacramento Union* reported:

> The party of Americans who started in pursuit found at Cook's Gulch, on Sutter Creek, the dead body of a Chinaman. They traced the robbers to Jackson Creek, a few miles below this village, and there found more of their work—one Chinaman mortally wounded and the body of Mr. Joseph Lake, a respectable citizen of the town. Mr. Lake was living, but speechless and he died in a few minutes. He had been shot twice and stabbed in the neck and his mule taken. The American party galloped on and soon overtook the Mexicans who had committed all these murders. The villains managed to escape with the loss of their horses, blankets, etc. and one or two of them was wounded. It is hoped they'll be captured tomorrow.
>
> This town is under the greatest excitement—A large meeting of the citizens was held this evening and severe measures were taken that must lead to the eventual capture of the murderers. Nearly the whole population has volunteered to turn out in the pursuit tomorrow. $1000 are [*sic*] offered for the head of Joaquin. His band is supposed to number over 50 men scattered over different parts of the country.[13]

---

[11] *Calaveras Chronicle* as reprinted in the *Republican*, February 2, 1853.
[12] *Republican*, January 26, 1853.
[13] Sacramento *Union*, February 15, 1853.

All of this was having a marked effect on the area. The *Calaveras Chronicle* complained that there was a noticeable decrease in the population along the Calaveras River. Some five hundred miners were leaving Carsons Hill for the Australian gold fields for fear of being robbed or murdered by Joaquín's band. Rumors were everywhere.[14] The *Republican* of February 16 reported Joaquín and his men had held up the Sacramento stage, killing the driver and two female passengers. The next day the report was dismissed as groundless. The same paper reported that Joaquín wore a coat of mail and receives a ball on his breast "with perfect indifference."

A large posse operating out of Jackson on February 15 was reported to be disarming every Mexican they found and arresting suspicious characters. When a Mexican woman betrayed the whereabouts of one of the outlaws, he was captured and brought into Jackson. Antonio Valencia was quickly recognized by several Chinese miners he had robbed. He was in jail for only a few minutes when a mob broke in and hauled him before a vigilante tribunal. "He was found guilty," reported the *Sacramento Union*, "and immediately escorted to that fatal Oak Tree fronting the Astor House which was now destined for the fifth time to bear a peculiar kind of fruit. He refused to confess or talk to a [C]atholic priest here."[15]

Reports were constantly circulating of teamsters being assaulted or missing. On February 20, five bandits entered a Chinese camp on the Calaveras River and killed or wounded several of the party. They took several thousand dollars, then moved on to a roadside store which they also plundered. Some two hundred other Chinese were robbed that day, the *Republican* noting that "Joaquin's spoils must have been some $30,000."[16]

A purse was collected at Jackson and a party of six men under deputy sheriff Charles Clark was quickly in the saddle. The possemen were John McNish, Gwynn Raymond, James Titcomb, John G. Ward, and David Pollock. Leaving Mokelumne Hill in a drizzling rain, the party followed reports of the outlaws through plundered Chinese camps. They kept on side trails when they could and knew they were on the right track at Camp Opera, where it was learned that four Mexicans had stolen a boat the night before. Here, seven more men joined the posse, making thirteen in all. Splitting into three groups at Winters Bar, the posse was able to cover

---

[14]*Republican*, March 9, 1853, and the *Calaveras Chronicle*, March 17, 1853.
[15]Sacramento *Union*, February 19, 1853. [16]*Republican*, February 23, 1853.

much more ground. Three Chinese had been killed at Rich Gulch the night before and $10,000 reported stolen.[17]

On the evening of February 22 Clark and his men learned that five Mexicans were in a nearby Chinese camp, and they promptly galloped to the scene. Spotting the posse charging down a hill, the bandits disappeared into a brush-covered hillside. One of the outlaws had been shot in the hand, but it was several minutes before the posse was reassembled and again galloped in pursuit. From the top of the hill they heard several pistol shots and made their way down a rocky hill to another Chinese camp. Here, amid scattered belongings and demolished tents, the posse found three dead miners and five others in their death agonies. Terrified survivors excitedly told Clark the bandits had left about ten minutes earlier, after taking some $3,000.

Spurring their lathered mounts off into the night, the posse lost the trail and returned to Foreman's Ranch for some rest. They again took up the chase the next morning, but were never able to catch up with their quarry. "There were five well dressed Mexicans," a posseman commented, "well armed and mounted on Beautiful animals." Another of the possemen wrote:

> I have been engaged a week in hunting Mr. Joaquin and his party, and we had a right lively time of it. . . . We followed them all over the county and, while we were on their trail they killed and wounded 15 Chinamen and stole seven or eight thousand dollars, We got one or two chances at them, but they were so well mounted that they beat us running all to hell.[18]

Gov. John Bigler finally responded to the frantic newspaper editorials, letters, and petitions by offering a $1,000 reward for the capture of the suspected Joaquín—one Joaquín Carrillo. It was not known yet just who this Joaquín was, or if there was more than one Joaquín in the band. Nor is it clear where the name Carrillo originated. Although the *San Joaquin Republican* noted the reward was "entirely inadequate," Bigler hastily responded that the amount was all he could legally offer. "Already," continued the *Republican*, "the citizens of this country have raised and expended more than that amount to stay the murderous band, but it is not yet done and it is clearly proved that Joaquín will not be taken by ordinary means."[19] An infuriated citizen of Calaveras County sent a press

---

[17]Ibid.

[18]*Republican*, February 26 and March 2, 1853. See also the *Alta*, February 28, 1853.

[19]*Republican*, February 26, 1853. The undated clipping is quoted from the Joaquin Murrieta Papers, Vault Bin 268, California State Archives, Sacramento.

clipping to his assemblyman, who in turn passed it on to the governor as a more realistic response to their constituents:

> When we consider that this county lies at the mercy of these ruffians, that there is no security for life or property and that the remote camps are nightly robbed and the inhabitants savagely butchered, we think the reward should have been at least $5,000 for the body of Joaquin and Reiz [sic] each and $1,000 for any of the subordinates. The conditions attached to this reward render it altogether negatory, [sic] for Joaquin will never be taken alive.[20]

It became increasingly clear that something had to be done, and quickly. But what? As the governor and legislature desperately hoped Joaquín would either be captured or killed, the bandits vanished almost as suddenly as they had appeared. There was hardly time for a collective sigh of relief before they reappeared, however.

Writing in his diary on March 14, 1853, Volcano miner John Doble gave a clear indication of the legendary status already acquired by Joaquín, even at this early date:

> The Indians that live on the Dry Sutter Amadore [sic] & Rancherie [sic] creeks ... are supposed to be incited to rob and steal by the band of outlawed Mexicans & Chileans known as Joaquin[']s band. There has been lately several murders committed near Jackson Amadore [sic] Drytown Campo Seco & Mokelumne Hill & two or three of the band have been taken up & he is said to wear a shirt of mail so that all who have yet shot at him have not affected him any in this neighborhood all has been quiet their range not being near here nor in this direction.[21]

Realizing their luck must run out if they stayed in the Calaveras area, Joaquín and his men headed south. Avelino Martinez later told Frank Latta that Joaquín wanted to go to Mariposa to look for an American who had abused him in the mines, which may or may not have been the case. Certainly, it was time to move on.[22] Probably moving at night in small and scattered groups, Joaquín rode with Martinez, Joaquín Valenzuela, and Ramon Soto as they made their way to the foothills near Quartzburg, where they set up a camp. Joaquín had mined in the area previously and had friends

---
[20]Ibid.
[21]John Doble, *John Doble's Journal and Letters from the Mines . . . 1851–1865*, Charles L. Camp, ed. (Denver: The Old West Publishing Company, 1962), 148.
[22]Latta, *Joaquin Murrieta and His Horse Gangs*, 54.

at the nearby Mexican village of Hornitos. Martinez remembered them having dinner in a Hornitos restaurant, in full view of everyone.

Hornitos was the locale of Rosie Martinez' fandango hall, a pleasure palace where the bloody but rich outlaws could enjoy themselves in relative safety. Frank Salazar, a lifelong resident of the old town, remembered the old residents talking of Rosie's place. It was underground, beneath another structure, and Salazar recalled well the ruins of the red tile floors that he had seen as a boy. The Martinez place would certainly appeal to the outlaws—there was even a tunnel from which they could make a quick exit, in time of trouble.[23]

Joaquín was now a hunted man whose life had changed forever. His hands were stained with the blood of dozens of victims, and the excitement of the chase was a euphoria he was unable to cast aside. He had had many close calls, but seemed unable to avoid conflict for long. In a dispatch from Mariposa dated March 6, 1853, the *San Joaquin Republican* announced the bandit's arrival:

> Our orderly and quiet community has been thrown into quite a state of excitement of late by the news which reaches us from time to time of the doings of the notorious Joaquin—who has recently paid us a couple of visits. Some two weeks ago he made his appearance with a dozen of his gang, in the town of Aronytas [Hornitos], a large Mexican camp on Burns' creek, about twenty miles from this place.... Last Thursday evening he repeated his visit to the same place, apparently alone. Two Americans who were present, recognized him and attempted to take him prisoner, but he shot both of them, wounding one in the arm and the other in the abdomen and succeeded in making his escape unharmed. Next day several Mexicans were taken into custody on suspicion of being connected with him.

This incident undoubtedly refers to a rustling raid on a Mariposa ranch on March 4. After enjoying their fling at the Martinez dance hall, Joaquín and his men were back in business again. No doubt they were gathering stock for a run down into old Mexico when they made a dash through the Willis Prescott ranch near Quartzburg. Following the rustlers into Hornitos that evening, Prescott tracked them to a tent on the outskirts of town, then sought out seven or eight other Anglos to help him with the capture. With a friend named Henry Crowell, Prescott entered the tent with a light and seized one of the suspects.

---

[23]William B. Secrest, *The Gold of Old Hornitos* (Fresno, Calif.: Saga-West Publishing Company, 1964), 5.

Frank Salazar was a lifelong resident of Hornitos and knew many of the pioneer residents. He is holding a sombrero that was reportedly the former property of Murrieta. *Author's collection.*

Suddenly, there was a series of explosions and flashes through the doorway. As clouds of gunsmoke filled the tent, Prescott took a bullet in the side and Crowell in the hip. Neither wound was serious, but in the confusion the several suspects fled and were quickly lost in the darkness. One of the possemen, Lee Vining, got off two shots, but his pistol misfired each time. The *Republican* noted:

> The people in the vicinity of Quartzburg are in arms and riding over the mountains and plains every day in search of Joaquin.... It was but a short time since Joaquin was recognized betting at monte in Ornitis [sic] against an American dealer; he got to drinking and betting very high and would in all probability have exposed himself to the dealer but for the timely entering of three of his band who carried him off by force. Will not Governor Bigler offer a reward, a sufficient sum to pay a party of men to seek him out and take him dead or alive?[24]

---

[24] *Republican*, March 12, 1853.

A rash of other local crimes were laid at Joaquín's door, the most notable being reported in the *Stockton Journal* of March 17:

> On Friday night five Frenchmen, camped on Bear Creek about 15 miles from Mariposa, were attacked in the night and the whole party murdered and robbed. It is supposed that the assassins belonged to Joaquin's band and were, perhaps, headed by the rascal himself.

Joaquín was meanwhile being reported all over the state by nervous travelers and others. At a road house near Placerville, three Mexican riders tried to sell a magnificent horse at an obviously low price. An old "Spaniard" who happened to be passing by thought he recognized Joaquín and gave the alarm. The vaqueros immediately spurred their mounts and disappeared down the road. A pursuing posse chased them for some distance, but they were lost at a spot called Spanish Camp on the Cosumnes River. The *San Diego Herald* reported a young Mexican who bore a "resemblance" to the daring Joaquín herding a band of some thirty-five horses south. Which one was the real "Joaquín," if either, is not known.[25]

Since there were indeed several bandits named Joaquín reportedly riding with Murrieta, it is apparent that between the names and the mobility of the gang there was a great deal of confusion. Until a few weeks earlier, not even the surname of the bandit leader was known—he was merely "Joaquin!" Names were being suggested by now, however. Joaquín Carrillo was one such name—Valenzuela, Moretto, and Muriati were others, but little was known for sure. Victims had supplied descriptions of the bandits but these, too, were often vague.

Trying to respond to the cries for help from the mining country, a resolution was introduced on March 26 before the California Assembly to offer a reward of $10,000 for "Joaquin." After whittling the amount down to $5,000, it was referred to the Committee on Military Affairs and unanimously recommended for passage. In a surprising move on April 14, however, Chairman José M. Covarrubias and a minority of the committee recommended the matter be postponed indefinitely.

"On more mature deliberation," the chairman wrote in his report,

> ... it has occurred to a minority of your committee that the principle involved in offering such reward is not justifiable in equity, nor would it be a safe and effectual mode of remedying the evil which we suffer. To set a price

---

[25]Both the Placerville and San Diego incidents were reported in the *Republican*, March 30, 1853.

upon the head of any individual who has not been examined and convicted by due process of law is to proceed upon an assumption of his guilt.

Assemblyman Covarrubias went on to remind his colleagues of the opportunities for mistaken identity or merely cupidity in the resolution. There was at the present time in the Assembly, he remarked, a memorial for relief concerning a victim of mistaken identity during the 1851 San Francisco vigilante uprising.[26]

"It may not be improper here to remark," concluded the chairman, "that there are citizens of this state, descendants of ancient and honorable families, who bear the name of Joaquín Carrillo—the name by which the individual is known for whose capture the reward is proposed to be offered.... One is a very respectable citizen of the County of Sonoma, and the other is District Judge of the 2nd Judicial district."[27]

It all made perfect sense to the legislature, but not to the citizens of Calaveras and Mariposa counties. Something had to be done, and the ranchers and miners began circulating a petition, hoping to keep up the pressure on the state.

During this same period in April, three heavily-armed Mexican vaqueros rode up to a ranch house on the Salinas plains, on the eastern edge of Monterey County. It was late at night, and the men told the rancher they were cattle buyers who had lost their way. The spokesman was a handsome young man, about twenty-one years old, wearing a false beard and mustache. He was carrying four pistols and a large knife. They were riding the best horses the rancher had ever seen. As a meal was being prepared, the rancher carried on a polite conversation with the three intruders.

When the vaqueros mentioned they were from the mines, the rancher asked what the latest word was of Joaquín. The leader glared at him and put his hand to his chest. "Sir, I am that Joaquin, and no man takes me alive or comes within one hundred yards of me so long as I have these good weapons."

The startled rancher then listened patiently as the man regaled him with tales of how he had been robbed and cheated and abused by Americans in the mines, and how he was now exacting his terrible revenge. He had been a great admirer of the Americans, but the treatment he had received had changed all that. He had lost some $40,000 to his persecutors and now vowed that he would "take the law into my own hands.... I'll rob—

---

[26]Joaquín Murrieta Papers.   [27]Ibid.

my track shall leave a trail of blood and he who seeks me shall bite the dust, or I will die in the struggle."

If the dialogue sounds like dime novel stuff, it must be remembered that it had been filtered through several people before being printed in the *San Francisco Herald* on April 18, 1853. Forget the language—the story makes too much sense not to be true. What bandit and killer would not tell a captive audience how he had been driven to a life of crime?! The article added that Joaquín had been seen a few days earlier in San Juan, San Jose, and some said, Monterey, where an aunt lived.

Meanwhile, a petition dated April 20, 1853, had been received at the state legislature at Benicia. It told of the desperate and ineffective efforts to capture Joaquín. Since the law seemed unable to protect the settlers, the petition strongly urged the legislature to authorize the raising of a party to track down Joaquín and his band of desperadoes.

The document concluded,

> We therefore, your memorialists and constituents, would respectfully petition our representatives in the Senate and Assembly now in session at Benecia [sic] to pass some special act immediately or at least before the adjournment of the present session, authorizing some discreet, prudent person to organize a company of twenty or twenty-five good horsemen, well armed and equipped and be so organized to be called the "California Rangers" and be required to traverse this county and other counties in the state for the purpose aforesaid for such length of time and to receive such compensation from the state treasury as our said representatives in their wisdom and patriotism may deed right and just—[28]

It was signed by 127 prominent residents of Mariposa County, including the recuperating William Prescott. The petition was read to the state senate on May 4 and referred to the Committee on Military Affairs. Before any action was taken however, another petition arrived from Mariposa County, this one signed by one hundred miners and ranchers. Harry Love personally presented the new petition, which urged the state to authorize the raising of a Ranger detachment of twenty men to be armed, equipped, and paid by the state. Extolling his bravery and experience on the Texas border, the petition strongly urged the appointment of Love as leader of the group.[29]

---

[28]"Petition from the Citizens of Mariposa County asking the passage of an Act to authorize the raising of a Company for the purpose of arresting Joaquin and his associate robbers," Joaquin Murrieta Papers. [29]Ibid.

The mining town of Mariposa, shown here in an 1859 print by Carleton Watkins, was where the Ranger legislation was initiated and where Harry Love's men made their triumphal entry with the head of Joaquín. *Author's collection.*

9
Ranger Days

Harry had apparently been in the Mariposa area for some time by now, although just what he was doing there is not known. There are no records of his having a mining claim in the county, but he may have had an informal arrangement with a mining partner.[1] Many Mariposa residents were Mexican War veterans who had heard of the famous express rider and explorer of the Rio Grande. This, and Love's dogged determination in the pursuit and capture of Pedro Gonzales, must have been the primary considerations in his selection as the Ranger leader.

Even though Gonzales had been acknowledged by Reyes Féliz to be one of Murrieta's men, the name Murrieta had not yet been attached to the ubiquitous bandit chieftain. They were getting close, however. On May 4 the *San Joaquin Republican* commented on the Salinas plains interview, stating that the bandit's real name was "Joaquín Muliati," although the governor's reward notice had officially designated Joaquín Carrillo as the fugitive. Clearly, the name problem would have to be resolved, and soon. He was still merely "Joaquín" in most accounts.

Name or no name, the legislature had stalled long enough. On May 17, 1853, an act creating the California Rangers under Captain Harry Love was signed and approved by Governor John Bigler. The company was not to exceed twenty men and would be in service for three months unless sooner disbanded. They were to supply their own arms, horses, equipment, and provisions, for which they were to be paid $150 a month per man. Although not specified, the $1,000 reward was still in effect.[2]

---

[1] A search of mining claims for Mariposa County for the early 1850s revealed only that a "G. Love," along with six others, filed a claim in September 1851. Mariposa County Book Records, 1, Notices, Locations of Mines.

[2] "An Act to authorize the raising of a company of Rangers," May 17, 1853. Joaquin Murrieta Papers.

A peculiar aspect of the act creating the Rangers was the naming of not one, but five, Joaquíns as the leaders of the outlaws. Finding it impossible to identify one individual bandit chieftain and knowing they must name *someone*, the legislators assembled a series of individuals who had been identified at one time or another in the press or by rumor. Named in the act were "Joaquín Muriati, Joaquín Ocomorenia, Joaquín Valenzuela, Joaquín Bottellier, and Joaquín Carrillo."

At this late date we can only speculate as to the origin of these names, but certain lines of reasoning make sense. Love and others lobbying at the capital for passage of the Ranger bill recalled the Bean slaying at Los Angeles and the mention of "Joaquín Murieta [*sic*]" as an associate of young Féliz and Pedro Gonzales. Joaquín Valenzuela, also known as "Ocomoreña" or "Nacamereño," was a well-known desperado, probably identified at some point as belonging to the bandit gang.[3] Joaquín Carrillo, the name of Murrieta's stepbrother, had already been identified by name on the governor's reward notice and so was therefore included.

This left only "Joaquín Botellier" unaccounted for. Apparently someone by this name had been recognized by a victim of the bandits and the first name of "Joaquín" had been enough to get him added to the list. Latta identifies this man as Joaquín Botellas, a brother of Refugio Botellas who was a California mail rider in the late 1840s. Instead of five bandit leaders, then, we have four, all of whom may or may not have led individual groups of Murrieta gangs. Despite all the hue and cry about the banditti, there were those still disturbed about the ambiguity of the whole matter. Commenting on the legislative act, the *Los Angeles Star* facetiously remarked:

> It is barely possible that THE Joaquin is included in the above enumeration, but if so, his identity is destroyed and with it all the notoriety he has acquired. A dangerous name is "Joaquin" and all who bear it must need to keep a sharp lookout, especially during the period of service of the twenty mounted rangers. The legal proprietors of some of the respectable names outlawed by the Legislature should petition for a rebaptism.[4]

---

[3] For verification of Joaquín Valenzuela's two nicknames, see the Los Angeles *El Clamor Publico*, June 5, 1858; the Santa Cruz *Pacific Sentinel*, May 28, 1858; and Myron Angel, *History* of *San Luis Obispo County, California* (Oakland: Thompson & West, 1883). This last source features an article by Walter Murray, one of the vigilantes who had hanged Valenzuela. Latta (p. 96) maintains that the remaining "Joaquin" was named Botellas, not "Botellier," and that his brother, Don Refugio Botellas, was an early California mail carrier.

[4] *Los Angeles Star*, June 4, 1853.

Love must have indeed been disturbed at the lack of information on his quarry. Still, he knew there were a great number of criminals out there, and he was anxious to get started. Once the Rangers were in the saddle he was sure they could narrow down the leads to the evasive "Joaquín," whoever he might be. Meanwhile, he had a company of Rangers to enlist. The *Republican* reported Love passing through Stockton on his way back to Mariposa from Benicia on May 20:

> Col. [*sic*] Harry Love, who has been authorized by the legislature to raise a company for the capture of Joaquin and his gang, passed through this city yesterday. An important power has been delegated to this gentleman and we hope that he will exercise it with vigor, yet with determination.

Only twenty-three years old when he arrived in California during the spring of 1849, William J. Howard came from a substantial Virginia family and was a veteran of the Mexican War. After a successful mining venture in Calaveras County, he settled in Mariposa County, where he established a pack train and tent store on Burns Creek, near Hornitos. With his brother Thomas, he bought 920 acres on the Fort Miller road where his store was located and established the Buena Vista Ranch, which became noted in the area for fine horseflesh. He also raised hogs, cattle, wheat, and barley, and acquired considerable property.[5] A contemporary visitor described the ranch located in

> the very beautiful valley of Buena Vista. . . . A capacious adobe building furnishes a pleasant retreat for the attendants on the rancho from the summer's heat, while a well, at convenient distance from the house, affords water of a most pure and excellent quality. . . . Near the road stands a very large corral built of rock taken from a neighboring sandstone quarry . . . higher up the valley is seen the barley field, embracing within its ditched fence some two hundred acres of land. . . .[6]

Howard's large horse herds were guarded by local Indians whose rancheria was nearby. Some fifty or sixty Indians worked for the brothers, harvesting their crops and tending the spacious gardens. It was a southern plantation in everything but setting.

---

[5]Jill L. Cossley-Batt, *The Last of the California Rangers* (New York and London: Funk & Wagnalls Corp., 1928), 90–93; John Outcalt, *History of Merced County, California* (Los Angeles: Historic Record Company, 1925), 167; *Merced County Sun*, May 3, 1890; *San Francisco Examiner*, December 17, 1893; *San Francisco Bulletin*, December 3, 1899; *San Francisco Chronicle*, April 21, 1907.

[6]The description of the Howard ranch is from an undated 1857 *Mariposa Democrat* article in Bertha Schroeder, *Mariposa News, 1850–1859*, unpublished typescript in collection of author.

If Howard did not know Harry Love personally, he certainly knew of him. In later years he recalled that Love came to him and asked that he help select his Ranger company: "Howard, you are more familiar with the fighting men of this part of the country. I wish you would pick the men you consider best suited for this undertaking."

As a veteran of both the Mexican War and a local Indian war, Howard was indeed in a position to help select men for the Rangers. Going one step further, Howard insisted that Love make his ranch the Ranger headquarters. Enlistments were quickly underway, all of the men selected having "smelt powder either in Mexico or Texas," as reported by Howard.

Even though the Rangers faced a difficult and dangerous mission, there was no problem acquiring recruits. Besides the salary of $150 a month, there was the $1,000 reward, which was a lot of money in mid-nineteenth-century America. Another $1,000 reward had been offered in Calaveras County, but even more important was the expectation of recovering stolen bandit gold. Anyone who read a newspaper could quickly total up an impressive amount of loot that might be located if the bandits were killed or captured. Far from a dearth of applicants, the Rangers had an oversupply, and there are indications several "unofficial" Rangers went along on various expeditions.[7]

A letter from one of the Rangers to the *San Joaquin Republican* dated May 30 listed the recruits of the Ranger company.[8] Patrick E. Connor, a Stockton resident and Mexican War veteran, was appointed first lieutenant of the group.[9] Charles Bludworth, a Louisiana native and local rancher, was appointed a second lieutenant. George W. Evans, veteran

---

[7]During the three-month life of Love's Rangers, a half-dozen of the men were replaced for one reason or another. Apparently there were a few others who tagged along from time to time just in case some bandit loot was recovered. Tom Mayfield and one L. R. Ketchum were two of the men mentioned, as was Jack Gordon, later a notorious Tulare County desperado. Another was a man named Kirker. Nothing is known of this latter character, and although the noted mountain man James Kirker comes to mind since he did come to California during the gold rush, he reportedly died in Contra Costa County in late 1852 or early 1853. None of these men show up in the 1852 Special Mariposa Census but, then, many of the actual Rangers do not show up in the census either. See Frank Latta's interview in the *Fresno Bee*, December 1, 1931. For data on Gordon see William B. Secrest, *Lawmen and Desperadoes* (Spokane, Wash.: The Arthur H. Clark Company, 1994), 152–156. Information on Kirker can be found in the biography by William C. McGaw, *Savage Scene* (New York: Hastings House, 1972).

[8]The new Ranger recruits are listed in the Stockton *San Joaquin Republican*, June 8, 1853. There are various degrees of information on these men, but most of them are quite obscure.

[9]Fred Rogers, *Soldiers of the Overland* (San Francisco: The Grabhorn Press, 1938), 9–10.

Looking like a real dude in his wedding clothes, William J. Howard was a seasoned Indian fighter and dangerous gunfighter when need be. He is seated here with his bride, Isabelle Holton. *California State Library.*

with an ugly saber slash scar across his forehead, was also appointed second lieutenant.[10] Another Texas border veteran, William W. Byrnes, secured his appointment by announcing he had gambled with Murrieta at Murphys and could identify him.[11] John Nuttall and William T. Henderson were the commissary officers.

The privates of the company were a conglomeration of politicians, ranchers, miners, and physicians: G. V. McGowan, Bob Masters, Major Walter H. Harvey, a Colonel McLane, George A. Nuttall, Lafayette Black, Dr. D. S. Hollister, Philemon T. Herbert, John S. White, Willis Prescott, James M. Norton, Coho Young, Edwin B. Van Born, and Dr. S. K. Piggott, company surgeon.[12]

---

[10]Material on William Howard, Charles Bludworth, and Walter Harvey is in the files of the author. In his biography and the four newspaper interviews he gave over the years, William Howard gave much information on the Rangers, although he was not present at the killing of Murrieta as he claimed, and his recollections must be used with a degree of caution.

[11]Secrest, *Lawmen and Desperadoes*, 70–75.   [12]*San Joaquin Republican*, June 8, 1853.

Besides being a Mexican War veteran, William W. Byrnes was a Southwestern scalp hunter, miner, rancher, and California Ranger who engaged in numerous personal encounters of the Navy Colt variety. This newspaper sketch was made from a photograph owned by his daughter. *Author's collection.*

Applicants for Ranger enlistment were expected to be Democratic in politics, although just how stringently this rule was applied is not known. Bigler undoubtedly made this clear—if there was to be any credit garnered for this expedition, it must be assigned to the governor and his party. Love was a Democrat, as was Pat Connor, the Howard brothers, Phil Herbert, and Major Harvey. It can be assumed that most, if not all, the others were also Democrats.

Whatever their politics, it was a tough crew. Connor was a great asset, having been an experienced company commander during the late war, where he had been badly wounded at Buena Vista. Charley Bludworth had been in at least one shooting scrape in the fall of 1851, when he had shot and wounded a man in Stockton. Bill Byrnes, another Mexican War veteran, had fought in a recent Indian war in El Dorado County. He was the first sheriff of Carson Valley in the Utah Territory and had been involved in various shooting scrapes. Mariposa assemblyman Phil Herbert had piloted the Ranger bill through the Assembly. He was a hard-nosed southerner who had knifed a fellow student in an Alabama college

Judge Walter Harvey was an early member of the Rangers, but soon resigned to pursue his political career. *Annie Mitchell Room, Tulare County Public Library.*

prior to fleeing to Texas.[13] Coho Young was the mail carrier between Fort Miller and Mariposa. Major Harvey was a political hack and a pal of Herbert. He had killed the noted Indian trader Jim Savage during the previous year and was then holding down a clerk's job in the legislature until some Democratic political opportunity arose. It seemed obvious that these local politicos saw a chance for higher office as a result of a successful bandit hunt. Local rancher Willis Prescott no doubt joined up in hopes of being able to even the score for Joaquín's shooting him. It was an impressive collection of adventurers, some of whom were destined to die with their boots on.

Bill Howard and his brother wanted to join up also, but apparently business affairs intruded. They were appointed supernumeraries, however, and as Rangers later dropped out, the Howards and others replaced them. For now the Rangers had their pick from the thoroughbred herds of the Buena Vista Ranch. It wasn't going to be a lack of good horseflesh that prevented the bandit's capture.

---

[13]William B. Secrest, "Mariposa Maverick," *Westways*, January 1977.

Love's men would be traveling light. The blazing hot San Joaquín summer was already upon them and their Navy pistols, rifles, and shotguns would be their heaviest gear. A tin plate and cup with a few provisions would be wrapped in their bedroll and tarp, tied behind their saddles. A pack animal would carry needed provisions. Already Love was sending out scouting parties to scout known bandit hideouts. On June 3, 1853, Ranger Pat Connor sent a letter to the *Republican* from Quartzburg:

> Tomorrow we start for the mountains—We have taken the horse that Mr. James Welch rode when he was shot, between San Jose and Santa Clara, about two months since, and we are now in pursuit of the Mexican who sold the animal in this place.[14]

On April 5 Welch had been traveling from Contra Costa County when he was attacked by two Sonorans at Mission San Jose. After receiving some fifteen knife wounds on the face, he was dragged half a mile with a rope around his neck. Some $350, a gold watch, revolver, his horse, saddle, and bridle were taken. Two suspects were apparently released for lack of evidence.[15]

Although he undoubtedly had various descriptions to go on, Love must have still been concerned at the lack of information on the bandit chieftain. Joaquín was described as a lithe and personable young Mexican by many, yet Billy Howard later recalled that the Rangers "were not looking for a young, fine-looking law-breaker, but for one Joaquin Murietta [sic], a stout, broad-shouldered man five feet, nine or ten inches high, and about 40 years old, was the description given by Bill Byrnes who had played cards with Murrietta [sic]."[16] This seems to be a description of Joaquín Valenzuela and indicates a faulty memory due to Howard's advanced years.

Meanwhile, the ranks of the Murrieta gang were still being thinned. Three Mexicans in Calaveras County had been identified as former Joaquín gang members and quickly skipped the area, while a suspect was picked up in Sacramento and retained for identification. In Vallecito, an American and a Mexican were arrested, as noted in a dispatch to the *San Francisco Herald*:

> Our camp has been the scene of unusual excitement owing to the arrest of two men supposed to be confederates of the Joaquin party.... They

---

[14]*Republican*, June 5, 1853.
[15]A report of the murder of Welch (or Walsh) was published in the *San Francisco Herald*, April 10, 1853.
[16]Lilbourne A. Winchell manuscript, collections of the Fresno City and County Historical Society.

had two stolen mules in their possession and from what the Mexican says, it was their intention, the night they were arrested, to steal the butchers' cattle. The Mexican was taken here ... the American was taken the same night at French camp; he is a desperate character [and] tried to draw his pistol, but was stopped by Forsyth, who swore ... he would blow his brains out.[17]

When Claudio had been killed, Joaquín reportedly appointed one Pedro Sanchez to his position of authority in the gang. A bully as well as a bandit, Sanchez stayed around Columbia and Martinez when other gang members had moved south. After several squabbles, he had threatened various Mexicans and otherwise terrorized the area. When he tried the same tactics on Albino Teba and chased him from a dance hall, Teba turned and warned him not to come any closer. Advancing with a knife in his hand, Sanchez was shot and killed by Teba, who immediately gave himself up to authorities. These events were related in a dispatch to the *Herald* that closed with "Joaquin is frequently called 'Carrillo, Cruz,' etc., but his real name is Joaquin Moriata [*sic*]."[18]

Even the law was making inroads on the gang. In late May 1852 one Jose Borella shot and killed a man named Janes at a Stockton dance house. After evading the law for some time, Borella was captured in late April 1853. Tried, convicted, and sentenced to death, he confessed to other murders and crimes.[19] According to the *Stockton Journal*:

> He acknowledged to being one of Joaquin's gang, and said that the deed for which he was to be executed was prompted by his leader, although Janes was not the intended victim. Another Mexican in the room had offended in some way and Borella was charged with a commission to kill him; and it was in attempting to carry out this murderous idea that he killed Janes.[20]

Borella was about twenty-seven years old and, despite carrying many scars from fights he had engaged in, the desperado fell apart as the gallows loomed before him. When hanged at Stockton on Friday morning, June 3, 1853, he trembled violently as the rope was placed around his neck.[21]

---

[17]Both notices of Joaquín gang members were in the *San Francisco Herald*, May 18, 1853. The Vallecito article was also in the *Herald*, July 2, 1853.
[18]*San Francisco Herald*, June 8, 1853.
[19]Jose Borella's shooting of William W. Janes (perhaps Jones) was reported in the *Herald*, April 22 and May 27 and 28, 1852.
[20]The *Stockton Journal* article was reprinted in the *Placerville Herald*, June 18, 1853.
[21]*Republican*, June 4, 1853.

Love and his men were kept quite busy in June investigating several murders and thefts in the Mariposa area. In a letter written to a friend, Stockton constable D. S. Clark, Love stated the Rangers had captured one thief and thirty-one stolen horses. In early June, the first supposed casualties of the campaign were announced in the *Republican*:

> A member of Captain Love's company who are in search of Joaquín's gang, sends us the report of the death of Major Harvey and Mr. (Coho) Young. Their bodies were found yesterday on the trail between the San Joaquin and the Frezno.[22]

It was quickly assumed that the "Major" had been killed by Indian friends of Jim Savage whom Harvey had treacherously shot down the previous year. The rumor proved false, however. Some days later the same paper printed a response from a Ranger who stated that Harvey had been elected a delegate from the new county of Tulare and had given up his Ranger affiliation. Coho Young had suffered a bad fall from his horse and also left the Rangers.[23] Galloping over the hot Mariposa plains quickly proved too much for Assemblyman Herbert, and he, too, soon found pressing business requiring his presence elsewhere.

In a dispatch dated June 18, a correspondent of the *San Francisco Alta* wrote that Love and some of his men had just returned from a scout with a captive Mexican cattle thief said to be Joaquín's brother. Two horse thieves had also been captured and sent to Quartzburg, under guard, for trial. The guards had no sooner returned to the Ranger camp than it was learned that the prisoners had been found on the road, "perforated by a half-dozen balls each."[24]

Although the *Alta* was Democratic in principle, it was antagonistic towards Governor Bigler and seldom passed up an opportunity to denigrate Love and his men. This must be borne in mind when the *Alta* and other papers made various innuendoes and accusations during and after the Joaquín campaign. A good example is reported in the *Alta* of June 24, when the paper made a more pointed reference to the incident noted above:

> Love's Rangers have determined to take the law into their own hands, on the singular ground that juries are disinclined to convict Mexican horse

---

[22] *Republican*, June 8, 1853.
[23] The deaths of Harvey and Young were also reported in the *Republican*, June 4, and the *Alta*, June 6, 1853. The correction was printed in the *Republican*, June 21, 1853.
[24] The June 18 dispatch to the *Alta* was published on June 20, 1853.

thieves! The two prisoners, who were shot on the way to Quartzburgh, [sic] were not, until after the discovery of the corpses, reported to have attempted to escape from their escort. Astonishing accuracy to have emptied a six-shooter into the body of a man in flight!

The Rangers would have ignored such an attack based on the last sentence of the article. It showed the writer's total lack of knowledge of his subject. Any of the Rangers could have performed that task. It was the implication that they were murderers, however, that prompted Pat Connor, or perhaps Bill Howard, to write from his Buena Vista ranch on July 6:

> The occurrence ... alluded to happened before the State Rangers were in existence and a short time previous to Capt. Love leaving the county with his petition to the Legislature. . . . I have been informed by respectable citizens of this place that those who shot the Mexicans were justifiable in so doing. . . . I am also informed that the act was reported to a magistrate in less than ten minutes after the occurrence.[25]

Although the *Republican* praised the work of the Rangers in ridding the area of bandits and horse thieves, a correspondent of the *Stockton Journal* had other ideas:

> Now I do not know that the Rangers have not faithfully performed every duty incumbent upon them and done everything in their power to accomplish the objectives for which they were organized, but the actual state of affairs here does not warrant the statements contained in the *Republican*. About two weeks ago two horses were stolen from Agua Frio by the Indians. They were retaken ... by a party of Mexicans who fell in with them. One of the Mexicans was wounded in the skirmish with an arrow. And last night Mr. Sharp, who lives within two miles of this place, had two horses stolen, and complaints of similar depredations are heard every day. There has been but one prisoner sent up by the Rangers, and he was a Mexican found in possession of a horse which was supposed to belong to a Mr. Welch who was murdered some time since, in Santa Clara County. I know of no testimony which connects him with the murder, nor do I know whether the horse had been identified.[26]

Harry Love must have bristled at such a report, but the Rangers were indeed having their own frustrations. Writing from Savage's Post on June

---
[25] *Republican*, July 12, 1853.
[26] The *Stockton Journal* article was re-printed in the *Alta*, July 31, 1853.

15, one of the Rangers commented that "We have made some arrests and captured some stolen animals. The men we have turned over to the civil authorities, but not in one case has there been a conviction, although stolen property has invariably been found in their possession. The only way to do the State service would be to take the law into our own hands." This was undoubtedly the genesis of the *Alta*'s attack, although they were confused as to the sequence of events.[27]

By keeping scouting parties out questioning victims and witnesses, Love picked up what information he could and put it together with press reports, letters, and news from travelers from other areas. Both Bill Howard and Pat Connor stated that a letter from a southern California officer had indicated Murrieta's gang was marauding in the area, and a newspaper report from San Diego seemed to validate the news. The bandits had been prowling between there and Los Angeles for some time stealing stock, but posses had pressed them so closely they had to abandon some seven or eight valuable horses that had broken down with fatigue. It was another indication of how fast the outlaws were moving about the state. The report continued:

> On the night of the 4th, an assault was made upon the ranch of Buena Vista about 30 miles distance away (from San Diego), further outrages were committed and more horses stolen. This is stated to be part of Joaquin's band and that enterprising individual himself is said to have been recognized in Los Angeles, on his way down the country. This report is strenuously doubted by many incredulous and obstinate persons who openly question the fact of the existence of that popular gentleman. But it is sufficiently ascertained that there are bandits in this locality and that most of the outrages are traced to one gang.[28]

The Rangers quickly prepared to move. Assigning Lieutenant Pat Connor and Bill Howard to keep on the trail of Welch's killer, Love selected four or five Rangers to patrol locally while he and the balance of his men saddled up and headed west, probably before dawn on about July 10, 1853.[29]

Although the weather was blistering hot, the lowlands of the San Joaquín Valley were a soggy mess. The past winter had seen devastating floods throughout the central valley, as well as a heavy snowfall in the Sierra. Now, the hot weather was rapidly melting the snow and, again,

---
[27]*Republican*, June 21, 1853.   [28]*Alta*, July 15, 1853.
[29]*Republican*, August 11, 1853.

the rivers and streams were dangerously high and overflowing. A resident of Fort Miller reported that "the waters of the Upper San Joaquín are so swollen by the melting of the snow in the mountains as to overflow their banks in many places."[30] The Mokelumne, Stanislaus, and Kings rivers were all flooding. An army officer with a topographical party seeking a railroad route through the area this same month wrote that "the valley was one vast sheet of water, from 25 to 30 miles broad."[31]

After crossing the San Joaquín River at Hill's Ferry, near the mouth of the Merced River, the Rangers could see off in the distance great clouds of dust raised by mustang herds, which often circled moving groups of riders. Large numbers of curious antelope also circled the Rangers, along with the wolves that stalked the herds looking for the old, weak, or young.[32]

The shimmering blue foothills of the coast range beckoned in the distance. Approaching San Luis Gonzaga from two sides, Love found no outlaws and headed up through Pacheco Pass toward the old Spanish mission town of San Juan.

---

[30] *San Francisco Herald*, June 20, 1853.

[31] House of Representatives, 33rd Congress, 2nd Session, Executive Document No. 91, *Reports of Explorations and Surveys to ascertain the most practical and economical Route for a railroad*, etc., 1853–4, vol. 5 (Washington: A. O. P. Nicholson, Printer, 1856). See also *San Joaquin Republican*, January 15 and 19, May 23, and June 14, 1853.

[32] Recollections of Zachariah T. Blankenship, a dictation in the G.W. Stewart Collection, California Room, California State Library, Sacramento.

10

The Long Trail to Cantua Creek

Situated in the Coast Range Mountains, between the San Luis Gonzaga Rancho and Monterey, San Juan Bautista was founded in 1797 as a mission and army post. After secularization in 1835, a collection of adobe buildings had grown up around the old church plaza, the village being called San Juan. The long adobe building that had housed the soldiers' families was converted to a tavern, while by 1849 Patrick Breen and his wife, survivors of the Donner party tragedy, were operating the town's United States Hotel. There were a few shops, along with scattered adobes of various residents and local rancheros.[1] As Love and his dusty Rangers rode along the tree-lined *alameda* leading to town, they must have eagerly looked forward to a drink at Breen's hotel bar.

Love's plan of action at that time is not known, but he obviously was not on a direct route to Los Angeles. While the angelic city may have been his ultimate goal, he was in San Juan because of horse thieves reportedly operating in the area. Although many of the wild horse roundups operated by Mexicans and others in the foothills were legitimate, Love knew that the bandit gangs mixed much stolen stock in some of those herds. At times, he split up his men so as to cover more ground. If he had no luck in the San Juan vicinity, he would work his way south, hoping to pick up other reports of illegal activities or intercept the gang by keeping wide-ranging scouts in the field.[2]

---

[1] For information on early San Juan Bautista by an early settler, see Isaac L. Mylar, *Early Days at the Mission San Juan Bautista* (Watsonville, Calif.: Evening Pajaronian, 1929). A broader history is by Charles W. Clough, *San Juan Bautista* (Fresno, Calif.: Word Dancer Press, 1996).

[2] The movements of the Rangers were reported in the *San Joaquin Republican*, August 11, 1853. In his *Joaquín Murrieta and His Horse Gangs*, Latta gives a much more detailed Ranger itinerary gleaned from various pioneers and their descendants. Love's final report to the governor is disappointing in its lack of detail, however. William Henderson's account in the Fresno *Expositor*, November 12, 1879, was written over twenty years later and, although one of the *(continued, next page)*

At San Juan Love purchased some supplies, then had a totally unexpected bit of luck by taking a certain prisoner. He quickly penned a note to the governor, then sent it north by courier:

San Juan, July 12, 1853
To his Excellency Govr Bigler
   Sir—I leave this place this night for the mountains. I have arrested a Mexican, Jesus, a brother-in-law of Joaquin's. He says he will take & show us to Joaquin if we will release him. I will try him a while to see what it will end in. There appears to be quite a number of horse thieves hid in the mountains back of this place and between here and the Tulare Valley. I hope I may make him useful to me in hunting them out. We get a few stray stock ever [*sic*] few days, but nothing of importance has occurred.
                        Your Obedient Servant
                        Harry Love,
                        Capt Cala Rangers[3]

Love did not make clear just how he had captured Jesús Féliz, but someone at San Juan must have pointed him out as being related to Joaquín— he would never have blurted out such information. When surrounded by Rangers, Féliz must have panicked, as indicated by his agreeing to betray Joaquín if the Rangers would release him.

Perhaps more personal motives prompted this betrayal. Joaquín had abandoned Jesús' brother Reyes Féliz to the tender mercies of the Los Angeles vigilantes the previous year. In addition, it was later determined that Jesús was merely a courier for the outlaws whom Joaquín may not have trusted to ride with the gang. These nagging aggravations might have festered in the mind of Jesús, and he did not need much encouragement to betray his notorious brother-in-law. Men have been betrayed for far less. This is all speculation, of course, but the scenario is interesting to consider. To be fair, Féliz family descendants have maintained that Jesús felt safe in guiding Love because he felt Joaquín had already left the area.

Love let it be known in San Juan they would be going to the coast,

---

(*continued from previous page*) better accounts of the fight, it is also sparse on the movements of the Rangers. Two accounts, one by William Byrnes' wife in the *Fresno Bee*, January 3, 1932, and one by his daughter in the San Francisco *Call*, April 3, 1892, are largely unreliable, although various details make it likely the genesis of the articles was indeed Byrnes. His wife's account appears to stem from the San Francisco *Alta*, April 2, 1873.

[3] Joaquín Murrieta Papers. For data on Vicente Jesús Féliz, see Latta, *Joaquín Murrieta and His Horse Gangs*, 104–106.

then scout through the southern counties. Promising to keep Féliz out of sight and release him the minute the outlaws were spotted, the Rangers kept their prisoner under close guard as they rode over to the Salinas plains, where they set up camp for the night. After dark, the Rangers hurriedly repacked their gear and again prepared to move.

Retracing their route back to San Juan, the Rangers and Féliz hid in a canyon near town the following day. That night they headed south as Féliz guided them along trails, across creek beds, and through dark gullies and canyons covered by sun-scorched grass and scattered oak trees.[4] The gang's hideout and roundup headquarters was some sixty miles away as the crow flies, so using the tortuous back route through the hills must have taken several days. On or about July 14, the Rangers took up positions behind a hill overlooking a large mustang-catching operation.

As Love and Féliz looked over the hill, both were startled at the scene below. There were hundreds of mustangs and vaqueros in the valley. Féliz thought Joaquín and his men had already left to begin their horse drive south. Love was amazed and worried at the number of men who were roping and branding the large herds of captured and broken mustangs. There were some sixty or eighty vaqueros at work—more than a match for Love's little band, which at this time was undermanned. Besides the stock corrals, there was an adobe cabin with several tents and brush huts off to one side. Dust and smoke from the campfires hung in the air until dissipated by an occasional hot breeze.

Love must have known if he had not already been spotted by a lookout, he would be soon, and quickly decided to move in close to see if they could identify any animals or men. It must have been a tense and curious scene. As the Rangers rode slowly through the herds of mustangs, sweating vaqueros at their branding chores looked up and followed their every move.

Riding slowly among the horses and men, Love noticed many of the animals were not mustangs, and he eased his animal towards a Californian or Mexican who seemed to be a leader. Love told him they were looking for strays and stolen stock and directed several Rangers to start checking the horses. The bluff worked—or at least the outlaws had been taken by

---

[4]The author worked in a West Side gypsum mine in the coast range hills in the 1940s and again visited the Cantua Creek area in the 1960s. This is hot, miserable country in the summer and is desolate and isolated, even today.

Patrick E. Connor was a Mexican War hero and a definite asset to the Ranger ranks. *California State Library.*

surprise and were confused as to what to do.[5] Apparently both groups identified each other, but Love continued to keep the outlaws off balance. He and several of the Rangers began taking names of all the vaqueros present, eventually running up a tally of over eighty names—probably all aliases. Several women were present and were also added to the list.

Seven or eight animals were identified as stolen and were confiscated. Meeting with no resistance, Love told the leader they were heading back to San Juan and bade them good day. Herding the confiscated stock ahead of them, Love and his men then slowly rode out of the camp and headed north.

None of the accounts of this meeting mention any bandits being recognized at this time. One wonders why Ranger Bill Byrnes did not spot Joaquín, but he may not have been present for one reason or another. Still,

---

[5]Both the *San Joaquin Republican* of August 11, 1853, and Henderson's recollection mention Love's parlaying with the large group of mustang catchers on Cantua Creek. None of Howard's accounts mention this meeting—another indication he was not along on the expedition.

the Rangers were confident that they had indeed been in the presence of some of Joaquín's gang. After a hurried conference, Love decided they had better follow the outlaws and wait for a favorable opportunity to attempt an arrest. It was their only option.

At the outlaw camp, consternation reigned supreme. Despite their lookouts, informants, and other precautionary measures, they had been tracked down by the dreaded Rangers. Abandoning the branding, they immediately prepared to take their horse herds south and within an hour were on the move. They moved fast, galloping easily over the west side of the San Joaquín plains in the baking July heat. At intervals they walked their animals, then again assumed the steady, miles-eating gallop south.

• • •

Meanwhile, as Rangers Connor and Howard were still searching for Welch's killer, they became involved with another band of thieves. An express office at Mormon Island had recently been robbed and, when two of the suspects were spotted at a horse-racing course on the Calaveras River, a Stockton deputy sheriff hurried to pick them up. Confronting the two outlaws, Deputy Edward Canavan called on them to surrender, but one, a man named Dawson, ignored the order. As Dawson moved away Canavan repeatedly told him to stop, but was ignored. "Shoot and be God damned," shouted the outlaw, and Deputy Canavan obliged him.

Leaving the desperately wounded Dawson behind, Canavan secured his other prisoner for the ride back. Pat Connor had been present at the shooting and accompanied the deputy and his prisoner to Stockton. In talking to Canavan, it was concluded that the prisoner and Dawson had planned to "fix" the race and swindle some of the gamblers present. It was also learned that Dawson had been in town trying to enlist another member for his horse stealing ring and had admitted to the Mormon Island robbery and the theft of one of the horses entered in the race. Connor had seized the stolen animal, described as a small black Spanish horse branded with a diamond on the shoulder.[6] The *Republican* reported:

> Capt. Connor received some further information respecting this desperate gang of thieves, and he is now in trace of them. We may expect some interesting developments.
>
> Dawson's wound is considered fatal; he is hourly getting worse. He

---

[6]*Republican*, July 19, 1853, and the *San Francisco Herald*, July 20 and August 4, 1853.

wishes to die and begged the doctor to give him sufficient laudanum to kill him.[7]

Connor returned to Mariposa, while Billy Howard remained in Stockton, where his horse, Winfield Scott, won two races at the local track on July 24 and 25.[8]

• • •

Back on the southern plains, Joaquín realized he was being followed as he skirted Tulare Lake on the west side of the valley. A result of the drainage of the Four Creeks area around Visalia, Tulare Lake was normally some sixty miles long and thirty-five miles wide. In 1853 it was much larger, as were the vast tule swamps surrounding it. In 1850, army lieutenant George H. Derby described the tules as extending into the lake for a quarter-mile, as far as the eye could see. On hazy days the lake appeared to be a vast, inland sea. Great clouds of geese and ducks were in flight or landing, while herds of wild horses, antelope, and tule elk skirted the area between the tules and the foothills. As soaked as the valley lowlands were, the surrounding plains were barren and hot.[9]

Just as Love must have had a lone scout far in advance of his main party to stay in sight of the horse herd and its drovers, Joaquín must have had scouts watching his back trail. By the time he reached Tejon Pass, the entrance to the mountains leading to Los Angeles, he was alarmed. With the band of horses they would never be able to lose the Rangers, and Love would just pick his time and place for a confrontation. The outlaws had the Rangers outmanned and outgunned, but worries remained. They quickly decided to split up, which would either discourage the Rangers or make them give up the chase.

Designating a group of his men to continue on to Sonora province in Mexico with the horse drove, Murrieta and a small contingent of his gang rode west, then skirted the coast range back to Cantua Creek. It seems inexplicable that he did this in view of the narrow escape he had just had with Love's Rangers. He might have been trying to rejoin his wife, who was at their Niles Canyon home. Possibly in his panic to get away, he was

---
[7] *Republican,* August 21, 1853.
[8] Although he always claimed otherwise, William Howard was not with the Rangers at this time. His previously cited accounts, however, were undoubtedly obtained from the other Rangers and are garbled, but reasonably accurate.
[9] F. F. Latta, "Little Journeys in the San Joaquin," *Tulare Daily Times,* 1937. As always, Latta's information and research is based on interviews with pioneers who knew early-day conditions.

Cantua Creek, in the western foothills of the coast range in Fresno County, was as desolate and blistering hot in Joaquín's day as in the 1960s, when the author took this photograph. The banks, quite tall and steep in places, provided good cover for an outlaw camp, but also allowed the Rangers to ride up and surprise Murrieta and his men. *Author's collection.*

just not thinking clearly. Other gang members headed in different directions.

Questioning some Indians at the Tejon, Love learned the bandits had bought some supplies, then split up.[10] Besides the horse herd going through

---

[10] Love does not mention the pursuit of the horse catchers to the Tejon in his official report, nor does the *Republican* account of August 11, 1853. Frank Latta's extensive research, however, indicates this was indeed the case. See Latta, *Joaquín Murrieta and His Horse Gangs*, 562–564. William Howard reported that the Rangers went as far as Los Angeles, but he may have been referring to the *county*. Alternatively, one of the Rangers may have said something to the effect of "We went nearly to Los Angeles," and years later all Howard remembered was the "Los Angeles" name. He made this same reference in all of his writings. Howard also mentions the Rangers obtaining information from Zapatero's Indians that Murrieta had passed that way heading north. This is consistent with a newspaper item in the *Sacramento Transcript*, August 23, 1853.

William Henderson is generally credited with being the Ranger who brought down Murrieta. He reportedly killed many Indians while on prospecting trips in the 1860s. *Madera County Historical Society.*

Tejon Pass, two other trails headed back north, skirting Tulare Lake. Already short Connor, Howard, and others who had returned to Mariposa with stolen horses, Love hated to split his force, but saw no alternative. Sending several Rangers to follow the east trail, Love led the balance in following the trail around the lake.

The heat must have been terrible that hot July day. Where the trails converged, the groups met up and continued along the sparse and rugged foothills to the general area where they had before met the horse runners. The scrub-covered plains of the San Joaquín shimmered in the blazing sun as Love camped in a secluded canyon to rest his horses and men. After sending out scouts, the Rangers prepared a dry camp and hoped to locate the outlaws the following day. Love must have been apprehensive. Had he allowed the outlaws time to escape by not attacking them when he had the chance? The Ranger leader must have slept little that night, wondering whether tomorrow would bring a confrontation or more frustration. Still, the men and horses had been on the move for over ten days and needed to have some rest.

The Rangers were up and running just before dawn. A scout called Love's attention to a glow and spiral of smoke to the north. They undoubtedly knew there was a water hole where Cantua Creek came out of the foothills—no one traveled that country without knowing where springs and creeks were located. In all likelihood Love had been avoiding that area, knowing the outlaws might very well camp there.

According to report, Love had only six men with him at this point. As they rode north, dawn was just breaking and Love must have circled to get downstream at Cantua Creek and keep the sun at his back. As they approached the smoke, the Ranger captain had a quick parley with his men. They could still see nothing, but Byrnes was probably ordered to take several Rangers across the creek and come up on the camp from the north side. Several others were motioned toward the south bank, while Love rode up the creek bed and was quickly into the camp. It was the morning of July 25, 1853.

"There were two Mexicans on guard," recalled Ranger Bill Henderson, "and they were taken prisoners and four more were found asleep in the bed of the creek.... Capt. Love began interrogating the Mexicans as to their business. They uniformly replied that they were catching mustangs."[11]

The Mexican camp was in the creek bed, by a spring, and the Rangers' approach had been unnoticed because of the high banks of the now-dry stream. The Mexicans had been taken completely by surprise.

Love began questioning the startled vaqueros and later reported the outlaws "appeared to have made some hard days['] marches previous, by the jaded looks of their horses."[12] One of the Mexicans, who was bathing the back of his horse in the creek bed, told Love angrily to direct his questions to him, as he was the leader of the group. The camp was in total confusion now. Several vaqueros who had been sleeping eased out of their blankets and eyed their horses. Others jumped to their feet. There is no way of knowing how many Rangers had surprised them. Love and another were probably in the creek bed, while others were up along the creek bank

---

[11] *Republican*, August 11, 1853.
[12] Love's comment in his report concerning the "jaded looks of their horses" also points to the long pursuit to and from the Tejon. Much of what had occurred during the Ranger's travels was omitted from Love's final report as a matter of brevity.

looking down at them. When Byrnes and his men suddenly appeared on the opposite bank, the outlaws must have thought Armageddon was at hand!

An account provided by one of the Rangers to the *Republican* gives some idea of the desperate action that now took place:

> As Capt. Burns [sic] entered the camp he looked at the leader and cried exultingly—"This is Joaquin Boys, we have got him at last." At the mention of the word Joaquin, seeing that he was recognized, the Mexicans threw off their cloaks and serapas [sic] and commenced firing and retreating. Joaquin himself was unarmed, having evidently just been awakened from a sound sleep, and in his hurry to get his horse forgot his weapons.[13]

The man washing his horse's back had been singled out as Joaquín and now the action was fast and furious. Moving quickly, the *vaquero*—later identified as "Three-fingered Jack"—scrambled to his feet with his pistol in his hand. He fired at Love, clipping a lock of hair from his head, then turned and sprinted for a horse, but was cut off quickly by a Ranger. As this action started, he two prisoners were brought up and closely guarded. Ranger Bill Henderson was closest to Joaquín and later described the action:

> [Capt. Byrnes] knew Joaquin very well and as soon as the latter caught sight of the Captain he jumped on his horse bare-backed and was off like the wind. Henderson raised his shotgun to fire at him, but his horse shied and the shot missed. Henderson followed in close pursuit.[14]

If the outlaws had been surprised while camping in the creek bed, Joaquín may have been out of the creek and bathing his horse at the adjacent spring. Engrossed in his work and with the sun at his back the approaching riders had gone unnoticed. Not thinking of anything but escape, he flattened himself against his horse's back, urging him up an incline and along the high creek bank. Henderson recalled:

> Joaquin, as an only hope, jumped his horse off the bluff some twelve feet high into the bed of the creek. Being bareback, he slipped from his horse and fell on his back on the ground. . . . Henderson followed him, and, as he sprang over the cliff he for the first time convinced himself that he was pursuing Joaquin. . . . Almost as quick as a flash Joaquin sprang to his feet and again mounted his horse. Henderson dropped his shotgun and pulled

---

[13] *Republican*, August 11, 1853.   [14] Fresno *Expositor*, November 12, 1879.

The death of Joaquín Murrieta as depicted by a Charles Nahl drawing published in the *California Police Gazette*. Author's collection.

out his revolver and, not desiring to kill Joaquin, shot at his horse with a view of breaking one of his thighs, but the ball missed the bone. They were both riding at a breakneck pace down the bed of the creek. Coming to a low place in the bank of the creek, Joaquin turned his horse to ride out, as he did so Henderson fired again at the horse, striking him in the same leg. ... The blood streamed from the wound, the ball having evidently cut an artery. Still the horses dashed ahead and as Henderson looked behind him he saw three other Mexicans riding forward to assist the fleeing criminal.[15]

As Joaquín rode for his life, his companions also made desperate efforts to escape. After firing at Love, Three-fingered Jack made a frantic dash

---

[15] His comment about Joaquín jumping his horse off a bluff "some twelve feet high" seems consistent with the creek banks, even today. In reviewing all these accounts, it is well to remember that reporters and participants such as Henderson were recollecting events that happened over twenty-five years earlier. Many place names were spelled phonetically at the time, and some sites mentioned had not yet appeared on maps. Also, dates were often haphazard at best.

A dramatic rendering of Joaquín Murrieta's death appeared in the July 23, 1905, San Francisco *Daily Evening Bulletin*. *Author's collection.*

on foot, stooping and dodging while turning several times to fire at his pursuers. The bullets of pursuing Rangers quickly sought him out, and he died in the gravel of the creek bed with Bill Byrnes' and Harry Love's pistol balls in his head. Apparently one of the outlaws was killed in camp, while another scrambled up behind a mounted companion and the two rode furiously down the creekbed. When a bullet slammed into the back of the extra rider, he slid to the ground, allowing the rider to get away. Henderson's report continues:

> Henderson was convinced that his only chance to capture Joaquin was to shoot him, as the Mexicans in the rear were already shooting at him, so he fired at the fleeing desperado and hit him in the small of the back, the ball passing through him. Still he clung to his horse and urged the animal forward. At this time John White, of the command, rode up and he also fired at Joaquin who was leaning forward on his horse, and the ball struck him just above the one fired by Henderson, and ranged upward. This caused

As leader of the California Rangers who tracked down Murrieta, Harry Love eclipsed even his Texas fame. An undated photograph, but probably taken during the early 1860s. *California State Library.*

him to fall from his horse, but mortally wounded as he was he still tried to escape, running at the best speed possible toward the hills. Henderson then fired at him and shot him through the heart . . . even then he had vitality enough to call out in Spanish to his pursuers to cease shooting as he had enough.[16]

Joaquín's gallant horse had apparently clambered out of the creek bed and the outlaw died in the low rolling hills at the foot of Los Tres Piedras—the Three Rocks. "Don't shoot any more," he reportedly cried out in Span-

---
[16]Fresno *Expositor*, November 12, 1879.

ish, "for I am dead."[17] As his wounded horse wandered off and collapsed, the most dreaded and hunted outlaw of old California lay in the brush and rocks and gasped out his few remaining breaths.

Several Rangers were still likely chasing outlaws who had managed to make their escape as Henderson and White dismounted and stared at the dead bandit leader. Charley Bludworth looked over at Joaquín, then at his horse as it lay whinnying and bleeding to death on the ground. At the sight of the beautiful, dying animal the Ranger openly wept.[18]

Looping a lariat under Joaquín's arms, one of the Rangers dragged the corpse back to the campground where Love and Byrnes engaged in an animated discussion. Several other Rangers ransacked the camp looking for stolen gold. Blankets were shaken out and saddlebags emptied, but no plunder could be found amid the bandit belongings.[19]

---

[17]Most accounts mention Joaquín's last words as being similar to what is used here. This quote is taken from the first Ranger account of the fight as published in the *Republican*, August 11, 1853.

[18]Charley Bludworth's weeping at the sight of Joaquín's dying horse is a tradition handed down in the family. Mary Annette Bludworth, Charley's daughter, told the story to her daughter, who passed it on to her children. The story was told to the author by Mrs. Joyce Wilson of Madera, Charles Bludworth's great-great-granddaughter. Letter, Mrs. Joyce Wilson to the author, November 7, 1995.

[19]Love's report mentions three bandits being killed, while the official Ranger muster roll notes only two. Either account may or may not have included Joaquín, which might explain the discrepancy. Avelino Martinez claimed there were at least eight dead bodies, but it seems odd that Love would not have mentioned this in his report. Two of Latta's reported dead were Pedro Gonzales and Juan Salazar. Barring several of each name in the gang, something is wrong here. Gonzales had been killed the previous year by Love, while Juan Salazar was killed several years later, as will be seen in a later chapter. It seems clear from his book that Latta was unaware of Love's killing of Gonzales and so was misled in relating this information. Both Love's report to the governor and the final Ranger Muster Roll are among the Joaquin Murrieta Papers in the California State Archives.

II

Heads You Win

Love knew he was not going to get any information from the large, well-built prisoner named Antonio Lopez, who was apparently a seasoned outlaw. He concentrated on the other captive, a scared young man named José María Ochoa. Only twenty-three years old, Ochoa claimed to have come up from Mexico with Murrieta, but denied engaging in any robberies. He must have been horrified as he identified the man who had been dragged into camp as Joaquín Murrieta, the bandit chieftain. López must have stared at his *compañero* in disgust.[1]

According to Love's official report, Murrieta, Three-fingered Jack, and two of the other outlaws had been killed. The rest had escaped. Although Latta's informants claimed up to eight outlaws had been killed, Love had only listed the four.

It was still early morning, but Love could already feel the sun beginning to bake the arid hills and plains around them. Calling Byrnes and Charley Bludworth over, the men discussed their next move. They had no time to rest on their laurels and celebrate the success of their expedition. The other bandits were escaping. More importantly, they needed to decide what to do with Joaquín's body. Millerton, a mining camp on the San Joaquín River, seemed the closest place to take the body, but they quickly realized that such a move would be impractical. The heat had been scorching on the plains for the past few days and would be no different today. They needed to cut off Joaquín's head for identification pur-

---

[1] William Howard always claimed Byrnes had cut off Joaquín's head and held it in front of Lopez demanding that he talk or he too would be beheaded. "Cut away," the outlaw reportedly growled, "I'll not talk." A good story, Howard might have heard it from one of the Rangers who were there at the scene. Several accounts mention that Lopez was surly and refused to talk. *San Joaquin Republican*, August 11, 1853. See also Howard's previously-cited accounts.

poses and, by fast travel, make it to Millerton or Fort Miller, where it could be immersed in spirits for preservation.[2]

Bill Byrnes is generally given credit for taking off Joaquín's head with his Bowie knife. It was perhaps an afterthought to hack off Three-fingered Jack's head also—and then his tell-tale hand. Taking a blanket from some of the captured bandit gear, some loose branches from a scrubby tree were placed in the middle and the three grisly trophies were tied up and secured on the back of Byrnes' saddle.[3] After again scouring the area for any stolen treasure, the disappointed Rangers gathered up what bandit gear and horses could be rounded up and prepared to move out.[4]

Love detailed Byrnes and John Sylvester to get the heads to Millerton or Fort Miller as quickly as possible. They were also to take the prisoner López along. Love and the remaining Rangers would pursue the bandits that had escaped. Ochoa had promised to cooperate, and Love took him along to identify some of the gang's hideouts. They would meet up at Millerton or Mariposa.

As Love and his men galloped off, Lopez was tied on his horse and the two Rangers set off in a northeasterly direction. Keeping their animals at a steady gallop, the three riders were soon within sight of the slough that stretched between the vast Tulare Lake and the San Joaquín River. It was a vast overflow swamp containing spring runoffs from the mountain streams and rivers. It was much marshier and wider now because of the recent snowmelt, and also quite dangerous. Many wild creatures had been trapped and drowned in its treacherous, tule-shrouded marshes.[5]

---

[2] Latta claimed the Rangers carried alcohol in several large tins in which to preserve any heads taken, but the alcohol was consumed during the expedition; see Latta, *Joaquin Murrieta and His Horse Gangs*, 595. If the heads had been carried in tin containers, the flesh might have been boiled from the skulls in that 100-degree summer heat.

[3] The wrapping of the heads and hand was described by ferryman Sam Bishop in the *San Francisco Chronicle*, August 10, 1891. Bishop's ferry was apparently located opposite the village of Millerton, as that is where the previously-cited Williamson survey party reported crossing this same month.

[4] The *Republican* of August 11, 1853, reported the Rangers had captured five six-shooters, two holster pistols, seven horses, and five saddles and bridles. The animals were all described and made available to anyone claiming ownership.

[5] An army map of the southern San Joaquín Valley dated July 25, 1853, shows the slough and tule swamp areas extending between Tulare Lake and the San Joaquín River. The marshy areas depicted were nearly twenty miles wide in spots. *Topographical Sketch of the Tulare Valley, Cal., July 25, 1853*, by Bvt. 2nd. Lieut. John Nugen, 2nd Inftry, in collection of author.

The shortest route to Millerton cut across the slough, but the Rangers could see it was some miles in width. Selecting what appeared to be the narrowest spot, they decided to try the crossing, but had not gone far when López' animal suddenly stepped in a hole. Mired in the sticky mud and tangled underwater foliage, horse and rider quickly disappeared under water. The Rangers' animals also became mired and, in trying to extricate their own panicked horses, they must have lost sight of López. Reining their animals around, Byrnes and Sylvester backtracked to where they had entered the treacherous bogs. On firm ground again, the two men anxiously sought some sign of López, but he was gone.[6] They hated to lose the prisoner, but at least they still had Ochoa and, hopefully, would apprehend others.

They headed north, following the slough to where it met the San Joaquín River. There were no ferries operating in the area at this time. The closest one was Hill's Ferry, some fifty miles north, which would have put them closer to Mariposa than Fort Miller. They had to cross at this juncture, swimming across the river alongside their horses. Once reaching the other side, they resumed their journey. It was just as well—this allowed them to avoid the Mexican villages at Las Juntas and the California Ranch. Both settlements were on the south side of the river and known as the resort of fugitives and stock thieves.[7] They probably did not know that Antone Lopez also kept his wife there. Heading east, they camped late that night on the river, then moved on at dawn.

Keeping up a steady pace up-river, Sylvester was now on familiar ground. The party crossed the southern portion of the Fresno River Indian Farm, a local Indian reservation that stretched between the Fresno and San Joaquín rivers. There was a ferry of sorts on the San Joaquín that was operated by one of the reserve employees who kept a whaleboat on a rope,

---

[6]The *Republican* account of August 11, 1853, states that Lopez "drowned himself and his horse as he was crossing the Tulare Slough." I doubt that the two Rangers would have known if their prisoner was accidentally, or purposely, drowned. It is possible they were sensitive about the possibility of their being considered negligent in the matter, however, and agreed on the published story. See also the *Republican,* August 4, 1853.

[7]Located on the south side of the San Joaquín River, both Las Juntas and the California Ranch were isolated Mexican villages, perhaps the oldest in the valley. Each was notorious for being the resorts of fugitives. L. A. Winchell, "The California Ranch: A Rugged West Side Beginning," *The Fresno Republican,* June 12, 1921, and Frank F. Latta, *El Camino Viejo a Los Angeles* (Bakersfield, Calif.: Kern County Historical Society, 1933). See also Charles W. Clough and William B. Secrest, Jr., *Fresno County: The Pioneer Years* (Fresno, Calif.: Panorama West Books, 1984), 38–43.

Samuel A. Bishop was an employee of the Fresno River Indian Farm in the summer of 1853, when he ferried two Rangers and a head across the river to Fort Miller. *Pen Pictures from the Garden of the World.*

which could get travelers across the often swift-running water. Sylvester may well have known the ferryman, a heavy-set, twenty-seven-year-old Virginian named Sam Bishop.[8] Both had been active in the late Indian troubles and Bishop, a former business associate of the late Jim Savage, was now teaching the reserve Indians to farm.

Edward F. Beale, California's superintendent of Indian Affairs, regarded Bishop as a valuable asset to the reserve system.[9] Besides being a farmer and blacksmith, Bishop's wife was the daughter of a principal Indian chief of the area and he had great influence among them. When not busy on the reserve, he or Indian employees operated the ferry, probably on a part-time basis.

As they climbed into Bishop's boat, the two Rangers told him of the fight with the outlaws and how they killed several of them, including the leader and his lieutenant. The Rangers' horses swam alongside the boat, and when they reached the opposite bank the ferryman asked them into his building. Years later Bishop recalled the incident:

---

[8] Information on Samuel A. Bishop is from Horace S. Foote, *History of Santa Clara County, California* (Chicago: Lewis Publishing Company, 1888), 657–660, and the author's personal collection.

[9] Beale's estimation of Bishop is reported in Voucher No. 42, Special Files of the Office of Indian Affairs, 1807–1904, M 574, Roll 33, National Archives.

I then asked the men what proof they had that they had killed Murrieta and his confederate. They smiled grimly as they pointed to a bundle which they had laid on a table. One of them removed the cloth and a number of green willow boughs were disclosed. These were spilled out when three ghastly objects met my gaze. They were two human heads and a human hand with only three fingers on it. I quickly recognized the repulsive features of Three-fingered Jack and the testimony of the mutilated hand was undeniable. The features of the other face were very light in complexion for a Mexican and I recognized it as the head of a dashing and handsome young man whom I had often seen riding around the vicinity of the reservation. I never suspected that he was the famous desperado. His features were very regular and somewhat pleasing. He had a very small mustache and did not appear to be more than twenty-one years old. I afterwards learned from Murrieta's relatives that was his age.[10]

The two Rangers agreed to placing the heads and hand in a small, empty whiskey keg Bishop offered them. "We then filled the keg with whiskey from a forty-gallon barrel that I had on hand," Bishop continued. "The keg was then securely strapped on the back of a mule that I hired to the officers for the purpose. They then continued on their way to Fort Miller."[11]

At the army post the two Rangers asked to see the post surgeon, Dr. William F. Edgar.[12] It is not clear whether the physician supplied them with alcohol in which to place their trophies, or whether they settled for the whiskey obtained from Bishop. It was undoubtedly Dr. Edgar who suggested the head of *Tres Dedos* was of little value. The heat and bullets in the skull had badly damaged the outlaw's features, and it was reportedly buried in the post cemetery. It was probably also Dr. Edgar who cut two slits in the skin of Joaquín's head, allowing a rawhide thong to be inserted to facilitate taking it from the keg for viewing purposes. This was also done to the hand.[13]

There must have been considerable commotion at the post when word was passed around about the Rangers and their grim trophies. A United States railroad survey party was camped there at the time, along with its

---

[10] *San Francisco Chronicle*, August 10, 1891.   [11] Ibid.
[12] Dr. William F. Edgar's presence at Fort Miller as assistant surgeon in 1853 is established by the post returns of that year. Letter, Mabel E. Deutrich, archivist, National Archives and Records Center, Washington, D.C., to the author, December 27, 1960. See also William F. Edgar, M.D., "Old Fort Miller," *Annual Publication, Historical Society of Southern California*, Vol. 3, 1893.
[13] The rawhide thong attached to Joaquín's head was noted by Mary Ann Strivens, an early Millerton pioneer, in the *Fresno Bee*, December 1, 1931. This is corroborated by an article in the *Sacramento Daily Union*, September 10, 1853.

Dr. William F. Edgar was a post physician at Fort Miller when Rangers Byrnes and Sylvester arrived with the head of Murrieta. The Rangers probably consulted with him as to how to best preserve the head. *Author's collection.*

escort of U.S. Dragoons under Lieutenant George Stoneman, later governor of California.[14] While waiting for Love and the balance of the Rangers to join them, Byrnes and Sylvester undoubtedly rode back down to the mining camp originally dubbed Rootville, but now renamed Millerton in honor of the nearby army post. It was largely a "rag town"— tents with a few frame and log structures. Here the head and hand were displayed in a local saloon. Curious miners and local merchants filed by the hideous objects as they were lifted from the keg by their leather "handles." The Rangers didn't buy their own whiskey that day!

First mention of Love's successful expedition was reported in the *San Joaquín Republican* of July 30, 1853:

> Headwaters of the San Joaquin, Fort Miller, July 26th.
> As an express is going to start from these diggings I hasten to inform you of the death of Joaquin, the robber, who has been such a curse in the country for some time. Captain Byrnes, one of the Rangers, and Mr.

---

[14]House of Representatives, 33rd Congress, 2nd session, Executive Document No. 91, *Reports of Explorations and Surveys to ascertain the most practical and economical Route for a Railroad, etc.*, 1853–4, vol. 5 (Washington, D.C.: A.O.P. Nicholson, Printer, 1856).

Sylvester arrived here yesterday evening with the heads of Joaquin and one of his band, whom they captured at a place called Singing River, about 140 miles from here. The remainder of the party are expected here this evening with two prisoners.... The weather is very warm—thermometer 115 degrees in the shade.

Love and his dust-powdered crew rode up out of the valley the day after Byrnes and Sylvester had arrived at the fort. The heat had been blistering on the plains, and there was little relief now in the foothills. They had Ochoa with them and were undoubtedly disturbed to learn of López' death. The Ranger captain was anxious to return to home base, and after crossing the river they arrived at the county seat of Mariposa on Sunday, July 31.[15] The town was a rough mining camp of the period, but tents and log cabins were being replaced by more substantial structures at this time. In June, a resident had described the town along Mariposa Creek:

> This town is improving very rapidly, and business of every description is in quite a flourishing condition. A goodly number of substantial houses have recently been erected, for dwellings as well as for stores. The warehouse of Mr. John McNamara, and the dwelling of Mr. William Phillips, are fine and imposing buildings.... There are in the place six grocery and provision stores.... Five clothing establishments, one tobacco store, two jewelry shops, two blacksmith shops, three hotels and one soda-pop manufactory.[16]

Love found the locals all up in arms about a recent flurry of Indian raids. Much valuable stock had been stolen, and the previous day a large meeting of citizens had met to solicit funds to sustain a volunteer group to take the field. They had postponed any action until Phil Herbert could talk to Love about the matter.[17]

Harry had no doubt looked forward to a few days' rest, but he knew it was important to obtain an interview with the governor as soon as possible. Setting up camp at Howard's Ranch, the Rangers looked after their horses and enjoyed a day of rest. On August 4 Love wrote out his official report to the governor, a two-and-a-half-page letter reporting on his movements and the recent fight at Cantua Creek.

There had been murmurs in the anti-Bigler press about a bogus Joaquín being brought in, but Harry was not too concerned. He was sure he had

---
[15]*Republican*, August 6, 1853.   [16]Ibid., June 4, 1853.
[17]Ibid., August 4, 1853.

the right man. Writing to his friend D. S. Clark in Stockon, he commented, "We have got the right Joaquin, and no mistake. The papers can say what they please, but I know what I say is true."[18]

Mariposa County sheriff John Boling had been given charge of the prisoner José Ochoa, who was duly tried before Justice of the Peace Abraham Powell on August 5. A lone document pertaining to the trial survives, signed by eighteen citizens, stating that Ochoa knew Joaquín Murrieta well and that he was a member of his band. It further mentions that the head now in possession of Captain Love was that of "the great robber and murderer, Joaquin Morietta [sic]."[19] The document was undoubtedly made up to add to the affidavits now being gathered identifying the head. On August 30, Sheriff Boling submitted a bill to the Mariposa County supervisors: for carrying the prisoner before Capt. Powell's court, $3.00; attending court, $3.00; for boarding the prisoner 21 days, $43.50.

On August 20 Ranger Bill Howard was detailed to escort the captive to the state capitol at Benicia, apparently because it was not known what else to do with him. He might have been needed later as a witness if any questions came up. For some reason Ochoa was kept in the jail at nearby Martinez, where he met a singular fate, as related in the *Los Angeles Star* of September 17, 1853:

> The prisoner taken by Love's Rangers at the time of the death of Joaquin was placed in the jail at Martinez for safe keeping. On the morning of the 4th instant the jailor found his prison empty and the body of the prisoner hanging from a neighboring tree. This act is supposed to have been committed by Mexicans who were fearful that he was about to make important disclosures in relation to the horse thieves who are now committing depredations in various parts of the state.

It has been suggested by later writers that there was something sinister about this lynching—that the Rangers had somehow engineered Ochoa's demise to keep him from blowing the whistle on Joaquín's bogus death. The truth of the matter is that locals in the Martinez area had been

---

[18]Ibid., August 6, 1853.

[19]The Justice Abraham Powell court document pertaining to the trial of Ochoa is among the Joaquin Murrieta Papers. Since the document is all in the same handwriting, signatures and all, it seems evident it was copied to be used along with the affidavits as proof of the bandit's identity. No other records of this hearing or trial have been located, and it has been suggested by some that the document is somehow a fraud. Sheriff Boling's payment requisitions, however, are proof enough of the document's authenticity. "Book of Supervisors Minutes," vol. A, 1852–53, Court of Sessions, Mariposa County Courthouse, Mariposa, California.

> for riding one week in search of Leach
> Williams & Irwin 50.00
> 6 Received Mexican Prisoner from Capt
> Loves Rangers 3.00
> Carrying him before Capt Powells
> Court 3.00
> Attending the same 3.00
> Boarding him 20 days 43.50
> Case of the People vs Long summoning
> Witness for Defendant Aug 2 .... 1.00

A portion of the log book of Mariposa Sheriff John Boling, showing he had "received Mexican prisoner from Capt Love's Rangers" and his resulting fees for taking him to court and boarding the outlaw for twenty days. A document in the California State Archives attests to the court hearing before Justice Powell's court, but all other court records have been lost. *Mariposa County Courthouse.*

coping with an excess of horse thieves for some time and were simply fed up. An illuminating article appeared in the *Sacramento Daily Placer Times & Transcript* of the time:

> Martinez, August 20th
> Messrs. Warren Brown, A.L. Brown and William Miles started in pursuit of the animals stolen from this place as mentioned in your yesterday's paper. Four of the seven were found near town, the balance were tracked to French Camp where the trail was lost. Upon this, Warren Brown remained in Stockton, William Miles took the Calaveras road and A.L. Brown the lower Mokelumne. At a hay stack, the latter gentleman found where some one had recently camped, and in damp ground near by, on close inspection, found tracks he knew from the fact of having shod the animals himself. In following the marks, he found a trail to a bottom

between wooded hills and there found the animals grazing and a Mexican lying, as he supposed, asleep under a tree. The Mexican sprung to his feet ... and fired twice at Mr. Brown, causing the beast he rode to rear and fall on a side hill. Mr. Brown's horse rolled over his fallen rider twice before he could extricate himself and when he did, the "Greaser" was partly covered by underbrush, running up a side-hill.[20]

With his right hand injured in the fall, Brown leveled his Navy Colt over a log with his left hand and made a sixty-yard shot that killed the retreating rustler. Three Americans were nearby but did not interfere, thinking that it was "Joaquin's band." The article closed with an ominous threat: "In conclusion we would say to horse thieves, try it again, for there are a few more of the same sort left and the same fate awaits them if caught in the act of thieving."[21]

Whether he was lynched by frightened Mexicans or crime-weary Anglos, young José Ochoa was just as dead.

• • •

Meanwhile, in the hills around Mariposa, there was an Indian problem. Love probably delegated one of his lieutenants to take a few men out on a scout to try and locate the guilty natives. Then, he began circulating in the area, seeking people who had known or could recognize Murrieta. On August 7 and 8 he took a series of depositions before the Quartzburg justice of the peace, J. H. Keen. Pedro Monka stated:

> I do solemly [sic] swear that the head Capt. Harry Love has is the head of Joaquin Muriati [sic], I having known him for eighteen years.

One Susan Banta swore:

> I do hearby certify that the head now in the possession of Capt. Harry Love is the head of Joaquin Muriati [sic], I having known him at San Luis Obispo and done some washing for him at various times.

Stephen Bond swore:

> I do heareby certify that the head now in the possession of Capt. Harry Love is the head of Joaquin Muriati [sic], I having knew him about 2 years on the Merced River.[22]

---

[20]San Francisco *Daily Placer Times and Transcript,* August 22, 1853.   [21]Ibid.
[22]Joaquin Murrieta Papers.

Bill Byrnes and others also made depositions, and Love felt he now had enough to proceed to Stockton, where he planned to collect more. He had already sent the head and hand ahead, as reported in the *Republican* of August 11:

> From Mariposa. Snelling's Ranch, August 8, 1853.
> Sir—Mr. Miller, the Deputy Sheriff of this county, arrived this morning on the stage from Mariposa, with five prisoners; convicts, all in harness, preparatory to their entering upon their services for the State in the penitentiary. They also have the keg, containing the head of Joaquin and the hand of Three-fingered Jack....

There was still a month of enlistment to serve out and Love was anxious to keep his Rangers in the public eye. He had hopes of maintaining his commission and keeping his men in the field. Anyone reading the California press knew there were still plenty of desperadoes and robbers out there, and the legislature might very well be convinced it would be good politics to keep them on duty for the rest of the year. Ordering a detachment of Rangers on patrol to keep an eye out for the Indian marauders, Harry and several others proceeded to Stockton, where they hoped to obtain a glass jar in which to exhibit the head and hand.

Riding across the plains toward Stockton, Love must have ruminated on his new-found fame. He had taken a gamble and won. What if he had not tracked down Joaquín? He might never have otherwise been able to live up to his Texas reputation here in California. But he had done it, and no one knew better than he just how lucky he had been. Searching for anybody on those bleak and blistering plains made looking for a needle in a haystack easy money. Still, there had been skill involved. He had learned much during those years scouting and riding the deserts of Texas and Mexico, and it had paid off now in this moment of triumph in California.

In Stockton, Pat Connor obtained a large glass jar and had a quantity of posters printed up advertising the exhibition of the head and hand. It was to be shown for one day only, August 12, at the Stockton House. The hours were 9 A.M. to 6 P.M. While his men took care of the arrangements, Harry looked up the editor of the *Republican* and did a little public relations work:

> In a recent conversation with Captain Harry Love we obtained some interesting information respecting the bands of Mexican guerrillas which

infest the country. As Captain of the State Rangers he has obtained a mass of information relative to their organization, their haunts and their leaders, that may be made of eminent use to our citizens.

The various bands of guerrillas extend from Sonora to Shasta, but their principal haunts and strongholds are in the coast range of mountains between Santa Clara and the Los Angeles valleys comprising a country 300 miles in length and from 20 to 50 miles in width....

Harry Love says that Joaquín, at a pinch, could have raised two thousand desperadoes; and he believes that such was that bandit's purpose, to scour the entire southern country, sack the small settlements, and before a body of troops could be raised announce himself at Sonora. The prisoner he took intimated as much.... Thus, we think, it would be desirable for the Rangers to be kept in the field.[23]

If Harry had laid it on a little thick—who was to say? Crime didn't cease with the death of Joaquín—hell, there were those who said Joaquín still wasn't dead! Who could say with certainty there was not still much work for the Rangers to do?

The exhibition was a resounding success. Many residents of the city filed past the bizarre display in the Stockton House, as reported in the *Stockton Journal*:

> THE HEAD OF JOAQUIN—This trophy was on display yesterday in company with the hand of 3-fingered Jack and attracted considerable crowds to its inspection. Capt. Love will send them below this evening and in the meantime he will return to his post at the head of the Rangers. The head does not appear natural, being discolored by the blood that has settled in the face and about the mouth. It is readily recognized, however, by these who knew the bandit, by the deep scar that marks the right cheek. There can be no doubt that this is the Joaquin whose depredations occasioned such terror in Calaveras Co. last winter.[24]

Various viewers recognized the head and offered to supply affidavits to that effect before a local justice of the peace. A man named N. B. Hubbell said he recognized the head as that of a man he had seen with Three-fingered Jack and one other near Vallecitos the winter before. He recognized Jack from Love's description and said he would have shot Joaquín then, but he had only a single-shot rifle to use against three men.

Five Mexicans came forward also, claiming they had known Joaquín since he was a youth in Mexico. Francisco Revarra stated that he had reared

---

[23] *Republican*, August 11, 1853.   [24] *Stockton Journal*, August 12, 1853.

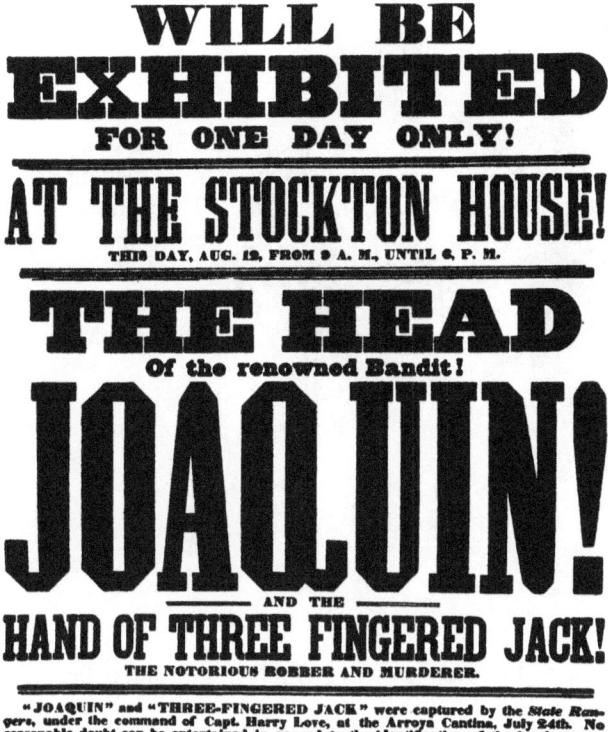

Broadside advertising the first exhibition of
Joaquín Murrieta's head in Stockton. *Author's collection.*

him and all agreed that the head in Love's possession was indeed that of the "notorious Robber, Joaquin Murriatta."

Harry added the new depositions to his collection. After assigning Rangers John Nuttall and Lafayette Black to take the display to San Francisco, Love returned to Quartzburg to assume command of his men. Apparently he had set up an appointment with Governor Bigler for the end of the month, and wanted to check in with his Rangers before heading for Benicia. Leading a group of his men, Love arrived in San Jose on August 23 with a Sonoran suspected of being involved in the murder of

The head of Joaquín as sketched from the original bottled exhibit. The features are exactly as the first contemporary reports detailed them, and the head was identified by many people who had known him in life. Overland Monthly, *November 1893*.

James Welsh.[25] The prisoner was securely ironed and delivered to the Santa Clara county sheriff.

In San Francisco Nuttall and Black set up their display in John King's Sansome Street saloon in mid-August. The arrangements are not known, but this time there was a charge of one dollar for a glimpse of the terrible trophies. Affidavits were displayed as the bay city residents filed past the large jar, then paused for a quick whiskey to steady their nerves—and stomachs.

When asked about several newspaper stories floating about claiming Joaquín was still alive in southern California, Nuttall or Black would point to the stack of affidavits. After thumbing through several of the statements, then again glancing at that ghastly head settled in the jar, most patrons were convinced. Besides, Joaquín had always been generally described as a good-looking young Mexican with flowing light brown hair, a scar on his right cheek, and light beard. This was an almost exact description of the head displayed by the Rangers, as reported in the *San Francisco Herald* at the time:

---

[25]Sacramento *Union*, August 29, 1853.

> The head itself is in a complete state of preservation and bears the impress of his character in every feature and lineament. It is that of a man about the middle size, apparently between twenty and twenty-five years old. The forehead is high and well developed, the cheek bones elevated and prominent and the mouth indicative at once of sensuality, cruelty and firmness. The hair, of a beautiful light brown with a golden tint, is long and flowing, the nose high and straight and the eyebrows which meet in the middle, dark and heavy. The eyes, now closed in death, are said to have been dark blue, with a keen, restless glance. . . . The face tapers off to the chin upon which, and on the upper lip, there is a thin beard like that of a young man who had never shaved. Under his right eye there is a small scar—the mark, no doubt, of some desperate conflict. The death of this monster is an occasion for general rejoicing, and all honor is due to the noble fellows who have rid the state of so terrible a scourge.[26]

This was the same description published in the Stockton paper before the head had been put on exhibition. There was no suggestion in the press of the time, or anywhere else, that an Indian head was being passed off as the noted bandit. How could there be? The head, as described, was obviously not that of an Indian. The Rangers had also stripped the corpse at the Cantua and noted various marks on the body. Besides the scar on the right cheek, he had another on his chest and a long scar across his back describing the course of a bullet. Two other bullet hole scars were on his leg. The confusion of names had now been resolved, and there seemed no reason to doubt that Joaquín Murrieta—one of the "Joaquins"—had indeed been killed by Love and his Rangers.[27]

Harry was probably on his way to the state capital when an article in the *Alta* was called to his attention. His eyes must have squinted with interest when he read the most pointed attack yet on the actions of the Rangers:

> It affords some amusement to our citizens to read the various accounts of the capture and decapitation of "the notorious Joaquin Murieta." The humbug is so transparent that it is surprising any sensible person can be imposed upon by the statements of the affair which have appeared in the prints. A few weeks ago a party of native Californians and Sonoreans [*sic*] started for the Tulare Valley for the expressed purpose of running mustangs. Three of the party have returned and report that they were attacked by a party of Amer-

---
[26] *San Francisco Herald*, August 19, 1853. Besides a display advertisement in the *Herald* August 18, 1853, there were also long articles on August 15, 19, and 26, 1853.
[27] *Republican*, August 11, 1853.

icans and that the balance of their party, four in number, had been killed; that Joaquin Valenzuela, one of them, was killed as he was endeavoring to escape and that his head was cut off by his captors and held as a trophy.[28]

The report, which had originated in Los Angeles, infuriated John Nuttall, who penned a long and angry letter to the *Herald*. After commenting extensively on the proofs secured by the Rangers that Joaquín had indeed been killed, Nuttall growled:

> As I have the good or bad fortune, as it may turn out, to be one of the aforesaid party that, in compliance with an act of our Legislature, pursued and captured a bloody wretch whose enormous and bloody deeds have justly alarmed the fears of the whole community, it is perhaps demanded of me that I should make a brief reply to an inuendo [*sic*] or an insidious attack, that I cannot regard in any other light but as having been prompted either by the most inexcusable ignorance of the effect of such a fabrication, or for the more wicked purpose of screening that infamous band who are still prowling at liberty, and who, for aught the public knows, have themselves through one of their own number, or by means of their stolen wealth, instigated the writing of the letter to which this is a reply.[29]

Love perhaps chuckled at the *Alta* story. Those boys were running in bad company if they had been with that crew. The Rangers knew who had been killed and had the affidavits to prove it. Why would they be gathering affidavits in areas where Joaquín was well known if they had a bogus head? And the Ranger leader wasn't finished yet. He would soon be collecting affidavits on that damned head in Calaveras and Tuolumne County, where Joaquín was very well known. A few months ago the *Alta* and some others of the anti-Bigler press were wailing about Joaquín and his gang terrorizing California. Now that the dirty work was done, these newspapers were wailing again—this time about the Rangers not getting Joaquín, or the wrong Joaquín, or something! Maybe he should have stuck a Navy Colt in some editor's ear and taken him along on the expedition as a witness. Still, only a few papers had raised any doubts about the Ranger's work. As he rode into Benicia, Love must have still been confident that most people were grateful for the dangerous work they had done. No matter what he thought or read, Governor Bigler certainly could not have second thoughts at this late date.

Apparently Love had not taken the head along to show the governor.

---

[28] *Alta*, August 23, 1853.   [29] *Herald*, August 26, 1853.

He brought all the affidavits, and, of course, Bigler had read many of the press accounts. They met in the governor's office, shook hands, and after some small talk Bigler leafed through the affidavits Love had produced from a leather binder. After a quick scanning of the papers, the governor scribbled out a document:

> It appearing satisfactory by the within affidavits that Capt. Harry Love has captured the notorious Robber, Joaquin, I therefore believe him entitled to the reward of $1000 offered for his capture.
> August 27, 1853 Benicia   John Bigler[30]

Thinking he had better cover himself just in case some of these adverse newspaper stories were taken seriously, the governor scribbled the following note at the bottom of the page and had Love sign it:

> This certifies that Joaquin could not have been taken alive and delivered to the authorities as he was mounted & endeavoring to make his escape when shot on my orders.
> Benicia August 27th 1853   Harry Love, Capt[31]

Love had apparently collected the Rangers three months' pay at this time, amounting to $450 per man. Curiously, the legislative appropriation for the Rangers was for $9,000 even—or three months' pay for only twenty men.[32] This suggests the Rangers were a man short, or Captain Love was paid separately—although there is no record of such being the case. With the reward split added in, they had nearly $500 apiece for their three-month outing and payday must have been a rousing occasion in the saloons of old Quartzburg.

Love planned a tour of the gold rush country to collect more affidavits and see if they could make a few dollars more by exhibiting their trophy. Dreams of capturing stolen bandit loot had long since evaporated, and hopes to have their commission renewed had also fallen on deaf ears. There was talk in the legislature of awarding them another $5,000 for their work, however, so perhaps more coin would be forthcoming in one fashion or another.

The Rangers were disbanded on August 28 and went their separate ways. Love apparently had business to take care of and sent Rangers Bill Henderson and Jim Norton to San Francisco to pick up the head and hand. Proceeding on the first leg of their tour, the Rangers arrived in Sacra-

---

[30]Joaquin Murrieta Papers.   [31]Ibid.
[32]The $9,000 Ranger payment was included in a list of 1853 legislative expenditures; see California State Legislature, "Statutes of California," 1853 (Sacramento: Government Printing Office, 1853).

mento about September 8, where they made provisions for their exhibit in the Whig Headquarters Saloon.[33] Governor Bigler was in town after a successful re-election campaign; it is curious that an opposition party saloon was selected in which to display the head. Arriving at the capitol shortly after his two men, Love took a room at the Niantic Hotel.

Although Whig in politics and very anti-Bigler, the Sacramento *Daily Union* heartily endorsed the results of the Rangers' expedition. "The evidence secured to identify this as being really the head of Joaquin," noted the *Union*, "is of a most satisfying nature."[34]

The display went on exhibition the next morning, being introduced by both an advertisement and a brief article in the *Union*. It was an immediate success. Henderson and Norton answered questions as the public filed by the horrid trophies hour after hour. A much longer article in the *Union* the next day was quite interesting:

> JOAQUIN'S HEAD— ... The head of the noted murderer is preserved in a glass jar, whose convex sides have the effect of magnifying the features into an unnatural expression. To obviate this object, a string is made fast to the crown of the head, by pulling which it is raised above the surface of the liquid and exhibited more in accordance with what it should be. A profusion of jet black hair falls below its ears, while the sightless orbs indicate them to have been possessed at one time of a flashing lustre, such as is common to a majority of the Spanish race.... Accompanying this bloody trophy is a right hand, containing three fingers and a thumb, believed to have belonged to Manuel [*sic*] Garcia, otherwise called "Three Fingered Jack." A hand, however, is much more difficult to be identified than a head, and as many people have lost one of their fingers, the proprietors of the head do not announce it, although well satisfied that they are correct in their belief that it is genuine.[35]

The article concluded by noting that the purpose of the exhibition was threefold; first, to allow those who knew "Joaquin Muriata [*sic*]" in life to identify him, so the Rangers could collect the various rewards; second, to gratify public curiosity to see the "most celebrated and infamous outlaw of his age"; and third, to discourage others from a life of crime or aiding Joaquín's compatriots who were still at large.

"Harry has completed his job...," reported the *Democratic State Jour-*

---

[33]Sacramento *Union*, September 9, 1853. Love's arrival in town was mentioned the same day in the Sacramento *Placer Times & Transcript*.   [34]Ibid.
[35]Sacrament *Union*, September 10, 1853.

> JOAQUIN'S HEAD—We would respectfully inform the citizens of Sacramento and surrounding country, that the head of JOAQUIN MURIATTA, the renowned robber and bandit, whose depredations were so numerous on the Calaveras and other portions of the country last winter, and who with part of his band was captured by Capt. Harry Love and his rangers on the Arrollo Cantuvo, in the Tulare valley, on the 24th July last, will be exhibited THIS DAY, at Vincent Taylor's Saloon known as Whig Head Quarters, opposite the Orleans Hotel. As there has been considerable doubts as to his being the genuine Joaquin, we have taken considerable pains to procure affidavits from persons who knew him in different parts of the State. Any one wishing to see said affidavits can do so by calling at Whig Head Quarters, which are true copies of sundry affidavits now on file in the Comptroller's office in Benicia.
> WM T. HENDERSON.
> s9   JAMES M. NORTON.

Sacramento newspaper advertisement advising the public that Joaquín's genuine head is in town and ready for viewing. *Sacramento* Daily Union, *September 10, 1853*.

nal. "They have rid the state of a merciless robber and murderer without committing any depredations themselves, and are entitled to the gratitude of the whole community."[36]

The Rangers were undoubtedly pleased and amused on September 13 when the *Union* published yet another notice of the exhibition in conjunction with a whimsical collection of old wives' tales about the continued animation of historical heads after decapitation. Love and his troops were packing up to move on when the inevitable political commentary was published in the Democratic *Times & Transcript* on September 15:

> JOAQUIN'S HEAD—Joaquin's head is being exhibited at Sacramento. It is to be seen there at the Whig Headquarters, the place where decapitated heads have been plenty since March last.

---

[36]Sacramento *Democratic State Journal,* September 12, 1853.

Love, Henderson, and Norton headed north and set up their trophies in Marysville, some forty miles above Sacramento. A discussion of heads and hands with a reporter appeared in the *Marysville Herald* of September 17, 1853:

> We held quite an interesting conversation with Capt. Love last evening, and among other things he informed us that the head would probably be given by the Rangers to some institution, or gatherer of notable things, where it might be safely preserved. The object in this exhibition is not to represent a bloody trophy, nor yet for the accumulation of money; and with regard to this latter, it is well to remark that the whole matter has been rather a source of expense than of profit to the gallant company....
>
> ...The object of the exhibition is simply to let it become fully known and established that the much dreaded assassin and robber is at last captured and slain.

During Harry's interview with the *Marysville Express* editor, a curious thing happened, as reported in the *Democratic State Journal* on September 16, 1853.

> While we were present, a Mexican was brought in who had known Joaquín since he was a boy of ten years of age. Previous to examining the head he stated that there was a certain mark on the cheek, and a mark under his chin. These marks were found in the designated places, and corresponded with the description given, exactly. The sheriff and his Deputy, Justices Danby and Filkins, all say that they recognize a striking resemblance in the features to one of the Mexicans arrested in 1851 for shooting Sheriff Buchanan. He [Buchanan] also recognizes the head. We learn that there is a sister of Joaquín[']s in this city at the present time. It would be well for the gentlemen now exhibiting this head, to get her to examine the head and give an opinion which will be conclusive.

Years later, in November 1879, a writer in the *Nevada City Transcript* claimed he was there the day Joaquín's sister came to view the head. Being aware of the relationship, he watched her closely as she stared at the trophy. She simply smiled. Later when a friend asked her if it was her brother's head she replied, "No sir, it is not; it is the head of Joaquín Gonzales. But say nothing. Let them think it to be my brother's head if they want to." Later, when her words were repeated to the captain, Love replied: "I know this to be the head of Joaquín Murietta [*sic*], and she says it is not because she is too proud to own it."

From Marysville, the Rangers headed east to set up the display in

Nevada City. They did not always obtain a mention in the local press, since various editors felt it was a barbarous exhibition and should be ignored. John Nugent, editor of the *San Francisco Herald*, summed up the thoughts of many on the grisly exhibition:

> Let this head and hand—shocking remembrances of great crimes—disappear from the public gaze. Their being hawked about in this fashion can but minister to a depraved curiosity, which should by all means be discountenanced in a civilized community.[37]

Word of mouth quickly spread the word, however, and when the crowds began to slacken, they moved on. From Nevada City, the Rangers headed south, where the trophies were exhibited at Auburn's National Hotel during the week of September 25.[38] Love is not reported as accompanying the exhibit at this time; perhaps he had lingered at one of the towns along the route.

From Auburn the men moved on to Placerville and Jackson, drawing good-sized crowds wherever they stopped. At Mokelumne Hill, Alfred Doten viewed the trophies and described the experience to a friend several years later:

> I was in Calaveras County at the time of [Murrieta's] bloody exploits, and when he was at last killed, and his head was exhibited, I was well acquainted with many Mexicans who knew Joaquin well, and they all testified to the identity of the head and agreed that this renowned bandit chief was now muerto [dead]. A Mexican woman at Mokelumne Hill, who had known Joaquin intimately from childhood up, was much affected on seeing his head, and shed tears over it. The story of his still being alive and active must have been gotten up by the lovers of the marvelous.[39]

At San Andreas several Mexican residents took offense at the display, and when Love shipped the head and hand south, the stage was followed. On the Stanislaus river, three Mexican riders stopped the coach and told the driver they had vowed to capture the head. After a brief parley, however, the coach was allowed to retain its cargo and move on.[40]

In Columbia, a former Murrieta mining partner reportedly recognized him at once, as did many of the other residents. A writer in the local *Columbia Gazette* was certainly impressed with the identification:

---

[37] *San Francisco Herald*, February 13, 1854. [38] *Auburn Herald*, September 24, 1853.
[39] Walter Van Tilburg Clark, ed., *The Journals of Alfred Doten, 1849–1903* (Reno: University of Nevada Press, 1973), 313. [40] *Republican*, November 1, 1853.

Joaquin was probably better known here than any other section of California, having long resided in this vicinity. A number of Mexicans and Americans recognized the head upon first sight. Among the number of those who recognized the head as that of Joaquin Muriatta [*sic*], was a Mexican who had known him in the State of Sonora, Mexico, from boyhood, and had been his partner in this vicinity. A number of the Chinese, who had seen him in his forays against their countrymen in Calaveras, recognized the head instantly, and gave certificates to that effect. Many may have had their doubts of the capture of this notorious robber chieftain before Captain Love's visit to Columbia, but the concurrent testimony of all who had known Joaquin, and saw his head, was so conclusive that there are now no doubts in the minds of the people up here that Harry Love and his gallant Rangers have performed to the letter all they promised to do when they started in pursuit of this notorious set of bandits.[41]

After several days in Columbia, Love put his trophies on the stage for the short trip to Sonora. Again there was trouble, as reported in the San Francisco *Daily Placer Times and Transcript* of October 26, 1853:

We learn from W.H. Owens, esq. the stage ... was attacked about 6 miles from Sonora at 10 Sunday night. Two volleys were fired, but no passengers were aboard so the stage kept going. The stage was also fired on the previous night. The head of Joaquin was exhibited at Mokelumne Hill and was expected to be on the stage both nights ... his gang suspected of the attacks in order to obtain his head. Since Captain Love and his rangers completed their service, Mexican horse thieves and bandits are having a good time in Southern California.

By October 21 Love and his two companions were back in Stockton.[42] The trip had been very successful. Besides a large number of affidavits from "respectable Americans," the Rangers had others gathered from Mexicans and some of the Chinese whose camps had been raided in Calaveras. The latter group "had recognized the head instantly and were exceedingly rejoiced at his capture," according to the *San Joaquin Republican*.

Harry and his men must have been weary of the whole business and anxious to get on with their lives. They held a meeting in Stockton and voted to leave the head of Joaquín in the hands of Pat Connor, who was now undersheriff of San Joaquin County. Connor was to dispose of the head in any way he thought proper for the best interests of the company.

---
[41]The *Columbia Gazette* quote was also published in the *Republican*, October 25.
[42]Love's return to Stockton was chronicled in the same issue of the *Republican*.

With the additional affidavits to bolster their claim to have slain Joaquín, the Rangers hoped to add pressure to a proposed bill before the legislature, requesting an additional appropriation for them.

The following month there was good news indeed. The previous winter, several San Francisco newspapers had advertised a $5,000 reward for the bandit Joaquín offered by Chinese of the city because he had killed so many of their countrymen. As it turned out, the report was not true, but when the Asian residents were informed of the situation, they collected $1,000 and gave it to a local judge for disbursement to the Rangers.[43]

The state capital was moved from Benicia to Sacramento in late February 1854, and Harry lobbied for his relief bill at the new location. He found some sympathetic ears, particularly when he explained that the $1,000 reward, split up twenty-one ways, came to a little over $40 each. This was hardly a generous sum for such doughty deeds as the Rangers had performed. And there had been other expenses during the campaign, such as ferry charges, supplies, and hotel bills. The following April, Assemblyman E. C. Springer of El Dorado County introduced a bill to provide $5,000 for the relief of Captain Love.[44] Phil Herbert and others supported the bill, but the San Francisco *Alta* was skeptical, as usual. "Of what Captain Love wishes to be relieved," grumbled the editor, "is not stated in the Legislative report, but probably it is of an empty pocket." The *Alta* editor knew as well as anyone the cost of traveling in California, and that the whole purpose of rewards was to reimburse posses for out-of-pocket expenses.[45]

A May 9 legislative committee report agreed that the Rangers should indeed be further compensated for their expenses. Volunteers for such dangerous work must be assured of adequate recompense, it said, or such expeditions would go wanting for personnel in the future. Governor Bigler signed the bill into law on May 15, 1854. The *San Joaquin Republican* of May 20 reported:

> CAPTAIN HARRY LOVE.—This gentleman paid us a visit yesterday. We rejoice to learn that justice was done to him by the Legislature and his claim against the State paid. It was through his courage and indomitable perseverance that the most infernal gang of rascals that ever infested any

---

[43]San Francisco *California Chronicle*, November 21, 1853, and the *San Francisco Daily Placer Times & Transcript*, November 21, 1853.
[44]*Journal of the Fifth Session of the Legislature of the State of California*, Sacramento, 1854.
[45]*Alta*, April 30, 1854.

country was broken up. The vote by which his claim was allowed is most complimentary to him. In the Assembly the vote stood: ayes, 43; nays 22. In the Senate he received 21 out of 26 votes.

It is not clear whether the legislative bill benefitted merely Love, or all the Rangers, but it was in Harry's name. Certainly his men felt they should all be included in the extra bonus, and indications are that Love had agreed to share the money. That the Rangers were uneasy about the matter is indicated by a letter Pat Connor wrote from Sacramento to his Ranger pal Bill Howard:

Sacramento, May 13, 1854

Dear Bill:

Harry Love's bill passed the Senate today by a large majority; he will not draw his money until Tuesday morning. I expect I will have some trouble to make him stick to his word; maybe not, altho I dread it. There will be hell in camp sure if he don't stick to his word.[46]

There is no record of whether Love "stuck to his word," although he undoubtedly did. Men like Connor, Byrnes, Charley Bludworth, and the Howard brothers were not likely to stand by while their captain refused to share a nice bonus. All but Connor were dangerous gunmen who had engaged in shooting scrapes both before and after the Joaquín adventure.

Any Ranger difficulties must have stemmed from a question of how to divide up this new reward windfall. Some had been with the campaign from the start, while others had dropped out, or joined late in the chase as others left. Harry might have threatened to keep it all if a fair resolution could not be agreed upon. Since there were no press reports of dissention in the Ranger ranks, it can be assumed the matter was settled amicably. Furthermore, none of the Rangers who afterward wrote of their experience complained of Love reneging on them.

---

[46]Cossley-Batt, *Last of the California Rangers*, 192–193.

12

Mary

Riding down the tree-shaded *alameda* leading to the old Mission Santa Clara, traveler Edwin Bryant was struck by the neglected structures and lands of the area. In that year of 1846, the primitive conditions seemed a clear indication of the paucity of government and laxness of the native Californians in maintaining their frontier domain. Bryant was surprised to find, among the miles of untilled fields, a garden enclosure at the old mission. There were some fruit trees and other plantings, but even these were showing a lack of care and decay.

As Bryant and his companions climbed down from their horses, a large woman emerged from one of the mission buildings to greet them. After obtaining water and engaging in small talk with the woman, the travelers moved on.

"Some excellent pears were furnished us by Mrs. Bennett," Bryant later wrote, "an American lady of amazonian proportions, who, with her family of sons, has taken up her residence in one of the buildings of the mission."[1]

Born in Georgia in 1803, Mary Swain Bennett came to California in 1845 with her husband, Vardamon, and their children. It was a traveling family. Vardamon's parents had not been pleased with his choice of a bride, and perhaps this had prompted their initial migration. They moved from Georgia to Tennessee and Arkansas in 1830, then migrated to Oregon in 1842. Still not satisfied, the family moved south into the Mexican state of California. By the time they took up a brief residence in the Sacramento Valley, they had eight children: Winston, Catherine, Dennis, David Jackson, Amanda, Mansel, Julia, and Samantha. There, they were again

---

[1] Edward Bryant, *What I saw in California* (New York: Appleton, 1848), 318.

A woman of great courage, stamina, and natural ability, Mary Bennett Love was also self-centered, greedy, avaricious, and often estranged from her own children. Far too independent in nature to get along with any man, Mary's marriage to Harry Love was a disaster. *Courtesy Conrado Family Archives.*

dissatisfied, and by 1845 the family was living in the small village called Yerba Buena, north of Monterey.[2]

In the scattered collection of adobe and frame buildings soon to be renamed San Francisco, Vardamon Bennett apparently could not make a living at his carpenter's trade, so he opened a saloon and bowling hall. A

---

[2]For biographical information on the Bennett family, see Mabel Dorn Early, "The Bennett Family," *The Pony Express*, September and November 1950; and Jeanette Rowland, "Widow Bennett," *News and Notes*, Santa Cruz Historical Society, June 1958. There is also some data in the "Pioneer Index" in Hubert Howe Bancroft, *History of California*, vol. 19 (San Francisco: The History Company, Publishers, 1888), 716–717. For a popular but inaccurate treatment, see Joan Barriga, "Mary Bennett, the Black Knight's Lady," *The Californians*, September/October 1990.

local resident described him as "a diamond of the first water—his house is always open and his face ever on the smile to receive customers . . . and when he laughs, ye Gods! . . . Bennett has a family and they are all family too, one in which is contained most of the bone and muscle of Yerba Buena."[3]

But there was trouble in the family Bennett. Business was dull in these years prior to the gold rush, and, when it became difficult to make ends meet, Mary took over the breadwinning chores to keep food on the family table—or so she claimed. San Francisco merchant William Heath Davis dealt with Mary in those early days:

> She was unmistakably the head of the family—a large, powerful woman, uncultivated, but well-meaning and very industrious. Her word was law, and her husband stood in becoming awe of her. Their children were respectably brought up, the family being supported by sewing, washing, ironing; raising chickens, turkeys and ducks. I trusted her for goods frequently, not knowing, or caring much, whether they were ever paid for; but they always were. She was an honest, good woman, and while not regarded as an equal by the better-cultivated and more aristocratic ladies, she was always pleasantly received in their houses.[4]

Mary was illiterate, but it never cramped her style; she had her sons do her reading and writing for her. When the Bennetts began quarreling over money matters, the six-foot, 200-pound Mary quickly wore down her meeker husband with her foul mouth and domineering nature. When it became apparent they could not reconcile their differences, Mary wrote to United States Consul Thomas O. Larkin at Monterey on June 6, 1845.[5] She complained that her husband had neglected his family, refused to support them, and even took any money earned by his children. More than likely, Mary was lying to get out from under a marriage in which she was no longer interested. She wanted her independence. When Larkin found her a place to live at the Santa Clara Mission, she took the children and headed south. They lived at the mission for a time, but soon traveled to the coast to live with two sons.

On June 25, 1845, Vardamon had written Larkin seeking his own custody of the children. The serious nature of their troubles is indicated by

---
[3]Joseph T. Downey, *Filings from an Old Saw* (San Francisco: John Howell Publishers, 1956), 5.
[4]Davis, *Seventy-five Years in California*, 149.
[5]George P. Hammond, ed., *The Larkin Papers*, 10 vol. (Berkeley and Los Angeles: University of California Press, 1952); vol. 3, pp. 182, 183, 223–225, 248, 268; vol. 4, pp. 101, 115.

another letter Larkin received from a Santa Cruz resident named Julius Martin. "I have one of old man Bennett's daughters aliving with me," he wrote, "and I shall go back to Gilroy's Ranch next weeke [sic] and have no house suitable for company and she wishes to come to Monterey and live with your wife for a short time as she is determined never to live with her Father nor mother anymore."

Mary took up residence in the Zayante Valley, a few miles north of the coastal village of Santa Cruz. There was much government land in the area, and, after filing on a claim, she prepared to farm with the help of her large brood of children. It was a hard life for a woman, but Mary was strong and tough, taking care of the younger children and doing the innumerable chores of those pioneer times. The Bennett boys also contributed to the larder. In December 1846 Mary traded some 53,000 shingles, probably split by sons Winston, Jack, and Dennis, for twenty-eight dollars' worth of goods from trader William Heath Davis.[6]

But tranquillity was not to be the lot of Mary Bennett. She quickly discovered that neighbor Isaac Graham was a rowdy ex-mountain man whose distillery and race track were the hangout for naval deserters, unemployed trappers, shiftless hunters, and gamblers. The small village of Zayante (now Felton) was a boisterous place, and not conducive to settlers raising families.

Graham was a frontiersman and trapper who had deserted his wife and family in Tennessee in 1830. In California he and a group of cronies had participated in a local political uprising and later were accused by the Mexican government of fomenting an insurrection. Forcibly taken to Mexico, where they were tried and acquitted in 1840, Graham returned, sued the government for his trouble—and collected. With the money—some $36,000—he bought the Rancho Zayante. He built a water-powered sawmill and distillery the following year and farmed his surrounding property. He never lost his "mountain man" mentality, however, and did things his own way, never giving any thought to the opinion of others.

Mary Bennett's worst nightmare came true when her oldest daughter was quickly and quietly wooed by Graham. Before the mother knew what was happening, Catherine had moved in with the old mountain man and all hell broke loose. An outraged Mary contacted Consul Larkin at Monterey and demanded Graham's housekeeping arrangements be broken up

---

[6]Original receipt in Huntington Library, San Marino, California.

Downtown Santa Cruz, California, in 1866, in a photograph by Lawrence & Houseworth of San Francisco. *California State Library.*

immediately. Larkin dispatched a hasty note to a justice of the peace at Santa Cruz, insisting the couple be separated promptly since, under the laws of both the United States and Mexico, any "children are illegitimate ... unless their parents are married by a competent authority."

José Bolcoff, the justice of the peace, called on Graham and was told that the woman would not be given up under any circumstances. Furthermore, Graham waved a piece of paper at the justice. It was a brief statement testifying to Graham and Catherine being married on September 26, 1845, "by one who was requested to read the ceremony." It was signed by Henry L. Ford, an American who had participated in some of the California troubles with Graham. Since neither were Catholic, the only other party who could have legally married them was Consul Larkin, but Graham complained that he could not make the trip to Monterey because of his "infirmities."[7]

---

[7]Doyce B. Nunis, Jr., *The Trials of Isaac Graham* (Los Angeles: Dawson's Book Store, 1967). The marriage and troubles between Graham and his wife and her family is related in great detail by a skilled historian in this intriguing work.

The unofficial scrap of paper did not pacify Mary Bennett. When both Larkin and Bolcoff refused to act further, however, there was nothing more she could do. Fed up with the Graham situation and the rough characters who inhabited the area, Mary packed up her younger children and moved to Santa Clara. She procured permission to occupy an adobe house in the orchard of the old mission and settled there, managing to stay out of the way for the most part during the Bear Flag Revolt and Mexican War. The Bennetts reportedly attempted reconciliations several times, but reunions never met with any success.

With the birth of Catherine's first baby in July 1846, Mary and her daughter apparently again reached some degree of accord. The child was christened Amanda (Mary's middle name) Ann Narcissa. In 1845, Vardamon Bennett had acquired two grants of land from Gov. Pío Pico. To do so he had joined the Catholic Church and assumed a new first name, Narciso. Catherine's baby was apparently given the modified name of her grandfather, Narciso Bennett.[8]

Meanwhile the older boys, Dennis and David Jackson Bennett, called "Jack" by the family, had been roving on their own, exploring the coast. Eventually Dennis bought six acres of land near town, and he and his brother decided to build a sawmill in the Zayante Valley, on the property formerly occupied by their mother. In 1848, after selecting a waterfall on San Lorenzo Creek, a tributary of the San Lorenzo River, the boys asked their father in San Francisco to buy the equipment they needed. Vardamon (now Narciso) must have escorted the sawmill machinery to the site, perhaps chartering a coastal schooner. Being a carpenter, he helped his sons set up their operation, obtaining lumber from Isaac Graham's sawmill. The waterfall supplied the power, and an overshot waterwheel drove the up-and-down saw.[9] Vardamon was drinking heavily at the time.

---

[8]The two Santa Clara land grants of Narciso Bennett are listed in Burgess McK. Shumway, *California Ranchos* (San Bernardino/Glendale, Calif.: The Borgo Press/The Sidewinder Press, 1988), 98–99. In the text of a state supreme court property dispute case, it is stated that "a tract of land claimed by the defendant Mary Love, as her separate property, it having been conveyed to her by her former husband, Narciso Bennett, to whom it had been originally granted by the Mexican government." *Shartzer v. Love,* 40 California Reports 93 (October 1870). Aware of Vardamon's property in San Francisco, Mary apparently never acquired a divorce and consequently obtained his estate upon his death.

[9]Information on the history of the Bennett sawmill is scanty, but some data can be found in an interview with Winston Bennett in the *Santa Cruz Sentinel,* May 1, 1888. See also Charlene Detlefs, *Brief History of the Falls/Love Creek* (Ben Lomond: Santa Cruz County, 1977), 1–10, typescript in Special Collections, Library, University of California at Santa Cruz. See also Santa Cruz *Frontier Gazette,* Spring 1958.

The boys were no doubt relieved that he had returned to San Francisco by the time Mary and her family appeared and took up residence in a cabin near the new sawmill. Winston Bennett owned local property also and worked with his brothers for a time, but soon left to settle in the Santa Clara area. Vardamon died the following year.

The year 1849 would have far-reaching effects on Mary Bennett and her family. Towards the end of the year, a stranger showed up on Isaac Graham's doorstep. He was six feet tall, stout of build, had long hair, and showed the effects of much travel. It must have been a stirring moment for the stranger as he introduced himself to his father. The startled and confused Graham could only stare and ask his grown boy into the house.

Jesse Jones Graham had been taken to Texas by his mother after his father had deserted them in Tennessee. He had grown up in the Lone Star State, participated in the Mexican War and, after somehow learning of his father's whereabouts in California, sought him out. Twenty-five years old at this time, Jesse's sudden appearance set in motion a chain of events that affected the Graham and Bennett families disastrously.

Any hopes for a peaceful relationship between Isaac Graham and Mary Bennett were now dashed to the ground. The Bennetts saw Jesse as a distinct threat. Certainly, at best, his sudden appearance was a major obstacle to the estate inheritance hopes of either Catherine or the two illegitimate daughters. If that was not enough cause for the Bennetts's concern, it soon became clear Isaac and Catherine were having their own marital problems due to his rough ways and sometimes cruel behavior. Even more significant was the fact that Jesse had said his mother was still alive in Texas. This meant old Graham was a bigamist. Catherine's marriage, if that was what it was, was even more invalid.

Early on the morning of March 31, 1850, Isaac and son Jesse left for San Jose to purchase livestock and attend a horse race. The depth of Graham's relationship with his wife can be gauged from the fact that she had delivered a stillborn child the previous evening. A sister was with her at the time, but Catherine decided she could no longer stay with such a man. Mary had been trying to get her to leave Graham for some time—to not just run away, but to also take all the money she could find in the house. Catherine must have finally concluded that her mother was right. Jesse was going to get it if she failed to do so. She deserved something and, with Graham away, now was the ideal time to make her move.

Mary appeared at the rancho that day and helped Catherine ransack the place. Some $7,000 was found, a considerable sum in those days. Apparently unknown to Catherine, her mother filched about half of the money, perhaps saying she would send it along when she was settled somewhere. Later Catherine would write to Graham:

> Mr. Graham . . . you know . . . I had good cause to leave you, but I should not have left you if it had not been for my mother. She laid the plan and got the man to go with me, and when the day came for me to go my heart rather failed me, but she came and tried to unlock the trunk with the other keys and when she could not she . . . took the ax and broke it and took the money off and assisted me off that night . . . if she had her way, you would not have been here today, for she tried to get me to poison you; and when I would not she would call me a fool, and say if she was in my place she would put a spider in your dumpling.[10]

John Palmer, a ranch handyman, was paid to go with Catherine and the two children. With his sister dressed as a man, Jack Bennett escorted the group to Santa Cruz, where they caught the first ship to San Francisco. Her next stop would be Honolulu.

When Graham returned from San Jose, his fury must have been monumental. Obtaining a warrant, he accompanied the sheriff in searching Mary Bennett's home, but none of the stolen money was found. Next he went after Catherine's sister, who had been at the house when he left. Accusing her of being an accessory in his wife's flight, Graham attempted to prosecute his sister-in-law, but she was released for lack of evidence.

Graham offered a reward and employed detectives in an effort to locate his wife, meanwhile keeping up a steady tirade of threats against the Bennetts in an effort to discover Catherine's whereabouts. Jesse Graham, very much caught up in his father's disastrous marital mess, also had various confrontations with them.

On the day they returned from San Jose, the two Grahams did not know what they were up against. Jesse was told to put fresh loads in a double-barreled shotgun kept at the house. Taking the weapon outside, Jesse was startled when he fired off one barrel and it exploded. With a blackened face, he showed his father what had happened. Noche, an Indian servant, was questioned as to the last person who had handled the gun. It was Dennis Bennett. Noche had seen him pound the barrel full of rocks, and had

---

[10]Catherine's letter was originally introduced at Jesse Graham's trial in 1888 and was reproduced in the *Fresno Daily Evening Expositor*, April 24, 1888.

not known the Grahams had returned in time to warn them. Jesse stared hard at his father. This was obviously a Bennett attempt to kill him.

Confronting the Bennetts at the first opportunity, Jesse accused them of attempted murder and again demanded they reveal Catherine's whereabouts. Mary still insisted she did not know where her daughter was, but she was concerned about Jesse's threats and obtained a restraining order from the local alcalde on April 22, 1850. Frustrated and probably furious, Jesse dropped into a Santa Cruz saloon afterwards and had a few drinks with friends before starting for home. What happened next was reported in the *San Francisco Daily Pacific News*:

> Jesse was ordered to give bail in the sum of $2,000. Not being able to obtain the sureties, the bond was doubled and he allowed to depart on his own recognizance, promising good behavior. He, however, followed Mrs. B. and on the road home overtook them about one mile from the Mission, fired with a double-barrel shotgun loaded with buckshot, upon Jackson, but missed him, and then discharged the other barrel at Mrs. B. before her son could offer any defense, having been thrown by his frightened animal. Five shot took effect upon her—two in her hip, the remainder in the legs, though none of them are dangerous.[11]

Jesse's story was that he had overtaken Jackson Bennett and his mother and had left the road and attempted to pass around them. "Both were heavily armed," he later recalled to a reporter, "and evidently meant to fight him.... When he got about opposite them Mrs. Bennett dismounted, drew a pistol and gave her son the command to fire ... and he fired. Graham fired at the same time, and young Bennett fell. He then gave Mrs. Bennett the benefit of the other barrel in the hips."[12]

Apparently convinced the Bennetts were determined to kill him and his father, Jesse left the wounded Mary and her son in the road while he rode furiously to the Bennett home. Three of Mary Bennett's daughters were in the yard as Jesse galloped up and asked if Dennis was at home. Told he was in the house, Jesse rode over to the doorway and called for him to come out. Dennis appeared and walked over to where the mounted Jesse sat, with his shotgun resting across the pommel of his saddle. The two exchanged a few words, when suddenly a shot rang out and Dennis sprawled on the ground. As the girls rushed over to their dying brother, Graham galloped off.

---
[11] San Francisco *Daily Pacific News*, April 27, 1850.
[12] *Fresno Daily Evening Expositor*, April 24, 1888.

California was six months away from becoming a state, and isolated areas such as Santa Cruz were still quite primitive so far as the law was concerned. Jesse stayed with his father for a time and later claimed he made several attempts to turn himself in, but the officials either were not available or interested. Knowing it was only a matter of time before the Bennetts would either assassinate him or compel local authorities to do something, Jesse said goodbye to his father and headed east. He had no sooner left the area than Jack Bennett offered a $2,000 reward for his apprehension, and the county offered $1,000 more.

The California gold rush was now under way, and Jesse easily lost himself in the mining country, perhaps acquiring some gold to boot. In Mariposa County he joined a Texas friend, Reuben Chandler. The two men mined together, but soon found themselves involved in a burgeoning Indian war. It would be many years later, in 1888, that Jesse would be tried for the Dennis Bennett killing and be acquitted by a hung jury and local public opinion.[13]

In May 1851 Isaac Graham finally located his wife, living in Oregon. He brought her and the two children back and the two engaged in a series of court squabbles, trying to recover the stolen money and acquire custody of the children. Eventually Catherine remarried and settled down to a more sedate life.

Mary Bennett had paid dearly for her scheming and the purloined Graham money, but her temperament and character would not allow her to accept any blame for what had happened. In their confrontation, Graham and Mary Bennett were the proverbial irresistible force meeting the immovable object. Strong, self-reliant, and insistent on doing things on her own terms, she could readily justify her actions in the tragedy that had enveloped her family. But that was in the past, and she got on with her life. Remaining at her farm in the area, she maintained various acquired property interests in Santa Clara, including the Mexican land grant of her ill-fated first husband, Vardamon.

---

[13]The tragic story of Jesse Graham and the Bennetts is well-told in Nunis, *The Trials of Isaac Graham*. The author is grateful to the late Nathan Sweet, Madera County historian, for his research into the Graham-Bennett troubles. See the Sweet materials in the June English Collection, Special Collections, Henry Madden Library, California State University, Fresno.

13
A Place Called Zayante

Harry Love's Rangers' reward money was bound to disappear fast in the gold rush economy of California. He had been on the move ever since he was a boy—had crossed oceans and deserts, fought in wars, explored mighty rivers, and chased bandits. He had done enough, but what next? Perhaps it was time to settle down.

George W. Evans had been a 2nd lieutenant in the Rangers and was a large Mariposa County property owner. Evans and his partner, Jacob Hill, owned the Louisiana Ranch, and were looking for a buyer in 1854. In September of that year they sold their property for $1,500, Evans having decided to relocate and take up land on the coast.[1]

Evans, an early Santa Cruz settler, might have accompanied Love on a trip over to the coast to look around in early 1854.[2] A leisurely ride to the Pacific was likely therapeutic after the excitement of the past year. They had heard of the old Monterey area when prowling about San Juan Bautista on the Joaquín chase. It was a country as yet not overpopulated by hordes of goldseekers—a land of redwood forests, sun-kissed beaches, and scattered old Spanish adobes.

If he did not yearn for the sea again, perhaps Harry liked the idea of locating on the coast. He could go into some kind of boat trade. He had also heard the lumber business was booming due to all the building going on in the state. In any case, it wouldn't hurt to do a little poking around. Certainly, few people could make mining pay.

It was a pleasant ride this early part of the year, up over the windy Pacheco Pass trail and through the hills to San Juan, where they would

---

[1] *Mariposa Gazette Centennial Edition,* April 1954.
[2] The Love-Evans trip to the coast in early 1854 is conjectural, and Love might very well have made the trip alone. Still, both men later moved to the same area and a trip at this time makes particular sense for Love, in lieu of his transactions later in the year.

have rested at Breen's hotel.[3] Moving on through the oak- and brush-covered hills, they rode across valleys where mustard seed was just beginning to blossom, along with wild oats, clover, and other grasses. Natives said the mustard grew so tall the horses could not see over it. A fledgling village was springing up in the Pajaro Valley—to be named Watsonville in a few years.[4] They were riding over the Rancho Bolsa del Pajaro, one of the large land grants of the area. They had heard much of these grants in recent years, as the government had been trying to establish ownership amid the tangled legal mess left by the Mexican government.

When the ocean first came into view, it was a breathtaking sight. If indeed Love and Evans made this ride to the coast together, they probably rode south down into the sprawling adobe village of Monterey. Harry would have enjoyed the crashing surf as they rode along the beach and later exchanged maritime talk with sailors in the cantinas and saloons of the town. They would have asked many questions of the locals to see what opportunities were available.

After a few days of relaxing, they perhaps rode north at a leisurely pace, covering the fifty-odd-mile crescent of cliffs and beaches skirting Monterey Bay to the straggling village of Santa Cruz. Again they talked to the locals about business opportunities and rode about questioning farmers, officials, and merchants. After hearing of the lumbering business being carried on to the north, the two men would have ridden the few miles along the trail to the Zayante Valley, where Isaac Graham's ranch and sawmill were located. The valley was about a mile in width and two miles long, with the San Lorenzo River and Zayante Creek coming together in its midst. It was a beautiful area of towering redwood forests amid mountain streams and rolling, brush-covered hills. Writing to his wife in Illinois, pioneer A. W. Rawson described the area in lyrical terms:

> I have seen and chosen Santa Cruz ... for a home ... up on the coast. This place has many advantages over others in respect to morals, social influence, family and amount of agricultural lands, gold mines, limestone ... with a decided advantage in point of fruits of all kinds, almost all garden vegetables can be had here the year round—strawberries are now ripe, new potatoes, plenty peaches, apples, pears, apricots, figs [and] cherries.[5]

---

[3] There was no road over Pacheco Pass at this time, just a well-traveled Indian and Mexican trade trail that had seen much use since the gold rush. See Brenda Burnett Preston, *Andrew and Susan Firebaugh, California Pioneers* (Rio Del Mar, Calif.: Rio Del Mar Press, 1995), 83–91.
[4] Betty Lewis, *Watsonville, Memories that Linger* (Fresno, Calif.: Valley Publishers, 1976), 1.
[5] A. W. Rawson Diary, Bancroft Library, University of California, Berkeley, California.

Others were not quite so charmed. Georgiana Kirby, in an 1852 diary entry, noted that "there were but few families, and those of the roughest sort. The Imuses, Hecoxes, Bennetts, Hollenbecks, Anthonys, Moores, and such as had not parted with their neat Yankee habits in housekeeping . . . there was no person, with the exception of Mrs. Sawin, whose manners and habits of living approached the lady-like."[6]

But Harry must have been impressed. It was an idyllic setting, isolated, yet with neighbors within riding distance and the village of Santa Cruz on the seashore a few miles south. In looking over the country he rode up the San Lorenzo River and stopped at the Bennett mill. Jack Bennett was probably still working there, but was discouraged about the lumber business. He had lost the mill and 160 acres in late 1851, when the sheriff had sold it to pay a $100 debt; apparently Mary had loaned him money before and now refused to help him again. Young Bennett must have been furious when the property was immediately sold to Thomas Byrd for $4,210. In early September 1853 the mill was again sold, this time to Charles P. Stevenson for $1,600.

It must have been one of those serendipitous moments. Bennett was weary of being tied down and confided that Stevenson was looking for a buyer. After roaming with his family all his life, Jack was again beginning to feel that vague stirring he knew so well.

The mill was situated on 320 acres, bounded by Mary Bennett's property on the north, Graham on the south, and on the east and west by more public land. Harry decided quickly to buy the place.[7]

At this time Love met Mary Bennett. The attraction must have been mutual, but in a practical rather than physical sense—both were large, unattractive people, but had qualities or assets that could be useful to each other. As the two rode around the property, Mary undoubtedly had immediate thoughts of corralling the big frontiersman. Harry was famous throughout the state as a Texas border hero and the conqueror of Murrieta. A strapping six-footer, he was everything Mary's previous husband was not—a strong, successful, no-nonsense type who could protect a woman and her family in this rough-edged pioneer country. Plus, she

---

[6] *The Journal of Georgiana Bruce Kirby, 1852–1860* (Santa Cruz, Calif.: Santa Cruz Historical Trust, 1987), 194.

[7] Charlene Detlefs, *Brief History of the Falls/Love Creek*, 5–7. The transactions are also recorded in "Books 1 and 2, Deeds," 1851–53, Santa Cruz County, California. A search of available deed transactions, however, disclosed no record of Love buying the Bennett mill.

A scene in the San Lorenzo Valley, California, showing the river and stands of pine trees i the area where Love's sawmill was located. Lawrence & Houseworth photograph, ca. 1866. *California State Library.*

needed a man to represent her in a male-dominated society. She had managed both Dennis's and Vardamon's estates and, according to Winston, ran them into debt through poor management. She was constantly involved in land deals, squatter troubles, and legal squabbles in a time when women were not taken seriously in such matters. She needed a strong man to intimidate the courts, judges, squatters, and lawyers with whom she was continually involved. In Harry Love she must have seen a man who could handle all her problems.

To Harry, the woman could only have represented stability in a frontier environment where American women were still a considered minority. Mary was large, tough, and a hard worker who was always on the move. She could be quite charming when necessary—friendly and fond of joking when it suited her purposes. Better still, she owned property. Besides her farm in the Zayante Valley, she owned various plots of land in the Santa Cruz area and was a claimant to the large Santa Clara County grant of her late husband. They must have grinned broadly at each other when they decided to marry. The world was their oyster; Harry was going to have a home. His world would no longer be the pitching deck of a ship, the cramped quarters of a keelboat, or the back of a half-wild mustang. Here, in the beautiful redwood forests of the Zayante Valley, he would sink his roots at last.

Returning to Sacramento, Harry lobbied for his relief bill in April and May, then returned to the coast. With some of Mary's children in attendance, they were married in Monterey on May 31, 1854.[8] There was no time to spend together since Harry had made previous plans; he caught the coastal steamer at Monterey for San Francisco.

• • •

It is not known just what Love's business in the East was, but on June 2 he boarded the *Yankee Blade*, which plied the coast between San Francisco and Panama. When the steamer returned the following month, the San Francisco *Alta California* reported a bizarre story:

> RUMORED SHOOTING OF MR. BINGHAM.—A singular report is brought by some of the passengers of the YANKEE BLADE in relation to the shooting of C. E. Bingham at Aspinwall. On the passage down, it is stated the passengers took offence at the relations existing between Mr. Bingham and Mrs. Woodward (Miss Susan Denin,) and that at Aspinwall a committee of seven of the passengers was chosen and that each one was furnished with a pistol, only one of which was loaded. They were then blindfolded and all fired at Bingham, who fell dead. This singular story is not fully confirmed, but we think there is no doubt from the statements of the passengers by the YANKEE BLADE, that Bingham was shot. It is further said that Capt. Harry Love was one of the committee.[9]

The *Alta* could be expected to denigrate Love as an anti-Bigler device, but, actually, about the only true statement in the report was that Bingham had indeed been shot after a flagrant relationship with the married Miss Denin. Little by little the true story emerged, beginning with a report in the Sacramento *Daily Union* of July 6:

> CONTRADICTED.—The S.F. "Sun," on the authority of Capt. Harry Love, not only denies the statement that he was concerned in the shooting of

---
[8]Church of Jesus Christ of Latter Day Saints, Monterey Stake, Genealogical Society, Seaside, California, microfilm. [9]San Francisco *Daily Alta California*, July 3, 1854.

C. E. Bingham, but states that he was on terms of friendship with the deceased, and actually saved him from violent treatment on the downward passage of the ship.

Since Harry was in the East by this time, this latter story was obviously obtained from a friend of Love who had returned to San Francisco. In succeeding weeks the whole story was pieced together, a timeless scenario in which Love had played a minor role.

• • •

Kate and Susan Denin were two New York actresses who had gone to California early in the gold rush. Susan married New York actor Fletcher Woodward, who accompanied the sisters to the West Coast, where they had done quite well. Woodward and the Denin sisters had recently fulfilled an engagement at San Francisco's American Theater with an actor and stage manager named C. E. "Ned" Bingham.[10]

Bingham had formerly been a theatrical manager in Marysville, where he perhaps assisted Love in exhibiting Joaquín's head. Although rumored to have a wife and family in the East, Bingham lived with a woman in San Francisco, then married one Emily Thorn. When the new bride's father took her away and began looking for Bingham, Ned moved on and took up with the Denin sisters' act. In the course of their performing, Woodward had noticed Bingham's interest in his spouse and became suspicious. Although Susan denied any improprieties, her husband insisted they return home for a visit in the hope that friends and family could dissuade her from any further suspected or real violation of her marriage vows.

Competition on the steamers traveling between the East and West Coasts was quite brisk at this time. The *Yankee Blade*, a new, 2,500-ton coastal steamer operating between San Francisco and Panama, was offering first-class rates at $175 and second-class at $150. Advertised to have all the latest conveniences, the ship was scheduled to clear the port on June 1 on her maiden trip down the coast.[11] When Love boarded, he found the steamer quite crowded and possibly renewed his acquaintance with Bingham during the first few days of the voyage.

---

[10]*Alta*, May 3 and 31, 1854.
[11]Ibid., May 20, 1854, and Donald G. Knight and Eugene D. Wheeler, *Agony and Death on a Gold Rush Steamer* (Ventura, Calif.: Pathfinder Publishing of California, 1990), 39–40.

Diaries, letters, and reminiscences of sea voyages during the 1850s make it plain that the principal entertainment aboard a cramped and crowded steamer was gossip. The ship was the immediate world of the passengers and their time was spent in petty intrigues, criticism, and splintering off into various groups. This must be borne in mind in light of what happened next.[12]

Shortly after leaving port, Woodward was startled to discover Bingham on board. He was even more disturbed after various comments suggested Susan had wheedled Bingham's ticket money out of him (Woodward) just prior to leaving. Passengers reported succeeding events to a New York newspaper later that month:

> Bingham soon put himself on very intimate terms with Susan; so much so that on the facts becoming public on the vessel the passengers were exceedingly indignant, and some of them manifested a disposition to throw the "roue" overboard. A crowd was got together near the bulwark ... and the transgressor would, it is supposed, have soon been missing, had not the Captain observed that something unusual was going on, and went to the scene of disturbance.[13]

After warning Bingham to curtail his behavior, Captain Henry Randall threatened to put him in irons if he did not break off his association with Miss Denin. The captain also promised to bring the matter to the attention of the American consul at Panama. This was apparently the incident where Love aided the captain in preventing any violence against Bingham.[14]

Far from being chastened by the episode, Bingham was shortly after observed walking about the deck with a slim and fashionably-dressed male companion who shied away from close scrutiny. It did not take the irate passengers long to realize that the errant Miss Denin had metamorphized into Bingham's new associate. "Revolvers were exhibited by Bingham during the whole time," noted a newspaper account, "and Mr. Van Alstyne [a passenger] states that Susan was also armed with a revolver."[15]

Disembarking on June 14 at Panama City, Harry and the other *Yankee Blade* passengers were taken ashore by small boats. The town itself was a decaying village of stone houses entirely surrounded by an ancient

---
[12] Oscar Lewis, *Sea Routes to the Gold Fields* (New York: Alfred A. Knopf, Inc., 1949), 48–56.
[13] *Troy* (New York) *Daily Budget*, June 28, 1854.
[14] *Alta*, July 3, 1854; *California Chronicle*, July 4, 1854; and Sacramento *Daily Union*, July 6, 1854.
[15] *Syracuse* (New York) *Standard*, June 25, 1854.

wall. Although a newspaper had been established, there was little indication of any enterprise in the city, travel across the isthmus being the only apparent business being conducted. A traveler commented:

> The people within and without the city have no occupations, no industry ... and everything invites and presages the time when a stronger and more vigourous race will supplant the indolent and degraded tribes with which these regions are now infested.[16]

Love and the other passengers made their own arrangements for travel across the isthmus. After dickering with natives, they mounted mules for the eighteen-mile trip east, to where the railroad was building westward. The weather was hot and humid, with occasional drenching rains making the jungle foliage steam. Soon they were riding along newly-laid railroad tracks where gangs of Jamaicans, Indians, and Chinese were laboring in the oppressive heat. High in the mountains, they boarded the cars for the final leg of the fifty-mile journey to Aspinwall, on the eastern side of the isthmus. The railway journey was a visual delight as the travelers enjoyed a beautiful jungle trip, with none of the hardships of prior years.

At Aspinwall the passengers found a new town, mostly built on stilts in the swamps surrounding the area. It was a deep-water port whose docks, warehouses, and railroad shops belied its true nature. Traveller Oscar Shafter described the town as a "miserable hole" filled with mixed-blood Indians and Negroes who made up with their fine physiques what they lacked in intellect and character. The St. Nicholas hotel, although named after the elegant New York house of the same name, was made up of two smaller structures that had been joined and given a second story. It was due to open soon, but quickly gained a reputation as a place where poor beds were the rule and worse food the custom. The City Hotel was the chief architectural attraction, boasting a dining room capacity of two hundred and a sixty-foot bar. By jamming cots side by side along its outside balconies, five hundred guests could be accommodated.[17]

There are conflicting stories of what happened next in the Denin saga. According to one account, it was generally conceded among the passengers that Bingham would be "taken off in one way or another." Susan had apparently broken from her husband by this time, and she and Bing-

---

[16]Flora Haines Loughead, ed., *Life, Diary and Letters of Oscar Lovell Shafter* (San Francisco: The Blair-Murdock Company, 1915), 42–45.

[17]*New York Herald*, June 24, 1854.

ham had fled Panama while Woodward attended to some business. It was the next day, when Woodward reached Aspinwall, that the situation reached a climax. Susan and her paramour had just left their hotel for the boat landing when a shot rang out. As Susan screamed, Bingham dropped to the ground with a bullet in the back. A nearby physician rushed over and pronounced the wound mortal. Woodward denied any involvement in the shooting, and there was no attempt to arrest him as he boarded the next steamer for New York.[18] Susan reportedly stayed with her badly-wounded lover, who recovered but was crippled for life. Possessing a superficial temperament, she left him after a short time and returned to New York.[19]

In early February 1857 Bingham was back in California and was given a benefit several months later at Marysville. To those who did not know his history, he would remark that he had lost the use of his legs in one of the filibustering expeditions in Central America. He had also lost a wife and two children. The full truth was that after Susan Denin had left him, the crippled Bingham returned to his family and accompanied them to Nicaragua to take up free land offered by filibusterer William Walker. When they were caught up in one of Walker's battles, Mrs. Bingham performed heroic service as a nurse. Both she and the two children died of cholera, after which the distraught and crippled Bingham returned to California.[20]

At Aspinwall, Harry boarded the Vanderbilt steamer *North Star* on June 16 for the second stage of his trip east. The ship arrived in New York on the afternoon of June 23. It was the fastest trip on record up to that time. The *New York Times* reports him on the ship's passenger list as "Captain Harry Love, who captured the renowned robber Joaquin," but oddly did not follow up with an article on the noted frontiersman.[21] It has been speculated Love was in the East seeking a commission in one of the new cavalry regiments then being formed. Perhaps it also provided an excuse for a brief visit home.

In early August Harry left New York on the first leg of his return to

---

[18] *San Francisco Herald*, July 3, 1854; *New York Times*, June 29, 1854; and Sacramento *Union*, August 11, 1854.

[19] *New York Times*, June 29, 1854; *Alta*, July 16, 1854; *New Orleans Delta*, June 22, 1854; and Sacramento *Daily Union*, July 18, 1854.

[20] Bingham's later life is constructed from the *Stockton Daily Argus*, February 12, 1857, and the *Marysville Herald*, April 7, 1857. See also Edmond M. Gagey, *The San Francisco Stage* (New York: Columbia University Press, 1950), 79.   [21] *New York Times*, June 24, 1854.

California.[22] Crossing the isthmus, he again boarded the *Yankee Blade* at Panama on August 18 and entered San Francisco Bay during the evening of August 31.[23]

• • •

There were no newspapers in the Monterey area, and apparently it took some time for news of the Love-Bennett nuptials to become known. On September 16, 1854, the *Columbia Gazette* reported:

> Captain Harry Love, the destroyer of the famous bandit Joaquin, turned Benedict just before his departure for the Atlantic States. He "weakened" to the charms of Miss Mary Bennett, of Santa Clara. Poor fellow, we only hope that some fine day he may not find himself discussing the wisdom of the remark of the elder Weller to his son Samivel, to "beware of the vidders."[24]

It was a sadly prophetic prediction.

Harry must have been glad to return to his new home at the sawmill and set out quickly to learn the business and the location of his markets. Although his own mill was water-powered, there were also several steam mills in the area. He could saw some 2,500 feet of lumber per day, but his production depended on the market and the season of year. Los Angeles and Santa Barbara were the principal markets after local consumption was satisfied, after which San Francisco and the inland towns provided business. He had high hopes for his new career. The lumber business in a fast-growing economy like California's was bound to be rewarding.[25]

---

[22] His return is reflected in the *Yankee Blade* passenger list published in the *California Chronicle*, September 1, 1854.

[23] The beautiful new *Yankee Blade* made one more trip to and from Panama before tragedy struck. Steaming through the Golden Gate on September 30, the ship headed south down the coast and into a heavy fog. Through a navigational error, the ship struck a jagged set of rocks just north of Santa Barbara. With a gaping hole in its bottom and water gushing into the hold, the ship perched precariously on the rocks while a few lifeboats struggled through the high waves to unload passengers on the nearby beach. Some twenty-five passengers were lost before a passing steamer began a rescue operation. The tragedy was made even worse when a gang of stowaway thugs began pillaging the damaged craft, attacking and robbing the passengers. More than $200,000 in treasure was on the lost ship, but much of it was later recovered. Knight and Wheeler, *Agony and Death on a Gold Rush Steamer*, 59–77.

[24] The *Columbia Gazette* marriage notice was furnished by Carlo M. DeFerrari of Sonora.

[25] For an appraisal of the local sawmills and markets, see the *Santa Cruz Sentinel*, April 16, 1859, and Joel W. Coolbaugh, "The Sawmill Era, a History of the Redwood Industry in Santa Cruz County, California," a paper for History 375, 1963, Stanford University, Stanford, California. See also Robert C. Rood, "The Historical and Environmental Impact of the Lumber Industry of the Santa Cruz Mountains," Geography and Environmental Studies Thesis, 1975, University of California at Santa Cruz, Santa Cruz, California.

Still, he learned quickly that there were difficulties. Despite the abundant forests of California, much lumber was being shipped to the new state from the East Coast, keeping the price down. Although there were two sawmills on his own property when Isaac Graham built his home, he had the lumber shipped in from the East. Quality was the main problem. In the primitive and portable California mills, a two-by-four-inch board might be two inches at one end, one inch on the other, and a half-inch in the middle.

Construction lumber was not the sole product of the mills, however. Chestnut oak, which grew extensively in the area, was a principal source of the tanbark used for tanning leather. The wood was then either used for charcoal, firewood, or manufactured into barrel heads and staves, rails, or picket fences.[26] Madrone was converted into charcoal and used in the manufacture of black powder. Large amounts of wood were also used to feed the furnaces of local lime kilns and paper mills.

Workers were no problem. Sawyers were cutting trees to the north and working west from the San Jose area. As they worked out a region or became dissatisfied, they would move on to other territory.

Two men could handle the sawing at a small mill, but the poor roads and trails made hauling difficult. For food and a few trinkets, Indians could be hired to drive the oxen that skidded the logs down from the timber stands. Oxen were much better to use than horses or mules, being stronger, steadier, and easier to handle.

Jack Bennett was apparently roaming again at this time. Mary wanted him to stay, but they could not get along; after selling her a piece of property for $400,[27] he left the following year to join William Walker's filibustering expedition in Nicaragua. There must have been someone helping at Love's mill at this time, for in November Harry was reported supervising the grading of a road from San Jose to the Stanislaus mines.[28]

In October 1854 Harry heard of a strange and brutal incident on the Monterey road. Six or eight Mexicans and Americans stopped at a road house on the Salinas River owned by a black man named Anthony. Anthony and his wife lived with his aged father, a young daughter, and

---

[26] *Santa Cruz Sentinel,* May 13, 1865.
[27] "Book 4, Deeds," July 20, 1854, Santa Cruz County, California. See also the *Santa Cruz Frontier Gazette,* Spring 1958.
[28] Latta, without citing a source, is authority for Love's road grading project. Latta, *Joaquin Murrieta and His Horse Gangs,* 579. Love would later build a road from his sawmill to facilitate taking his lumber to town.

a Portuguese handyman; they apparently made a comfortable living serving travelers from San Jose and the San Joaquín Valley. It was nine o'clock in the evening, and after the riders tied their horses they ordered supper and were promptly served.

Following the meal, Anthony was passing around cigars when he was suddenly seized from behind by one of his "guests." While the innkeeper was being bound, one of the Anglos announced that they were robbers and if Anthony would give up his money no harm would come to them. His wife quickly left the room and returned with some $2,000 just as the bandit leader stepped forward.

"I am Joaquin's brother. I want the world to know that if Joaquin is dead, his brother lives!"

The leader now struck the old man on the head, knocking him senseless. Both the wife and child were struck down, as was Anthony. Announcing the handyman must go with them, the bandits then blew out the lights. Anthony came to his senses first and in the darkness managed to escape, but he had not gone far when the sky lit up behind him. Looking back, he gasped to see the house in flames. In its dispatch, the *San Jose Semi-Weekly Tribune* noted:

> A person who just arrived from the scene of this most horrible and fiendish transaction, states that he saw the charred bodies of Anthony's wife and daughter, his father, and the Portuguese. The Coroner, who went over this morning, has not yet returned—but from him we will probably have more particulars.[29]

Whether this was, in fact, Joaquín's brother or some bandito looking for glory, is not known, but the ambiguous use of Joaquin's name indicates uncertainty in the Mexican community as to the fate of the now-famous bandit. Love could always reiterate that if the Rangers had been kept in service, this type of crime would not be so common, and the *Tribune* would not be complaining about "the frequent occurrence of such foul deeds among us."[30]

From time to time other provocative Murrieta questions would be raised in the press, and Harry would be asked the same old questions in the grogshops of the Zayante Valley and Santa Cruz. There were those who did not want to believe the Rangers had been successful and, although well-aware that political motives invariably prompted such questions, it

---
[29] *San Jose Semi-Weekly Tribune*, October 24, 1854.   [30] Ibid.

still bothered him on occasion. A letter to the *Alta* in March 1855 irked him especially and he was quick to respond:

> Mr. Editor: I observe in your issue of the 24th inst., a letter from San Ramon signed "H.", in which he ["H."] asserts that the "notorious Joaquin Murieta [*sic*] was alive, and had just returned from Sonora with eleven men, well armed, etc., and was going to the upper country to revenge the death of a poor devil called Gregorio Lopez, who, having some slight resemblance to him, had fallen a victim to Love's thirst for the reward offered for his [Murrieta's] head." Now this is to state to the said "H.", whoever he may be, that Harry Love knew Joaquin Murieta, and knows he is dead —which fact is certified to by some of the most reliable men in the State— and that Harry Love never thirsted for the reward offered for Murieta's head, and is ready to answer for his intentions to "H" or anyone else.
>
> Harry Love.[31]

In stating that he "knew" Murrieta, Love can be forgiven being caught up in the moment. He must have been weary indeed, however, due to these naysayers who had plagued the Rangers from the start. The following year, the endless rumors struck even closer to home after a series of organized horse thefts in the nearby Pajaro Valley. The *Santa Cruz Pacific Sentinel* reported in late October 1856:

> The native Californians say that the band is under the direction of the celebrated robber chieftain Joaquin Murietta [*sic*] who has returned from Mexico; we were told yesterday that he had been seen in this county by a man who knew him, and that a partner of his called Pantellon stayed overnight two or three days ago in Watsonville. We have no doubt that Pantellon has been seen in Watsonville and has been in its vicinity for several days; is connected with these horse stealing operations, the natives say he murdered an American a short time [ago] in the mines for the purpose of getting his horses; as to Joaquin, we give the story for what it is worth; it is however proper to state that nearly or quite all of the native population believe that he is still alive, and that he paid a dollar to see the head exhibited as his at San Francisco.[32]

In time Harry was able to shrug his shoulders at such tales. He knew the Mexicans were a proud people and many would never admit that Joaquín had indeed been killed. He had brought back his head, collected

---
[31] The offending *Alta* letter appeared on March 24. Harry's response was printed in the issue of March 28, 1855.
[32] *Sentinel*, October 25, 1856.

affidavits as to its identity, and exhibited it through the areas where he was best-known. There was nothing else he could do.

A series of events connected to the above article indicated how easy it was to confuse Murrieta with the other "Joaquíns" and former gang members who were still at large. Besides engaging in stock theft, a group of bandits pounced on the Las Cruces ranch situated just north of Santa Barbara, as reported in the *Santa Barbara Gazette* of June 17, 1856:

> A party of 6 Mexican desperadoes entered two of the dwelling houses and stole money from each, amounting in all to about $200. In one of the houses two of the accursed gang bound with a strong cord the hands of a widow lady some 60 years of age who resides there, and committed violence upon her person. One Tomas Romero, a resident of the Montecito, who was tarrying at one of the houses was shot in the breast. . . . The ball has been extracted by Dr. Gustavus Milhauss, but it is feared that the wound will prove fatal.

News of the crime was quickly brought to Santa Barbara, along with two account books of a cattle dealer who had passed through the area recently. It was feared the outlaws had also killed him and stolen his stock. Posses were promptly formed, a nine-man sheriff's party being augmented by other ranchers along the road towards the Las Cruces ranch. In a few days, a dusty, weary posse returned with several prisoners. "They brought in two Sonorians [*sic*] . . . ," reported the *Gazette*, "who will be examined before a magistrate today. Another Sonorean [*sic*] named Jesús, against whom there is some evidence, succeeded in making his escape. Being mounted on a fleet horse, he eluded all pursuit."

The two prisoners were none other than Juan Salazar and Joaquín Valenzuela, both former members of Murrieta's old gang. The escaping bandit was conceivably Valenzuela's brother, Jesús. The two suspects were examined before Justice of the Peace V. W. Hearne in Santa Barbara, where Salazar was fully identified as the "scoundrel who bound and choked the old lady" at the Las Cruces ranch. Although the proof against Valenzuela "did not appear to be very clear," both men were jailed to await the next court term.[33]

Valenzuela was apparently acquitted for lack of evidence, but Salazar was tried on August 9, 1856, and sentenced to ten years at San Quentin. But Juan's race was not yet run, as reported in the *Gazette* of August 14:

---

[33] *Santa Barbara Gazette*, June 19, 1856.

PRISONER ESCAPED. Juan Salazar, convicted of rape at the last term of the Court of Sessions . . . affected his escape from jail last evening, during the absence of the sheriff and his deputy. Salazar was assisted in his escape by a party of ten or twelve persons who first made an entrance into the building though the back door of the Sheriff's office, and after a vain attempt to demolish the door opening from this room into the jail, they pushed in the window of the county clerk's office, through which they entered and cut a passageway into the jail. Search was immediately instituted, but nothing can be learned of the whereabouts of the prisoner.[34]

Juan was quickly back in business. When Isaac Williams, a large Los Angeles rancher, lost two fine horses in early October, he and his brother were quickly on the trail. At San Luis Obispo the stolen animals were found in the possession of some Californios who had taken them from a supposed thief. The animals were readily given up to the owners. At Soledad, Williams learned Juan Salazar and a one-eyed man had stolen some horses from a local rancher. Wishing to aid in the pursuit of the rustlers, Williams followed their trail to Watsonville, where a group of vigilantes had discovered the whereabouts of the thieves. It was learned that the outlaws fit the description of Salazar and his one-eyed partner, who were traveling with others of the gang.

Nosing about in the Spanish-speaking community, it was learned that Salazar had a woman he usually stayed with up on the Pajaro River. Williams and a vigilante posse descended on the woman's house about two o'clock in the morning. They caught Juan asleep and quickly had him in custody. Several others were in the room also, and when one broke and ran he was shot, but still made his escape. The *Santa Cruz Sentinel* of November 15 chronicled the closing scenes of Juan Salazar's misspent life:

> On leaving with the prisoner they concluded to take him down to some private house in the valley; whilst on their way thither, they made every pledge for his security if he would tell the whereabouts of his companions, but nothing could they get out of him, and in traveling on whilst near a thick patch of mustard, he made an attempt to break and, being pursued some fifty yards, was shot and killed.[35]

The vigilantes had several other run-ins with outlaws and shot and lynched at least two more in the Pajaro Valley. It was hard justice, but the

---
[34] *Santa Barbara Gazette*, August 14, 1856.
[35] *Sentinel,* November 15, 1859, and the *San Jose Tribune,* November 26, 1856.

papers were constantly recording stock thefts and the ranchers had had enough. The *Sentinel* noted that the coroner's jury on October 20 had found that "We the jury have examined the body of Juan Salazar, and believe he came to his death by being shot by a navy revolver from the hands of some unknown person."[36]

Joaquín Valenzuela had successfully fled the area and was laying low. He obtained work on a southern San Joaquín Valley ranch and must have been startled to learn of the death of Salazar and others in the Pajaro Valley. It seemed a particularly appropriate time to go straight, but then banditry had always been a part-time business.[37]

---

[36] *Santa Cruz Sentinel,* November 8, 1856.

[37] Valenzuela had gone to work for David Alexander, a prominent southern Californian, as will be seen later.

14

Byrnes

Although life was hard in the Zayante Valley, a good sign of progress was the talk of a wagon road over Pacheco Pass.[1] Settlers were taking up land on a steady basis. Neighbors helped each other as needed. Food was seldom a problem, since game abounded in the surrounding mountains and nearly everyone tended a garden and a few fruit trees, raised some chickens and a few hogs, and kept a milk cow. Chores were never-ending, and even the children were kept busy making candles and soap, hoeing the garden, tending stock, or gathering firewood.[2] But the pioneers celebrated hard, too, holidays and weddings always being an excuse for gatherings that might last all night or several days.

When Patty Reed was married on Christmas Day 1856, settlers gathered from miles around. A daughter of James Reed, Martha Jane "Patty" Reed and her family had barely survived the horrors of the Donner party tragedy in the high Sierra during early 1847. Reed was a former San Jose resident who was managing the Rancho Rincon property that adjoined Isaac Graham's land. The wedding was held at a cabin in an area called Hazeldell and, despite the threatening weather, guests arrived steadily all day.[3]

When Harry and Mary Love rode up, there were dozens of children scampering around the cabin, while off to one side an Indian tended a hog and beef being barbecued. The Loves were introduced to Frank Lewis, the

---
[1] Andrew D. Firebaugh was given permission to build a road over Pacheco's Pass by the Merced County Board of Supervisors on February 7, 1856. As work progressed there were sporadic notices in the *Santa Cruz Sentinel* since the road was so important to the area. See Preston, *Andrew and Susan Firebaugh, California Pioneers,* and the *Santa Cruz Pacific Sentinel,* December 18, 1856.
[2] Mussey, *A Book of Country Things,* 72–77.
[3] There is an account of the Reed wedding and information on the Reeds and other pioneers of the area in Tom McHugh, *Hazeldell Charivari, Christmas at Zayante, 1856* (Santa Cruz, Calif.: Penny Press Publishing Company, Inc., 1959).

happy groom, who was a merchant and a San Jose city council member. Mary knew that old Graham, her former son-in-law, would be there and probably studiously ignored him. While the women prepared food and gossiped, the men retired to various sanctuaries and brought out their pipes, cheroots, and jugs of liquor. Later, there was fiddle playing and dancing. The *Sentinel* editor published his eyewitness comments a few days later:

> The wedding was attended by numerous friends of the family—and barring the thoughts of the respected parents, of parting with their accomplished daughter—everything was happiness and glee. Our friend R.K. Vestal was the party selected to administer the justice called for—which he did in good style.... The person who bore off the valuable prize was Mr. Frank Lewis of Santa Clara county, much to the discomfiture of the beaux in this vicinity.[4]

• • •

From time to time Harry would hear news of his old Ranger comrades. George Evans was a neighbor, and they occasionally bumped into each other in Santa Cruz or on the trail.[5] Pat Connor was undersheriff for San Joaquín County and had recently made a run for the office of county clerk.[6] Billy Howard was in law enforcement also, as a deputy sheriff in Mariposa County, where he and his brother still operated their Buena Vista Ranch.[7]

Howard was in the news at this time as a result of a shooting scrape on his ranch. A group of men returning from Kern River stopped and asked the brothers if they might stay a few days in an unoccupied house on the Howard property. They were given permission to do so, but promptly took advantage of the situation, as reported in the *California Chronicle* of May 10, 1855:

> A few days since the occupants were asked to vacate the premises as the owners wanted to make improvements, &c. This they refused to do, stating at the same time that they intended to hold the claim. Capt. Howard told Mr. Champlain [Chamberlain], one of the occupants, that he would let him have a horse to go to Mariposa and satisfy himself that the land

---

[4] *Sentinel,* December 27, 1856.
[5] George Evans is listed on the delinquent tax list in the *Sentinel,* January 3, 1857. The following month he is reported taking the census for the county's school children.
[6] *San Joaquin Republican,* August 4, 1853.
[7] William Howard was at various times a rancher, Snelling stable owner, deputy sheriff, lawyer, and district attorney. See the *Fresno Morning Republican,* January 6, 1924.

in dispute was recorded, surveyed and paid for; and that if he did not find the title to the property good, he could get free possession. But nothing would do; he had possession of the house and intended to keep it. Capt. Howard then remarked to him that both parties could not live in the same house; at which time Champlain grabbed his pistol and attempted to rise and draw. The Captain fired at Champlain and killed him instantly. He immediately gave himself up to the civil authorities.

Howard was easily acquitted at a justice court hearing, and was no doubt disturbed that he was forced to kill a man resulting from an act of kindness on his part.

Love may have also heard that Bill Byrnes had recently taken up residence across the bay in Monterey. In late 1853 Byrnes had parlayed his Ranger service into a job as a guard at the new state prison at Point San Quentin, above San Francisco. He stayed with it for a little over a year, but at that early date neither the prisoners or the keepers wore uniforms, and guards frequently felt no better off than their wards.[8] Byrnes claimed some land nearby and built a cabin, but he was drinking hard also and may have left after various official investigations in early 1855.

This same year, Byrnes appeared in Monterey, where he married a woman named Marion Ross.[9] Looking about for a job to support his new bride, Byrnes obtained a position as the bodyguard of wealthy landowner Lewis F. Belcher, known as "The Big Eagle of Monterey."[10] Belcher wielded much influence in Monterey and Santa Clara Counties and, in assuming his protection, Byrnes would play a part in one of the most bitter feuds of the American West.

Love and other residents of the area were well aware of the origins of the Roach-Belcher troubles.[11] It had all started on Christmas Eve 1852,

---

[8] Bill Byrnes' stint as a prison guard is documented in various state legislative documents; see *Document No. 25, In Senate [session 1855] Report of Committee Relative to the Condition and Management of the State Prison* (Sacramento: B. B. Redding, State Printer).

[9] *San Francisco Call*, April 3, 1892, and *Fresno Bee*, January 3, 1932. Both articles also mention Byrnes' prison service.

[10] There are various contemporary newspaper notices of Byrnes being employed by Belcher as a bodyguard. See the *Sentinel*, June 28, 1856.

[11] The so-called Roach-Belcher feud was one of the noted vendettas of Pacific Coast history. The feud has been ably chronicled by Paul P. Parker, "The Roach-Belcher Feud," *California Historical Society Quarterly*, March 1950, and in Nita Harrell, *The Sanchez Treasure* (San Juan Bautista, Calif.: San Juan Bautista Historical Publishers, 1975), 30–206. See also Edward McGowan, *San Jose Pioneer*, May 15, 1880, and the *Santa Cruz Surf*, December 31, 1901. The author has gathered material on this feud for many years and is grateful to Santa Cruz historian Phil Reader, who has generously shared his own collections of county history on these events.

when wealthy ranchero José María Sánchez had tried to cross the rain-swollen Pajaro River and drowned. Owning some 30,000 acres of property in the area of San Juan, Sanchez acquired great herds of cattle, sheep, and horses, which he parlayed into a small fortune in the early days of the gold rush. Sanchez' young wife, Encarnación, was left with three children and an estate of some $300,000. Men have died for far less.

Illiterate and ignorant of business affairs, as most Hispanic women were in those days, Encarnación married a young Boston attorney named Thomas Godden, who immediately began dipping into family funds. About the time that he had a gambler friend named Samuel C. Head appointed guardian of the estate, Godden was killed in a steamer explosion on San Francisco Bay.

Head began siphoning off estate funds as soon as was practical. In selling forty barrels of beans, $30,000 in gold dust was found secreted in one of the barrels, indicating Sanchez had used the containers as a bank. This discovery caused another ripple of interest among men determined to acquire control of an estate of such immense wealth.

Eventually caught in his fraudulent practices, Sam Head was convicted in June 1853 of trying to appropriate some $68,000. Encarnación, by this time, was becoming concerned for herself and the six children. Besides being robbed by husbands and administrators, squatters were camping on her lands and rustlers were stealing her cattle. She was particularly concerned with the $80,000 of the estate that had been willed to her children.

When Lewis Belcher recommended his friend Sheriff William Roach as administrator of the Sanchez estate, the widow must have thought her troubles were over. A big, tough Irishman who had come to California with Stevenson's Regiment during the Mexican War, Roach was a political power in Monterey and a terror to lawbreakers. He had many friends, but was uncompromising and avaricious. Appointed administrator by judge Josiah Merritt, Roach resigned his sheriff's post and immediately hauled off the $80,000 in question so as to better protect it.

In June 1853 the widow married again—this time pairing up with a San Juan physician named Henry Sanford, a friend of Lew Belcher. The good doctor soon convinced his bride to let him handle the estate funds. When he conveyed the message to Roach, the ex-lawman demanded an overblown payment for his guardianship. Sanford offered a more reasonable settlement, but Roach turned it down and refused to give up the estate funds until his demands were met. Furthermore, when one of the Sanchez children wanted to get married and asked for her share of the estate, Roach refused on the basis of her not being twenty-one years of age.

It was not long before Sanford and Belcher were accusing Roach of embezzling estate funds, and Belcher and fellow bondsman David Jacks both resigned. When Sanford brought suit against the newly-appointed bondsmen to indemnify the estate, Judge Merritt denied the suit. Belcher and Sanford then hired attorney David S. Terry of Stockton to obtain a change of venue to San Joaquin County, on the grounds that Judge Merritt was taking bribes from Roach.

The case had no sooner been transferred to Stockton when Belcher received word in late February 1855 that Roach had left for Mexico to avoid the Stockton hearing. Ordering Bill Byrnes and several others to pursue the fleeing ex-sheriff, Belcher warned them to kill him only as a last resort. They caught up with the fleeing guardian at San Buenaventura and cornered him in the old mission. Ordering his companions to keep an eye on their quarry, Byrnes quickly rode to Santa Barbara, where he obtained a warrant for the fugitive and the services of Sheriff Russell Heath. Roach was soon staring through the bars of the Stockton County Jail.[12]

The situation quickly went from bad to worse. When ordered by the Stockton court to give up the estate funds he held, Roach refused and was ordered to stay in jail until he complied with the judge's order. Fuming, Roach still refused to reveal the location of the treasure to lawyer Terry. Feeling his home would certainly be searched now, Roach contacted his brother-in-law, Jerry McMahon, and had him take the treasure to a more secure hiding place. Now only McMahon knew where the gold was buried.

McMahon had been disturbed for some time at Sanford and Belcher's criticism of his sister's husband. On March 15, 1855, McMahon caught Dr. Sanford in Monterey's Washington Hotel bar, and the two engaged in a brief shouting match laced with obscenities. When the doctor drew a pistol, someone grabbed his arm and the weapon was discharged harmlessly into the ceiling. McMahon left but soon returned, as reported in a dispatch to the *San Jose Semi-Weekly Tribune*:

---

[12] *San Jose Semi-Weekly Tribune*, April 3, 1855.

Upon entering the room again, he exclaimed, "Where is Dr. Sanford?" and upon perceiving him immediately drew his pistol and fired, the ball taking effect on Sanford, passing through his heart. Dr. Sanford them drew his pistol out and fired at McMahon, his shot also taking effect and penetrating the heart of McMahon. Sanford then started for one door and McMahon for another door. As Sanford passed out, McMahon . . . fired another shot at him, and then dropping his pistol immediately fell. Sanford fell at the same time. . . .

The body of Dr. Sanford was carried away today to be delivered to his wife and friends at his rancho.[13]

The first blood of the feud had now been shed. Bill Roach, languishing in the Stockton jail, finally could stand it no more and told lawyer Terry where he could find the hidden Sanchez funds. Terry had no sooner left for Monterey, however, when Roach offered to share the gold with jailor Franklin Foote if he would release him. Foote agreed to the plan, and the two men rode desperately for the coast. While Roach went into hiding near Monterey, Foote galloped on and beat Terry to the Roach home. It was then Foote learned that the treasure had been re-hidden by Jerry McMahon, and McMahon was dead. No one now knew where the Sanchez gold was hidden.

The feud simmered as the combatants jockeyed for position. Roach stayed hidden and went abroad only when surrounded by bodyguards. Belcher was shot at many times as he traveled between his ranches, but Byrnes and his other guards were able to shield him, and he was never hit. He kept up the pressure to recover the Sanchez funds from Roach's bondsmen, but was able to obtain only a few thousand dollars.

Roach fired his attorney, Pacificus Ord, and hired Isaac Wall, a former Monterey assemblyman and then collector of the port, as his new lawyer. When Wall and a popular shoemaker and ex-constable named Thomas Williamson left Monterey with a pack animal on the afternoon of November 6, 1855, it was assumed by some they were taking money to Roach at his hiding place.

Wall and Williamson's bodies were discovered late the next morning, some twenty-five miles south of town on the Buena Esperanza Rancho. Both had been shot through the back of the head, lassoed, and dragged over the side of a ravine. Their equipment was scattered over a wide area, indicating a search had been made for money, but $1,000 in a money belt

---
[13] *San Jose Semi-Weekly Tribune*, March 20, 1855.

on Wall had been missed by the robbers. Both victims were young men in their thirties and very popular in the community.

A posse was quickly organized by Sheriff John B. Keating, who had obtained a warrant for Anastacio Garcia. The warrant was based on a witness who had overheard the bandits dividing the loot from the killings. The murderers had been alerted by Wall's Indian servant, who was a danger to the gang and later killed by Garcia.[14]

A noted desperado and bandit, Garcia had been involved in the killing of a constable at a Monterey dance hall in 1854. He was a native Californian, about thirty-three years old at this time, six feet tall with swarthy complexion and thick, curly black hair.

Keating, his undersheriff Joaquín de la Torre, Charles Layton, A. C. Beckwith, and several others comprised the posse that rode up to Garcia's thatched adobe home at a place known as El Tucho, some twelve miles from Monterey. It was sometime after four in the morning. The place had a tough reputation and was surrounded by large oak trees, willows, and thick brush. Dismounting, Keating directed de la Torre, Layton, and Beckwith to go to the rear door while he knocked at the front. At the rear, Mrs. Garcia opened the door and told the officers her husband was not at home. Saying they had a warrant, the undersheriff stepped into the dark house, which was only lit by a candle carried by the woman. Suddenly Garcia leaped out from behind his wife's skirts and shot de la Torre dead. Several confederates in the house now began firing through the door at the possemen. Layton went down first with a mortal wound, then Beckwith, both men staggering or crawling off into the darkness. Garcia and his *compañeros* now rushed from the house and into the surrounding thickets, firing from their cover and wounding Sheriff Keating's brother George and a posseman named Coleman. The Monterey *Sentinel* of November 17, 1885, had mixed feelings about the shootout:

> Too much bravery amounts to rashness—the result at any rate shows this much—four men wounded, and we are afraid two of them dangerously. It is a great wonder that half a dozen were not killed, as one of the nine actors of Friday morning's scrimmage informs us that the bullets flew around like cold peas on a hot shovel, or words to that effect; for the balls flew around as quick as a man could snap his fingers.

---

[14] *Sentinel*, November 17, 1855. For details not readily available at the time, see the *Sentinel*, May 12, 1877.

Citizens of Monterey were aghast at what was suspected to be the latest toll of the feud. Posses scattered up the Salinas Valley and the coast, making frantic efforts to track down Garcia and his accomplices, but none could be found.

Meanwhile, unable to remain a widow for long, the widow Sanford married again the following year. George Crane, her new husband, was a handsome attorney from Virginia who promptly began pressing the attack on Roach and his bondsmen, but with little success.

No one knew when the next outburst of violence would take place, but residents of the area waited warily. On the night of June 19, 1856, the Big Eagle of Monterey was drinking at the Washington Hotel bar with lawyer Truman Beeman. He had reportedly sent Byrnes off on an errand, but there was a good crowd on the premises and Belcher took the opportunity to relax. Apparently his other bodyguards were not around, either. What happened next was chronicled in the *Santa Cruz Pacific Sentinel:*

> Mr. Lewis T. Belcher was shot last night at the Washington Hotel, about ten o'clock while talking to a friend at the bar. The shot was fired by an assassin from behind a pillar in the corridor; at the same time the billiard room adjoining the bar was full of people. The shot was no doubt from a revolver and took effect in the abdomen, making a large hole.... Mr. Belcher lingered on until two o'clock this afternoon when he died. He leaves a wife and child.[15]

Before dying Belcher had named Roach and five others as being in on the plot to kill him. "They did not give me a chance," the Big Eagle of Monterey groaned on his death bed, "but shot me down like a dog. They were afraid to meet me face to face. My poor wife and child, God knows how they will fare in this country so full of lawyers and laws and such bad justice." Anastacio Garcia was suspected of being involved in Belcher's death, since he was now thought to be in Roach's employ.

In late October, Garcia was finally located in the south. His wife had been watched, and when she boarded a coastal steamer for Los Angeles she was followed by Tom Clay, a Monterey schoolteacher. Clay observed the rendezvous of Garcia and his wife, then quickly contacted the Los Angeles sheriff's office. A small posse under command of undersheriff W. H. Peterson was promptly in their saddles and took Garcia into custody after intercepting him on the road. The *Los Angeles Star* of October 25 commented:

---

[15] *Pacific Sentinel,* June 28, 1856,

Mr. Peterson rode up to him and asked his name which he at once told. He was then asked for arms when he exhibited a pistol which was taken from him. He again was asked the same question when he produced another six shooter; and on a third demand he drew from his legging a large knife, fourteen or sixteen inches long. Garcia made no resistance, for Mr. Peterson on coming up with him levelled his double-barreled shotgun upon him, whilst Mr. Getman took his weapons.

Garcia was promptly escorted to the northbound steamer *Senator* at San Pedro and returned to Monterey. In December the grand jury brought in five murder indictments against him for the murders of Wall, Williamson, de la Torre, Layton, and the Indian servant of Wall who had tipped off the outlaws. In later years, Garcia's wife confessed her husband had admitted to fourteen murders.

Just what happened next depends on the storyteller. Some said Garcia was a threat to those who knew of his Roach connection, while others claimed word was circulating that friends of the outlaw had vowed to rescue him from his cell. On the morning of February 17, 1857, the jailer made the following entry in the Monterey jail register: "Anastacio Garcia charged with murder found strangled in his cell this morning."[16] Actually, Garcia had been hung to an overhead beam in a jail corridor with his feet tied to a log. His head had been nearly severed from his body.[17]

The terrible feud had burned itself out. It was years later, in early September 1866, that William Roach, whose actions had triggered the tragic feud, was found dead after returning from a local election in Watsonville. His crushed and mangled body was found at the bottom of a roadside well. His old feud enemies were at first blamed for his death, but evidence over the years suggested he had been killed by some Mexican and Indian laborers who resented their treatment at his hands.[18] So far as is known, the treasure that Roach had fought so hard to possess was never located.

Bill Byrnes was among those accompanying the body of Lew Belcher to San Jose for burial on the morning of June 21, 1856.[19] With Belcher's death he was out of a job. Telling his pregnant wife he would be in touch with her when he found another position, he was soon on the move again. As usual, what he was really seeking was adventure.

---

[16] A copy of the Monterey jail register is owned by John Boessenecker, who provided the Garcia entry to the writer.
[17] *Sentinel*, February 28, 1857.
[18] *Watsonville Pajaro Times*, September 8, 1866.
[19] *Sentinel*, June 28, 1856.

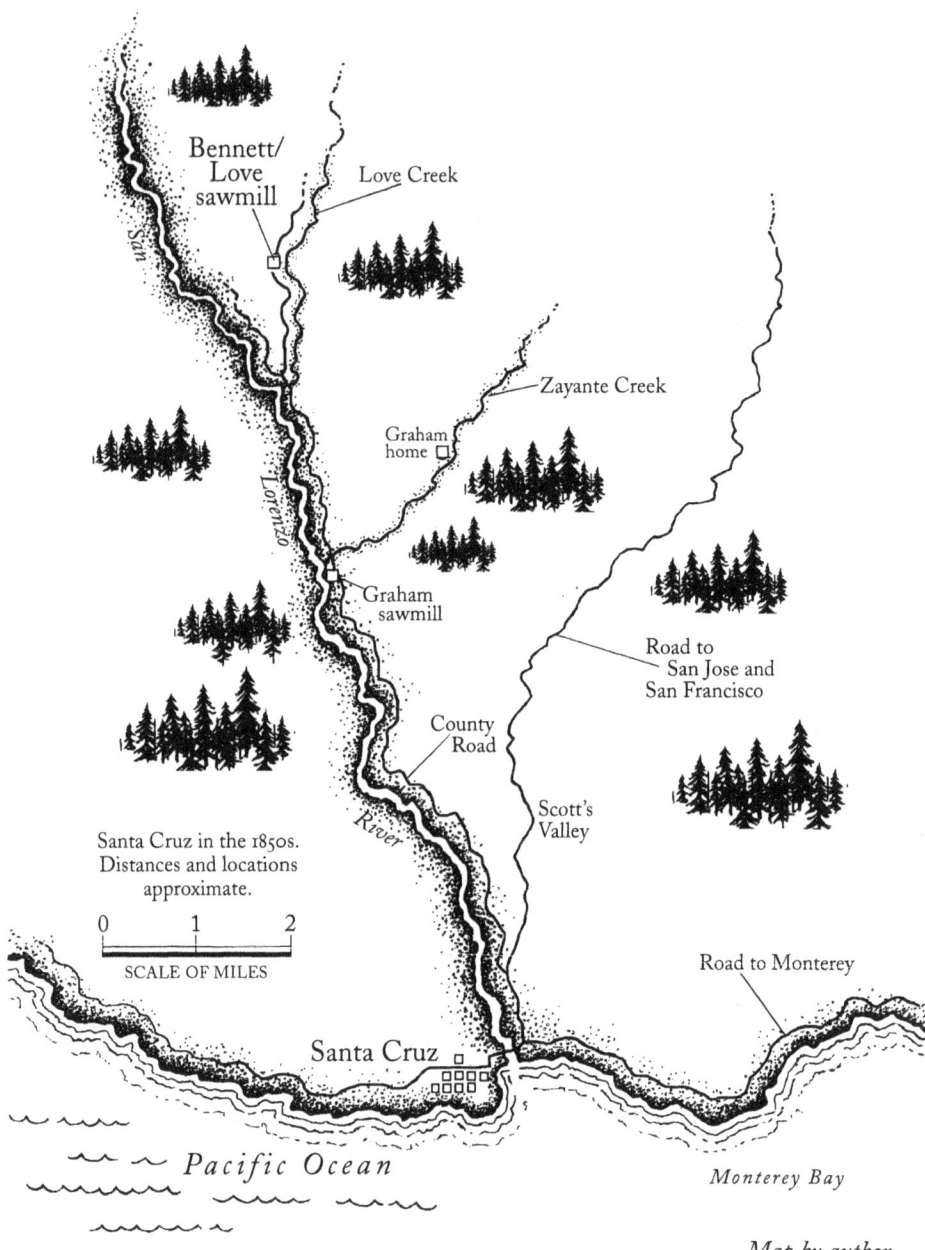

15

The Violent Land

In early 1858, Harry's Ranger comrade Charley Bludworth was a featured player in one of old California's most desperate shootouts. The new county of Merced had been carved out of the western portion of Mariposa County in 1855; Bludworth was one of the commissioners who formed the political entity and was also elected to be its first sheriff.

Snelling, or "Snelling's Ranch" as it was known in the early days, was the county seat of the new county at that time.[1] Four generations of Snellings had come in 1851 to California from Missouri. They purchased property in what was then Mariposa County, including a hotel on the road to the mines. A blacksmith shop and a few other buildings sprouted around the hotel. When the village became the county seat in 1856, a small courthouse was built on property donated by the Snelling family and, in appreciation, the town was named after the family. Benjamin Snelling was its patriarch, and when a post office was established at the hotel in October 1853, his son William was appointed first postmaster. There was a race track near the village, and it was a lively place when crowds of horse owners gathered in the hotel saloon prior to a contest.[2]

Everyone for miles around knew the Snellings, and Bludworth took

---

[1]Charley Bludworth's ranch was near Snelling, and before leaving for his stint with the Rangers, he had given power of attorney to a friend in case anything happened to him. Upon his return, he was leaving a Snelling saloon one night when he was struck from behind and knocked unconscious. Friends came to his aid and he recovered, but he was never quite sure whether his friend was hesitant to relinquish his power of attorney, or whether one of Joaquín's gang had been stalking him that night. Told to the author by Jerry Wilson, husband of Joyce Wilson (who is the great-great-granddaughter of Charles F. Bludworth), on December 23, 1975.

[2]Information on Charles F. Bludworth, the Snelling family, and their namesake town is from a variety of sources: *History of Merced County* (San Francisco: Elliot & Moore, 1881), 86; John Outcalt, *History of Merced County* (Los Angeles: Historic Record Company, 1925), 108–113, 148, 130; correspondence with the late Mrs. Bertha Schroeder, Mariposa County (*continued, next page*)

a romantic interest in William's granddaughter, Frances White. Her brother Ben was also a good friend and probably stood up for him when Charley and Frances were married. Mrs. Bludworth was pregnant with their first child when her world erupted in a cloud of gun smoke in December 1857.

A string of tragic events had been initiated some time before when William C. Edwards and a man named West had engaged in a saloon game called "Crack-a-loo." It was a simple contest whereby two or more men tossed coins at a crack in the floor. The owner of the coin that came closest to the crack won. Suddenly, in the midst of the game, there was an argument and the two men shouted at each other, and then engaged in a brief brawl. Friends interceded, but when Edwards and West left the room they were muttering threats and curses. They were disagreeing over a twenty-five-cent bet![3]

Details of the feud that now simmered are scanty, but West's brother-in-law, William Snelling, voiced his opinion of the confrontation and incurred the wrath of Edwards. Friends of both parties engaged in threats, and on several occasions pistols were drawn. The two groups seemed to be on a collision course, with none of the partisans pausing to point out the trivial disagreement that had sparked the trouble.

A showdown occurred on Saturday evening, December 5, 1857. Both Snelling and Edwards had eaten dinner at the hotel and exchanged dirty looks across the room. Edwards left the room first and was standing in the hotel bar when Snelling got up and walked through the doorway. With a pistol in his hand, Edwards whirled on the postmaster, catching him by surprise. "There's Snelling now," he snarled, "the son-of-a-bitch!" He fired, the bullet ripping into Snelling's side and through his lungs, knocking him into a partition. As his eyes glazed and he slumped to the floor, Snelling pulled his derringer and fired at his attacker. The bullet missed its target as Edwards jumped behind a counter, then rushed out the front door.

Leaping from the porch into the road, the gunman plunged into the arms of sheriff George Turner, who was crossing the street. Turner wrenched the pistol from Edward's hand, but was thrown off balance as the killer scrambled into a nearby thicket, where he quickly disappeared.

(*continued from previous page*) historian, concerning her research on the Snelling family, Schroeder to the author, October 28 and November 4, 1976; and genealogical information also provided by Mrs. Joyce Wilson.

[3] *Mariposa Democrat*, January 28, 1858.

Rancher Charles F. Bludworth was acting second lieutenant of the Rangers, a member of the committee that created Merced County, and the new county's first sheriff. He was also a dangerous gunman when necessary. *Courtesy Jerry and Joyce Wilson.*

In the hotel barroom, William Snelling's horrified family gathered around him. Dr. Jeff Goodin, a local physician and family friend, quickly examined the fallen man, then shook his head. He could not live.

As family and friends tended the dying Snelling, Charley Bludworth and several others quickly began tracking the killer. They were out several days, but had lost the trail. By the time they returned, William Snelling was dead.[4]

Far from recoiling in horror at the tragedy, the feuding parties intensified their threats and promises of vengeance. William Stevens, an Edwards partisan, made talk that he would shoot Bludworth at the first opportunity, but Charley was a family man now and hoped to avoid trouble. When he heard that Stevens and two cronies named Jim Wilcox and E. J. Barclay were in Snelling and still making threats, Bludworth decided he could no longer avoid a showdown. He was going to pick his own time

---

[4]Edwards' shooting of William Snelling is reported in the *Stockton Daily Argus,* December 7, 1857. Articles on the big shootout at Snelling also appeared in *Mariposa Democrat,* January 28, 1858, the *Stockton Daily Argus,* January 29, and the *San Francisco Daily Alta California,* January 27, 1858.

and place, and not be ambushed like his wife's grandfather. Accompanied by Dr. Goodin and brother-in-law Ben White, Charley rode into town, the trio tying their horses across from the courthouse on Saturday afternoon, January 23. What happened next was recounted in the *Stockton Daily Argus* of January 29, 1858:

> On Saturday, Stevens, in company with several friends, came to Snelling[']s and while sitting in the Sheriff's office, Bludworth entered suddenly and addressing Stevens, remarked with an oath that he, Stevens, was the first man who had threatened to kill him, or something to that effect, at the same time drawing a single barrelled pistol and shooting him in the breast. After this, Stevens rose and attempted to draw a revolver—Bludworth clinched with him and drew his, shooting him again. Stevens finally fell dead. While this was going on, a man by the name of Barclay interfered and struck Bludworth with his revolver, the pistol at the same time going off. Upon this, Dr. Goodin, one of Bludworth's friends, drew a revolver and shot Barclay—Barclay fired in return, and was himself finished by a man by the name of White, who shot him and afterwards broke his skull with a pistol. Another of Steven's friends, a boy by the name of Wilcox, shot several times at Goodin, who finally fell, having received five shots. Stevens and Barclay died immediately—Goodin lived about four hours.

Bludworth and Ben White had come through the fight untouched by bullets, although nearly forty rounds were reportedly fired in a few seconds. They immediately turned themselves over to the shaken sheriff, who had been present during the whole scrap. After an examination before Justice Webster, the two men were held to $2,000 bail.

Dr. Goodin's death was particularly tragic, as he was quite popular and had a large circle of friends. Clarissa, William Snelling's widow, had the uncomfortable task of writing to Dr. Goodin's wife back in Missouri. After describing events leading up to the tragedy, she tried to console one who had lost a husband in a senseless quarrel in a faraway and lawless land:

> Merriposa City, California, January 30, 1858
> ... I know it will be a great shock to you to hear of the Dr.['s] death. I can deeply simpathize [*sic*] with you in your bereavment [*sic*]. Just seven weeks before the Dr.['s] death my dear husband was killed by the same party. The Dr. stood over him until he died. He died with his arms around the Dr.['s] neck for he loved him as a brother. He had bin a brother to me since Mr. Snelling[']s death. . . . I will send you one of his curly locks. I cut it off with my own hands. I thought perhaps it would be some com-

fort to you to gaze once more on the locks of him that was once so dear to you. It seems indeed hard to have a companion murdered by such savage hearted men as to be left to tread the rough path of this unfriendly world alone. . . .

Clarissa Snelling[5]

Edwards, meanwhile, had disappeared completely. A $1,500 reward was offered by the Masons—both Snelling and Dr. Goodin being prominent members of the fraternity. A report said he been arrested in San Jose, but it turned out to be erroneous. Actually, he had made his way over the mountains to the Carson Valley area in what would later be Nevada. He sought out a local rancher and gambler named Lucky Bill Thorington, who had a reputation for helping people in trouble. Thorington aided the fugitive, but when Edwards killed a Honey Lake cattleman to obtain possession of his stock, Lucky Bill also became linked to the crime.[6] Thorington's son was sent to Merced County to collect a debt owed Edwards, and it was not long before Bludworth and his friends learned of the fugitive's whereabouts. On June 26, 1858, the *San Andreas Independent* reported:

> EDWARDS, THE MURDERER—We learn that a party, consisting of 3 persons, well armed, have gone over to Carson Valley for Edwards, the murderer of young Snelling. The party (consisting of messrs, Bludworth, Gooden [*sic*] and Stevens) are friends and relatives of the murdered man and they are determined to bring the body of Edwards back to California with them, dead or alive.

But they were too late. Lucky Bill had been hanged by vigilantes on June 19, while Edwards had been taken to Honey Lake Valley where he, too, was strung up. A supposed accomplice of Edwards was also lynched by the Honey Lake vigilantes, making in all seven victims of that deadly chain of events originating with a game of Crack-a-loo and a twenty-five-cent wager!

Tried and acquitted for the Stevens killing, Charley Bludworth went on to a prominent career in Merced County. Although defeated in another run for sheriff in May 1865, he was elected constable the following September. He died on December 7, 1869, survived by his wife and four children.

---

[5] Clarissa Snelling's letter is courtesy of Charles Merrill.
[6] Michael J. Makley, *The Hanging of Lucky Bill* (Woodfords, Calif.: Eastern Sierra Press, 1993), 64–70. For contemporary accounts see the *Alta*, July 4, 1858, and the *Placerville Mountain Democrat*, June 26 and July 3, 1858.

• • •

Harry had, meanwhile, been forced to conclude that his sawmill was not the guaranteed investment he had thought it to be. There were few decent roads in the area, and hauling lumber from his mill was a difficult job. He finally had to build a road known as the "Harry Love Grade" along the San Lorenzo River to more easily transport his lumber to market.[7] In addition, as the timber stands were worked out, the skid roads to take the logs to the mill needed to be extended further and further. Even more challenging was the competition of the many other sawmills in the area. Isaac Graham had two mills in the valley, and there were many others, including those at Pescadero, Williams' mill at Butano, another at Rincon, two on Branciforte Creek, and two others at Soquel.[8]

During this period Harry and his wife were dealing in property, both in paying debts and acquisitions. Mary had power of attorney over her son Dennis's six acres near town, and in October 1854 it was sold for $600 to attorney B. C. Whiting. The property was some fifteen miles from their own claims and jointly owned by Harry, Mary, Jack Bennett, and Mr. and Mrs. G. C. Shelby. Although Harry's name was used in titling the deed, he probably had little to do with the transaction. When notary D. G. Gregory recorded the document, he noted that Mary acknowledged "in an examination separate and apart from and without the hearing of her husband that she executed the same freely, and voluntarily in her own right and as the attorney in fact" for the parties involved. This was the legal custom of the time to prevent husbands from pressuring their wives. Perhaps interested in the property's invesment value, Harry bought it back in September 1855 for $100 less than its previous price.[9]

The Loves were in Santa Clara in mid-May 1856 when they heard of exciting events in San Francisco. A vigilance committee organized in the bay city during 1851 hanged several criminals and chased others out of town. Things were calm for a time, but for the past few years there had been outrageous election frauds, a burgeoning crime rate, and complaints concerning the local courts. When gambler Charles Cora shot and killed the U.S. marshal in the city in November 1855, there was a tremendous

---

[7]Detlefs, *Brief History of the Falls/Love Creek*.   [8]*Santa Cruz Pacific Sentinel*, April 16, 1959.
[9]The Whiting sale is recorded in *Volume 2, Deeds, 1854, Santa Cruz County, California*. The re-sale to Love is in *Volume 3, Deeds, 1855, Santa Cruz County, California*.

outcry. On May 14, 1856, a sleazy politician named James P. Casey shot a local newspaper editor who had threatened to publish Casey's New York prison record. It was the final straw. Under their 1851 leader, William T. Coleman, the vigilantes again organized in droves and took over the city.

Harry had been working hard and was probably grateful for an excuse to go to the city. And he smelled excitement. It is not known if he went to San Francisco as a spectator or participant but, after talking to friends and getting caught up in the excitement, he found himself enlisting in Bailie Peyton's regiment of vigilantes.[10]

There is no date on Harry's enlistment paper, but he may have been among the huge force which took Casey and Cora from the county jail, trying and hanging them on May 22. Two more criminals were hanged and many banished before the committee voluntarily disbanded. Harry rode at the head of a cavalry company in a final vigilante parade on August 18, 1856.[11] Love had briefly returned home before this, since he and his stepson Mansel Bennett sold two lots in Santa Cruz to Francis R. Brady for $100 in July 1856.[12] Earlier, in November 1855, Harry and Mary had sold a piece of coastal property to Mansel for $5,000. Mary acquired this property before her marriage.[13]

In December 1856 Love decided to lease his mill to Mowry W. Smith for $2,400 per year so he could concentrate on farming.[14] Besides some forty acres of hay, Harry was raising corn and other crops now and felt more comfortable letting someone else worry about keeping the mill busy.

In all of these dealings, Harry noticed his wife was very manipulative and controlling. He had expected to share in her property holdings, but although she agreed to her husband being appointed guardian of her children, she always insisted on sole control of her property. At the same time, she expected Harry to manage the lawyers in her various legal affairs and

---

[10]Love's application for enrollment in the vigilantes is in the Huntington Library, San Marino, California; William P. Frank, Curator Hispanic, Cartographic and Western Manuscripts, to the author, February 19, 1997.

For treatments of the 1856 San Francisco vigilantes, see Robert M. Senkewicz, S.J., *Vigilantes in Gold Rush San Francisco* (Stanford, Calif.: Stanford University Press, 1985); Hubert Howe Bancroft, *Popular Tribunals, Vol. II* (San Francisco: The History Company, Publishers, 1887); and Doyce B. Nunis, Jr., ed., *The San Francisco Vigilance Committee of 1856, Three Views* (Los Angeles: The Los Angeles Westerners, 1971).   [11]San Francisco *Daily Herald*, August 19, 1856.

[12]The Brady sale is recorded in *Volume 3, Deeds, 1856, Santa Cruz County, California.*

[13]The Mansel Bennett transaction is in *Volume 3, Deeds, 1855, Santa Cruz County, California.*

[14]The leasing of Love's mill to Mowry Smith is recorded in *Volume 3, Deeds, 1856, Santa Cruz County, California.*

dealings with squatters.[15] As he tried to dismiss these concerns, he gradually realized just how little he had known of this woman at the time of their marriage. He had always got along with women quite well at a distance, but he knew now that he was a neophyte when it came to a close relationship. Throwing himself into his work, he could only hope time would smooth out this situation.

One day Mary received word that Jack had died in Nicaragua of yellow fever. Harry had liked Jackson, and it was hard to think of him buried in a jungle grave so far away. Winston was seldom around, but he had gotten to know step-sons Jack and Mansel and knew his wife must be terribly upset over her son's death, particularly since they had quarreled before he left. Harry handled the probate matters with their San Francisco lawyer, as evidenced by the following letter:

> Santa Cruz, May 24, 1858
>
> Gen. [John] Wilson
> Dear Sir: I send inclosed ten dollars to file the papers in the case of D.J. Bennett. Mr. Porter has been appointed administrator. He will send you the papers this week. You must do what you think best in the matter. If we can't get the law, the thousand dollars will be very acceptable. Mrs. Love sends her respects to you and family. We will come to the city in July.
> Yours Truly, Harry Love[16]

• • •

Harry enjoyed the hunting and fishing in his area, and when a party of Santa Clara sportsmen came over for a day of relaxation on the banks of the San Lorenzo River, they found more sport than they bargained for. While fishing about six miles above the Love mill, their sport was rudely interrupted by the sudden appearance of a large grizzly bear. The party's rout seemed to amuse the *Sentinel* editor mightily:

> We would not be understood to say that they took to flight, they merely affected a masterly retreat at a rate of running that would be called swift,

---

[15]Mabel Dorn Early, a great-granddaughter of Mary Bennett Love, told Frank Latta that Mary was always used to running her own business and family and "she objected to Mr. Love having anything to say about either." See Latta, *Joaquin Murrieta and His Horse Gangs*, 301–304. This is underscored by the fact that Mary frequently signed documents with "Mary Bennett" instead of "Mary Love." She would also sometimes add "formerly Mary Bennett" beneath her signature. Mary was illiterate, but would dictate her signatures be written in this way.

[16]The letter concerning David Jackson Bennett's estate is in the Bancroft Library, University of California, Berkeley, California.

and which, being up hill, was considered inconvenient. His royal highness pursued the even tenor of his way, curious to investigate the cause of the intrusion in his dominion. He finally retired. . . . Bears and trout are said to be plenty up on the San Lorenzo.[17]

In April 1858 two Frenchmen named Bartolo Baratie and M. Borel assumed ownership of the San Juan Capistrano Ranch, some forty miles east of San Luis Obispo. It was a lonely locale—and dangerous. For years the coastal stretches of El Camino Viejo connecting the old missions had been a bandit's paradise. Walter Murray, a San Luis Obispo resident, wrote in 1858 that "scarcely a month has passed without the disappearance of several travelers or the finding of dead bodies or skeletons on the roads." In late November 1857 two Basque cattle buyers had been murdered while on a cattle-buying trip. When one of the murderers was caught, he was turned loose by a jury of fellow native Californians, infuriating many of the local residents.[18] Artist Henry Miller, traveling the road in 1856, wrote of seeing "part of a human skeleton bound to a tree; part of the bones had fallen to the ground, the flesh had all gone and only some dried skin was remaining. The skull laid on the ground, cleft in two towards the left temple."[19]

A group of native California vaqueros rode up to the Baratie and Borel rancho on May 10, 1858. Claiming to be mustang catchers, the men bought some food and rode away. The next morning the gang returned and murdered both ranchers, ransacking the house and terrorizing Baratie's wife and Mexican servants. Several of the gang took the two servants away with orders to kill them. Instead, they were told to keep quiet and turned loose, apparently the outlaws feeling they would not testify against their own countrymen. It was a bad mistake. Mrs. Baratie was also taken to a place of safety and released.

Rafael Herrada, known as El Huero, was the leader of the gang, the others being Santos Peralta, Miguel Blanco, Desiderio Grijalva, one Luciano, and Froilan Servan. Fleeing the scene of the murders at the San Juan Capistrano Ranch, the killers remembered that they had stopped the previous day at the ranch of Jack Gilkey, who could now tie them to the area of the crime. Riding up to where Gilkey was hoeing in his field,

---

[17] *Sentinel*, June 5, 1858.   [18] *Sentinel*, June 25, 1858.
[19] Henry Miller, *Account of a Tour of the California Missions, 1856: The Journal and Drawings of Henry Miller* (San Francisco: Book Club of California, 1952), 24. Additional material on the murders is reported in the *Sentinel*, May 29, June 25, and July 17, 1858. See also Angel, *History of San Luis Obispo County, California*, 300–301.

the rancher was shot through the head by Grijalva. The murderous bandits then disappeared into the brush-choked countryside.

One of the servants, Ysidro Silvas, gave the alarm at the rancho of Captain David Mallagh. Taken to town and interviewed by the sheriff, Silvas was given a tour around town to see if he could recognize any of the killers. He quickly pointed out Santos Peralta, whose alibi was easily demolished. When Silvas identified some trinkets found on Peralta as being the property of the Baraties, the sheriff knew he had some hard evidence against the killers.

A vigilante group quickly assembled. That night, Peralta was taken from his cell and lynched. The next morning, when word was received that a group of the robbers was hiding near town at the ranchito of an associate of the killers named Pío Linares, the vigilantes rode forth, taking Silvas along with them. El Huero, Blanco, Grijalva, and Servin were identified by Silvas before the outlaws made a hasty getaway.

Back in town, the vigilantes organized two posses to track the killers. Within a month Linares had been killed in a battle with the vigilantes, and Blanco and Grijalva were captured and hanged after a hearing. Luciano was caught when returning to town and confessed to being a participant in the crime. He, too, was quickly lynched.

One of the vigilante groups had struck paydirt of another sort. Checking all likely hiding spots as they headed south, the posse rode into the San Emigdio rancho of David Alexander, located southeast of present-day Bakersfield. Although quite wealthy, Alexander's home was a rough, stuccoed adobe with a crude stone floor and primitive furniture.[20] It was surrounded by the huts and houses of his Indian laborers and *vaqueros*. In speaking with Alexander, the vigilantes learned the notorious Joaquín Valenzuela was a vaquero on the ranch. This was the same Valenzuela who was named by the legislature as one of the five Joaquíns and who had escaped punishment for the Las Cruces ranch rape and robbery. With Alexander protesting vigorously, Valenzuela was seized and hustled back to San Luis Obispo by the posse.

Valenzuela had lately been associated with Jack Powers, the Santa Barbara gambler now being sought as the leader of all these outlaws. His brother, Jesús Valenzuela, was also wanted as one of the bandits. Joaquín

[20]William H. Brewer, *Up and Down California in 1860–1864, The Journal of William H. Brewer* (Berkeley and Los Angeles: University of California Press, 1966), 385–386.

was given the usual hearing in which he was charged with the kidnapping of a young American girl on the San Joaquín River and various other crimes. He stated he had not committed any crimes for the past year and seemed to think this should exonerate him. When told he must die, he asked to dictate several letters, one of which was to David Alexander:

San Luis Obispo, May 21st 1858

Dear Mr. Alexander—
I send you my last farewell in a few hours I will not be any more of this world. Give my last love to my dear wife and I hope I shall see her again in the other world. For what I owe you, you can take what I have got at your place and the balance give to my dear wife and if there is not enough I can not pay you any more. Give my best respects to Don Julian and his wife and to all the people on the rancho also to Miguel and his family in particular to Cessimera and his family—to Dolores and his family. I recommend to you my poor wife. I think I shall confess before I suffer death and I hope you will forgive me everything I have done to you. I am forever yours,
Joaquin (X) Valenzuela[21]

All large and isolated ranches, such as Alexander's San Emigdio, kept a general store for the use of their employees and travelers. It seems clear from Valenzuela's letter that he "owed his soul to the company store," as the song goes. After dictating several other letters, Joaquín was hanged, going quietly to his death. Some were not pleased with this manner of vigilante justice and, knowing little of the background of such distant happenings, *El Clamor Publico*, a Los Angeles Hispanic newspaper, published a blistering diatribe protesting the lynchings:

> Such is justice in this country, where it is pretended that there are laws, rights and liberty! They lie! Here, when they pretend to punish one crime, they commit another greater than the first.
> ... A few days later this rabble, calling itself the PEOPLE, publicly executed in San Luis Obispo an innocent man named Joaquin Valenzuela, commonly known by the nickname Nacamereno. Don David W. Alexander, who just arrived in town, and at whose ranch this poor man was employed, said that he was seized while at work and while among his family and that he had never strayed from his home. Here is another bloody example which will eternally mark the reformers of righteousness and justice in San Luis Obispo.[22]

---

[21] Joaquín Valenzuela's letter is from the originals in Spanish, Vigilante Papers, San Luis Obispo Museum, San Luis Obispo, California.   [22] Los Angeles *El Clamor Publico*, June 5, 1858.

Other papers, closer to the scene and facts, were more tolerant of the lynchings. Harry Love must have smiled grimly when he read the accounts in the *Santa Cruz Pacific Sentinel.* He was undoubtedly convinced that two more of the Joaquíns (Valenzuela and his alias) had paid their dues to society. Perhaps he relived the Joaquín days again while regaling friends with a story he had told a Marysville editor in late 1853:

> We learn from Capt. Harry Love, who is now in our city, that about a year since the somewhat notorious Joaquin Valenzuela, then residing on the Merced River, Mariposa County, was suspected of various illicit practices and driven from his place of refuge by the populace. In his house was found a little American girl about six years of age, light complexion, fair hair and blue eyes, which Joaquin's wife said had been given to them in Marysville some two years before. The girl is represented as being very pretty. She was called Ann, but no other name known. She could not speak English, and has no recollection of her parents. She was taken by the citizens, and on application to the County Judge, John Ruddle, Esq., was appointed her guardian with whom she now resides. She is now well cared for, but it is suggested that perhaps some of our citizens . . . might throw some light upon the matter which would lead to tracing her paternity.[23]

The *Sentinel* report of the lynching was brief and to the point:

> The next day a party of men headed by the sheriff went in pursuit of the murderers, saw them once on a mountain, but lost them again. They returned to town with a Sonorian named Joaquin Valenzuela, alias Joaquin Ocomorenia, one of Joaquin Muriata's [sic] crowd or gang of robbers. A Vigilance Committee was formed instantly. They tried Joaquin, found him guilty of murder, rape and kidnapping an American child on the Merced River some time ago. He was then hanged.[24]

Joaquín Valenzuela had been described by Walter Murray, one of the San Luis Obispo vigilantes, as one who "owes justice a score which fifty lives can never pay. He was hung in full sight of the whole people of San Luis, in broad daylight, by the united voice and assistance of all the respectable men of the county, and died acknowledging his guilt, asking pardon of his friends and warning all malefactors not to tell their secrets . . . thus you lose yourself."[25]

---

[23]Sacramento *Democratic State Journal,* September 16, 1853.
[24]*Sentinel,* May 29, 1858.
[25]*Sentinel,* June 25, 1858.

16

Santa Cruz

A government survey of Santa Clara indicated that much of the town was located on Vardamon (Narciso) Bennett's Spanish land grant, now claimed by Mary.[1] In a lawsuit she had affirmed that the grant had been conveyed to her by her former husband, yet in a prior lawsuit she had testified that the grant had been originally granted to her by the Mexican government in 1845. Records of the grant stated it had been given to "Narciso" Bennett in 1845, but Mary did not hesitate to lie to retain the land. The grant itself consisted of two tracts of land containing numerous renters, which, when patented in 1871, made up just over 358 acres.[2]

When Mary heard the news from Santa Clara, she must have beamed. The claim, noted a newspaper report, "covers most of Santa Clara . . . embracing all the protestant churches, school houses and colleges and, in fact, all the business portions of the town. The citizens have been holding meetings every day since the making of the survey." Harry and his wife caught the first stage for Santa Clara and found large meetings taking place nearly every night. Settlers who for years had assumed they were on government land were now furious at the prospect of losing everything. To solidify their claim, which had earlier been confirmed by the U.S. District Court, the Loves hired one H. S. Washburne to survey their tract, giving him a $200 note in payment.[3]

---

[1] Santa Cruz *Pacific Sentinel,* May 9, 1857.
[2] In Shumway, *California Ranchos,* 98–99, the Bennett grant is noted as being "made in 1845 by Governor Pico in two grants to Narciso Bennett."
[3] In *Charles Maclay v. Harry Love and Mary Love,* 25 California Reports, 367 (July term, 1864), Mary states "in 1845 the Mexican Government granted to the defendant, Mary Love [then Mary Bennett] a tract of land lying in the present county of Santa Clara." Yet in *Shartzer v. Love,* 40 California Reports, 93 (October term, 1870), Mary had testified "that a tract of *(continued, next page)*

Mary must have complained bitterly about the confused state of these old land grants and the mess left by the Mexican government. It would be years before all the titles would be straightened out and, in fact, she would never live to see them settled completely.

Harry was having difficulty leasing his mill and was becoming weary of the steady stream of legal problems engendered by his wife. He did what was necessary, but it all took time and money and was especially distracting during planting and harvesting time. Squatter problems on the Bennett properties produced more legal troubles. In a letter to their lawyer, Mary seemed to indicate that she now considered the mill a part of her holdings, although still excluding Harry from her own real estate ventures:

Santa Cruz, Nov. 30th, 1858

Gen. Wilson

Sir—Mr. Love saw Lidel [?] the other day after you left and he was glad to take a lease of me—So he is now my servant—He says that the other parties have not tried to dispossess him yet—Please remember a Sawyer to run my mill—

Yours, Mary Love[4]

Harry's road from his mill down to town had served its purpose for some years, but now the rutted thoroughfare desperately needed upkeep and repairs. It was little more than a trail, actually, but was getting more and more use as settlers from the north commuted to town. He had built a bridge over the creek to facilitate his and others' travel, but in discussing

---

(*continued from previous page*) land claimed by the defendant Mary Love, as her separate property, it having been conveyed to her by her former husband, Narciso Bennett, to whom it had been originally granted by the Mexican government." Mary never did have a problem with shading the truth.

[4] Mary's letter to her lawyer, John Wilson, is in the John Wilson Collection, the Bancroft Library, University of California, Berkeley, California. "General" John Wilson, a lawyer and Whig politician, came to California from Missouri in 1849. He was appointed as an Indian agent at Salt Lake City and as a naval agent at San Francisco. In San Francisco he practiced law, ran a hotel, and engaged in land speculation. Henry L. Ford married Wilson's daughter Susan on September 1, 1851. Ford had deserted the army in the East in 1842 and fled to California, where he engaged in the Micheltorena campaign and was a member of the Bear Flag party and Frémont's Battalion. He lived in San Jose, Santa Cruz, and San Francisco, engaging in buying and selling stock. Later he was an Indian agent in northern California. His wife and infant son died in 1852, and Ford himself was killed by the accidental discharge of his pistol in July 1860. One wonders if Mary realized her lawyer, John Wilson, was the father-in-law of Henry Ford, the man who had "married" daughter Catherine to Isaac Graham? See Fred B. Rogers, *Bear Flag Lieutenant* (San Francisco: California Historical Society, 1951), 7, 43–53.

the matter with neighbors, it was decided to petition the Board of Supervisors to make it a county road.

On February 6 Harry and his neighbor Otis Ashley presented their petition and signatures to the board of supervisors in Santa Cruz.[5] Both men were appointed road commissioners to aid the surveyors inspecting the road. The proposed new county road would run from Love's mill down the San Lorenzo River, through Ashley's and Isaac Graham's property, to a point where it connected with the San Jose and Santa Cruz road running through Hiram Scott's ranch. They were to report back at the next scheduled supervisor's meeting.

The recent government surveys had caused consternation locally just as in Santa Clara and other parts of the state. On February 26, 1859, a large settlers' meeting had convened at the Santa Cruz courthouse, elected officers, and formed a committee to draft by-laws and regulations for the organization. The serious problems of the local landowners were set forth in a statement issued by William Blackburn, president of the group:

> The late survey as made by the United States Surveyor of course respects none of the boundaries heretofore recognized by all—but in many instances separates a man's house from his improvements and leaves him in a measure homeless. Our object, therefore, is to settle our boundaries amongst ourselves, equitably, and to prevent the unprincipled few, who have been accidentally favored by this survey, from despoiling his neighbor.
>
> ... Three-fourths of the inhabitable part of the county is covered with Spanish grants, outside of which a numerous population have sought places for settlement, and for the last ten years many have improved these locations, and made them their homes. ...
>
> It is asserted by a few, whom this survey favors—that this is a Vigilance movement; but such is not the case, as in nearly all newly settled districts in the Western States, where the inhabitants have been allowed to pre-empt lands, like associations have been formed.[6]

The settler-squatter problems were the cause of much violence throughout the state, but the Santa Cruz pioneers were determined to avoid the shooting confrontations that had bloodied Santa Clara, Sacramento, and other areas. The grant situation was so serious and frustrating that Tulare County, in the San Joaquín Valley, was using their lack of grants as an inducement for settlers. The October 1859 *Visalia Delta* noted:

---

[5] *Pacific Sentinel*, February 11 and March 5, 1859. Notice of the settlers' meeting appeared in the *Sentinel*, March 5, 1859.   [6] Ibid., March 5, 1859.

SPANISH GRANTS—It will be pleasant for those who intend to immigrate to this county to know that there is not a single Spanish Grant located within the boundaries of Tulare County.... Persons who desire to locate and improve permanent homes for their families, can be assured of a good title, that of the United States—no other is known here.[7]

In early March the supervisors adopted Harry's and Otis Ashley's report on the location of the new county road.[8] It was not until November, however, that the road was declared a public highway and that those living along the route were responsible for all repairs and upkeep.

• • •

As isolated as they were, the Santa Cruz pioneers frequently found diversion with traveling entertainers who found their way to the coast. Lecturers, minstrels, ventriloquists, and occasional acting troupes graced the local halls, but in early October 1859 a particularly unusual show was announced in the *Sentinel*:

ELEPHANT AND CIRCUS SHOW.—On Tuesday next the Elephants will visit Santa Cruz. Of course "Young America" will have to be gratified by a sight, and of course "Old America" will have to accompany the children. Afternoon performance at 2 o'clock, for the convenience of families and children.[9]

It was a rare treat. These were the first elephants on the West Coast, and many Californians had never seen such beasts outside the pages of a book. The show promised to be well-attended. When the two elephants, Victoria and Albert, landed at San Francisco in mid-May of that year, they already had had an illustrious and well-travelled career. The two behemoths had been purchased in Ceylon and were taken to the Cape of Good Hope at an early age. After being exhibited in Europe for some years, they were brought to America around 1856, where they toured the East and wintered in New York.[10]

Early in December 1858 Victoria and Albert boarded the ship *Wanderer* at New York and spent the next 159 days at sea. Special cubicles sixteen

---
[7]*Visalia Delta*, October 8, 1859.
[8]The adoption of Love and Ashley's road proposal appeared in the *Sentinel* of November 11, 1859.
[9]*Sentinel*, October 7, 1859.
[10]Information on the history of the animals was obtained from the San Francisco *Daily Alta California* and the San Francisco *Daily Evening Bulletin*, May 18, 1859. See also Stuart Thayer, "The Elephant in America, 1840–1860," *Bandwagon*, September–October 1991. Additional material was provided by the Circus World Museum, Baraboo, Wisconsin. Fred Dahlinger, Jr., director, Library and Research Center, to the author, February 27, 1996.

feet long, nine feet wide, and eight feet tall had been constructed for them, and they managed the long journey with no problems other than some weight loss. In San Francisco the elephants and circus performed under a specially-made canvas tent and had a very successful showing.

Moving south, the caravan of wagons and the two elephants performed at Redwood City and San Jose, then headed towards Sacramento. On the road they overtook an Indian driving an ox team. "The fellow," noted a press account, "hearing them approach, looked behind and seeing the strange-looking animals close at his heels, he became greatly alarmed and 'broke' for the hills leaving his team to care for themselves."[11] The scene must have been repeated endlessly as the show traveled to Placerville and a string of gold camps in the Sierra.

There must have been tremendous excitement as the two elephants crossed through Pacheco Pass and lumbered along the mountain roads toward the coast. There was a show at San Juan Bautista on October 9, one at Watsonville the next day, and then the entourage plodded into the outskirts of Santa Cruz on the 11th. The show cost one dollar, and hundreds showed up for the two and seven o'clock showings.[12] Victoria and Albert were the star performers, but owner John Wilson also headlined two talking ponies, Dashaway, the world's smallest horse, a clown, an Indian rubber man, and a variety of equestrian and other acts. We do not know if Harry and any of his family attended, but they probably did.

For those who could not afford the show, it was nearly as much fun to watch the circus pack up and prepare to leave. As the line of wagons and elephants began their march down the coast, Sheriff John Porter was suddenly reminded that Wilson & Company had failed to obtain a license for their exhibition. The lawman quickly rectified his error, and the procession moved on towards Monterey where they were exhibited for two days. Then, it was on to San Luis Obispo and Los Angeles.

• • •

Although the ranks of the Joaquíns had been thinned by the hanging of Valenzuela, Harry's Ranger veterans had recently been reduced by one also. An early arrival in the area, John Sylvester is mentioned in Mariposa County court records as being appointed a county auctioneer in December 1850. He was conspicuous in the Mariposa Indian War and

---
[11] San Francisco *Daily Evening Bulletin*, June 20, 1859.
[12] The *Sentinel*, October 14, reported large crowds at Watsonville and Santa Cruz.

later ran for sheriff against John Boling. Everyone liked John Sylvester and knew he could be counted on in a tight spot. Harry must have seen one of the many press reports of his death that circulated in late July 1859.

Sylvester had ranch property in Fresno County and was taking some horses south early that month, when he passed through Visalia. He was last seen on a trail near Fort Tejon, but the next day his riderless horse was captured at a nearby ranch. His saddle and blankets were covered with blood, and the commandant at nearby Fort Tejon was quickly notified, as reported in the *Tulare Record and Fresno Examiner* of July 23:

> We learn by the last mail that the body of Mr. John Sylvester, of Fresno County, has been found a short distance from Fort Tejon, and that he was murdered by a native Californian who has been arrested and is now secured in the Los Angeles County jail. Too much credit cannot be given to Col. B.L. Beall, U.S.A. commanding Fort Tejon, for his prompt and energetic action.[13]

Colonel Benjamin L. Beall of the First Dragoons had indeed acted quickly. He dispatched Sergeant Fritz and Private Crowley of Company K to ride to Los Angeles and obtain a civil officer to investigate the disappearance. Returning with Deputy Sheriff Billy Warren, circling buzzards helped the party locate Sylvester's body in a ravine. The rancher had been knifed twice, then dragged with a lariat off the trail. A suspect named José Olivas had been seen riding with Sylvester and had eaten with him at a stage stop. He was promptly arrested and deposited in the Los Angeles County jail. Although circumstantial evidence indicated Olivas was the killer, the case against him was not deemed strong enough, and after a hearing at the November term of court he was released.

Olivas, however, was a bad apple and could not stay out of trouble for long. He was picked up on a horse theft rap and thrown into a cell with Boston Dainwood and three of his gang in 1863, after they had seriously assaulted a Los Angeles police officer. All had long criminal records, and the local citizens were weary of their presence.[14] On the night of November 21, all five were taken from their cells and hanged from beams along the corridor in front of the courthouse.[15]

---

[13] *Tulare Record and Fresno Examiner*, July 16, 1859. See also the *Stockton Daily Argus*, July 26 and 29, 1859.

[14] *Tulare County Record*, September 3 and 10, 1859. See also Clarence Cullimore, *Old Adobes of Forgotten Fort Tejon* (Bakersfield, Calif.: Kern County Historical Society, 1949), 38.

[15] *Los Angeles Star*, November 28, 1863, and the *Visalia Times Delta*, November 26, 1863.

Harry was happiest when the mill was leased and he could hear the saw while he worked on his farm and gardens. The mill had been leased to two men named Farnham and Pope, but in November the partnership was dissolved. Hugo F. Hihn took over the operation as an agent for Harry, continuing to advertise for a lessee.[16] The 1860 Santa Cruz agricultural census showed Love to have 320 acres of improved land with his farm, valued at $3,000.[17] He had $200 worth of machinery, one horse, two cows, twelve oxen, twenty-five hogs, and forty acres in hay. His stock was valued at $800. His net worth did not seem like much, but he was working hard and had a home at last. In early October of the previous year he had stopped by the *Sentinel* office and dropped off one of his garden beauties:

> Capt. H. Love left at this office a raddish [sic], or beet, or something of a vegetable nature, so large that if we can charter the elephants we intend to send it to the Santa Clara Agricultural Fair for the edification of the scientific and curious.[18]

He was spending much time in Santa Clara also, helping with Mary's farm and squatter troubles.[19] Only one of the Bennett children was living with them at this time, twenty-two-year-old Julia. In the 1860 Santa Clara census, Harry combined both his and his wife's property, listing the value of their real estate at $100,000 and personal property at $8,000. Oddly enough, Harry and his family were also listed in the Santa Cruz census that year. His land was valued at $5,000 with personal property at $1,200. Besides Mary, Mansel and Julia Bennett were enumerated as also living on the property.

It was a busy year. In April Winston and Mansel sold two Santa Cruz lots to their mother for $75,[20] while Harry was hauled into court on a perjury charge in early August.[21] He was easily acquitted, but it was time-

---

[16] A display ad in the *Sentinel*, November 29, 1860, announced the dissolution of the Farnham-Pope partnership and Hugo Hihn as the new agent.

[17] The 1860 Santa Cruz County Agricultural Census was obtained from the Ellis Collection, Santa Cruz County Public Library, Santa Cruz, California.   [18] *Sentinel*, October 7, 1859.

[19] Love's listing in the 1860 census for both Santa Cruz and Santa Clara counties indicates he was constantly traveling between the two towns.

[20] The record for the Bennett sons' sale of real estate to their mother is in Volume 5, Deeds, 1860, Santa Cruz County, California.

[21] Santa Cruz County Court of Sessions, Book No. 2, August term, 1860. The existing records are meager and difficult to read to the extent that the cause of the action is obscure. Suffice it to say that he was acquitted. See the *Sentinel*, August 17, 1860.

consuming and aggravating. In December Mary was also in court winning a judgement against S. J. Lynch, probably a Santa Cruz squatter.[22]

In 1860 Mary bought $27 worth of goods from one Charles Maclay, who had acquired the $200 note given to surveyor Washburne in 1857. Since Harry had signed the note also and the property had been acquired prior to her marriage, Mary and her attorney thought they saw a technicality whereby she could avoid the debt. They lost the case, but appealed to the California state supreme court.[23]

This same year, Mary brought another case before the supreme court. In January 1854 she had signed a note promising to pay her lawyers, Wallace and Ryland of San Jose, $500 upon obtaining a judgement of any kind in a then-pending Santa Cruz court case. When the case ended and she did not pay, she was taken to court and lost. She again appealed to the supreme court, which upheld the lower court ruling.[24]

This type of legal scenario seemed to be an increasing pattern of her life. Harry was perhaps particularly annoyed by another of her unscrupulous legal maneuvers, as reported in the San Jose and Santa Cruz presses in August 1861. Mary had engaged a Santa Cruz resident named Thomas B. Hart to locate land claims that she might have an interest in acquiring. In the course of their business dealings, Hart loaned Mary money occasionally, for which he received a contract for land at the time certain surveys were made. Eventually, Mary gave Hart a note for $1,000, but later claimed the note was fraudulent and had him indicted for forgery. It was a bad mistake. Hart was acquitted at his trial, with Mary being stuck with both her lawyer's fees and the $1,000 note. Her growing reputation for such legal shenanigans was alluded to in the *San Jose Mercury:*

> The testimony of witnesses proved the good character of the plaintiff, and that of defendant bad; therefore, we think no candid mind could form any other opinion than that Mr. Hart is an injured and much abused man, and entirely innocent of the charge set forth in the indictment.
>
> Mr. Hart has had the misfortune to be the victim of circumstances. He has been involved in a former suit in which he was indicted by the Grand Jury on the testimony of T.J. Ditmar, for grand larceny, which could not be sustained against him. It is believed by many that it was a concerted movement on the part of Ditmar and Mrs. Love to ruin Mr. Hart by incar-

---

[22] Mary was represented by John Wilson in the Lynch case, *Sentinel*, December 13, 1860.
[23] *Charles Maclay v. Harry Love and Mary Love*, 25 California Reports 367 (July term, 1864).
[24] *Bostic v. Love*, 16 California Reports 69 (July term, 1860).

ceration in prison, thereby making it easier for Mrs. L. to sustain her charge of forgery, and to avoid paying the note, all of which, we are pleased to chronicle, has been happily frustrated.[25]

Land problems continued to be a plague in California throughout the 1850s and 1860s. The Mexican land grants, titles that had been guaranteed by the Treaty of Guadalupe Hidalgo, were riddled with fraud, forgeries, and sloppiness. The California Land Act of 1851 had sought to hasten title hearings by transferring them from Congress to local government, but they remained a hornet's nest of problems. By themselves they were trouble enough, but government public lands were often found to overlap mission, pueblo, and rancho grants. Federal title hearings, local legislation, and court rulings complicated or confounded, rather than settled, the problem. The grants and government land steadily being taken up by settlers were constantly being occupied by squatters, who stubbornly disputed ownership and caused seemingly endless and expensive litigation. Squatter organizations, championed by some newspapers, lawyers, and judges, became quite powerful politically and were soon electing their own candidates.[26] The local *Sentinel* was speaking directly of Harry Love and his neighbors when it wrote:

> In this county, many of our oldest settlers upon the public lands yet unsurveyed, eagerly embraced the opportunity of acquiring homes with a secure title by locating under the Public Land laws. Men who had gone into our mountains, endured for many years the solitude and hardships of such a life, built roads, and, in short, given the country all its civilization, invested their hard-won earnings in the purchase of lands in this manner. This is a matter of common notoriety with us, and no one, who knows what this county was twelve or fifteen years ago, would deny the privations and dangers suffered by these old settlers. Such men knew nothing of the law's intricacies and supposed, as all men did, that their certificate of purchase vested a good title in them. By the very labors of these men, the wilderness was subdued, the forests became filled with homes, and their lands rapidly increased in value.[27]

Yet the courts and Congress still batted these land problems back and forth, and legitimate settlers seldom knew, from day to day, the fate of their property interests. The import of the situation was nowhere more

---
[25]The *San Jose Mercury* comments on the Hart case are reprinted in the *Sentinel*, August 8, 1861.
[26]Paul Gates, "The California Land Act of 1851," *California Historical Quarterly*, December 1971.
[27]*Sentinel*, December 22, 1866.

apparent than in early 1866, when a group of squatters fenced off and built a small house one night on public land set aside for the Santa Cruz County Courthouse. This problem was quickly resolved the next night when a crowd of townspeople met, burned down the squatters' house and fence, and ran them out of town. But the problems were seldom resolved so simply, and squatters became a way of life in frontier California.

Mary had had much trouble with squatters, but Harry was enduring a different set of problems. In early October 1861 he saw smoke billowing up about a mile and a half away from home. Riding toward the smoke, he discovered neighbor James King had set fire to some brush and had lost control of the blaze. Harry and others did what they could to try and contain the fire, but made no headway and soon returned to look after their own property. By October 4, the fire reached Harry's property and destroyed several miles of fencing and some 150 acres of grass. It was another catastrophe Harry did not need.

He took neighbor King to court, suing on charges of setting a fire and destroying his property. Damage was set at $1,500, but the amount must have been considered inflated. When the jury found for the plaintiff, Love won a mere $60 settlement.[28]

He was still also helping Mary with her land problems and in late July of the following year wrote a land commissioner in San Francisco:

> Santa Clara, July 28, 1862 Mr. Williams
> Dear Sir I will come to the citty [sic] tomorrow week with two or three witnesses to give testimony in the Bennitt [sic] clame [sic]. Mrs. Love has notifyed Mr. Gould of the fact alsow. if it is possible I would like to have them comenced the same day so they can come back on the same boat as time is money with farmers at this time.
> If you can take testimony on that day pleas drop me a line.
> Yours Truley, H. Love[29]

The letter, in Harry's miserable handwriting, indicated his concern about taking time away from the farm during harvest. He had stopped advertising his mill for lease in February 1861, but fate was to take the matter out of his hands.

---

[28] *Case No. 364, District Court, 3rd Judicial District, December, 1861.* Santa Cruz County.
[29] *Transcript of the Proceedings in Case No. 260, Isaac Graham, et al, Claimant vs. the U.S. Defendant for the place named "Zayanta."* Library, University of California at Santa Cruz, Santa Cruz, California.

17

Flash Floods and Fierce Fires

Frontier California was a sprawling paradise of forests, plains, and mountains—a seemingly inexhaustible natural empire out of which a rich and ever-growing economy was being established. Although the squatter troubles were one early indication of surfacing problems, there were many others.

By 1861 there had been years of unrestrained lumbering in the San Lorenzo Valley. Paper mills, tanneries, and lime kilns on the outskirts of Santa Cruz required a constant supply of firewood to function, as did the local gunpowder mill, which used local madrone wood to manufacture black powder. The sawmills along the rivers and streams of the valley supplied all this wood, as well as building lumber for a large surrounding area, which included many coastal areas to the south. The chestnut oak was also still being heavily logged for its tanning bark.

Meanwhile, no attempt was being made to replant the clear-cut areas of the forest, while the skid roads down which the oxen hauled the logs became ever longer. These roads, furrowed deeper year by year by the logs and oxen, pointed like great fingers directly to the sawmills—a potential peril which no one, at that early day, could foresee.[1]

In early October 1861 another fire, probably emanating from a hunter's camp, swept along the southwestern rim of the mountains surrounding the San Lorenzo Valley. From Soquel, just south of Santa Cruz, the fire raged some forty miles up the coast. A black pall of smoke hung over the mountains, while at night "the red, glaring light of the fire seen flashing high up in the air . . . presented a view fearfully grand and picturesque."[2]

---

[1] Robert C. Rood, "The Historical Geography and Environmental Impact of the Lumber Industry of the Santa Cruz Mountains," Thesis, double major in Geography and Environmental Studies, May 15, 1975, University of California at Santa Cruz, Santa Cruz, California.
[2] *Pacific Sentinel,* October 10, 1861.

Stage road in the rugged Santa Cruz Mountains.
Harry Love's sawmill was in this beautiful wilderness,
where he thought he had found a home at last.
From Vischer's Pictorial of California, *California State Library.*

Large acreages of timber were destroyed, adding yet another factor to the danger of erosion in the cleared areas.

December 1861 and early January 1862 were characterized by heavy rains throughout California. As the storms continued day after day, the settlers in the valleys watched helplessly as the rivers and streams began to rise. There was extensive flooding in the Sacramento and San Joaquin valleys, and although Santa Cruz and Monterey counties escaped the main storms, the settlers watched uneasily as the creeks ran full. Then, during the week of January 8, a steady, drenching rain engulfed the coastal areas. By late Saturday, January 11, the San Lorenzo River had risen three feet above the previous high-water mark of 1852.

Harry and the other settlers quickly became alarmed at the rising streams and river. Suddenly, flash floods came racing down the streambeds and skid roads, inundating most of the sawmills and sweeping others away. "During the whole of Saturday," noted the *Sentinel*, "the river was filled with drift wood, timber and lumber, and frequently immense redwood trees which had been washed out by the roots, would be seen speeding down the current."[3] Several complete barns were observed cascading down the swollen river, one actually being washed out to sea. Agricultural and property damage in the area was immense.

Below the valley, the town of Santa Cruz and surrounding villages were partially flooded also as the raging waters washed out all the dams on the river. Residents worked desperately to re-channel the river as it gobbled up property, and hastily cut a new channel closer to town, but to no avail. After several weeks of persistent storms, the rains let up, the weather alternating between a few days of bright, crisp sunlight and snow in the mountains. The settlers and industries located in Harry's valley had been hit especially hard. At the end of the month, the *Sentinel* listed some of the damages in and around town:

> On the river above town damage to a large amount was done—Duncan & Warren's tannery is a total loss, and cannot be set down at a less figure than $20,000. The paper mill, in the loss of dam, flume and out buildings, and the material injury to the mill and machinery, will be $10,000 or $15,000. Graham's, Hicks', Love's and Bryant's saw mills were all swept off, as well as every dam on the river. Miller's saw mill was damaged. McPherson's saw mill and dam were injured to a considerable extent.[4]

Harry's sawmill was gone. It had been located high above the river, but the torrent that cascaded down Love's Creek swept everything before it. It is not known if anyone immediately figured out the logistics of just what had happened. It was fate—one of Mother Nature's cruel pranks. Just how much other property he lost is not known.

It is possible that he was relieved in a grim sort of way. Although he had invested everything he had in the mill, it had never been the money-making project he had envisioned. Having the mill on the tax rolls while it was inactive half the time was hardly worth it, and lease advertisements in the local press added to his costs. The good news was that he could now forget the mill and concentrate on farming. In any case, the farm was all he had now.

---

[3] *Pacific Sentinel*, December 12, 1861, and January 17 and January 30, 1862.
[4] Ibid., January 30, 1862.

By mid-February the stages to San Jose and Watsonville had resumed their schedules, and the rebuilding of the area was well under way.[5]

Harry threw himself into his farmwork, cutting firewood and tanbark oak for the mills as extra income. He never had to really worry about his family, however. As the years went by Mary paid little attention to her husband's farming efforts, and probably somehow blamed him for the loss of the sawmill. She hated living in the mountains and finally refused to do so, dashing Harry's hopes for a normal family life. He did what he could to avoid arguments, taking her on visits to the McCuster farm near Watsonville to see her daughter and grandchildren. But nothing seemed to help. More and more she took care of herself, and finally she just stayed in Santa Clara, looking after her property interests.

Valley residents received word that Isaac Graham had passed away in November 1863. His health problems, brought on by a life of frontier excesses, had reached a point where he sought medical treatment in San Francisco. It was too late, however, and he died on November 8. "He had a powerful frame," commented the November 14, 1863, *Sentinel*, "a persuasive address, an unerring eye with the rifle, and that daring which is always a concomitant of strength and power. He was of litigious spirit and in his prime had both friends and enemies, but his last years of childlike age had pacified all enmities and he left none but friends behind him." Mary Love had probably sneered at that last comment.

In May 1864 Harry was dealt another harsh blow as reported in the *Sentinel*:

> INCENDIARISM—The dwelling and tool house of Capt. Harry Love who lives in the San Lorenzo Valley about seven miles from town were burned to the ground on Thursday night. Capt. Love is sure that the fire was the work of an incendiary, as it originated in a tool house, several feet from his dwelling house, in which there had been no fire for some time. The entire contents of the two buildings were also burned and Capt. Love himself narrowly escaped.[6]

It was a terrible blow. He was living alone at this time, and, after salvaging what he could, friends helped put up a new cabin. His crops had been harvested and a few months later he was back busily tending his garden and hay fields.

---

[5]Stagecoach travel between Santa Cruz, San Jose, and Watsonville was reported restored in the *Sentinel*, February 20, 1862.   [6]*Sentinel*, May 14, 1864.

The following year Harry was asked to ride in the annual Fourth of July parade in Santa Cruz. He was fifty-five years old at this time and, although careless in his dress, he was a commanding figure as he rode about town on visits and errands. There were few streaks of grey in his beard and locals often referred to him as the "Black Knight of the Zayante," after the Walter Scott character.[7] Riding in the parade must have been a much-needed ego boost, and he put on his best clothes. The *Pajaro Times* described him as a "tall, manly figure, with sparkling eyes, long curling hair falling far down his shoulders, with his knightly sword hanging by his side."[8] The sword had been presented to him by a Mexican gentleman whom he had rescued in the mountains during his Texas days.

Harry was pretty much back to normal in November 1865, when the *Sentinel* published the following notice:

> TALL CORN—We have been shown a sample cornstalk, fourteen feet high, Yellow Dent variety, a fair sample of a 25 acre field, raised by Harry Love, on the San Lorenzo bottom seven miles from Santa Cruz, which almost surpasses belief in thrift and yield. The aforesaid cornstalk, on last election day, afforded the "Black Knight of the Seyante" [*sic*] a ponderous flagstaff with which he marched to polls and deposited his democratic vote, in true Jacksonian style, for Henry Hare Hartley, well knowing his candidate to be true, in word and deed, to the platform on which he stood. The crop of corn was planted on the 11th of May, in full ear by the first of August and now all ripe and housed. The sample cornstalk can be seen at Plumb's Sample Rooms, Elliott's Wholesale Liquor Store, Main street.[9]

In January 1866 B. F. Watkins, a squatter on a corner of Mary's land grant in Santa Clara, responded to Mary's suit of ejectment. The case had been dragging on for years and illustrated the convoluted legal problems that undoubtedly fueled the Loves' personal difficulties. Mary had acquired her title in April 1854, just prior to her marriage to Harry Love. The following November, both she and Harry had signed a note to pay the legal firm of Howard and Perley one-tenth of the land if they would prosecute their land claim before the United States Land Commission.

Watkins squatted on the property in January 1855, claiming some twelve and one-half acres. Mary was furious, but since her claim had not been confirmed yet, there was little she could do. This may have been an early

---
[7] Just who applied the title "Black Knight of the Zayante" to Harry is not known.
[8] Bancroft, *History of California, Vol. 7, 1860–1890*, 203.
[9] *Sentinel*, November 4, 1865.

breach in the Loves' relationship. She had married Harry as insurance against just this sort of thing. Watkins was a damn squatter. Why couldn't Harry run him off—scare him—do *something*? After talking tough to the fellow several times, Harry probably said there was nothing they could do but leave it up to the lawyers. It was Mary's way to keep pushing until something happened, then claim it was the other person's fault. But Harry would not cooperate. He was not going to beat up some poor farmer just because land titles in California were a mess.

In February 1863 Watkins acquired lawyer Howard's title to the property, based on the 1854 note signed by Harry and Mary—which still had not been paid. Mary had denied the contract for years, finally acknowledging it in January 1861 when the title was confirmed. Now she contended, with the connivance of her lawyer, that the 1854 note was invalid not only because of the statute of limitations, but because she was married at the time the note had been signed and, as such, had no power to make an executory contract.[10]

• • •

In March 1866 there was a great deal of support for a new road recently surveyed from the San Lorenzo Valley into Santa Cruz. The county supervisors had appropriated $1,000 for the project, and it was estimated that $9,400 would be needed to complete the job. The road was desperately needed, and in early April, at a meeting held at Ashley's school house on the river, nearly $1,500 was contributed. Harry, a farmer named Hicks, and one George Otto were appointed to seek further contributions, and it seemed the road was well on its way.[11]

• • •

In the spring groups of fishermen began prowling the banks of the local streams and the San Lorenzo River. A party of San Franciscans had good luck near Harry's old mill site and sent several baskets of trout home to their families.[12] The old Ranger was surprised on May 5 when Ben Kooser brought a mutual friend, William Biven, by for a visit and some fishing.

As editor and owner of the Stockton *Herald*, William Biven had decided to take a vacation trip to the coast in late April. He caught a riverboat

---

[10]*Love v. Watkins*, 40 California Reports, 547 (January term, 1871). It was typical Mary—again trying to avoid a debt.   [11]*Sentinel*, March 31 and April 14, 1866.
[12]Ibid., May 5, 1866.

for San Francisco, then boarded a stage to San Jose. From there he changed coaches for the trip south past Gilroy and over the coast range to Watsonville, which he reached on May 3. It was a pleasant trip, which the editor described in an entertaining series of letters to his paper.

By May 4, Biven was in Santa Cruz, where he looked up a former Stockton acquaintance, Ben Kooser, who was presently editing the *Sentinel*. Delighted by the unexpected visit, Kooser promised to drop everything and take Biven for a tour of the area, "if my credit is good for a horse and buggy."[13]

The next morning the two men made a tour of the shoreline, taking in the crashing surf and drift logs along the sandy beaches. Both had known Love "of the shaggy locks" in the palmy days of '53, when he had brought the now-famous head and hand to Stockton.[14] After stopping by Kooser's residence for some fishing worms, the two men headed into the shady glens and tree-shrouded mountains north of town to visit Harry. It was a beautiful ride, with wildflowers and coveys of quail on every side. Only one stretch of road made Biven nervous—a cut allowing passage for only one vehicle with a 200-foot drop to a mountain brook below. After this they drove on more rapidly, crossing several mountain streams of cold spring water. Biven wrote an interesting account of the day:

> Passing by a pleasant pine grove, we saw Harry Love's house before which had gathered a number of "mountaineers" who were spending the day in a social manner, such as bantering, wrestling and foot racing. Before we had stopped, we were called to ride up through the gateway which invitation we promptly accepted. Although it had been thirteen years since we had seen Harry Love, we could not mistake him. His form is peculiarly fitted for mountain life; he would look misplaced anywhere else. He received us with that hospitality for which he is so well noted, and soon we felt as if we had been accustomed to daily stopping in to chat with him. He invited us with those that were already there, to his pine grove, under which we were soon seated drinking lager beer—for lager had found its way even in these mountains. After some conversation, Love assured us he would take us to where we could find plenty of trout. He first took us to his mountain meadow, which requires no irrigation, and which last years raised corn, the stalks of which were over fourteen feet high. While hunting for more worms, Harry Love started for the group of visitors to explain the cause of his leaving them, when we suddenly heard "high words," and

[13]Stockton *Daily Evening Herald*, May 17, 1866. [14]Ibid.

looking we saw signs of a fight between Love and a stout fellow upwards of six feet high. He was taller than Love, but Harry had advantage in "make up." Starting forward as peace-maker (when we first arrived we had been taken for a preacher) we heard Harry tell his opponent that he "would take nothing back, and in a fight he was only eighteen years old"—that he ordered him to leave his enclosure, because he was a Mormon, one who was a member of the "Destroying Angels," and that he was concerned in the Mountain Meadow massacre—and no such man was wanted to visit him. We approached the crowd that had gathered about Love and the Mormon and asked him to show us the trout stream. Obeying the laws of hospitality, as is natural with him as it is to show his likes or dislikes immediately to a man, he excused himself for delaying us and led the way over ground covered with wild strawberries, some just commenced ripening, and by long lines of wild gooseberry bushes that were laden with its berries. Upon reaching a mountain brook, gurgling here and lying quiet there, with its clear and cold water, Love pointed up the side of a mountain and said, "a quarter of a mile up you can find plenty of grizzlies." Kooser said he hadn't lost any grizzly lately, and had none to find.[15]

After a few hours of fishing, the two visitors noted the declining sun and knew it was time to start back. On the way back, Harry showed them several bee trees that he planned to despoil later for his own use. Back at his cabin, Harry assured them that there was still several hours of sunlight after it was hidden behind the mountains.

> Not withstanding our haste, our kind and obliging host would not hear of our departure until we would partake of a lunch with him, in which excellent coffee with the real cream, and fresh butter, made us forget even Kooser's driving! ... Our visit in these mountains was a day of pure enjoyment.[16]

Later in the month great black clouds came rolling in from the sea, causing concern among the farmers around the state. Harry and his neighbors in the valley looked anxiously at the sky, as all had recently seeded crops and had newly-mowed hay lying in the fields yet. Much grain was also already standing tall in their fields. Then the rain began. It was slow and steady at first, but at times torrents came down, inundating the fields. The damage was devastating throughout the state. The *Sentinel* reported:

> THE RAINS—The late rains have done much damage in this county, breaking down standing grain—especially early sown wheat and barley and vol-

---
[15]Ibid.   [16]Ibid.

unteer oats and grass. The hay crop, which was mown, is probably injured twenty per cent. Nearly every farmer ... was now plowing up their newly mown fields and planting beans. Messrs. Davis & Crowell [sic]—of the lime kilns—had five hundred tons of heavy grass just newly mown as the rain commenced falling and the damage is considerable.[17]

Harry's farm suffered accordingly, although the extent is not known. With all the crop losses, other consequences of such heavy rains were becoming apparent. Santa Cruz had been flooded to some extent, but it might have been much worse. A small dam just north of town had barely withstood the onslaught of the rising river, and such warnings could no longer be ignored, as noted in the February 2, 1867, *Sentinel*:

> The large forests of redwood and other timber now covering the mountains are rapidly being leveled. The wood is disappearing, and large tracts are now barren where, not many years ago, we beheld mighty forests. The disappearance of timber and the cultivation of a country never fails to have a potent effect upon the weather.
>
> The waters can rush over these barren hills and throw themselves into the channel of the San Lorenzo with less opposition than formerly. This facility increases as the timber disappears—and were we to speculate as to the results, we should inevitably come to the conclusion that a bulkhead that can now scarcely stem the torrent of the stream would be inadequate to the task in another year.

Despite the bad weather, the new San Lorenzo Road was underway, and in mid-October the *Sentinel* had reported: "There are now twenty men at work grading, under the supervision of Mr. A. Googen, from Gold Gulch Flat.... About one hundred and fifty rods have been graded during the last two weeks, and it is confidently expected that the whole road will be completed before the first day of January."[18]

•   •   •

Harry continued to have squatter troubles with his land. Throughout the 1860s he was caught up in property disputes, resulting in a string of court appearances. He and other local property holders lived in a constant state of apprehension, never knowing from day to day how some new law or court decision might affect their title.

Finally, the old Ranger threw up his hands. Dreams of a home and

---

[17] *Sentinel*, June 2, 1866.   [18] *Sentinel*, October 13, 1866.

financial security seemed impossible, no matter how hard he worked. Mary had been living in Santa Clara for the past few years and would not return to the farm, despite several visits and pleas from him. Dan and Catherine McCusker visited Mary in May 1864 and witnessed several of the Love arguments. "It was pretty rough," Catherine later complained, "and I did not want to hear it and tried to avoid it."[19]

Dan McCusker said Mary had "asked him [Love] at the time . . . to live with her—to provide for her and to behave himself." Harry had responded that "he would be damned if he would do it—he never would live with her or be about the ranch home . . . in Santa Clara again." Harry could not make her understand that he could not support the two households. "He got very mad," McCusker continued, "and got up and threw a bucket of milk out into the yard."[20]

Back home, Harry was not sure just what he was going to do, but when Charles Brown, a Santa Cruz lumberman, proposed buying his 640 acres, the old Ranger took his offer. It is not clear how Harry had doubled his acreage, but it is possible that he was also selling some of Mary's property. Brown was in no hurry to assume control of the property and told Harry he could stay and farm until he made up his mind what he was going to do. In May 1867, Harry accepted Brown's offer of $300 for his property and had the deed recorded.[21]

Early the following month, he was assaulted by yet another disaster. On June 15, 1867, the *Sentinel* reported:

> FIRE BY AN INCENDIARY—Harry Love informs us that on last Sunday, about 12 o'clock, he was apprised of the fact that his entire crop of newly cut and partly cocked hay, some hundred tons, valued at six hundred dollars, was on fire. Harry is having trouble about his land, and it is supposed this has something to do with the burning of his hay. Whoever the incendiary may be, he ought to be brought to punishment, as there is no safety in the community where such villains are allowed to circulate.[22]

It was another devastating blow to Love's farming enterprise. It is not known if he proffered charges against anyone for the fire, but the absence of court records indicates there was probably not enough evidence to pros-

---

[19] *Love vs. Love*, Case 627, District Court, Third Judicial District (December term, 1867), Santa Cruz County, California.   [20] Ibid.
[21] Detlefs, *Brief History of the Falls/Love Creek*. See also Volume 4, Mortgages, 1867, Santa Cruz County, California.   [22] *Sentinel*, June 15, 1867.

ecute. Harry could do little else but keep his pistol handy and stay on a constant alert.

The following month yet another disaster ravaged the valley. It originated just a mile from Harry's place, when a party of men lost control of a fire while trying to smoke out a hive of wild bees. As great clouds of black smoke were seen north of town, word of the blaze soon spread. Rumors were quickly passed around as mounted men were seen galloping out of town, trying to get some idea of the extent of the fires. It was quickly determined the conflagration was moving south toward Santa Cruz, as noted in the *Sentinel* of July 13:

> The fire, noticed last week, spread far and near, destroying everything perishable in its route, and threatened even the town of Santa Cruz—and the citizens of the town were alarmed by the ringing of bells. . . . On Saturday the fire burned nearly to the grove where the Fourth was celebrated, and was only stopped by back-firing, on a line at right angles with the coast, by citizens en masse, who reached the scene of conflagration in wagons, on horseback and on foot. On Tuesday and Wednesday the powder-mills and paper-mills were in great danger, and the employees turned out in great numbers to fight the devouring element. Many people from Santa Cruz assisted and night and day for four days helped fight and fire against fire, to save private property. Davis & Cowell's lime kilns and the kilns of Samuel Adams suffered most by the loss of valuable timber, staves, hoop-poles, etc. The burning of Glasswell's mill and buildings and the Caldwell residence is about all the houses we have heard of being destroyed, although most of the farmers and other residents up the coast had removed their furniture and other goods down to the beach for safety. . . . At night the forked flames lit up the western sky in lurid glare, while the crackling and roaring of flames, mingled with the dull sound of falling trees, struck the beholder with awe.[23]

The distance from Love's farm over the mountains to the coast was some six or eight miles. Although few dwellings were lost in the San Lorenzo Valley, much stockpiled lumber in the neighboring hills was destroyed. Harry lost 100 cords of tanbark, while John Sprague lost 300 cords and George Gitchel 70. Hundreds of other cords were lost along the coast also. The Glasswell mill was destroyed, along with some thirty outbuildings and 20,000 feet of redwood fenceposts. The total value of the consumed cut lumber was reported to be $30,000.[24]

---

[23]Ibid., July 6, 1867.   [24]Ibid., July 13, 1867.

Harry must have wondered what could happen next. Although still undecided about what his next move was to be after selling his place, he was again brought back to the situation he was in. He must have wondered if he should have stayed with the sea, or perhaps gone in with a partner who was knowledgeable about business matters. He was reminded of Fred Hihn, who was quite wealthy through real estate and various other business ventures, and Isaac Graham, William Blackburn, and Jacob Snyder, who had also obtained wealth through shipping and good investments. But there was no use kidding himself—he was not a businessman and had to make a decision soon. He must have been depressed and discouraged as he worked in his fields waiting for the next calamity to strike.

The San Lorenzo road, meanwhile, was bogged down in politics. Harry's friend Fred Hihn was feuding with county auditor T. T. Tidball, who refused to draw warrants for the appropriations the county had made for the road. Tidball insisted the action was illegal, and the matter was now in the courts. The road was sputtering along on donations, but in August 1867 Harry and several other concerned citizens wrote a letter to the *Santa Cruz Times* asking that Tidball make a complete accounting of what public moneys had been appropriated for the road's construction. Tidball responded that some $750 in warrants had been drawn and given to Hihn, and the remaining $250 would be released when properly demanded.[25] Tidball was inferring that Hihn had not made a proper accounting for any funds received, but in an article to the *Sentinel* on August 24, 1867, Hihn published a detailed accounting of all moneys received and expended that he had received from Tidball.

The bickering petered out after this, and by September the *Sentinel* reported:

> SAN LORENZO ROAD—There is a chance that this road will now be speedily built. The Supervisors have appropriated $1,000 for the purpose, and renewed efforts will be made to complete the road before the rainy season sets in.[26]

There would be a good road from the valley into town at last. Since his name does not appear on lists of private contributors to the road, Harry seems to have worked behind the scenes on various committees overseeing the project. He had no money to spare. The road seemed unimportant

---

[25]Ibid., August 17 and 24, 1867, and *Santa Cruz Times,* August 17, 1867.
[26]*Sentinel*, September 14, 1867.

now, anyway, as personal problems took precedent over nearly everything else.

Harry's marriage was in a shambles. The longer he knew her, the more Mary seemed incapable of close relationships, particularly with men. She could appear charming and helpful to outsiders, but her domineering personality and independent ways kept her husbands, and often her children, at arm's length. Once the children had moved away and could visit her on their own terms, the relationship seemed to improve.

The husbands did not fare so well. Vardamon apparently could cope with her so long as the family was on the move, but after settling in San Francisco Mary's controlling ways quickly surfaced and the relationship began falling apart. She left him for lack of support yet, ironically, when he died a few years later in 1849, he was quite wealthy—undoubtedly a result of property he held in San Francisco. According to son Winston, Vardamon left an estate of $150,000 at his death. Always wily and shrewd, Mary apparently had never gotten a divorce for this very reason. She was still Vardamon's wife and now successfully claimed the estate and the Santa Clara land grant. Winston later accused his mother of running the estate into debt through poor management.

There were stories at the time of her poisoning Vardamon by putting a venomous spider in a dumpling, but Winston denied these tales. Since the accusation originated with her own daughter Catherine, though, it must be given serious consideration.

Harry apparently gave up on the relationship. He could not fathom this woman and did not know what to do. His Santa Clara visits never worked out and inevitably resulted in more fights. Why couldn't she understand that he could not support two separate households? He could barely support himself.

Finally, the inevitable happened. On August 28, 1866, Sheriff Albert Jones served Harry with a divorce summons from Santa Clara.[27] It could not have been unexpected, but Harry had no intention of travelling back and forth to Santa Clara for the various hearings. On September 15 he applied to the Santa Clara County Clerk for a transfer of the case to Santa Cruz County, which was finally effected on July 24 of the following year.

---

[27] *Love vs. Love*, Case 627, District Court, Third Judicial District (December term, 1867), Santa Cruz County, California.

18

The End

For some time Harry had been considering a run for justice of the peace of his township. His friends had encouraged him, and he was sure he could handle the job. Three-fifths of the local litigation came before justices of the peace, making it an important office and one that took a big load off the regular courts. The justices had jurisdiction in cases up to $300, administered oaths, issued writs of attachment and subpoenas, and had the power to seize and sell property. They could also summon and impanel juries, issue criminal warrants, and had wide powers pertaining to law enforcement. A township constable executed the decrees of the justice court.[1] Harry must have felt that with all the legal wrangles of the past few years, a JP job would be a cinch.

The more he thought about it, the more he liked the idea. There was no salary, but the fees could be quite lucrative and he would not be put out of business by fire or flood.

On October 12, 1867, Harry ran an announcement in the *Sentinel*, the editor giving him a courtesy notice in the same issue:

> CANDIDACY—Attention is directed to announcement notice of Captain Harry Love who is an aspirant for the office of Justice of the Peace. Capt. Harry is a pioneer citizen of this county, and probably as well known as any other man in it, having identified himself with its interests, both in a civil and military capacity, and suffered from flood and fire, in the washing away of his mill and the incendiary burning of his hay—the entire earnings of a year of toil—last hay-cutting. Harry feels competent for just administration of the office, and we invite a perusal of his card.[2]

---

[1] A good account of nineteenth-century justice of the peace duties and jurisdiction appeared in the *Santa Cruz Sentinel*, September 30, 1865. The office was established in 1849, with justice courts instituted in the following year. See the *California Constitution of 1849*, art. VI, secs. 1, 14 and *California Statutes of 1850*, 179.

[2] The *Sentinel* article on Love's candidacy appeared on October 12, 1867, but the "announcement notice" referred to could not be located.

Harry was indeed widely known in the area by now and probably expected his fame to guarantee his election. He called on all of his township neighbors and made it a point to look up others he had not met. Making up a quantity of *cartes de visite* from a photograph taken by local photographer E. P. Butler, Harry passed these out to newcomers in the area, hoping they would be impressed. Quite popular at the time, the small visiting cards showed Harry in a seated pose with his revolver exposed at his side.[3] He was the conqueror of Joaquín, the personification of the lawman—and hopefully, the ideal representative for justice of the peace.

The old Ranger must have been quite nervous as October 16, election day, finally arrived. He remembered how nervous he had been when the legislature had voted on his $5,000 reward. There was no reason to believe he would be any less successful now. He spent the next ten days waiting for election results to be posted outside the *Sentinel* office. When word spread that results were being put up, Harry left the saloon and made his way through the crowd. There were seven candidates, and it took him a few seconds to compare the figures. With 170 votes, he had come in fourth.[4] Friends patted the big Ranger on the back and tried to cheer him up as they made their way back to the saloon.

After losing the election, Harry was hardly in the mood to take up Mary's divorce action, but he had no choice. In her complaint she had alleged her husband had deserted her in June 1864 and since then had refused to provide her with any provisions or live with her. Further, he had refused to acknowledge her as his wife despite her assertions that she had "faithfully discharged her duties as his wife." In a written statement, Harry denied all of this, stating categorically that he had never refused to return to her or allow her to return to him. The case did not get under way until late October 1867.

A succession of witnesses were summoned, and Mary suffered a serious setback when sons Mansel and Winston refused to appear or testify. Daughter Julia Adams recalled her mother saying Harry refused to live

---

[3] An original *carte de visite* (or visiting card) of Love's sitting portrait was owned by Mansel Bennett, who had lived with Harry at various times. This photo, now in the collections of the Holt-Atherton Center for Western Studies, University of the Pacific, Stockton, California, is printed on the back: "E. P. Butler, Santa Cruz, Cal." Butler had a studio on Pacific street in Santa Cruz during the 1860s, but occasionally traveled to surrounding towns where he set up a temporary shop. He specialized in "all the latest styles of pictures—sun pearls, enameled cards, ambrotypes, photographs, carte de visites, etc." See the *Santa Cruz Sentinel*, October 14, 1865, and the *Santa Cruz Sentinel News*, August 8 and 22, 1954. [4]*Sentinel*, October 26, 1867.

with her or support her, but she had never heard him make that statement. Her sister Samantha gave some irrelevant testimony, then also refused to testify further. Thomas W. Wright could contribute little of importance, either. Catherine and Dan McCusker appeared next, and were apparently the only witnesses who could or would give pertinent testimony.

Catherine testified that during a visit to her mother in Santa Clara in May 1864, Harry had said he would not live with Mary or provide for her—"she can provide for herself," she reported him saying. She claimed her mother was destitute at the time and had "scarcely anything to keep house with or to eat." Catherine had visited for about six days, during which time either Mary or Dan McCusker had furnished provisions. Once, when Mary had asked Harry to get some flour, he replied he had no money. She then gave him money for a fifty-pound sack that he then purchased. Catherine's assertions of poverty must have sounded rather hollow when her mother's many property interests were considered.

Dan McCusker testified next. He also recalled the May 1864 visit when he had heard Harry say he would neither live with, nor provide for, Mary. But all the testimony, or lack of it, did little more than underscore the couple's mercurial relationship.

On December 14, 1867, Judge McKee finally dismissed the action, charging Mary for the court costs.[5] Harry was off the hook, but his relationship was as unstable as ever—probably worse. Still, he would let things cool down and take it from there. Perhaps he would take a trip to Santa Clara and see what the lay of the land was. There seemed little else he could do at the moment.

As he began settling his local affairs, Harry must have looked back on those happy days when he first rode into the valley. It was springtime, a time of renewal and rebirth—a time for fresh beginnings. Here he would begin his new life with a family, a home, and the sawmill. He would supply lumber for the construction of homes, communities, bridges, wagons, and boats. He would take part in building a great new state from a wilderness.

But none of his dreams or plans had worked out. As he looked out over the valley, the enormity of his failures must have settled heavily on his shoulders. Far from being a new beginning, his marriage, farming, and sawmill ventures seemed to be a downhill spiral into bankruptcy and oblivion.

---

[5] *Love vs. Love*, Case 627, District Court, Third Judicial District (December term, 1867), Santa Cruz County, California. See also the *Sentinel* for August 17 and 31, 1867.

In mid-December 1867, friends and neighbors were informed that Love was giving up the farm and moving to his wife's place in Santa Clara. He probably said little of the reconciliation, but everyone knew of his situation. Harry had failed. He had failed in his business and his marriage, while his wealthy and independent wife was establishing a substantial farm of her own outside Santa Clara. He put on his best face. He would be "running" the farm for Mary—it was too much for her alone, and so on.

After selling and giving away whatever personal property he could not pack in his wagon, Harry hitched up his team. Since 1858 there had been a good road through Hiram Scott's valley, to the east, and over the mountains to San Jose. The Santa Cruz Turnpike Company was a toll road and, although precarious and only six or seven feet wide in places, the journey to San Jose took only about five hours. It was an easy trip.

On December 21 the *Sentinel* commented on the loss of their neighbor:

> GONE FROM OUR GAZE.—Capt. Harry Love, of Joaquin notoriety, and who for many years has been a resident of the San Lorenzo Valley, has emigrated to Santa Clara, where, he informs us, he will be pleased to receive any and all of his numerous Santa Cruz friends. Harry has got a heart in him as large as that of a bullock, and no man ever entered his dwelling without sharing its hospitality.

Crossing the mountains gave Harry plenty of time to think. He must have been apprehensive about just why he was going to Santa Clara, when it made more sense to be heading in the opposite direction. There was little or no chance things could ever be the same between them again, and it was humiliating to be chasing after her this way. It wasn't like Mary was a beautiful woman he couldn't forget—far from it; she was plain, mean, and overweight. But he was fifty-seven years old now and had lost everything. He still wanted a home. If they tried, maybe they could still make it work. They would never be lovers again, but maybe they could be friends—companions for these twilight years of their lives.

And she owed him. All these years of running her errands, her embarrassing attempts to cheat people and avoid debts, the endless lawsuits and dealing with her lawyers—he deserved something. Hell, if it hadn't been for all the time spent on her foolishness, he would have had more time for farming and been more successful. He took another pull on the jug at his side. It didn't matter. He was homeless and broke. There seemed to be no choice but to go to Santa Clara. There had to be a payback for all those wasted years.

It was a beautiful trip. In riding through the tall pines and lofty canyons the solitude was almost overwhelming.[6] Except for the birds chirping in the trees and the distant call of a hawk, the woods gave the impression that there was no one else in the world. Sometimes the quiet was something you could almost reach out and touch. Then, the jingling and creaking of a team and wagon or some pack mules would suddenly appear to break the mood.

In the past, the trip had been a good time to think—to sort out problems and look for answers. This time, however, there seemed to be no answers, only wishful thinking and a terrible foreboding.

Harry paid his fifty-cent toll at Hiram Scott's cabin, then later probably stopped at Mountain Charley McKiernan's place for a drink.[7] Charley was one of the earliest settlers in the Santa Cruz Mountains. He raised stock and hunted for a living and had lost a chunk of his skull in a fight with a grizzly bear in May 1854. A San Jose physician fashioned a silver plate out of two Spanish coins to cover the hole in his skull, but there was little they could do for his terribly scarred face and body. Everybody liked Charley, although San Jose pioneer Tom Fallon was said to have thought that the grizzly had carried off most of his brains in that fight.[8]

Coming down the winding grade into the foothills, Harry could see the scattered farms and villages off in the distance. A traveler of the time wrote:

> The Santa Clara Valley is the most fertile and lovely in California. At the point where we came into it, it is about six miles wide, its bottom level, a fine belt of scattered oaks four or five miles wide covering the middle. It is here all covered with Spanish grants, so is not cultivated, but near San Jose, where it is divided into farms, it is in high cultivation; farmhouses have sprung up and rich fields of grain and growing orchards everywhere abound.[9]

As he made the last leg of his trip into Santa Clara, Harry must have been apprehensive. Mary was living on Grant Street, on the outskirts of

---

[6]Richard A. Beal, *Highway 17, the Road to Santa Cruz* (Aptos, Calif.: The Pacific Group, 1991), 67–72, and Leon Rowland, *Santa Cruz, The Early Years* (Santa Cruz, Calif.: Paper Vision Press, 1980), 73–74. See also the *Sentinel*, May 5, 1866. Highway 17 is a beautiful drive today and must have been much more so in the pristine days of Harry Love.

[7]"Ghost Towns of the Santa Cruz Mountains," *San Jose Mercury Herald*, April 22, 1934.

[8]Thomas M. Enery, ed., *California Pioneer: The Journal of Captain Thomas Fallon* (San Jose, Calif.: Inishfallen Enterprises, 1978), 88.

[9]Brewer, *Up and Down California, in 1860–1864: The Journal of William H. Brewer*, 169–170.

town at the time.[10] She probably had a small frame house and some outbuildings on her property. There were plans for a new two-story home with construction beginning soon. Winston was living in Santa Clara at the time, as was daughter Clementhia. Harry probably got a cool reception from Mary, but he would settle for that. He stored his belongings in the barn and prepared to also bunk there.

The reconciliation was probably doomed when Harry was unable to repay neighboring rancher William Trenouth for a loan. A fifty-year-old Englishman who had emigrated from Australia a few years before, Trenouth probably enjoyed the frontiersman's stories of his travels and adventures, while Harry admired his friend's family and fertile fields. With his wife, six children, and successful farm, Trenouth had everything Harry had longed for. He must have sensed the big Ranger's envy when he made him his first loan. Well-aware of the property interests of Harry's wife, he was not overly concerned about the return of his investment.

When he was unable to make any repayments, Harry probably told Trenouth to sue.[11] It seemed the only way to get any payback from Mary. The two men remained friends when Trenouth took Harry and his wife to court in January 1868 to collect the $1,025 debt. Mary was undoubtedly bitter and unforgiving when Trenouth won the suit, since the payment was specified by the court to be in gold.

Harry helped out on the farm and kept busy for several months, but Mary remained cold and distant. There were still legal problems—lawyers to see and hearings to attend together. Mary had no doubt failed to pay him for any of the work he was doing on the farm. She had always found excuses to avoid paying liabilities, and Harry's debt was no different. By April Harry was again borrowing from Trenouth, who apparently sympathized with his situation.

Mary had begun building her new house in early 1868. She hired a carpenter named Calvin Russell, and by June the place was nearing completion. Harry stayed away most of the time, but he must have felt

---

[10]Mary Love's home was on the northeast edge of town, while Vardamon's old land grant was across town—to the west. The grant was in a well-developed agricultural area and had been whittled down considerably from its original size. See 1866 plat maps in *Historical Atlas of Santa Clara, California* (San Francisco: Thompson & West, 1876).

[11]Documents pertaining to the William Trenouth lawsuit are in the Harry Love Probate Records on file in the Santa Clara County Clerk's Office, San Jose, California. Harry's later loans from Trenouth are also indicated in papers and debts recorded in Love's probate records. Personal information on Trenouth was gleaned from *United States Census, Santa Clara County, California, Population Schedules, 1870*.

increasingly morose watching the new house going up and knowing he would never live there. Mary must have glared in contempt at the man she could not seem to drive away. He was never going to get anything out of her, so why didn't he leave?

Driving a final wedge between them, in April Mary hired a young man named Christian "Fred" Eiversen to help out around the place.[12] Mary was so heavy now that she needed help with her chores and in getting in and out of her buggy. The move was meant to embarrass Harry further, emphasize that he was not wanted, and demonstrate that young Eiversen would be paid while Harry was still waiting for his wages. To make matters worse, Mary circulated stories that Love had beaten her and Eiversen had been hired as protection.[13]

The old Ranger refused to totally leave the premises, but he must have stayed away for periods of time. He could hardly ignore the situation, however, and on his first confrontation with the handyman Harry told him he must leave. "I was hired and am paid by Mrs. Love," commented Eiversen, "and I'm not leaving until she says so." When Harry threatened his life if he didn't leave, Eiversen just walked away.[14]

After several such run-ins, Love became so abusive and loud that Eiversen sought to have him put under bonds. The judge, however, had other ideas. He ruled that a husband had the right to keep people who were offensive to him off his wife's premises, and the situation continued to simmer into the summer.

We know little of Love's movements at this time, but he was increas-

---

[12] Almost nothing is known of Christian Eiversen. He has not been located in any local Santa Clara or state source, either before or after the gunfight, and must have left the area and perhaps the state soon after the shooting. Micki Mistretta, local research volunteer, Santa Clara Historical and Genealogical Society, to the author, November 8, 1996. Mrs. Sibylle Zemitis, California Section, California State Library, to the author, October 16, 1996.

[13] Mary told a reporter for the *San Jose Mercury* that she refused to live with Love because he beat her. This directly contradicted her divorce action, in which she swore that Harry refused to live with her and she wanted him to return. The only descendant of the Bennett family to comment on the situation was Mrs. Mabel Dorn Early, a Santa Cruz attorney who died in 1969. Mrs. Early was a granddaughter of Catherine Bennett McCusker, and in several interviews with Frank Latta made no mention of Love beating his wife. She maintained the trouble between the two originated in Mary not wanting Harry to have any say in her family or business transactions. Other indications that no such beatings ever took place are an absence of legal charges filed by either Mary or any of her children. Furthermore, it is difficult to imagine Mansel Bennett keeping a *carte de visite* of a stepfather who beat his mother. To the best of the author's knowledge, the single source for this beating story was in the *San Jose Mercury* of July 2, 1868. See Latta, *Joaquin Murrieta and His Horse Gangs*, 301–306, as well as Mabel Dorn Early, "The Black Knight of Zayante," *The Pony Express*, November 1953.

[14] San Jose *Weekly Patriot*, July 3, 1868.

ingly frustrated by the situation. Again, he should have walked away. He had lost. There was no hope and nothing here for him any more. In June 1868 he had borrowed sixty more dollars from his friend Trenouth, but that could not go on forever. He missed working in the fields, but spent most of his time in Pete Lozier's saloon brooding and plotting a way out of his terrible situation.

When Harry confronted Eiversen at the house on Saturday, June 22, he angrily warned the handyman to leave, but again to no avail. "Love came here last Saturday," later recalled Calvin Russell, "and kicked up a fuss and tackled Fred [Eiversen] and then tackled me and I don't know what for."

When he saw Mary and Eiversen on a business trip in San Jose the following Saturday morning, he was furious. Climbing onto his express wagon, Harry knew it was time to do something—anything. He whipped up his team for Santa Clara.[15]

It is not clear just where Love was staying at the time. It was either with a friend such as Trenouth, or perhaps he was just sleeping out in his wagon. At eleven o'clock that morning, he drove up to Mary's new house where carpenters and painters were busily at work. Calvin Russell later recalled:

> [He] unharnessed his team and said he was Harry Love. He was armed with a double barreled shot gun, pistol and sheath knife. He took his station at the gate, locked it and showed me the key. As I went to dinner I asked him to go to dinner with me. He said he could not. He said if that man Fred came in there, he would have to walk over his dead body. I went to dinner and stayed as long as I could and make my time good and when I came back to work he was there waiting at the gate. I asked him to come to the house and help me put up some jamb and told him no one would disturb him. He ripped out a great oath and said he was going to stop there.[16]

J. L. Duff was painting on the roof and also came down to eat. He, too, spoke briefly with Love and noticed he had a small bag of crackers and a pot of tea. Harry remarked, "That's the way Texas Rangers lived when they camped." From time to time Harry would walk to his wagon and take a pull on a bottle there.

---

[15] Events leading up to the deadly encounter between Love and Eiversen are based on newspaper accounts in the *San Jose Patriot* (July 3, 1868), the *San Jose Mercury* (July 2 and 9, 1868), and the Santa Clara County *Coroner's Inquest of Harry Love* (June 29, 1868), now in the collections of the Santa Clara County Museum.

[16] The coroner's report contained the eyewitness statements of Calvin Russell, Dr. A. B. Caldwell, Dr. Whipple, Dr. L. Robinson, J. L. Duff, Charles S. Kidder, and Clementhia Bennett.

Mary Love's home in Santa Clara, California, where Harry Love was killed in a senseless shooting and brawl. The structure was torn down many years ago. *Author's collection.*

Clementhia Bennett had arrived at the construction site about nine o'clock that morning. Her mother had asked her to keep an eye on the place until she returned from a business trip to San Jose with Eiversen. The daughter had remained in the house most of the morning but, after eating, several of the workmen had warned her of Love's presence and threats. "That old fool Love," remarked a man named Owens, "has come to take possession of the place." Russell also warned her that there was liable to be trouble, and that she should keep an eye out for her mother so as to warn her.

Harry had called an Indian farmhand out of a nearby cornfield and was talking with him at the gate when Clementhia came out of the house. Without saying anything, Harry unlocked the gate and let her through out to the road. She had seen her mother's buggy coming down the street and now rushed towards it waving her arms. Eiversen reined up in a cloud of dust just as Clementhia grabbed the animal's bit. She quickly explained that Love was at the gate and there was liable to be trouble. Offering Eiversen the key to her house, Clementhia told him to drive her mother there, but at that moment Mary began screaming, "There he comes! There he comes!"

The Santa Clara shootout between Harry Love and Chris Eiversen as depicted in *Frank Leslie's Illustrated Newspaper*, August 15, 1868. *Author's collection.*

Mary's screams had frightened the horse and as it danced about in the road Harry shouted something that was unintelligible. As Mary yelled, "He will shoot you!" Eiversen jumped from the buggy, but the handyman was already drawing his pistol. Love fired a blast from his shotgun now, a few pellets striking Eiversen in the face, with one glancing off Clementhia's hand as she tried to quiet the horse. The handyman now coolly advanced upon Love's position at the gate, firing shots of his own, both of which missed. Harry fired the other barrel of his shotgun, then drew his pistol and fired several more times, hitting Eiversen in the arm. But he kept coming. Mary and her daughter must have huddled by the buggy as the shooting continued.

Harry had been kneeling before, and he was scrambling to his feet now as Eiversen rushed up to the gate. Leaning over the fence, he fired at point-blank range, the bullet striking Love high on the right arm and shattering the bone. With a yelp of pain, Love struck at Eiversen with the empty shotgun, then sprinted for the house. With blood gushing from his wound, Love called for Russell to save or protect him as Eiversen leaped over the fence in pursuit.

"Come in and I'll protect you," said Russell, but Love had already turned to face his attacker as Eiversen slammed him hard on the head with his pistol. The old Ranger dropped, but struggled upright only to again be clubbed down. Russell and one of the painters at this time rushed out and separated the two men.

As Love was helped to his feet by the two workers, Eiversen stepped back, muttering that he had been shot. He was bleeding from his face and arm, but his wounds appeared to be superficial. Duff and Russell then carried Love to the back of the house, where he was laid out on the ground. He was bleeding badly and talking wildly about being murdered. "The women were murderers," he babbled, "and had hired the German to kill him." The workmen sent for a doctor, then did what they could to stop his bleeding as Harry continued to rave and went into shock.

It was early afternoon when Doctors Whipple and A. B. Caldwell arrived at the farm. Dr. Caldwell later described the scene:

> I arrived here about two o'clock this afternoon: deceased was lying on the ground back of this building very bloody and shot in the right shoulder. The orifus where the ball entered breaking the Humorus was about two or three inches below the shoulder joint. The bone was slivered into fragments or that part of it was broken badly. His head was cut and bruised as from blows with a pistol or bludgeon. Soon after other Med gentlemen arrived and held consultation about the propriety of amputating the arm.[17]

Harry's arm was terribly shattered and, after removing some bits of bone, the two physicians sent for another doctor to corroborate their diagnosis. It was three o'clock before Doctor L. Robinson arrived, and the three agreed to amputate the wounded arm at the shoulder socket. Chloroform was administered to the raving patient, but it never seemed to fully take effect.

"He was continually raving," reported Dr. Caldwell, "like he was intoxicated from the delirium caused by the blow on the head. I think this was the reason the Chloroform did not produce the proper effect; did not examine the head to see if the skull was fractured. While dressing the arm he was very much excited and talked incoherently and just as we were

---
[17]Ibid.

putting in the last suture he attempted to raise up and fell back and expired. The amputation had been performed about half an hour when he expired."[18]

By now, neighbors had begun gathering and events of that bloody afternoon were being passed from person to person. When Harry Love's name was mentioned, bystanders crowded closer trying get a glimpse of the body. There was undoubtedly a blanket over the corpse now, and all that remained visible of the noted frontiersman were the great splotches of blood which spattered the yard.

Captain Love's name had long since lost its luster. People who saw him recently could hardly associate the dashing Texas hero and Ranger who had tracked down Murrieta with the shabby old man in the battered hat driving his express wagon around town. He was just an old farmer. His failed marriage, various legal problems, and disheveled appearance all served to make his colorful past a distant or forgotten memory. Harry Love had gasped out his last few breaths on the afternoon of June 29, 1868, but the Black Knight of the Zayante had died in the San Lorenzo Valley some years ago.

News of the tragedy was announced to the San Francisco newspapers in the following brief dispatch:

> SANTA CLARA, June 29th, '68—A shooting affray took place between Capt. Harry Love and a German, on the ranch of the former. The German was in the employ of Mrs. Love. Some seven to ten shots were exchanged, both parties being twice struck. Capt. Love's arm was shattered so as to render amputation necessary, under which operation he died. Capt. Love was a member of the Society of California Pioneers. The German will recover.[19]

Later, many of the inland papers picked up the much more detailed account in the *San Jose Patriot*, and for a brief moment the old Ranger again gained prominence. He hadn't been heard from in years, and now he was dead. A few days later the *Visalia Delta* noted:

> DEATH OF HARRY LOVE—Harry Love, an old resident of California and well known to many persons in this county, died at the residence of Mrs. Love, near Santa Clara, on the 23 ult [*sic*]. He got into an altercation with a German employee, when they exchanged several shots, Love receiving his death wound.[20]

---

[18]Ibid.
[19]*Sentinel*, July 4, 1868.
[20]*Visalia Delta*, July 8, 1868.

Real insight into the tragedy, obviously written by someone acquainted with the family, was reported closer to home in the San Jose *Patriot* of July 3, 1868:

> A TRAGIC AFFAIR—DEATH OF HARRY LOVE, THE TEXAS RANGER. Ever since the marriage of Harry Love, the Texas Ranger, with the widow Bennett, eight or ten years ago or more, there has been from time to time turmoils in the family— quarrels—separation, law-suits, reunions and a separation again. In fact there has been no harmony in the family, and their domestic affairs have too often been the subject of ventilation by courts and gossips. The woman has never borne an enviable reputation, and there are persons who know them both well, who maintain that Harry Love, with all his faults, was the best of the two and the least to blame in the troubles of their married life. . . . It seems that of late there was a sort of reconciliation between the parties, a kind of half-reconciliation, whereby they were for a time enabled to live together under the same roof—but there was no sympathy, no unity of feeling—no disposition, on the part of the woman at least, to forget the past—no yearning for a happier comingling of thought and affection. Harry Love felt that he was only tolerated there, and he imagined that the great obstacle to the re-establishment of true marital relations in the family was in the person of Christian Eiversen, a German laborer employed by the wife to work upon the place.[21]

The *San Jose Mercury* seems to have obtained their information from Mary. Referring to Love as a man of "immense frame—although a great braggart and of questionable personal bravery," the *Mercury* article made serious charges against the late Ranger captain:

> His wife by a second marriage, Mary Love, is a wealthy landowner. She has refused to live with her husband for a number of years on account of his cruelty to her. She says that he was in the habit of beating her cruelly at such times as he could find her alone and unprotected. It was partly for her own protection that she employed Eiversen a few weeks ago to work on her farm and live in her house.[22]

All this was so much nonsense, of course. Mary had accused Harry of refusing to live with *her* in her recent divorce action. Now she was claiming she had left him. And, if Mary had ever been "cruelly" beaten, as she claimed, she would have been the first to file battery charges against her husband. Certainly, if she hadn't, one of her many children would have

---
[21] Most other notices were reprints of the *San Jose Patriot* article.
[22] *San Jose Mercury*, July 9, 1868.

done so. Yet no such charges were ever filed. Mary was lying again, as she had so many times before, but Harry could no longer defend himself.

In a long article appearing in the *Santa Cruz Sentinel* on July 4, Harry's personal history was reported at some length, although exaggerated or erroneous. The *Patriot*'s account of his death was repeated, along with fond memories of their former neighbor in the San Lorenzo Valley:

> In common with the many friends of the deceased in this county and throughout California, we sincerely regret his untimely taking off. Harry Love was long a resident of this county and his eventful life with the many exploits by flood and field, would fill a large volume.... The captain is an intelligent, generous man, with considerable of the bravado that has characterized many of our noted frontiersmen.

An inquest held at the scene of the tragedy came to the conclusion that Love had been killed by Christian Eiversen with a pistol fired in self defense. This is not really accurate, since the cause of death was not from the pistol wound, but from complications resulting from the amputation. Although there was talk of the botched surgery at the time, Love apparently died from a combination of shock, too much chloroform, and loss of blood. Intoxication may have played a part also, but this was never discussed.

Eiversen was examined before Justice Billings on Monday, July 3, and quickly discharged on a plea of self-defense.[23] Everyone had hailed his coolness under fire and his bravery had been the one saving grace of that final, sordid incident. Certainly, no semblance of the gallant Harry Love of an earlier time had been present that tragic day.

Apparently there was no public funeral—at least none was mentioned in the press. Hopefully, a few old friends were present when he was laid to rest in the Santa Clara city cemetery, where he lies today in a recently marked grave.[24]

---

[23] *San Jose Weekly Patriot*, July 3, 1868. The handyman's disappearance after this is so complete, one wonders if the shooting might have been something more than a happening prompted by Love's rash action. Not that Mary would have paid Eiversen to kill Love, but she knew how to tantalize Harry. She would have told Eiversen Harry had beat and threatened her and how her husband would kill him if he got the chance. "Don't take any chances," she might have suggested to the handyman, and Harry helped things along when his pride led him to the final confrontation on Grant Street.

[24] Over the years the record of Harry Love's burial place became obscured due to the Santa Clara Mission City Memorial Park register book becoming difficult to read, and the gravesite being unmarked. At the time the author first visited the site in the early 1980s, it was thought by some that the name in the register read "Mary Love," instead of "Harry Love." When the author and several friends looked at the register, however, we all agreed that the register read "Harry" and not "Mary." The actual gravesite had been unmarked for many years.   *(continued, next page)*

The End

Winston Bennett, one of Mary's boys, paid for Harry Love's burial expenses out of his mother's estate funds. *California State Library.*

And so it was over. John Erkson was appointed administrator of Harry's estate, but there was little property to deal with. Gathering together the meager belongings of the late frontiersman, the following list of items were deemed of too little value to warrant a public auction:

> One double barrel shotgun   One express wagon
> One wolf skin   Two pair of blankets
> One pair buckskin gloves   One black vest
> One lot dirty shirts & drawers $1.50 cash
> One set of harness   Two horses
> One trunk[25]

In May 2003 the author was asked to participate in the erection of a memorial marker to be placed on Love's grave. The headstone was a project of the Mountain Charlie Chapter #1850 and Joaquín Murrieta Chapter #13, E Clampus Vitus, a fraternal organization dating back to gold rush days. Besides aiding in the accuracy of the text on the stone, the author was a speaker at the event. At long last, Harry has a marker on his grave.

[25] *Harry Love Probate Records* (Santa Clara County Clerk's Office, San Jose, California) contain his property list and many other documents pertaining to his debts and estate. Winston Bennett paid Love's funeral expense of $150 on November 1, 1869.

Harry Love's grave was lost for many years, and when it was located there was no headstone to mark it. On March 29, 2003, the author was a speaker at the marking of the grave by several chapters of E Clampus Vitus. *Courtesy of Eric Carlson.*

Harry's legacy was valued at $382.50. It seemed an odd coincidence that a wolf skin was among his pitifully few belongings. The wolf, the origin of his name—where it all began. It had probably been killed prowling near his farm stock in the San Lorenzo Valley. Once a living, dynamic thing, now it was only a shell. Soon it would be forgotten dust—like Harry.

The estate was instantly in debt, the three physicians charging $100 apiece for their surgery, which nearly ate up what the property was worth. William Trenouth was owed some $465, including over $275 worth of interest. Other debts dragged on for some time.

When Mary became ill late that year, she went to live with her daughter Catherine near Watsonville. Mary had always enjoyed eating, and Catherine had to continually remind her she would soon weigh 400 pounds if she made no effort to control herself. While crocheting one day Mary suddenly looked up and said, "There now, you see, I never did get to weigh 400 pounds." Then she lay back and died. The *Santa Clara News* reported her passing on December 25, 1868:

> Mrs. Mary Love, relict of the late Harry Love, died suddenly on Saturday last of heart disease at the residence of her son-in-law, Mr. McCusker, near Watsonville where she was temporarily staying. Her age was 65 years, 1 month and 24 days.... Mrs. Love had been ailing for the last three or four years with the disease from which she died. She appeared in excellent health and spirits but moments before she was stricken down. She was sitting down when the fatal attack came. She exclaimed, "I am gone," and died almost instantly without a struggle. Mrs. Love was interred in the Watsonville grave yard. She was possessed of considerable property, chiefly in real estate.

Winston Bennett was appointed administrator of his mother's estate. It seemed poetic justice when his stepfather's burial costs and other debts were paid out of the estate funds. It was much too late to calm the waters of their troubled marriage, and they were both gone now, but in the end Mary had to share her wealth with Harry after all.

In the beautiful, shaded forests a few miles above Santa Cruz, a barely noticeable creek meanders down through the woods and junctures with the San Lorenzo River at the tiny mountain hamlet of Ben Lomond. Few modern residents realize the area was once home to a daring adventurer and frontiersman who played a singular role in the settlement of early California. Known as "Harry Love's Grade" in the early days, the road running along the creek now is simply "Love Creek Road," after the creek which also bears his name.

Thus, a recently-erected headstone on his grave, a small wandering creek and a winding mountain road are the only monuments commemorating this tragic pioneer.

Dr. Jordan's Museum moved many times over the years. This woodcut depicts the displays at his Kearney Street address, as illustrated in the 1876 edition of his booklet, *The Philosophy of Marriage and Manhood Power*. The museum was strictly an advertising gimmick for his quack medical practice. Murrieta's head and many other displays were destroyed during the 1906 earthquake. *Author's collection.*

Epilogue

Although the head of Murrieta was exhibited in California for more than fifty years, reports and suggestions that the bandit had not been killed were current even before the head was put on display. The most curious item was published in the San Francisco *Herald* of August 19, 1853:

> Senor Editors Herald
>
> As my capture or supposed capture seems to be the topic of the day, I will, through your kindness, inform your readers of your valuable paper that I still retain my head, although it is proclaimed through the presses of your city that I was recently captured.
>
> Joaquin Carrillo

This must have startled Love and his men and raised eyebrows around the state. There was little comment in the press, however, and it was, apparently, fast realized that this man (if the letter was genuine) was another of the Joaquíns listed in the original state reward notice. According to Latta, this man was Murrieta's half-brother, who had left with Joaquín's widow for Mexico the day the letter was posted. This is speculation, however, based on Latta's interviews with several aged pioneers.[1] A more realistic explanation of the letter is that it was a hoax, executed to do what Hispanics are doing to this day—trying to convince the public that the famed Mexican bandit had not been killed. The origin of the letter, however, has yet to be resolved. The captured prisoner, Ochoa, the identifications in the affidavits, and other evidence all left little doubt that Joaquín Murrieta was the outlaw leader who had been killed and decapitated.

Love's response to the *Alta* correspondent in 1855 has been given ear-

---

[1] Latta, *Joaquin Murrieta and his Horse Gangs*, 628.

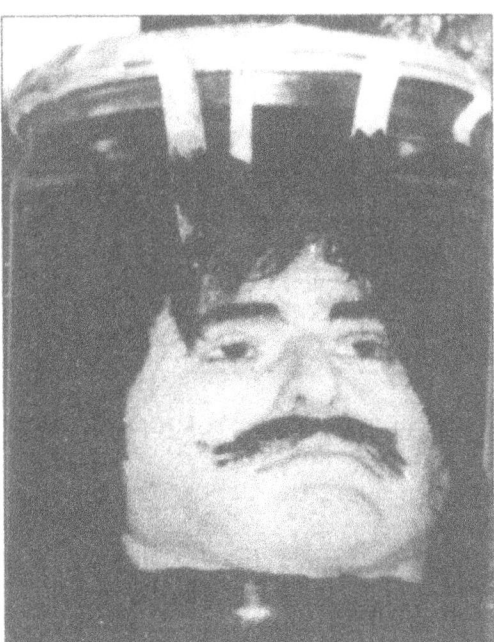

A fraudulent wax "head" of Joaquín Murrieta, made up for the Old Town Museum, New Almaden, California, some fifty years ago. After the museum's demise, the head resurfaced from time to time as the real trophy. *Author's collection.*

lier, but most such accusations were even more nebulous. Usually, accounts were second- or third-hand and mention a sister or brother, and sometimes Joaquín's mother, as disavowing the identity of the head. Vague tales of letters from Mexico, saying Joaquín was alive, were sometimes alluded to, as well.

A typical tale was published in the *Alta* on November 10, 1879. Writing from Tucson, Arizona Territory, Alfred A. Green, a dishonest California lawyer, related how in 1857 he had been sent to San Buenaventura by the mayor of San Francisco to obtain testimony on a local boundary problem. While visiting the old mission at that place, Green had some interesting discussions with a young resident priest. When the conversation turned to some of the area bandits, the name of Murrieta inevitably surfaced.

Swearing Green to secrecy, the priest related how, just the previous month, he had been called to Los Angeles to officiate at the wedding of a young man named Murrieta. Curious, the priest asked if the groom was related to the famous outlaw. To his surprise, the young man said he was

Joaquín's brother. "Is it true the Americans got the head of your brother?" asked the priest. "No, Senior Padre," was the response, "but see for yourself." And with this he produced a letter from Joaquín written from Mexico. In it, he advised his relatives in California to sanction the stories of his death to protect him from any bounty hunters coming after him in Mexico. "All the family," continued the brother, "have told the Americans who brought the head for us to identify that it is the head of my brother Joaquin, and we still tell all persons the same story whenever we are questioned about it."

Green also claimed that his brother had traveled extensively in northern Mexico and had heard stories of Joaquín living in the area after his supposed death in California. Green's story is typical of these nebulous "letter" tales, replete with relatives in on a plot to throw the authorities off the trail of the hounded Joaquín. This writer has talked with present-day Hispanics who tell similar stories, but all such tales suffer from the same weakness—*no such letter has ever been produced or published!*

From time to time, articles on Murrieta in the San Francisco press would generate other tales of the "escape" genre. A long piece in the *San Francisco Chronicle* of February 6, 1881, gave a general survey of the Murrieta story and wasted no emotion on the bandit's sordid career in crime. He was described as having coarse, black hair, a dark complexion, and dark eyes. A widely circulated rebuttal appeared in the Monterey *Californian*, the author claiming some personal knowledge of his subject:

> He had very intellectual features, light complexion, soft, light brown hair and was truly a handsome man. The head said to be his, now on exhibition at Jordan's Museum, is no more the head of Joaquin Murietta [*sic*] than it is our head The authorities had to kill someone to get the large reward, so they killed an Indian and got a couple of men who had never seen him to swear it was Joaquin Murietta. Nobody who had extended acquaintance with him was ever shown the body. And lastly, he was not killed at all. He succeeded in eluding the authorities and going to Sonora, his old home, where we have reason to believe he is yet living in peace and quiet.[2]

Claiming to have "studied the history of this robber chief pretty thoroughly," the Monterey *Californian* author makes statements illustrating

---

[2] Rebuttals of the February 6, 1881, *San Francisco Chronicle* article appeared in the *Monterey Californian* and were reprinted in the Visalia *Weekly Delta*, March 11, 1881, as well as the Eureka (Nevada) *Daily Sentinel*, March 5, 1881.

a seeming lack of background in his subject. Although his description of Joaquín's features tallies well with contemporary descriptions, his comment that the Rangers had "killed an Indian and got a couple men who had never seen him swear it was Joaquín Murietta [sic]" is ludicrous. Contemporary descriptions of the head in the jar characterize a young Mexican, and not an Indian. No one at the time suggested that an Indian head was being displayed by the Rangers. More important, Sam Bishop, who saw the head when he ferried the two Rangers across the San Joaquín, certainly knew an Indian head from a Mexican; he was married to an Indian woman at the time. He not only said it was a young Mexican's head, but claimed to have later discussed the matter with several Murrieta relatives!

The *Californian* comment that "Nobody who had extended acquaintance with him was ever shown the body [head]" is also patently ridiculous. Love and his men exhibited the trophy in Stockton, San Francisco, Sacramento, and throughout the mining country. The Rangers would have had to be crazy to try to pass off a bogus head as that of the widely-known bandit chieftain. The head was exhibited in all the areas where Murrieta had lived, robbed, and murdered. He was identified by Mexicans who had known and worked with him, by Chinese who had been robbed by him, and by many others. Further, he was identified by the prisoner, Ochoa, at his Mariposa court hearing. The Rangers did everything possible to establish the identity of the head, and any open-minded observer might reasonably conclude that the Murrieta story has now come full circle.

From Ridge's fairly accurate (ignoring the conversations) initial biography of the bandit, to Joseph Henry Jackson's conjecture that Murrieta was primarily a fictitious character, to historian Frank Latta's oral history interviews, we can make a good case now for starting over at the beginning. The real story has been staring us in the face for the past 140 years, but no one has recognized this until now. Love and his Rangers really did get the right man, after all!

A new wrinkle to the "escape" genre was promoted by Latta in his book, *Joaquin Murrieta and His Horse Gangs*. After many years of research, interviewing pioneers and family members, Latta came out with yet another version of how Murrieta escaped death at Cantua Creek that hot July morning. Latta contended that Joaquín's horse handler, an Indian called Chappo (more correctly, Chapo—"Shorty" in Spanish), was killed and beheaded instead. This version was obtained from an elderly claimed associate of Murrieta named Avelino Martinez. Claiming to have helped bury the bodies after the fight, Martinez said that he recognized Chappo's headless body by his belt buckle. But Latta then went on to shoot down his own story by writing that Martinez described Chappo as having long hair, chopped off just below the collar in a "dutch boy" style cut. This haircut neither matches any of the contemporary descriptions, nor the drawing made directly from the exhibited head (which matches contemporary descriptions).

It was Latta's further assertion that Murrieta had been in the area during the fight at Cantua Creek and, later, helped bury the bodies. With a companion (Latta speculates that it was Joaquín Carrillo), Murrieta then visited Monterey before heading for his home in Niles Canyon. During the night, the two riders were intercepted by a posse looking for other outlaws, and Joaquín was shot in the leg and his horse killed. Riding double, Murrieta and his companion made their escape in the darkness and, some hours later, arrived at the adobe home in Niles Canyon. But Joaquín had lost too much blood. He died after requesting that he be buried beneath one of the rooms of the house, so the Americans would never know they had killed him. His plea was granted, and Joaquín's wife, sister, and her small son, and whoever had brought the dying bandit home, laid him to rest. The boy, Tomas Procopio Bustamante, later purportedly told his wife of the burial, and it was kept a family secret until she told Latta in 1936.

This was Latta's startling new revelation. It flew in the face of all the other "escape" stories in that no Murrieta descendant interviewed by Latta ever told him Joaquín had returned to Mexico after his supposed death. This helped to verify Latta's story, but canceled out all of the "escape" stories that had the outlaw returning to Mexico and living out his old age. Both versions cannot be right.

After reviewing all of the evidence, this writer believes Joaquín never returned home for the simple reason that he was killed that day at Cantua Creek.

The burial within the Niles Canyon adobe also became suspect when a team of amateur historians and archaeologists attempted to locate the adobe site and excavate within the walls. By comparing the present-day surrounding mountains and terrain to old photographs of the area, Charles W. Callison and some fifty workers began digging on July 15, 1986. "If we prove Latta correct and find the body, we win," stated Callison. "Even if we don't find the body and prove Latta was wrong, we win."

Although Callison believed his team had uncovered the foundation of the house, careful and extensive excavation produced no indication of a grave site. By July 29, the project was abandoned. Latta's story was relegated to the list of other unverified tales.

Callison took a positive approach to the failed project, however. "Beyond a doubt, the dig was still a success," he said. "We proved there was no grave, which is just as important as proving there was one." Still, others of the team were unsure of the results. Further study of maps and comparisons of old photographs with the modern site indicated to some that there had been a miscalculation on the adobe site. There were hopes that another dig could be initiated at a future time.[3]

Frank Latta's nearly-lifelong pursuit of material for Joaquín Murrieta and his horse gangs yielded much valuable data, and his book is the starting place for any study in this field. Yet, as Latta's life wound down and he worked to finish his saga, it seems that he lost focus on occasion and was overwhelmed by his mountain of research. Most agree the book would have been more valuable—and readable—if much of the material had been reduced to addenda or footnotes. But he had to do it his way, and we must be grateful for his efforts.

A variety of Hispanic writers have tackled the Murrieta story over the years, but always with disappointing results.[4] While grudgingly admitting that their hero was a bandit, the qualification of his being driven to outlawry and the assumption that he was a "Robin Hood" or a "patriot"

---

[3] The Callison dig was widely covered in the press, the first quote being taken from the *San Francisco Chronicle*, July 26, 1986. Mr. Callison was kind enough to send the author his eighteen-page résumé of the dig, along with detailed maps; Callison to the author, September 15, 1986. The *San Francisco Chronicle*, July 31, 1986, reported the conclusion of the dig.

Dianne C. Klyn participated in Callison's dig and shared her experiences, sketches, and photographs with the author. With the cooperation of Frank Latta's daughter, Monna S. Olson, she also authored a condensed, and more easily digested, version of Latta's book; see *Joaquin Murrieta in California* (San Ramon, Calif.: The Publishing Place, 1989). Klyn to the author, July 10 and 17, August 27, and September 10, 1990; February 20, 1995.

[4] Such authors as Manuel Rojas (*Joaquin Murrieta, "El Patrio,"* Mexicali, Baja California: privately published, 1986) and Michael Romero (*Joaquin Murrieta, The Life of a Legend*, Soledad, Calif.: the author, 1979) have published studies of Murrieta based on earnest, if sometimes superficial, research. The overriding theme in both works is that Joaquín Murrieta is some kind of nationalistic hero, rather than a bloody bandit; terms such as "Chicano social banditry" are used to foster this contradiction of the facts. To state that Murrieta was a "Chicano guerilla" and that he fought "against the oppression of his people" is to ignore the fact that Murrieta and Claudio not only robbed their own people, but were pursued by them frequently. Claudio and his men, it should also be noted, were killed by a posse made up of both Anglos and Hispanics!

is never too thinly disguised. This seems to be an angry, nationalistic tradition, a stick in the eye of the Anglos who usurped so much Mexican territory in the nineteenth century. If Joaquín can be made a hero, his victims are, therefore, villains.

And this is too bad. The Hispanic writers have the background of heritage and culture that might open doors to an in-depth study of a worthwhile subject. Yet they seem content to utilize the previous research of others, while keeping afloat the tired (and false) tales of the social bandit who was forced into a life of crime. It is the rather obvious ploy of making Murrieta's criminal life more palatable by the suggestion of higher motives for his actions. The idea that Murrieta was not a murderous thief but a "Chicano guerrilla leader" leading some kind of patriotic insurrection is ignoring a mountain of evidence to the contrary. Further, it is insulting to the thousands of decent Hispanic pioneers to whom he caused great distress, grief, and shame. Still, despite the realities of history, Murrieta remains a folk hero to Hispanics in California and Mexico.

The guarded animosity of Hispanic writers is well represented in the work of Arnold Rojas, an old *vaquero* and late-blooming writer. In several wonderful books of reminiscences dealing with early California *vaquero* lore and traditions, Rojas included tales of Murrieta reflecting the typical attitudes of Mexican-American writers. "There is no proof that Murrieta ever robbed anyone," stated Rojas. "That he took revenge for the outrages committed against him . . . cannot be denied, however." It can be "denied," though, since these "outrages" cannot be proved, either. Later in the same paragraph, Rojas admitted, "Since records are so meagre, for a picture of Murrieta we must depend on the stories of old people whose hazy memories unfortunately mix fact and fable indiscriminately."[5] Combined with his own lack of sources and dates, Rojas invalidated anything he has written about Murrieta by such statements.

The truth is, Murrieta and his men robbed their own countrymen as readily as they robbed Anglos. The theft of horses from the Corona ranch is easily verified by newspaper reports and the confession of Reyes Féliz, as is the robbing of a group of Mexican miners at Chinese Camp in late August 1852. And it was the robbing of a Mexican traveler that led to the killing of Claudio and several of his men. There were numerous other instances, but the point is apparent. Further, the bloody rampage of the

---

[5] Arnold R. Rojas, *These Were the Vaqueros, Collected Works of Arnold R. Rojas* (Sutter, Calif.: author, 1974), 221.

Murrieta gang in the winter of 1853 could hardly be justified by any cruel treatment received in the mines. No rational person slaughters innocent people, primarily inoffensive Chinese, for the crimes of others.

Actually, Murrieta and some of his men may have needed little if any prodding to turn outlaw. They were just boys. Joaquín was said, and looked to be, in his early twenties in 1853. At the time of their deaths, Reyes Féliz was only sixteen, while Claudio was reportedly only nineteen. But children matured much earlier in those days. Boys were doing the work of men at an early age, while girls were married at age fourteen and earlier. The attacks on the Marsh home, the Santa Clara ranch massacre, and the murders near Marysville the following year were so brutal and conscienceless that it is difficult to believe this was the work of disgruntled Mexican miners. Robbery, and perhaps beatings, might be the reaction of decent men driven to crime. The savage murders attributed to Murrieta, Claudio, and others of the gangs are more the work of boys away from home and running amuck. The boasting of Claudio in the Santa Clara jail is clearly the action of a juvenile delinquent, eager to be feared by his peers as a ferocious bandit and murderer.

• • •

In cleaning up the loose ends of the Murrieta story, we inevitably come to the strange saga of a woman who claimed to have been married to Joaquín. There is no evidence to substantiate her claim but, during her lifetime, Mariana Andrada was widely known as "Joaquín's widow."

She first came to public notice in 1874 during the search for a later Mexican outlaw, Tiburcio Vasquez. Boyd Henderson, a reporter for the *San Francisco Chronicle*, accompanied the posse of Sheriffs Harry Morse and Thomas Cunningham as they searched the west side of the San Joaquín Valley. Thinking Joaquín's so-called "widow" might have news of the outlaws, the lawmen sought her out where she was staying with a sheepherder on Kettleman's Plains, in what is now western Kings County. In an article in the *Chronicle* that same year, Henderson reported:

> Joaquin's widow, now forty-three years old, is a woman of medium height, and though rather stout is of finely-developed proportions. Despite her age, her loose mode of life, her present fondness for aguardiente, and a scar extending across her face from nose to ear, she is not by any means a homely or repulsive-looking woman. Her lips still retain their fine curves,

This tintype is reportedly the only known likeness of Mariana Andrada, who claimed to be the widow of Joaquín Murrieta. It seems to show her as described in an 1885 Fresno newspaper as "past fifty, fat and flabby" but "more cunning and designing than she looks."
R. C. Baker Museum.

and her teeth are a marvel of perfect preservation. It required no very strong draughts on the imagination to believe that twenty years ago she possessed a figure which was a model of grace.[6]

Mariana went on to relate how Joaquín had caught her in a dalliance with another man and had shot her twice in the arm, then slashed her face and breasts and left her for dead. There were those who later said her scars "had been acquired in a fandango hall brawl," but to the end of her days she stuck to her "widow of Joaquín" story.

---

[6] *San Francisco Chronicle*, May 17, 1874. The late Dr. Raymund F. Wood's *Mariana La Loca, Prophetess of the Cantua and Alleged Spouse of Joaquin Murrieta* (Fresno: Fresno County Historical Society, 1970), is a biography of this mysterious woman. Since 1970, other details of her life have become known.

The age Mariana gave Henderson would make her born about 1831, which tallies fairly well with what little is known of her early life. In 1935, Dr. G. H. Phillips, a Hanford dentist, recalled the old woman he had known around the turn of the century:

> She was about 70 years old and certainly no one would have believed that weather-beaten, wrinkled face of hers ever could have charmed the Mexican bandit. I confess that for a time I disbelieved her claims, but later I learned from an old resident, Mrs. Jack Sutherland.. that she knew Mariana in Sonora in the gold rush days and that she was a very fine-looking girl. She also vouched for the fact that Mariana was the sweetheart of Murieta [sic].[7]

After the Henderson interview, Mariana dropped from sight for some time but, by the late 1870s, she seems to have conceived the idea of a religious revival as a means of acquiring wealth. Some said that she had been living with local sheepherders and would roam the area around Las Tres Piedras—also known as Three Rocks or Joaquín Rocks—looking for her old paramour's buried gold. It was in this vast wasteland that she began preaching to the isolated Mexican and Portuguese sheepmen of the area.

In the fall of 1882, the Jesuit fathers of Santa Clara College petitioned the archbishop of San Francisco to gather information on the life of a noted early priest, Fr. Magin Catala, the "Holy Man of Santa Clara." A commissioner was authorized to travel about the state and gather information from people who had known this "holy man," who had died in 1830. Word of the interest in Father Magin eventually reached Mariana, who began to devise a way to capitalize on the late priest.[8]

First indications of Mariana's scheme were reported in the Fresno *Daily Expositor* in late April 1883. In a long interview with "an intelligent Basque Frenchman" named Pedro Lascelle, the article reported that many people were gathering in the Cantua Creek area to hear the preaching of the reincarnated spirit of Father Magin, the long-dead priest. According to Lascelle, he had talked to the mysterious person who could heal the sick,

---

[7] *The Fresno Bee*, October 7, 1935. John (Jack) Sutherland was a large rancher and cattleman who had come to Fresno County in 1857. Before that, he was a prospector in the gold rush country. For Sutherland's mining and ranching ventures in the early 1850s, see J. D. Mason, *History of Amador County, California* (Oakland: Thompson & West, 1881), 85, and Clough and Secrest, *Fresno County—The Pioneer Years*, 120, 146, 165.

[8] Raymund F. Wood, *Mariana La Loca, Prophetess of the Cantua & Alleged Spouse of Joaquin Murieta* (Fresno: Fresno County Historical Society, 1970), 20–50.

relieve the distressed, and address people by their proper name without knowing them. "He has sent out word to all who want to be saved to go and see him, and if they believe on him they shall not die."[9]

Mariana was preaching that the world was coming to an end that spring and all who believed in her would be saved. As the word spread, throngs of Mexicans, Portuguese, Basques, and other minorities gathered at the Three Rocks to hear Mariana's preachings—which included her acquisition of all the property of her subjects, since they would soon no longer need it. With the aid of several associates, Mariana produced "miracles," including Father Magin speaking out of a rock, mysterious pictures appearing at night, and a "devil," garbed in black, who rode about collecting money and jewelry from the faithful. Eyewitnesses at the time estimated that between 350 and 400 people were camped about the Three Rocks waiting for the great day of salvation.[10]

Of course, the whole thing was a fraud. One of Mariana's associates was a magician and another a ventriloquist. The new-fangled magic lantern of the time flashed pictures on a large boulder while the ventriloquist produced voices from the rocks. As impressive as her special effects were, Mariana made a mistake in naming a precise date for the end of the world—May 16, 1883. When the date arrived and nothing happened, the faithful became fidgety, and Mariana became scared. She quickly revised her doom date to a more nebulous time frame—"within three years."

Meanwhile, in the summer of 1883, strange stories began circulating from the west side of the valley. Particularly curious was an article in the Livermore *Valley Review* in July 1883. Under the heading "Joaquin Murietta's [sic] Widow," it was reported:

> The plan to increase the number of converts is to harbor all criminals and protect them from the hands of the law. And, every Spaniard or Mexican that accidentally strayed into camp or near it, to take them captives, confiscate their stock, jewelry, money, etc. and if they would not take the necessary oath, to lock them up by night and guard them by day until they would take the "robbers' oath" and become members of the band. This had been done, until today she reigns over a band of murderers, cutthroats and robbers that number over 300. Some four weeks ago Anton Roucher and an Italian started out looking for stock and fell into this camp, the she-devil took them prisoners and confiscated everything. Anton Roucher is

---
[9] San Francisco *Daily Morning Call*, May 2, 1883, as reprinted from the Fresno *Daily Expositor*.
[10] Ibid.

still there and his family are very anxious to have the authorities go after him and take him away from this hellhole on earth. Tuesday, a Mexican spy came in and reported these facts, and also that Juarez, the escaped murderer from the Martinez jail, was among the gang and that Ignacio Romero, his companion, had died there after being shot by Constable Fitzgerald and that the shot had penetrated one side and passed through him. Also, that he saw several familiar faces of desperadoes, horse and cattle thieves among the gang.[11]

The article closed by recommending that officers look into the situation. Actually, as early as mid-May 1883, Fresno County deputy sheriff Jim Meade made a trip to the area, but he found no gathering of outlaws.[12] An accompanying reporter described the various services without any reference to any resident criminals. But the strain was beginning to tell on everyone. As her converts began drifting away, Mariana took to drink. The intense preaching and trickery of the past few years had worn her down. A drunken prophetess quickly discouraged new converts and others of her flock. By 1885, only a handful of the faithful remained and the "Prophetess of the Cantua" decided that desperate measures were called for. In July, she apparently fatally poisoned the daughter of a family that was leaving. Mariana had grimly predicted they would "start for home, but come back crying." The child's father, Delfino Carona, had been skeptical of Mariana from the start, and quickly had her in the Fresno jail on a murder charge. Lack of witnesses and other evidence resulted in an acquittal, and Mariana walked out of court and down Mariposa Street a free woman.[13] But she had milked her religious scam dry, and the hills around Three Rocks were no longer host to crowds of fanatical followers.

In December 1890, Mariana again came into prominence when a petrified man was discovered in the area of Cantua Creek. The body, weighing some 415 pounds, was brought into Fresno and examined by various physicians and scientists who all pronounced it genuine. A few months later, the petrified corpse was being displayed in San Francisco while controversy raged over identification, as noted in the San Francisco *Bulletin* of April 13, 1891:

---

[11] The Livermore *Valley Review* article was reprinted in the San Jose *Daily Herald*, July 20, 1883, and the San Francisco *Call* of the same date.
[12] *Fresno Daily Expositor*, May 30, 1883.
[13] *Expositor*, July 17, 1885, and Wood, *Mariana La Loca*, 56–62. See also *The Fresno Bee*, November 8, 9, and 10, 1935, for Frank Latta's interviews with participants in Mariana's religious scheme.

At the time of the discovery considerable interest was excited among the old settlers around Fresno as to its identity, and numerous theories were advanced. A very romantic, and not improbable story in connection with the affair comes from the widow of Joaquin Murieta [*sic*], the once famous California bandit. She states that about thirty-two years ago Murieta and his band murdered a young Spaniard and buried his body on the banks of the Cantua creek, where they were then camped. She even located the grave to within a few yards of where the body was found. On the strength of her narrative the relatives of the murdered Spaniard set up a claim to get possession of the petrified body, but there being no marks by which to identify it, they failed to establish a claim. The body is so perfectly preserved that the corns on the feet can be easily distinguished.

The "petrified man" was later declared to have been carved out of sandstone by an itinerant Italian sculptor who happened to be in the area.

The "widow's" saga came to a sordid end on April 12, 1902. Known by this time as Mariana La Loca, or "Crazy Mariana," she lived with an old woodcutter named Gabriel near Hanford. She was intoxicated that day as she walked down the road paralleling the railroad tracks toward the small village of Kingston in southern Fresno County. The engineer of the California Limited saw her a quarter of a mile away and watched as she approached the intersection where the road crossed the tracks. As the train roared toward the crossing Mariana hesitated, as if confused, then stepped directly in front of the onrushing locomotive. By the time the train had stopped and the engineer and fireman had raced back to where the crumpled body lay, Mariana was dead. She was buried in Hanford's Catholic Cemetery.[14]

But what of Mariana's claim to have been Murrieta's wife? Although various researchers have looked into her claim and found it wanting, there are still nagging questions relating to her story. What of the Hanford dentist who was told by early cattleman Jack Sutherland's wife that Mariana had, indeed, been one of Joaquín's women? And the petrified man story? Teodora Arredondo, who was involved in Mariana's religious scam, said she had first met Mariana at the funeral of one of Murrieta's old gang members. She seems to have had some tie-in with the famous bandit, but just what that connection was will perhaps forever remain a mystery.

The final question is perhaps the most provocative of all. Mariana was

---

[14]*Hanford Journal,* April 12, 1902.

buried under the name "Ana Andrada" and is so listed in the Kings County coroner records. Her age is given as "about 70 years." Could it be that in reality she was Ana Benitez, whom Joaquín had left at San Gabriel after the Bean killing?[15] *Quien sabe?* We'll probably never know.

[15] *Los Angeles Star*, December 4, 1852.

Bibliography / Principal Sources

BOOKS

Allen, George W. *Love History and Genealogy*. La Porte, Ind.: Allen Press, 1937.

Andrews, John R. *Ghost Towns of Amador*. New York: The Carlton Press, Inc., 1967.

Angel, Myron. *History of San Luis Obispo County, California*. Oakland: Thompson & West, 1883.

Angel, Myron, and Fairchild, M. D. *History of Placer County, California*. Oakland: Thompson & West, 1882.

Bancroft, Hubert Howe. *Popular Tribunals, Vol. 2*. San Francisco: The History Company, 1887.

———. *History of California, Vol. 3, 1860–1890*. San Francisco: The History Company, 1890.

Bauer, K. Jack. *The Mexican War, 1846–1848*. New York: Macmillan Publishing Company, 1974.

Beal, Richard A. *Highway 17, the Road to Santa Cruz*. Aptos, Calif.: The Pacific Group, 1991.

Bell, Horace. *Reminiscences of a Ranger*. Santa Barbara: Wallace Hebberd, 1927.

Bieber, Ralph, and Averam B. Bander, eds. *Exploring Southwestern Trails, 1846–1854*. Glendale: The Arthur H. Clark Company, 1938.

Borthwick, J. D. *Three Years in California*. Edinburg: William Blackford & Sons, 1857.

Branda, Eldon Stephen, ed. *The Handbook of Texas, A Supplement*. Vol. 3, Austin: The Texas State Historical Association, 1976.

Brewer, William H. *Up and Down California in 1860–1864*. Berkeley and Los Angeles: University of California Press, 1966.

Brown, D. McKenzie. *China Trade Days in California*. Berkeley and Los Angeles: University of California Press, 1947.

Browning, Peter, ed. *Bright Gem of the Western Seas*. Lafayette, Calif.: Great West Books, 1991.

Bryant, Edward. *What I Saw in California.* New York: Appleton, 1848.
Buffum, Edward Gould. *Six Months in the Gold Mines.* Los Angeles: The Ward Ritchie Press, 1959.
Cazneau, Mrs. William L. *Eagle Pass or Life on the Border.* Robert Crawford Cotner, ed. Austin: Pemberton Press, 1966.
Chamberlain, William Henry and Wells, Harry L. *History of Yuba County, California.* Oakland: Thompson & West, 1879.
Cleland, Robert. *The Cattle on a Thousand Hills.* San Marino: The Huntington Library, 1951.
Clough, Charles W. and William B. Secrest, Jr. *Fresno County, The Pioneer Years.* Fresno: Panorama West Books, 1984.
Coker, Caleb, ed. *The News from Brownsville, Helen Chapman's Letters from the Texas Military Frontier, 1848–1852.* Austin: Texas State Historical Association, 1992.
Collins, Carvel. *Sam Ward in the Gold Rush.* Stanford, Calif.: Stanford University Press, 1949.
Colton, Walter. *Three Years in California.* Stanford, Calif.: Stanford University Press, 1949.
Cossly-Batt, Jill L. *The Last of the California Rangers.* New York and London: Funk & Wagnalls Corporation, 1928.
Cullimore, Clarence. *Old Adobes of Forgotten Fort Tejon.* Bakersfield: Kern County Historical Society, 1949.
Davis, William Heath. *Seventy-five Years in California.* San Francisco: John Howell, Publishers, 1929.
DeVoto, Bernard. *The Year of Decision: 1846.* Boston: Little, Brown & Company, 1943.
Doble, John. *John Doble's Journal and Letters from the Mines . . . 1851–1865.* Denver: The Old West Publishing Company, 1962.
Dobyns, Henry F., ed. *Hepah, California! The Journal of Cave Johnson Coutts.* Tucson: Arizona Pioneers Historical Society, 1961.
Donovan, Frank. *Riverboats of America.* New York: Thomas Y. Crowell Company, 1966.
Downey, Joseph T. *Filings From an Old Saw.* San Francisco: John Howell, Publishers, 1956.
Eisenhower, John S. D. *So Far From God, The United States War with Mexico, 1846–1848.* New York: Random House, Inc., 1989.
Enery, Thomas M., ed. *California Pioneer, The Journal of Captain Thomas Fallon.* San Jose: Inishfallen Enterprises, 1978.
Fite, Gilbert C. *The Farmer's Frontier, 1865–1900.* New York: Holt, Rinehart and Winston, 1966.
Foote, Horace S. *History of Santa Clara County, California.* Chicago: Lewis Publishing Company, 1888.

Gagey, Edmond M. *The San Francisco Stage.* New York: Columbia University Press, 1950.
Garner, William Robert. *Letters from California, 1846–1847.* Berkeley and Los Angeles: University of California Press, 1970.
Hammond, George P., ed. *The Larkin Papers.* 10 vols. Berkeley and Los Angeles: University of California Press, 1952.
Haney, Kenneth. *Gold Rush by Sea.* Philadelphia: University of Pennsylvania Press, 1941.
Hart, Herbert M. *Pioneer Forts of the West.* Seattle: Superior Publishing Company, 1967.
Harrel, Nita. *The Sanchez Treasure.* San Juan Bautista, Calif.: San Juan Bautista Historical Publishers, 1975.
Historical Atlas Map of Santa Clara County, California. San Francisco: Thompson & West, 1876.
Hoover, Mildred Brooke, Hero Eugene Rensch, and Ethel Grace Rensch, rev. by William N. Abeloe. *Historic Spots in California.* 3rd edition. Stanford, Calif.: Stanford University Press, 1966.
Kelly, Pat. *River of Lost Dreams.* Lincoln and London: University of Nebraska Press, 1986.
Kirby, Georgiana Bruce. *The Journal of Georgiana Bruce Kirby, 1852–1860.* Santa Cruz: Santa Cruz Historical Trust, 1987.
Klyn, Dianne C. *Joaquin Murrieta in California.* San Ramon: The Publishing Place, 1989.
Knight, Donald G., and Eugene D. Wheeler. *Agony and Death on a Gold Rush Steamer.* Ventura: Pathfinder Publishing of California, 1990.
Koch, Margaret. *Santa Cruz County, Parade of the Past.* Fresno: Valley Publishers, 1973.
Lamott, Kenneth. *Chronicles of San Quentin.* New York: David McKay Company, Inc., 1961.
Lang, Herbert. *History of Tuolumne County.* San Francisco: B.F. Alley, 1882.
Lang, Margaret Hanna. *Early Justice in Sonora.* Sonora, Calif.: The Mother Lode Press, 1963.
Langum, David J. *Law and Community on the Mexican California Frontier; Anglo-American Expatriots and the Clash of Legal Traditions, 1821–1846.* Norman and London: University of Oklahoma Press, 1987.
Latta, Frank F. *El Camino Viejo á Los Angeles.* Bakersfield: Kern County Historical Society, 1933.
———. *Joaquín Murrieta and His Horse Gangs.* Santa Cruz: Bear State Books, 1980.
Lewis, Betty. *Watsonville, Memories that Linger.* Fresno: Valley Publishers, 1976.
Loughhead, Flora Hanes, ed. *Life, Diary and Letters of Oscar Lovell Shafter.* San Francisco: The Blair-Murdock Company, 1915.

Lydston, G. Frank, M.D. *Panama and the Sierras.* Chicago: The Rintar Press, 1900.
Makey, Michael J. *The Hanging of Lucky Bill.* Woodfords, Calif.: Eastern Sierra Press, 1993.
Marryat, Frank. *Mountains and Molehills, or Recollections of a Burnt Journal.* London: Longman, Green and Lonmans, 1855.
McGaw, William C. *Savage Scene.* New York: Hastings House, 1972.
McHugh, Tom. *Hazeldell Charivari, Christmas at Zayante, 1856.* Santa Cruz: Penny Press Publishing Company, 1959.
Miller, Henry. *Account of a Tour of the California Missions, 1856: The Journal and Drawings of Henry Miller.* San Francisco: Book Club of California, 1952.
Mussey, Barrows. *A Book of Country Things.* Brattleboro, Vt.: Stephen Greene Press, 1965.
Mylar, Isaac L. *Early Days at the Mission San Juan Bautista.* Watsonville, Calif.: Evening Pajaronian, 1929.
Nadeau, Remi. *The Real Joaquin Murieta.* Corona del Mar, Calif.: Trans-Anglo Books, 1974.
Nunis, Doyce B. Jr., ed. *The San Francisco Vigilance Committee of 1856, Three Views.* Los Angeles: Los Angeles Westerners, 1971.
———. *The Trials of Isaac Graham.* Los Angeles: Dawson's Book Store, 1967.
O'Neal, Paul. *The Rivermen.* New York: Time-Life Books, 1975.
Outcalt, John. *History of Merced County, California.* Los Angeles: Historic Record Company, 1925.
Peck, Lt. John J. *The Sign of the Eagle.* Foreword and Commentary by Richard Pourade. San Diego: Copley Books, 1970.
Perkins, William. *William Perkins' Journal of Life at Sonora, 1849–1852.* Berkeley and Los Angeles: University of California Press, 1964.
Preston, Brenda Burnett. *Andrew and Susan Firebaugh, California Pioneers.* Rio Del Mar, Calif.: Rio Del Mar Press, 1995.
Rasmussen, Louis J. *San Francisco Passenger Lists*, vol. 2. Colma, Calif.: San Francisco Historic Records, 1966.
Ridge, John Rollin (Yellow Bird). *The Life and Adventures of Joaquin Murieta.* Norman: University of Oklahoma Press, 1955.
Rogers, Fred B. *Soldiers of the Overland.* San Francsco: The Grabhorn Press, 1938.
Rojas, Arnold R. *These Were the Vaqueros.* Shafter, Calif.: the author, 1974.
Romero, Michael. *Joaquin Murrieta, The Life of a Legend.* Soledad, Calif.: the author, 1979.
Rowland, Leon. *Santa Cruz, The Early Years.* Santa Cruz: Paper Vision Press, 1980.
Ruxton, George Frederick. *Adventures in Mexico.* New York: Outing Publishing Company, 1915.
Secrest, William B. *The Gold of Old Hornitos.* Fresno: Saga-West Publishing Company, 1964.
———. *Joaquin, Bloody Bandit of the Mother Lode.* Fresno: Saga-West Publishing Company, 1967.

———. *Lawmen and Desperadoes*. Spokane, Wash.: The Arthur H. Clark Company, 1994.
Senkewicz, Robert M. *Vigilantes in Gold Rush San Francisco*. Stanford, Calif.: Stanford University Press, 1985.
Shumate, Dr. Albert, ed. *Boyhood Days, Ygnacio Villegas' Reminiscences of California in the 1850s*. San Francisco: California Historical Society, 1983.
Shumway, Burgess McK. *California Ranchos*. San Bernardino, Calif.: The Borgo Press and Glendale, Calif.: The Sidewinder Press, 1988.
Smith, George Winston, and Charles Judah. *Chronicles at the Gringos: The U.S. Army in the Mexican War, 1846–1848*. Albuquerque: University of New Mexico Press, 1968.
Smith, Justin H. *The War with Mexico*. 2 vols. New York: The Macmillan Company, 1919.
Sonnichsen, C. L. *Roy Bean, Law West of the Pecos*. New York: The Macmillan Company, 1943.
Soulé, Frank, John H. Gihon, and James Nisbet. *The Annals of San Francisco*. New York: Appleton, 1854.
Stoddart, Thomas Roberson. *Annals of Tuolumne County*. Sonora, Calif.: Tuolumne County Historical Society, 1963.
Tolbert, Frank X. *The Day of San Jacinto*. New York: McGraw Hill Book Company, Inc., 1959.
Varley, James F. *The Legend of Joaquín Murrieta*. Twin Falls, Id.: Big Lost River Press, 1995.
Vielé, Teresa Griffin. *Following the Drum*. New York: Rudd & Carleton, 1858.
Wislizenus, A., M.D. *Memoirs of a Tour to Northern Mexico*. Glorieta, New Mexico: The Rio Grande Press, Inc., 1962.
Wood, Raymund F. *California's Agua Fria, The Early History of Mariposa County*. Fresno: Academy Library Guild, 1954.
———. *Mariana La Loca, Prophetess of the Cantua and Alleged Spouse of Joaquin Murietta*. Fresno: Fresno County Historical Society, 1970.

Journals

Butler, Steven R. "Alabama Volunteers in the Mexican War, Part Two." *Alabama Genealogical Society Magazine* 23 (1991).
Canfield, Eli. "In the Twilight of his Years, Eli Canfield Recalls his Boyhood in Arlington, 1817–1831." *Vermont History* (Spring 1972).
Early, Mabel Dorn. "The Bennett Family." *The Pony Express* (September–November 1950).
———. "The Black Knight of Zayante." *The Pony Express* (November 1953).
Edgar, William F., M.D. "Old Fort Miller." *Historical Society of Southern California*. Annual publication, 1893.
Gates, Paul. "The California Land Act of 1851." *California Historical Society Quarterly* (December 1971).

Latta, Frank F. "Murietta Rides Again." *The Pony Express* (September 1962).
Parker, Paul P. "The Roach-Belcher Feud." *California Historical Society Quarterly* (March 1950).
Ramey, Earl. "The Beginnings of Marysville." *California Historical Society Quarterly* (March 1936).
Rogers, Fred B. "Bear Flag Lieutenant." *California Historical Society Quarterly* (March 1951).
Roper, William L. "The Duel on Horseback, Roy Bean in Old Town." *San Diego Magazine* (October 1972).
Rowland, Jeanette. "Widow Bennett." *News & Notes, Santa Cruz Historical Society* (June 1958).
"Spanish Pioneer Homes of California." *Magazine of American History* (January and June 1890).
Standart, Sister M. Colette, O.P.. "The Sonora Migration to California, 1848–1856: A Study in Prejudice." *Southern California Quarterly* (Fall 1976).
Strickland, Rex W. "P.T. Herbert: Ante-bellum Resident of El Paso." *Password, Quarterly of El Paso Historical Society* (April 1960).
Wood, Raymund F. "New Light on Joaquin Murrieta." *Pacific Historian* (Winter 1970).

UNPUBLISHED MATERIALS

Baratie, Mrs. Andrea. 1858 statement in Vigilante Papers, San Luis Obispo Historical Society, San Luis Obispo, California.
Bennett, Mary. Receipt to William H. Davis, December 4, 1846; DA 35 in Collections of Huntington Library, San Marino, California.
Blankenship, Zachariah. Interview by Frank F. Latta in George W. Stewart Collection, California Room, California State Library.
Coolbaugh, Joel W. "The Sawmill Era, A History of the Redwood Industry in Santa Cruz, California." A Paper for History 375, 1963 (Stanford University) Library, Special Collections, University of California at Santa Cruz, California.
Detlefs, Charlene. *Brief History of the Falls / Love Creek.* Ben Lomond, Santa Cruz County, California, 1977. Typescript in Special Collections, Library, University of California at Santa Cruz, California.
Love, Harry. Two letters 1859 and 1862, in *Transcript of the Proceedings in Case No. 260: Isaac Graham et al, Claimant vs. The United States, Defendant, for the place named "Zayanta."* Special Collections, Library, University of California at Santa Cruz, California.
———. Letter to John Wilson. John Wilson Collection, Bancroft Library, University of California, Berkeley.
Love, Henry [Harry]. Application for enrollment in 1856 San Francisco Vigilance Committee. In collections of the Huntington Library, San Marino, California.

Love, Mary. Letter to John Wilson in John Wilson Collection, Bancroft Library, University of California, Berkeley.
Monterey County Marriage Records, 1850–1860. Microfilm in Church of Jesus Christ of Latter Day Saints, Monterey Stake, Genealogical Society, Seaside, California.
Rawson, A. W. Diary, in the Bancroft Library, University of California, Berkeley, California.
Rood, Robert C. "Historical and Environmental Impact of the Lumber Industry on the Santa Cruz Mountains." 1975, Geography and Environmental Studies, Thesis, University of California at Santa Cruz, California.
Schroeder, Mrs. Bertha. "Mariposa News, 1850–1859: Gleanings from California Newspapers." Unpublished typescript in collection of author.
———. Correspondence October–November, 1976.
Sweet, Nathan. Materials in June English Collection, Special Collections, Henry Madden Library, California State University, Fresno, California.
Valenzuela, Joaquín. Letters 1858, in Vigilante Papers, Collections of San Luis Obispo Historical Society, San Luis Obispo, California.
Wilson, Mrs. Joyce. Letter to author, November 7, 1995, and other materials, including photographs, reminiscences and Bludworth family genealogy.
Winchell, Lilbourne. Manuscript materials in collections of Fresno City and County Historical Society.

Government Documents

Book of Supervisor's Minutes, Volume A, 1852–1853, Court of Sessions, Mariposa County, Mariposa, California.
Books 1 and 2, Deeds, 1851–1853; Book 2 and 4, Deeds, 1854; Book 3, Deeds, 1855; Book 3, Deeds, 1856; Book 5, Deeds, 1860, County Recorder's Office, Santa Cruz, California.
Bostic, Leslie vs. Mary Love, No. 2607, WPA No. 12739, 1860. California State Archives, Sacramento, California.
Chapman, Major William W., to Harry Love, January 30, 1849, in Chapman Letter Book, collection of Caleb Coker.
Chapman, Major William W. to Major General Thomas S. Jessup, June 8, 1849; Records Group 92, Records of the Office of the Quartermaster General, Consolidated Correspondence File 1792–1890 National Archives, Washington, D.C.
Chapman, Major William W., to Harry Love, March 4, 1850; Records Group 92, Records of the Office of the Quartermaster General, Consolidated Correspondence File 1794–1890. National Archives, Washington, D.C.
Chapman, Major William W., to Major E.B. Babbitt, September 14, 1850; Records Group 92, Records of the Office of the Quartermaster General, Consolidated Correspondence File 1794–1890. National Archives, Washington, D.C.

California State Legislature, "Statutes of California." Sacramento, Government Printing Office, 1853.
Document No. 25, in Senate [session 1855] Report of Committee Relative to the Condition and Management of the State Prison. Sacramento: B.B. Redding, State Printer.
House of Representatives, 33rd Congress, 2nd Session, Executive Document No. 91, *Reports of Explorations and Surveys to ascertain the most practical and Economical Route for a Railroad, etc. 1853–1854*, Vol. 5. Washington, D.C.: A.O.P. Nicholson, Printer, 1856.
Journal of the Fifth Session of the Legislature of the State of California. Sacramento: B.B. Redding, 1854.
Joaquin Murrieta Papers, Bin 268, California State Archives, Sacramento, California.
King, Captain John H., to Brevet Major George Deas, Assistant Adjutant General, April 10, 1850; Records Group 393, Letters Received, Western Department and Department of U.S. Army Commands, National Archives, Washington, D.C.
King, James, vs. Harry Love, Case No. 364, District Court, 3rd Judicial District, December 1861. Santa Cruz County, California.
List of Convicts on Register of State Prison at San Quentin. Sacramento: State Printing Office, 1889.
Love vs. Love, Case No. 627, District Court, Third Judicial District, December, 1867. Santa Cruz County, California.
Love, Harry, Probate Records, 1868. Santa Clara County Recorder's Office, San Jose, California.
Love, Mary, vs. B. F. Watkins, 40 California Reports 547 (January Term, 1871).
Maclay, Charles, vs. Harry Love and Mary Love, No. 3527, WPA No. 4886, 1862. California State Archives, Sacramento, California.
Maclay, Charles, vs. Harry Love and Mary Love, 25 California Reports 367 (July Term, 1864).
Mariposa County Special Census, 1852, California History and Genealogy Room, Fresno County Public Library, Fresno, California.
People of the State against Harry Love, Perjury, Santa Cruz County Court of Sessions, Book 2, August Term, 1860.
Santa Cruz County Agricultural Census, 1860. Ellis Collection, Santa Cruz Public Library, Santa Cruz, California.
Shartzer, Hiram, vs. Harry Love and Mary Love, 40 California Reports 93 (October, 1870).
U.S. Population Schedules, 1850 Census, Tuolumne County, California.
U.S. Population Schedules, 1860 Census, Santa Clara County, California.

U.S. Population Schedules, 1860 Census, Santa Cruz County, California.
U.S. Population Schedules, 1870 Census, Santa Clara County, California.
Volume 4, Mortgages, 1867. County Clerk's Office, Santa Cruz, California.

CALIFORNIA NEWSPAPERS

Auburn Herald
Benicia Gazette
Calaveras Chronicle
Calaveras Prospect
Columbia Gazette
El Clamor Publico
Fresno Bee
Fresno Expositor
Fresno Republican
Los Angeles Star
Livermore Valley Review
Mariposa Gazette
Mariposa Democrat
Marysville Appeal
Marysville Herald
Merced County Sun
Pajaro Times
Placer Times & Transcript
Placerville Herald
Placerville Mountain-Democrat
Pleasanton Times
Sacramento Democratic State Journal
San Francisco *Alta California*
San Francisco Bulletin
San Francisco Call
San Francisco Call-Bulletin
San Francisco Chronicle
San Francisco Examiner
San Francisco Herald
San Francisco Pacific News
San Francisco Picayune
San Jose Mercury
San Jose Patriot
San Jose Pioneer
San Jose Semi-weekly Tribune
San Jose Visitor
Santa Barbara Gazette
Santa Cruz *Sentinel*
Santa Cruz *Pacific Sentinel*
Santa Cruz *Surf*
Stockton Argus
Stockton Herald
Stockton Journal
Stockton *San Joaquin Republican*
Stockton Times
Tulare County Record
Tulare Times
Tulare Record & Fresno Examiner
Tuolumne Courier
Visalia Delta
Visalia Times-Delta

OTHER NEWSPAPERS

American Flag (Mexico)
Congressional Globe (Washington)
Corpus Christi Star
Houston Telegraph
Mobile Register & Journal
New Orleans Bee
New Orleans Picayune
New York Herald
New York Times
Sandusky (Ohio) *Clarion*
Syracuse (New York) *Standard*
Troy (New York) *Daily Budget*
Washington Star
New Orleans Delta

Index

Abernathy, Seaburn, 57
Acklin, William M., 59, 60
Adams, Julia Bennett, 173, 227, 246
Adams, Ramon, 13
Adams, Samuel, 241
Agapito (traveler), 84
Agua Fria, Calif., 131
Aguila, José, 95 n. 13
Akop (Chinese), 107
Alabama, 23, 27–28, 32, 33, 60, 126
Alameda (San Juan Bautista, Calif.), 135
Alameda County, Calif., 60, 60 n. 22, 79
Alameda Creek, Calif., 60
Alamo (San Antonio, Texas), 15
Alexander, David, 198 n. 37, 218, 219
Allen (packer), 42
Allen, Ethan, 20
Alviso, José, 102
Amador, Calif., 114
Amador Creek, Calif., 114
American Camp. *See* Columbia, Calif.
American Flag (newspaper, Matamoros, Mex.), 15, 16, 44
American Theater (San Francisco), 188
Andrada, Ana. *See* La Loca, Mariana
Andrade, Mateo, 85
Ann (captive girl), 220
Anthony (innkeeper), 193, 194
Anthony family (Santa Cruz, Calif.), 185
Anza Trail, Calif., 51
Apaches, 43, 49
Arizona Territory, 264

Arkansas, 173
Armstrong, G. M., 39
Arredondo, Teodora, 51
Arroyo de Cantua, Calif., 163. *See also* Cantua Creek, Calif.
Ashley, Otis, 223, 224
Ashley's schoolhouse (Santa Cruz, Calif.), 236
Aspinwall, Panama, 187, 190, 191
Astor House (Jackson, Calif.), 112
Auburn, Calif., 169
Austin, Texas, 45, 46
Australia, 74, 112, 250
Avisimba (near San Jose, Calif.), 102

"B.R.," 107 n. 6
Babbitt, E. B., 63, 65, 66
Bad Company (Joseph Henry Jackson), 13
Bakersfield, Calif., 218
Banta, Susan, 158
Baratie, Bartolo, 217, 218
Barber, E. G., 58
Barclay, E. J., 211, 212
Barumas (murderer), 103
Basques, 217, 272, 273
Bay State Ranch, Calif., 108, 110
Baylor, Captain, 34
Beale, Edward F., 152
Beall, Benjamin L., 226
Bean, Joshua, 98, 99–100, 101–103, 107, 122, 276
Bean, Roy, 100

Bear Creek, Calif., 117
Bear Flag Revolt, Calif., 178, 222 n. 4
Bear Mountain, Calif., 107 n. 6
Beaurais, A. B., 84
Beckwith, A. C., 205
Beeman, Truman, 206
Belcher, Lewis F., 201–206, 207
Bell, Horace, 98, 103
Belt's Ferry, Calif., 87, 88
Ben Lomond, Calif., 261
Benicia, Calif., 119, 123, 156, 161, 163, 164, 165, 171
Benítez, Ana, 101, 102, 103, 276
Bennett, Amanda, 173
Bennett, Catherine. *See* McCusker, Catherine Bennett
Bennett, Clementhia, 250, 252 n. 16, 253, 254
Bennett, David Jackson, 173, 176, 178, 180, 181, 185, 193, 214, 216, 216 n. 16
Bennett, Dennis, 173, 176, 178, 180, 181, 182, 186, 214
Bennett, Julia. *See* Adams, Julia Bennett
Bennett, Mansel, 173, 215, 216, 227, 246, 246 n. 3, 251 n. 13
Bennett, Mary. *See* Love, Mary Swain Bennett
Bennett, Narciso. *See* Bennett, Vardamon
Bennett, Samantha, 173, 247
Bennett, Vardamon (Narciso), 173–176, 178–179, 182, 186, 221, 221 n. 2–3, 243, 250 n. 10
Bennett, Winston, 173, 176, 179, 186, 216, 227, 243, 246, 250, 259 n. 25, 261
Bennett family, 173, 174 n. 2, 175, 185
Bennett–Love sawmill, 178, 178 n. 9, 185, 185 n. 7, 192, 193 n. 28, 214, 215, 222, 223, 227, 233, 236, 245, 247
Bennington, Vt., 20
Bester (rancher), 57
Betts, Ike, 110
Big Bar, Calif., 84
Bigler, John, 14, 113, 116, 121, 126, 130, 136, 155, 161, 164, 165, 166, 171, 187
Billings, Justice, 258

Bingham, C. E. (Ned), 187–188, 189, 191
Bingham, Emily Thorn, 188
Bishop, Samuel, 150 n. 3, 152, 152 n. 8–9, 153, 266
Bishop's Ferry, Calif., 150 n. 3
Biven, William, 236, 237
"Black Knight of the Zayante" (Harry Love), 235, 256
Black, Lafayette, 125, 161, 162
Blackburn, William, 223, 242
Blackhawk Indian War, 22
Blanco, Miguel, 217, 218
Blankenship, Zachariah T., 133 n. 32
Bludworth, Charles, 124, 126, 148, 148 n. 18, 149, 172, 209, 209 n. 1–2, 210, 211–212, 213
Bludworth, Mary Annette, 148 n. 18
Boessenecker, John, 207 n. 16
Bolcoff, José, 177, 178
Boling, John, 156, 156 n. 19, 226
Bond, Stephen, 158
Borel, M., 217
Borella, José, 81, 129
Boston, Mass., 20, 22, 202
Botellas, Joaquín, 122, 122 n. 3
Botellas, Refugio, 122, 122 n. 3
Botellier, Joaquín, 122, 122 n. 3
Bottellier, Joaquín (alias), 122
Bowen, Isaac, 77
Brady, Francis R., 215
Branciforte Creek, Calif., 214
Brazos Santiago, Texas, 63, 65, 69
Breen, Patrick, 135
Brent, Thomas L., 41
Brisano, Jesus, 107
Brown, A. L., 157–158
Brown, Charles, 240
Brown, Warren, 157–158
Brownsville, Texas, 16, 36, 39, 45–46, 47, 69, 70, 71
Bryant, Edwin, 173
Bryant, William Cullen, 87
Bryant's sawmill (Santa Cruz, Calif.), 233
Buchanan, R. B. "Buck," 77–78, 79, 108, 110, 168

Index 289

Buena Esperanza Rancho, Calif., 204
Buena Vista (battle, Mexican War), 126
Buena Vista Ranch, Calif., 123, 127, 131, 132, 155, 200
Buena Vista Valley, Calif., 123
Buffum, Edward G., 99
Burita, Mex., 28
Burnett, Peter, 57
Burns Creek, Calif., 87, 115, 123
Bustamante, Tomas Procopio, 267
Butano, Calif., 214
Butler, E. P., 246, 246 n. 3
Byrd, Thomas, 185
Byrnes, Marion Ross, 201
Byrnes, William W., 125, 126, 128, 135 n. 2, 138, 143–144, 146, 149–155, 159, 172, 201, 201 n. 8–10, 203, 204, 206, 207

Cajon Pass, Calif., 100
Calaveras Chronicle (newspaper), 106, 109, 112
Calaveras County, Calif., 54, 79, 105, 113–114, 118, 123, 124, 128, 160, 164, 169, 170
Calaveras River, Calif., 84, 110, 112, 139
Calaveras road, Calif., 157
Caldwell, A. B., 252 n. 16, 255
Caldwell residence, 241
California, 13, 14, 17, 23, 36, 41, 42, 47, 48, 49, 50, 52, 53, 54, 56, 59, 65, 71, 73, 75, 80, 87, 99, 104, 107, 119, 121, 122, 123, 132, 148, 152, 154, 159, 162, 164, 170, 171, 173, 176, 177, 179, 182, 183, 188, 191, 192, 193, 202, 209, 212, 213, 217, 224, 226, 229, 230, 231, 232, 236, 249, 256, 258, 261, 263, 264, 265
California Chronicle (newspaper), 200
California gold rush, 13, 17, 41, 42, 49, 73, 74
California Land Act of 1851, 229
California Limited (railroad train), 275
California Militia, 99
California Ranch, Calif., 151, 151 n. 7
California Rangers, 14, 15, 17, 19, 59, 119, 121–172, 183, 194, 201, 209, 225, 236, 239, 240, 246, 250, 251, 255, 256, 266

California State Assembly, 117, 119, 172
California State Assembly, Committee on Military Affairs, 117, 119
California State Legislature, 119, 122, 123, 131, 164, 165, 171–172
California State Senate, 119, 172
California Supreme Court, 228
Californios, 50, 58, 61, 75, 137, 163, 173, 197
Callison, Charles W., 267–268, 268 n. 3
Camargo, Mex., 25, 30, 31, 32, 32 n. 15, 39, 40, 41
Camp Opera, Calif., 112
Campbell, Reuben P., 38 n. 29
Campo Seco, Calif., 83, 114
Cañada Molino Vallejo, Calif., 60
Canavan, Edward, 139
Canfield, Eli, 21
Cantua Creek, Calif., 14, 135, 137 n. 4, 138 n. 5, 140, 143, 155, 163, 266, 267, 272–275
Cape of Good Hope, 224
Carona, Delfino, 274
Carly, Joseph, 82
Carrillo, Jesús, 50
Carrillo, Joaquín (alias), 122, 129
Carrillo, Joaquín, 60, 113, 117, 118, 121, 122, 263, 267
Carrillo, Joaquín Manuel, 50
Carrillo, Juan, 50
Carrillo family, 50
Carrollton Railroad Depot, Texas, 27
Carson, James H., 61, 61 n. 24
Carson Valley, Calif., 213
Carson Valley, Nevada, 126
Carson's Hill, Calif., 112
Casey, James P., 215
Catala, Magin ("Holy Man of Santa Clara"), 272, 273
cattle trade, 23 n. 12, 13
Cazneau, Jane Matthews, 66 n. 8
Cessimera family, 219
Ceylon, 224
Chamberlain, Mr. *See* Champlain, Mr.
Chamberlain, Sam, 34
Champlain, Mr. (Chamberlain), 200, 201
Chandler, James, 30, 31

Chandler, Reuben, 182
Chapman, Helen, 35, 44–47
Chapman, William, 35, 36, 38–39, 41, 43, 45, 47–48, 63–66, 69–71
Chapman, Willie, 48
"Chappo" (Murrieta gang member), 280
Cherokee Ranch, Calif., 111
Cherokees, 13, 41, 42
Chihuahua, Mex., 36, 38, 40–41
Chileans, 59, 114
China trade, 23 n. 12
Chinese, 53, 83, 107, 108, 111, 112, 113, 170, 171, 190, 266
Chinese Camp, Calif., 83, 269
circus, 224, 225
City Hotel (Aspinwall, Panama), 190
Clark (posse member), 79–80
Clark, Charles, 112, 113
Clark, D. S., 130, 156
Clay, Tom, 206
Clements, Mr., 65
"Cloudy" (outlaw). See Féliz, Claudio
Coast Range Mountains, Calif., 75, 89, 108
Cochran (posse member), 79–80
Cocks, Henry, 84
Coker, Caleb, 36 n. 26
Coleman (posse member), 205
Coleman, William T., 215
Colorado River, 49
Columbia, Calif. (American Camp), 53, 54, 81, 82, 129, 169, 170
Columbia Gazette, 169, 192
Comanches, 36, 37 n. 27, 70
Connor, Patrick E., 124, 126, 128, 131, 132, 139, 142, 159, 170, 172, 200
Contra Costa County, Calif., 128
Cook's Gulch, Calif., 111
Cora, Charles, 214, 215
Corona, Yrenero, 93, 95, 102, 269
Corpus Christi, Texas, 25, 43, 45, 69
Corpus Christi Star (newspaper), 43, 45
Cosumnes River, Calif., 111, 117
Cottonwood Creek, Calif., 91, 94
Courtney (horse owner), 104

Couts, Cave J., 49
Covarrubias, José M., 117–118
Cowell (lime kiln owner, Santa Cruz, Calif.), 239, 241
crack-a-loo (game), 210, 213
Crane, Encarnación Sanchez Sanford, 202, 206
Crane, George, 206
"Crazy Mariana." See La Loca, Mariana
crime in California, 76 n. 7
Crowell, Henry, 115, 116
Crowley, Private, 226
Cruz, Cheverino, 105
Cruz, Joaquín (alias), 129
Cuesta del Conejo, Calif., 102
Cunningham, Thomas, 270

Dainwood, Boston 226
Danby, Justice, 168
Dashaway (horse), 225
Davis (lime kiln owner, Santa Cruz, Calif.), 239, 241
Davis, William Heath, 175, 176
Davis and Cowell (lime kiln owners, Santa Cruz, Calif.), 239, 241
Dawson (outlaw), 139, 140
De Ferrari, Carlo M., 53 n. 7
de la Torre, Joaquin, 205, 207
Democratic State Journal, 167
Democratic Times & Transcript (newspaper), 167
Denin, Kate, 188
Denin, Susan. See Woodward, Susan Denin
Dent's Ferry, Calif., 91
Derby, George H., 140
Desha, Robert, 27, 28, 30, 31, 32, 34
Dickenson's Ferry Calif., 88
Ditmar, T. J., 228
Doble, John, 114
Dolores family, 219
Don Llano, N.M., 43
Donner party, 135, 199
Dorsey, Caleb, 81–83

Doten, Alfred, 84, 169
Douglas, James, 84
Douglas, Stephen, 22
Dry Creek, Calif., 114
Drytown, Calif., 114
Duartes, Antonio, 107
Duff, J. L., 252, 252 n. 16, 255
Duncan and Warren's tannery (Santa Cruz, Calif.), 233
Dyer, Herman, 21

Eagle Mountain, N.M., 42
Eagle Pass, Texas, 64, 66
Edgar, William F., 153
Edwards, William C., 210, 211, 213
Eiversen, Christian "Fred," 251–255, 257, 258
El Camino del Diablo (road, Sonora, Mex.), 51
El Camino Viejo (road, Calif.), 217
El Clamor Publico, 219
El Dorado County, Calif., 126, 171
"El Huero." *See* Herrada, Rafael
El Paso, Texas, 41–42, 43, 47, 63, 65, 70
El Tucho, Calif., 205
Eleuterio (outlaw suspect), 102
Elliott's Wholesale Liquor Store (Santa Cruz, Calif.), 235
Ellis, Charles, 109, 110
Elmore, Rush, 27
Empresario (brig), 33
Erkson, John, 259
Escobosa, Miguel, 81
Espinosa, Manuel, 84, 85
Evans, George W., 124, 183, 184, 200
Exploration of the Rio Grande (report), 71

Fallon, Tom, 249
Farlia, Claria. *See* Féliz, Claudio
Farnham (sawmill lessee), 227, 227 n. 16
Feather River, Calif., 77
Féliz, Claudio (Claria Farlia), 51, 54, 56, 57, 58, 61, 75–79, 81–85, 107, 110, 129, 270
Féliz, Jesús, 51, 51 n. 4, 60, 136, 137

Féliz, Reyes, 51, 51 n. 4, 54, 61, 76, 78, 79, 81, 82, 84, 91, 92, 98, 101–103, 107, 110, 121, 122, 136, 269, 270
Féliz, Rosa (Rosita), 51, 52, 60, 79, 263, 281
Felton, Calif., 176
Filkins, Justice, 168
Firebaugh, Andrew D., 199 n. 1
Fitzgerald, Constable, 274
Florida Indian troubles, 22, 35
Foote, Franklin, 204
Ford, Henry L., 177
Ford, Susan Wilson, 222 n. 4
Foreign Miners' License Act (Calif.), 52 n. 6, 53
Foreman's Ranch, Calif., 108, 113
Forno, Captain, 27
Forsyth (man), 129
Fort Brown, Texas, 28, 30, 32, 35, 36, 38, 39, 43, 44–45, 48, 63
Fort Duncan, Texas, 70
Fort Marcy, N.M., 41
Fort McIntosh, Texas, 67, 68, 69, 70
Fort Miller, Calif., 89, 127, 133, 150, 151, 153–155
Fort Miller road, Calif., 123
Fort Polk, Texas, 28
Fort Tejon, Calif., 226
Four Creeks area, Calif., 140
Franklin House, La., 27
Fremont Battalion, 222 n. 4
French Camp, Calif., 129, 157
French Hill, Calif., 56
French miners in Calif., 105, 117
Fresno, Calif., 274, 275
Fresno County, Calif., 226
Fresno County Jail, Calif., 274
Fresno Daily Expositor (newspaper), 272
Fresno River, Calif., 61, 130, 151
Fresno River Indian Farm, Calif., 151
Fresno Slough, Calif., 150, 150 n. 5, 151 n. 6
Fritz, Sergeant, 226

Gabriel (outlaw), 79
Gabriel (woodcutter), 275

Gaines, Edmund, 33, 33 n. 19
Gallagher (murder victim), 77
Garcia, Anastacio, 84, 205, 206–207, 207 n. 16
Garcia, Bernardino (Three-fingered Jack), 81, 92, 94, 144–145, 149, 150, 153, 159, 160, 166
Gardiner (murder victim), 77
Gatewood, Jeff, 110
Georgia, 32, 173
Getman, Mr., 207
Gibbes, C. D., 75
Gila River, 74
Gila Trail, 47
Gilkey, Jack, 217
Gilroy, Calif., 237
Gilroy's Ranch, Calif., 176
Gitchel, George, 241
Glasswell's mill (Santa Cruz, Calif.), 241
Godden, Thomas, 202
Gold Gulch Flat, Calif., 239
Gonzales, Carmine, 38
Gonzales, Pedro, 81, 91, 92, 97–98, 98 n. 1, 102, 107, 121, 122, 148 n. 19
Goodin, Jeff, 211–213
Googen, A., 239
Gordon, Jack, 124 n. 7
Gould, Mr., 230
Graham, Amanda Ann Narcissa, 178
Graham, Catherine. *See* McCusker, Catherine Bennett
Graham, Isaac, 176–182, 184, 185, 193, 199, 200, 214, 222 n. 4, 223, 234, 242
Graham, Jesse Jones, 179–182
Graham's sawmill (Santa Cruz, Calif.), 233
Grant Street (Santa Clara, Calif.), 249
Gray, M. B. "Mustang," 34
Green, Alfred A., 264–265
Green, Sam, 55
Gregory, D. G., 214
Grijalva, Desiderio, 217–218
Gulf of Mexico, 34, 43
gunpowder mills (Santa Cruz, Calif.), 231, 241

Gurietta, Joaquín (alias), 79

"H.," 195
Hall, John, 110
Hamilton (rancher), 57
Hanford, Calif., 272, 275
Hanford Catholic Cemetery, Calif., 275
Harney, General, 44
Harrington, Mr., 57
Harry Love's Grade, Calif. (road), 214, 261
Hart, Thomas B., 228
Hartley, Henry Hare, 235
Harvard College (Cambridge, Mass.), 56
Harvey, Walter H., 125, 126, 127, 130
Hazeldell, Calif., 199
Head, Samuel C., 202
Heard, William, 15, 16
Hearne, V. W., 196
Heath, Russell, 203
Hecox family (Santa Cruz, Calif.), 185
Henderson, Boyd, 270, 272
Henderson, William T., 59, 60, 125, 135 n. 2, 138 n. 5, 143, 144–145, 145 n. 15, 146–147, 165, 166, 168
Herbert, Philemon T., 125, 126–127, 130, 155, 171
Hermosillo, Mex., 85
Herrada, Rafael (El Huero), 217, 218
Hicks (farmer), 236
Hicks' sawmill (Santa Cruz, Calif.), 233
hide trade, 23 n. 12
Hihn, Fred, 242
Hihn, Hugo F., 227, 227 n. 16
Hill, Jacob, 183
Hill's Ferry, Calif., 133, 151
Hipólito, Eduviges, 50
Hipólito, Jesós, 50
Hispanics. *See* Mexicans
Holabird, Samuel B., 68
Hollenbeck family (Santa Cruz, Calif.), 185
Hollister, D. S., 125
"Holy Man of Santa Clara." *See* Catala, Magin

Honcut Creek, Calif., 76
Honey Lake Valley, Calif., 213
Honolulu, Hi., 180
Hornitos, Calif., 87, 115–116, 123
Houston, Sam, 15, 16
Howard (attorney), 235
Howard and Perley (attorneys), 235
Howard, Thomas, 123, 126, 127, 172
Howard, William J., 123–124, 126, 127, 128, 131, 132, 138 n. 5, 139–140, 140 n. 8, 141 n. 10, 142, 149 n. 1, 156, 172, 200–201, 200 n. 7
Howard's Ranch. *See* Buena Vista Ranch
Howe, Julia Ward, 87
Hubbell, N. B., 160
Hudson, Walter, 68, 69
Humbug, Calif., 82

Imus family (Santa Cruz, Calif.), 185
Indians, 16, 36, 37, 38, 39, 40, 41, 42, 43, 44, 49, 50, 51, 64, 68, 69, 70, 75, 90, 94, 95, 98, 99, 100, 102, 103, 104, 114, 123, 127, 131, 141, 152, 158, 190, 193, 207, 218, 266
Ione Valley, Calif., 105, 106
Isleta, Texas, 42
Italians, 274

Jacks, David, 203
Jackson, Calif., 105, 106, 111, 112, 114, 169
Jackson Creek, Calif., 111
Jackson, Joseph Henry, 13, 266
Jamaicans, 190
Janes (murder victim), 129
Jenkinson (murder victim), 77
Jesuits. *See* Society of Jesus
Jesup, T. S., 70
Jesús (Sonoran), 196
Jesus, Senora, 101
Joaquin Murrieta and His Horse Gangs (Frank Latta), 266
Joaquin Rocks (Tres Piedras). *See* Three Rocks
Jones, Albert, 243
Jordan's Museum (San Francisco), 265
Juarez (murderer), 274

Julian, Don, 219

Keating, George, 205
Keating, John B., 205
keelboats, 23 n. 13, 48, 63–66, 64 n. 3, 67 n. 11
Keen, J. H., 158
Kell Ranch, Calif., 58
Kentucky, 33, 54, 99
Kern (Mexican war volunteer), 30–31
Kern River, Calif., 200
Ketchum, L. R., 124 n. 7
Kettleman's Plains (Hills), 270
Kidder, Charles S., 252 n. 16
King, James, 230
King, John, 162
King, John H., 67, 68
Kings County, Calif., 270
Kings River, Calif., 133
Kingston, Calif., 275
Kirby, Georgiana, 185
Kirker (California Ranger), 124 n. 7
Kirker, James, 124 n. 7
Klyn, Dianne C., 268 n. 3
Kooser, Ben, 236–238
Kottinger, J. W., 84

Lafayette Square (New Orleans), 27
Lake, Joseph, 111
land grants, California, 178, 182, 184, 186, 199, 221, 223–224, 229–230, 235, 249
Lang, Bill, 55
Laredo, Texas, 67, 69
Larkin, Thomas O., 175–176, 177
Las Cruces, Calif., 196, 218
Las Cruces Ranch, Calif., 196
Las Juntas, Calif., 81, 92, 151, 151 n. 7
Las Muertos, Calif., 109
Lascelle, Pedro, 272, 273
Latta, Frank Forrest, 14, 50 n. 3, 51 n. 4, 60 n. 22, 81, 81 n. 18, 87 n. 1, 92, 92 n. 12, 95 n. 13, 114, 122, 122 n. 3, 135 n. 2, 140 n. 9, 141 n. 10, 148 n. 19, 149, 150 n. 2, 193 n. 28, 216 n. 15, 251 n. 13, 263, 266–267, 268, 274 n. 13

Layton, Charles, 205, 207
Leary, John, 82, 83
Lewis, Frank, 199, 200
Lidel (land lessee), 222
lime kilns (Santa Cruz, Calif.), 193, 231, 239, 241
Limpia Creek, Texas, 43
Linares, Pio, 218
Lincoln, Abraham, 22
Ling, Sergeant, 68
Lipan Indians, 43
Livermore Valley, Calif., 84
Livermore Valley Review (newspaper), 273
Longfellow, Henry Wadsworth, 87
López, Antonio, 81, 149, 149 n. 1, 150–151, 151 n. 6, 155
López, Benito, 102, 103
Lopez, Gregorio, 195
Los Alamos, Calif., 94, 95
Los Angeles, 79, 83, 84, 85, 94, 97–98, 102, 122, 132, 135, 136, 140, 156, 160, 164, 192, 197, 206, 219, 225, 226, 264
Los Angeles County Courthouse, 226
Los Angeles County Jail, 226
Los Angeles Star, 95, 97, 98, 99, 100, 101, 104, 122, 156, 206
Louisiana, 23, 26, 28, 30, 33, 124
Louisiana Ranch, Calif., 183
Love, Henry (Harry): birth and early years, 20–22; seafaring days, 22–23; early romance, 23, 34; relocates to Mobile, Ala., 23, 27; Mexican War enlistment and service, 27–34; career as dispatch carrier and express rider, 35–48; career as keelboatman and explorer, 48, 63–71; joins gold rush to California, 73–74; undertakes first hunt for Joaquín Murrieta, 88–92; captures Pedro Gonzales, 97–98, 107; presents petition to form California Rangers, 119; appointed head of Rangers, 121–122; organizes Rangers, 123–128; early Ranger operations, 128, 130–133; captures Jesús Féliz and narrows down Murrieta's whereabouts, 135–139, 140–143; final battle with Murrieta and his men at Cantua Creek, 143–148; concludes Ranger operations, documents and exhibits Murrieta's head and Three-fingered Jack's hand, 149–150, 155–156, 158–171; concludes Ranger compensation issues, 171–172; relocates to Santa Cruz, Calif., and purchases Bennett sawmill, 183–185; meets and marries Mary Swain Bennett, 185–187; travels to East Coast via Panama, involvement in Bingham-Denin controversy, 187–192; activities in lumber business, 192–193, 214–215; dogged by questions of killing "real" Murrieta, 193–196; presence at Lewis-Reed wedding, 199–200; involvement in San Francisco Vigilance Committee of 1856, 214–215; real property and legal difficulties, 214, 215–216, 221–222, 223–224, 227–230, 235–236, 239–240; farming activities, 215, 222, 227, 234, 235; decline of marriage and divorce proceedings, 215–216, 243, 246–247; road-building activities, 222–223, 236, 239, 242–243; flooding of property, 231–234, 238–239; house and crops destroyed by fire, 234, 240–242; hosts traveling party in San Lorenzo Valley, 236–238; unsuccessful candidacy for justice of the peace, 245–246; financial ruin of, final controversies with wife and death, 247–256; obituaries of, inquest re: death, estate settlement and burial, 256–260
Love, John, 20
Love, Mary Swain Bennett, 173–182, 185, 192, 199, 214, 215, 216, 216 n. 15, 221–222, 227, 228–229, 234, 235–236, 240, 243, 246, 249–254, 256, 257, 258, 258 n. 23–24, 260–261
Love Creek Road, Calif., 261

Love sawmill. *See* Bennett-Love sawmill
Lower Mokelumne Road, Calif., 157
Lozier, Pete, 252
Luciano (outlaw), 217, 218
Lynch, S. J., 228, 228 n. 22

Maclay, Charles, 228
Mallagh, David, 218
Mallard, Joseph S., 97, 98 n. 1
Mapimi, Mex., 37, 38
Mariano (outlaw), 105
Mariposa, Calif., 14, 81, 87, 92, 97, 98, 114, 115, 117, 121, 123, 126, 127, 130, 140, 142, 150, 151, 155, 158, 159, 200, 209, 212, 266
Mariposa County, Calif., 74, 87, 97, 103, 118, 119, 123, 156, 159, 182, 183, 200, 209, 220, 225
Mariposa County Board of Supervisors (Calif.), 156
Mariposa Creek, Calif., 155
Mariposa Indian War, 225
Mariposa Street (Fresno, Calif.), 274
maromas (rope dance), 101
Marsh, John, 56, 57, 58, 79, 270
Marsh's Landing, Calif., 56
Marshall, Ben, 54, 55, 55 n. 10, 56
Marshall, Manuel, 55 n. 10
Marshall, Thomas, 55 n. 10
Martin, Julius, 176
Martinez, Calif., 129, 156, 157, 274
Martinez, Avelino, 92, 114, 148 n. 19, 267
Martinez, Rosie, 115
Marvin, William, 61
Marysville, Calif., 77, 78, 79, 168, 188, 191, 220
Marysville Express, 168
Marysville Herald, 77, 168
Marysville vigilance committee, 77–78
Massachusetts, 20, 45, 56, 87
Masters, Bob, 125
Matamoros, Mex., 15, 16, 26, 28, 30, 31, 35, 36, 38, 44, 45
Matamoros Flag (newspaper), 35
Mather, George, 77

Mayfield, Thomas Jefferson, 124 n. 7
Mazatlan, Mex., 73
McColloch (Mexican War officer), 31
McCulloch, Ben, 34
McCusker, Catherine Bennett Graham, 173, 176–178, 179–180, 180 n. 10, 182, 222 n. 4, 240, 243, 247, 251 n. 13, 260
McCusker, Dan, 240, 247, 261
McCusker farm, Calif., 234
McFarland, Jim, 59
McGowan, Edward, 15–16
McGowan, G. V., 125
McKee, Judge, 247
McKiernan, Mountain Charley, 249
McLane, Colonel (California Ranger), 125
McMahon, Jerry, 203–204
McNamara, John, 155
McNish, John, 112
McPherson's sawmill and dam (Santa Cruz, Calif.), 233
Meade, Jim, 274
Melones, Calif., 59
Mendez, Juan, 92
Mentoria (steamer), 63
Merced, Calif., 158
Merced County, Calif., 209, 213
Merced River, Calif., 61, 87, 133, 220
Merritt, Josiah, 202, 203
Methodist Church, 46
Mexican War, 16, 20, 25 n. 1, 34, 35, 39, 50, 54, 98, 99, 121, 123, 124, 126, 178, 179, 202
Mexicans (Hispanics), 15, 16, 25, 36, 50, 52, 53, 56, 59, 60, 64, 75, 76, 77, 78, 79, 80, 81, 82, 83, 84, 89, 90, 101, 105, 107, 109, 110, 111, 112, 113, 114, 115, 117, 118, 128, 129, 130, 131, 135, 137, 143, 144, 145, 146, 156, 158, 159, 160, 168, 169, 170, 193, 194, 195, 196, 207, 217, 266, 268–269, 273, 274
Mexico, 23, 25, 26, 27, 28, 30, 35, 36, 39, 44, 49, 52, 57, 61, 70, 73, 75, 79, 80, 82, 98, 115, 124, 149, 159, 160, 170, 176, 177, 195, 203, 263, 264, 265, 281
Mexico (Calif. town), 102

Mexico City, Mex., 71
Miguel (man), 219
Miles, William, 157
Milhauss, Gustavus, 196
Miller (deputy sheriff, Mariposa County, Calif.), 159
Miller, Henry, 217
Miller's sawmill (Santa Cruz, Calif.), 233
Millerton, Calif., 149–150, 150 n. 3, 151, 154
Mission San Jose, Calif., 128
Mission Santa Clara, Calif., 173
Mission Santa Cruz, Calif., 181
Mississippi, 33
Mississippi River, 22
Missouri, 33, 209, 212
Mitchell, Hyman, 53
Mobile, Ala., 23, 27–28, 30–31, 33–34
Mobile Register (newspaper), 27, 30, 34
Mobile Volunteers (Mexican War), 31
Mokelumne Hill, Calif., 79, 106, 112, 114, 169, 170
Mokelumne River, Calif., 133
Monclova, Mex., 44
Monka, Pedro, 158
Montecito, Calif., 196
Monterey, Calif., 52, 84, 85, 110, 119, 135, 174, 175, 176, 177, 183, 184, 187, 192, 193, 201, 202, 203–204, 205, 206, 207, 225, 267
Monterey Bay, Calif., 184
Monterey Californian (newspaper), 265, 266
Monterey County Grand Jury (Calif.), 207
Monterey County, Calif., 118, 201, 232
Monterey Sentinel (newspaper), 205
Monterrey, Mex., 40
Moore family (Santa Cruz, Calif.), 185
Moretto, Joaquín (alias), 117
Moriata, Joaquin (alias), 129
Mormon Island, Calif., 139
Mormons, 238
Morse, Harry, 270
Mountain Meadows massacre, 238

Muliati, Joaquín (alias), 121
Muriati, Joaquín (alias), 117, 122
Murphys, Calif., 54–55, 60, 125
Murray, Walter, 217, 220
Murrieta, Jesús Carrillo, 55
Murrieta, Jesús, 50, 55
Murrieta, Joaquín, birth and early years, 50; immigration to California, 50–52; early mining and criminal career, 52–56, 58–60; begins career in horse thievery, 60–61, 75–76; crimes in Yuba County, 76–79; continued criminal activities in California gold rush country, 79–82, 85; murders Allan Ruddle and escapes, 87–92; heads to southern California and is captured by Indians, 93–95, 98; involvement in murder of Joshua Bean, operations in southern California, 101–104; California legislature takes action against by creating Rangers, 117–118, 119, 121–122; confusion among multiple Joaquíns, 122–123; Ranger campaign against, 128–133, 135–139; retreats to Cantua Creek area, final battle with Rangers and death, 140–148; decapitation and preservation of head, 150–155; head authenticated and displayed throughout California, 158–171; lingering questions relating to outlawry, death, and burial of, 193–196, 263–270; possible relationship to Mariana La Loca, 270–276
Murrieta, Joaquín Juan, 81
Murrieta, José, 50
Murrieta, Martin, 81
Murrieta, Vicenta, 79
Murrieta family, 50
mustangs, 61, 133

Nacamereño, Joaquin (alias, Joaquin Valenzuela, q.v.), 122
Natchez, Calif., 76
National Hotel (Auburn, Calif.), 169

Negroes, 190
Neva (steamer), 28
Nevada, 213
Nevada City, Calif., 169
Nevada City Transcript, 168
New England, 45, 66
New Mexico, 35, 38
New Orleans, 22, 27, 28, 34, 45, 63, 71
New Orleans (steamer), 73
New Orleans Daily Delta (newspaper), 45
New Orleans Picayune (newspaper), 27, 28, 31
New York, 19, 45, 52, 74, 188, 189, 190, 191, 215, 224
New York Daily Times (newspaper), 19
New York Times (newspaper), 191
Niantic Hotel (Sacramento, Calif.), 166
Nicaragua, 191, 193, 216
Niles Canyon, Calif., 60 n. 22, 141, 267–268
Noche (Indian servant), 180
North Star (steamer), 191
Norton, James M., 125, 165, 166, 168
Nueces River, Texas, 25, 68
Nugent, John, 169
Nuttall, George A., 125
Nuttall, John, 125, 161, 162, 164

Oak Tree (Jackson, Calif.), 112
Ochoa, José María, 14, 52, 81, 149, 150, 151, 155, 156–158, 263, 266
Ocomoreña, Joaquín (alias), 122
Ocomorenia, Joaquín (alias), 122, 220
O'Donnell (soldier), 68
Olivas, José, 226
Olson, Monna S., 268 n. 3
Ord, Pacificus, 204
Oregon, 48, 173, 182
Orestimba Creek, Calif., 93
Otto, George, 236
Owens (bystander), 253
Owens, W. H., 170

Pacheco, Juan Perez, 91–92

Pacheco Pass, Calif., 75, 76, 89, 91, 133, 183, 184 n. 3, 199, 199 n. 1, 225
Pajaro River, Calif., 197, 202
Pajaro Times, 235
Pajaro Valley, Calif., 184, 195, 197, 198
Palace of the Governors (Santa Fe, N.M.), 41
Palmer, John, 180
Palo Alto (battle, Mexican War), 28
Panama, 187, 188, 189–191
Panama City, Panama, 189
Panoche Pass, Calif., 19
Pantellon (outlaw), 195
paper mills (Santa Cruz, Calif.), 193, 231, 233
Parras, Mex., 36
Peralta, Santos, 217–218
Perkins, William, 91
Perley (attorney), 235
Pescadero, Calif., 214
Peterson, W. H., 206–207
petrified man (hoax), 274–275
Peyton, Bailie, 215
Phillips, G. H., 272
Phillips, William, 155
Phoenix Quartz Mills, Calif., 108–109
Pico, Pío, 178, 221 n. 2
Pico, Salomón, 102
Piggott, Dr. S. K., 125
Placer County, Calif., 74
Placers Seco, Calif., 53, 54
Placerville, Calif., 117, 169, 225
Platt, William H., 27
Point Isabel, Texas, 26, 28, 30
Point San Quentin, Calif., 201
Polk, James Knox, 25
Pollock, David, 112
Pope (sawmill lessee, Santa Cruz, Calif.), 227, 227 n. 6
Porter, John, 225
Porter, Mr. (administrator), 216
Portsmouth, Me., 22
Portsmouth Square (San Francisco), 74
Portuguese, 273

Powell, Abraham, 156, 156 n. 19
Powers, Jack, 218
Prescott, William, 119
Prescott, Willis, 115–116, 125, 127
Prospect Hill (Los Angeles), 103
Pueblo de Murrieta, Mex., 50

Quartzburg, Calif., 19, 114–115, 116, 128, 130, 131, 158, 161, 165

Raiford, Phillip H., 27
Rains (ferry operator), 110
Rancheria Creek, Calif., 114
Rancho Bolsa del Pajaro, Calif., 184
Rancho Rincon, Calif., 199
Rancho Zayante, Calif., 176
Randall, Henry, 189
Rangers (Joshua Bean company), 99–100
Rawson, A. W., 184
Raymond, Gwynn, 112
Read, Felipe, 102, 103
Reader, Phil, 200 n. 11
Real de Bayareca, Mex., 102
Redwood City, Calif., 225
Reed, James, 199
Reed, Martha Jane "Patty," 199
Reed family, 199, 199 n. 3
Reiz (outlaw), 110, 114
Reseca de la Palma (battle, Mexican War), 28
Revarra, Francisco, 160
Revolutionary War, 20
Rich Gulch, Calif., 113
Richards, Robert J., 50 n. 3
Rico, Juan, 101, 102
Rico, Juanita, 101
Ridge, John Rollin, 13, 91 n. 9, 95 n. 13, 266
Rincon, Calif., 214
Ringgold Barracks, Texas, 39, 63, 64, 65, 69, 70
Rio Grande River, 16, 17, 20, 25, 26, 27, 28, 30, 31, 33, 36, 39, 42, 45, 48, 63, 65, 67, 69–70, 71, 121
Roach, William, 202–204, 206–207

Roach-Belcher feud, 201–207
Robinson, L., 255
Rodgers (Indian scout), 41, 42
Rojas, Arnold, 269
Roma, Calif., 102
Romero, Ignacio, 274
Romero, Tomas, 196
Rootville, Calif., 154
Roucher, Anton, 273, 274
Ruddle, Allan, 87–91, 92 n. 12, 103
Ruddle, Anne Elisabeth, 87 n. 1
Ruddle, John, 87, 220
Ruddle family, 89, 103
Russell, Calvin, 250, 252, 252 n. 16, 255
Ruxton, George Frederick, 38 n. 28
Ryland (attorney), 228

Sacramento, Calif., 105, 112, 128, 165, 167, 168, 171, 172, 187, 223, 225, 266
Sacramento Daily Placer Times & Transcript (newspaper), 157
Sacramento Daily Union (newspaper), 166, 167, 187
Sacramento Phoenix (newspaper), 14–15
Sacramento Union (newspaper), 76–77, 78, 79–80, 110, 111, 112
Sacramento Valley, 173, 232
St. Nicholas Hotel, 190
Salazar, Frank, 115
Salazar, Juan, 81, 92, 148 n. 19, 196–197, 198
Salinas, Calif., 84, 193
Salinas plains, Calif., 58, 118, 121, 137
Salinas River, Calif., 193
Salinas Valley, Calif., 84, 206
Salkmar, Frederick, 76
San Andreas, Calif., 107, 108, 109–110, 169
San Andreas Independent (newspaper), 213
San Antonio, Texas, 38, 39, 42, 43, 45, 46, 63, 65, 66
San Buenaventura (Ventura), Calif., 97, 203, 264
San Diego, Calif., 98, 100, 101, 132
San Diego Herald (newspaper), 117
San Elizario, Texas, 42

San Emigdio Rancho, Calif., 218, 219
San Francisco, 13, 15, 53, 55, 58, 73, 83, 118,
  161, 162, 165, 169, 171, 174–175, 178, 179,
  180, 187, 188, 192, 195, 201, 214–215, 216,
  224, 225, 230, 234, 237, 243, 256, 263,
  264, 265, 266, 272, 274. *See also* Yerba
  Buena
San Francisco Bay, 202
San Francisco Bulletin (newspaper), 275
San Francisco Chronicle (newspaper), 13,
  265, 270
San Francisco Daily Alta California (newspaper), 53, 55, 57, 58, 61, 130, 132,
  163–164, 171, 187, 195, 263, 264
San Francisco Daily Pacific News (newspaper), 181
San Francisco Daily Placer Times and Transcript (newspaper), 170
San Francisco Evening Picayune (newspaper), 73
San Francisco Herald (newspaper), 58, 60,
  78, 103, 119, 128, 129, 162, 164, 169, 263
San Francisco Ranch, Calif., 100
San Francisco Sun (newspaper), 187
San Francisco vigilance committee, 15,
  214–215
San Gabriel, Calif., 94, 98–104, 276
San Gabriel Mission, Calif., 98
San Gabriel River, Calif., 99
San Jacinto (battle of, Texas) 15–16
San Joaquin County, Calif., 54, 170, 200,
  203
San Joaquin County Court of Session, 54
San Joaquin County Jail, 203
San Joaquin Republican (newspaper), 75,
  83, 89, 107–108, 111, 112, 113, 115, 121, 124,
  128, 130, 131, 139, 144, 154, 159, 163, 170,
  171–172
San Joaquin River, Calif., 56, 61, 75, 81, 89,
  130, 133, 149, 150, 150 n. 5, 151, 154, 219
San Joaquin Valley, Calif., 61, 93, 94, 97,
  102, 103, 128, 132, 136, 139, 142, 150 n. 5,
  163, 194, 198, 223, 232, 270. *See also*
  Tulare Valley

San Jose, Calif., 52, 57, 58, 78, 79, 81, 85, 92,
  102, 119, 128, 161, 179, 180, 193, 194, 199,
  200, 203, 207, 213, 223, 225, 228, 234,
  237, 248, 249, 252, 253, 258, 270
San Jose City Cemetery (Calif.), 258
San Jose Mercury (newspaper), 228, 257
San Jose Patriot (newspaper), 256, 257, 258
San Jose Semi-Weekly Tribune (newspaper), 194, 203
San Juan Bautista, Calif., 119, 133, 135–137,
  138, 183, 202, 225
San Juan Capistrano Ranch, Calif., 217
San Juan River, Mex., 31
San Lorenzo Creek, Calif., 178
San Lorenzo River, Calif., 178, 184, 185,
  214, 216, 217, 223, 232, 235, 236, 239, 261
San Lorenzo Road, Calif., 239, 242
San Lorenzo Valley, Calif., 231, 234, 236,
  241, 248, 256, 258, 260
San Luis Gonzaga, Calif., 89, 91, 95 n. 13,
  103, 107, 133, 135
San Luis Obispo, Calif., 85, 158, 197, 217,
  218–220, 225
San Luis Obispo vigilance committee,
  218–220
San Pedro, Calif., 207
San Quentin (California State Prison),
  76, 85, 196, 201
San Ramon, Calif., 195
Sánchez, José María, 202, 204
Sánchez, Pedro, 81, 129
Sandoval, Cypriano, 102, 103
Sandusky, O., 71
Sanford, Henry, 202–204
Santa Ana, Calif., 15
Santa Barbara, Calif., 192, 196, 203, 218
Santa Barbara County Court of Sessions
  (Calif.), 197
Santa Barbara County Sheriff (Calif.), 197
Santa Barbara Gazette (newspaper), 196
Santa Clara, Calif., 17, 128, 160, 173, 175,
  178, 179, 182, 186, 192, 214, 216, 221, 223,
  227, 230, 234, 235, 240, 243, 247, 248,
  249–258, 261

Santa Clara Agricultural Fair, 227
Santa Clara College, 272
Santa Clara County, Calif., 131, 162, 186, 200, 201
Santa Clara County Clerk, 243
Santa Clara County Jail, 270
Santa Clara Mission, Calif., 175
Santa Clara News (newspaper), 261
Santa Clara Valley, Calif., 249
Santa Cruz, Calif., 17, 176, 177, 180, 181, 182, 183, 184–185, 186, 194, 195, 197, 200, 206, 215, 216, 221, 222, 223, 224, 225, 227–228, 230, 231, 233, 235, 236, 237, 239, 240, 241, 248, 249, 261
Santa Cruz County, Calif., 232, 243
Santa Cruz County Board of Supervisors, 223, 228, 236
Santa Cruz County Court House, 230
Santa Cruz County Grand Jury, 228
Santa Cruz Mountains, Calif., 249
Santa Cruz Pacific Sentinel (newspaper), 195, 198, 200, 206, 216, 220, 224, 227, 229, 233, 234, 235, 237–239, 240, 241, 242, 245, 246, 248, 258
Santa Cruz Times (newspaper), 242
Santa Cruz Turnpike Company, 248
Santa Fe, N.M., 38–39, 41, 43, 49
Savage, James D., 127, 130, 152
Savage's Post, Calif., 131
Saw Mill Flat, Calif., 81
sawmills (Santa Cruz, Calif.), 178, 178 n. 9, 185, 185 n. 7, 192, 192 n. 25, 193 n. 28, 214, 215, 222, 223, 227, 233, 236, 241, 245, 247
Scott, Hiram, 223, 248, 249
Seibels, John I., 27
Senator (steamer), 207
Servan, Froilan, 217–218
Shafter, Oscar, 190
Sharp, Mr., 131
Shasta, Calif., 160
Shelby, Mr. and Mrs. G. C., 214
Sheldon, John, 59
Sherman, William, 36–38

Sierra Nevada Mountains, Calif., 52, 81, 132, 199, 225
Silva (outlaw), 85
Silva, Esteban, 85
Silvas, Ysidro, 218
Sinaloa, Mex., 50
Singing River, Calif., 155
Smith, Digby, 57
Smith, Mowry W., 215
Smith, William F., 42
Snelling, Calif., 159, 209–210, 211, 212–213
Snelling, Ben (son of Benjamin), 210
Snelling, Benjamin, 209
Snelling, Clarissa, 212–213
Snelling, William, 209, 210–211, 213
Snelling family, 209, 210, 211
Snelling's Ranch, Calif., 159, 209
Snow (murder victim), 59
Snyder, Jacob, 242
Society of California Pioneers, 23 n. 11, 256
Society of Jesus (Jesuits), 272
Socorro, Texas, 42
Soledad, Calif., 197
Soliz (outlaw), 79
Somers (brig), 75
Sonoma County, Calif., 118
Sonora, Calif., 50, 51, 52, 52 n. 6, 56, 58, 59, 60, 76, 81–83, 91, 102, 103, 160, 170, 195, 272
Sonora, Mex. (province), 49–52, 55, 75, 85, 102, 140, 160, 170, 265
Sonora Herald (newspaper), 83
Sonoranian Camp (Sonora, Calif.), 52, 85
Sonorans, 49–52, 56, 75, 95, 97, 128, 161, 163, 196
Sonorean Camp, Calif. *See* Sonoranian Camp
Sonorian Camp (Yuba County, Calif.), 77, 78
Soquel, Calif., 214, 231
Soto, Ramon, 81, 92, 114
Spaniards, 61, 88
Spanish Camp, Calif., 117

Spanish Main, 22
Sprague, John, 241
Springer, E. C., 171
stage lines, 234, 234 n. 5
Stakes (judge), 102
Stanislaus mines, Calif., 193
Stanislaus River, Calif., 52, 81, 85, 110, 133, 169
steamboats, 22, 48, 56
Stevens, William, 211–213
Stevenson, Charles P., 185
Stevenson's Regiment (Mexican War), 52, 202
Stockton, Calif., 53–54, 56, 76, 82, 88, 91, 92, 123, 124, 126, 129, 130, 139, 140, 156, 157, 159–160, 163, 170, 203, 204, 212, 237, 266
Stockton City Recorder's Court (Calif.), 53
Stockton Daily Argus (newspaper), 212
Stockton Herald (newspaper), 236
Stockton House (Stockton, Calif.), 159, 160
Stockton Journal (newspaper), 82, 88, 117, 129, 131, 160
Stockton road, Calif., 87
Stoddart, Thomas Robinson, 56 n. 13
Stoneman, George, 154
Strivens, Mary Ann, 153 n. 13
Sullivan's Creek, Calif., 83
Sutherland, John, 272 n. 7
Sutherland, Mrs. John, 272, 275
Sutter Creek, Calif., 111, 114
Swain, Mrs., 185
Swain, Mary. *See* Love, Mary Swain Bennett
Sylvester, John, 150–155, 225, 226

tanneries (Santa Cruz, Calif.), 231, 233
Taylor, Zachary, 25–26, 27, 28, 30, 31, 33, 35, 41, 98
Teba, Albino, 129
Tehachapi Mountains, Calif., 94–95, 97
Tejon Pass, Calif., 94, 95, 102, 103, 140, 141–142

Tennessee, 173, 176, 179
Terry, David S., 203, 204
Texas, 15, 16, 20, 22, 23, 25–26, 28, 33, 34, 35, 39, 42, 46, 74, 87, 97, 119, 124, 125, 127, 159, 179, 182, 185, 235, 256, 257
Texas, Army of, 15
Texas Rangers, 28, 34, 252, 256, 257
The Headquarters (saloon, San Gabriel, Calif.), 98
The Major Babbitt (keelboat), 63, 65, 70
Thorington, Lucky Bill, 213
Thorn, Emily. *See* Bingham, Emily Thorn
Thornton, Seth B., 26
Three Rocks (Joaquin Rocks, Tres Piedras), Calif., 76, 92, 94, 147, 272, 273, 274
Three-fingered Jack. *See* Garcia, Bernardino
Tidball, T. T., 242
Tinaja de los Dragones, Mex., 38
Titcomb, James, 112
Treaty of Guadalupe Hidalgo (1848), 35, 52, 229
Trenouth, William, 250, 250 n. 11, 252, 260
Tres Piedras. *See* Three Rocks
Trevesia (desert, Chihuahua, Mex.), 36
Trinidad (outlaw), 79
Tucson, Ariz., 264
Tulare County, Calif., 223, 224
Tulare Lake, Calif., 61, 97, 140, 142, 150, 150 n. 5
Tulare Record and Fresno Examiner (newspaper), 226
Tulare Slough. *See* Fresno Slough
Tulare Valley (San Joaquin Valley, q.v.): 61, 136, 163
Tunis Creek, Calif., 94
Tuolumne County, Calif., 52, 74, 102, 164
Tuolumne River, Calif., 85, 88
Turley (soldier), 68
Turner, George, 210
Turnerville, Calif., 108

United States, 19, 23, 25, 28, 31, 34, 41, 153, 175, 177
United States Agricultural Census (Santa Cruz County, Calif.), 227
United States Army, 27–28, 34–35, 43
United States Army, Dragoons, 36 n. 25, 154
United States Army, Eighth Military Department, 39
United States Army, First Artillery, First Infantry, 28
United States Army, First Dragoons Regiment, 34
United States Army, First Dragoons, Company K, 226
United States Army, First Infantry, G Company, 67
United States Army, Ninth Military Department, 39
United States Army, Quartermaster's Department, 35
United States Army, Second Dragoons, 26
United States Army, Western Division, 33
United States Army engineers, 43, 65
United States Barracks (New Orleans), 28
United States Census, Santa Clara County, 227
United States Census, Santa Cruz County, 227
United States Congress, 25, 33, 229
United States District Court (Calif. land claims), 221
United States Hotel (Sacramento, Calif.), 78
United States Hotel (San Juan Bautista, Calif.), 135, 184
United States Infantry, Sixth Regiment, 31
United States Land Commission (Calif.), 235
United States Military Academy (West Point), 25
United States Surveyor (Calif.), 223

Ures, Mex., 50
Utah, 126

Valdez, Pablo, 84, 85
Valencia, Antonio, 81, 112
Valenzuela, Jesús, 218
Valenzuela, Joaquín (alias), 117, 122
Valenzuela, Joaquín, 81, 92, 114, 122, 122 n. 3, 128, 164, 196, 198, 198 n. 37, 218, 219, 220, 225
Vallecito, Calif., 128, 160
Vallejo, José de Jesús, 60
Van Alstyne, Mr., 189
Van Born, Edwin B., 125
vaqueros, 56, 79, 80, 81, 93–94, 117, 118, 137–138, 143, 217–218, 269
Varley, James, 14
Vasquez, Teodore, 78–79
Vasquez, Tiburcio, 270
Ventura, Calif. *See* San Buenaventura
Vermont, 20–22, 47
Vestal, R. K., 200
Victoria and Albert (elephants), 224, 225
Vielé, Egbert, 66–69
Vielé, Teresa Griffin, 66 n. 9, 68 n. 13
vigilance committees, 77–78, 102–103, 105, 214–215, 218–220, 223
Villegas, Tony, 92
Villegas, Ygnacio, 92
Vining, Lee, 116
Virginia, 123, 152, 206
Visalia, Calif., 94, 140, 223, 226
Visalia Delta, 223, 256

Walker, William, 191, 193
Wall, Isaac, 204–205, 207
Wallace (attorney), 228
Wallace, W. P., 39
Wallace and Ryland (attorneys), 228
Wanderer (ship), 224
Ward, John G., 112
Ward, Sam, 87–88
Warren, Billy. 226
Washburne, H. S., 228

Washington, D.C., 71
Washington, John M., 39, 39 n. 31
Washington, John S., 41, 44
Washington Hotel (Monterey, Calif.), 203, 206
Watkins, B. F., 235–236
Watsonville, Calif., 184, 195, 197, 207, 225, 234, 237, 260–261
Watsonville cemetery, Calif., 261
Webster, Justice, 212
Welch, James, 128
Welch, Mr., 131, 132, 139
Welsh, James, 162
West (crack-a-loo player), 210
West Indies, 22
Whig Headquarters Saloon (Sacramento, Calif.), 166, 167
Whipple (doctor), 252 n. 16, 255
White and Courtney (horse owners), 104
White (horse owner), 104
White, Ben, 212
White, Frances, 210
White, John S., 125, 146
Whiting, B. C., 214
Whiting, William H. C., 42, 43
Wilcox, Jim, 211
wild horses, 61, 75, 133
Williams, Benjamin, 54
Williams, Isaac, 197
Williams, Mr., 230
Williams' sawmill (Butano, Calif.), 214
Williamson, Thomas, 204–205, 207
Willow Springs, Calif., 79–80
Wilson, Gen., 222
Wilson, Jerry, 209 n. 1

Wilson, John, 216, 222 n. 4, 228 n. 22, 225
Wilson, Joyce, 148 n. 18, 209 n. 1–2
Wilson, Lt. Col., 28, 30
Wilson, Mortimer, 57
Wilson and Company, 225
Winfield Scott (horse), 140
Winters Bar, Calif., 112
Woll military road, Tex., 43
Wood (murder victim), 58
Wood, Ray, 14
Wood's Creek, Calif., 82
Woodbeck, Peter, 108
Woodward, Fletcher, 188–189, 190–191
Woodward, Susan Denin, 187–189, 190–191
Wool, John E., 35
Worth, William, 39, 43

Yackee Camp, Calif. *See* Yaqui Camp
Yankee Blade (ship), 187–189, 192
Yaqui Camp, Calif., 107–108, 111
Yaquis, 49
Yerba Buena, Calif., 73, 174–175. *See also* San Francisco
Yorktown Gulch, Calif., 83
Young, Coho, 125, 127, 130
Yuba County, Calif., 76, 79, 110
Yuba River, Calif., 77, 78, 79

Zapatero, Chief Jose, 94–95
Zayante area (Santa Cruz, Calif.), 176, 183, 184, 256
Zayante Valley (Santa Cruz, Calif.), 17, 176, 178, 184, 186, 187, 194, 199

The Man from the Rio Grande:
A Biography of Harry Love, leader of the California Rangers
who tracked down Joaquín Murrieta
by William B. Secrest
has been produced in an edition of 750 copies.

The typeface used is Caslon.

www.ingramcontent.com/pod-product-compliance
Lightning Source LLC
Chambersburg PA
CBHW031429160426
43195CB00010BB/672